The Atlantic in
World History,
1490–1830

The Atlantic in World History, 1490–1830

Trevor Burnard

BLOOMSBURY ACADEMIC
LONDON • NEW YORK • OXFORD • NEW DELHI • SYDNEY

BLOOMSBURY ACADEMIC
Bloomsbury Publishing Plc
50 Bedford Square, London, WC1B 3DP, UK
1385 Broadway, New York, NY 10018, USA

BLOOMSBURY, BLOOMSBURY ACADEMIC and the Diana logo are
trademarks of Bloomsbury Publishing Plc

First published in Great Britain 2020

For legal purposes the Acknowledgements on p. ix constitute an
extension of this copyright page.

Cover design by Tjaša Krivec
Cover image is a composite of *Vintage World Map* and
Intricate illustration of nautical symbols
(© Man_Half-tube/Getty Images)

A catalogue record for this book is available from the British Library.

A catalog record for this book is available from the Library of Congress.

ISBN: HB: 978-1-3500-7353-1
          PB: 978-1-3500-7352-4
        ePDF: 978-1-3500-7355-5
       eBook: 978-1-3500-7354-8

Typeset by Integra Software Services Pvt. Ltd.
Printed and bound in Great Britain

To find out more about our authors and books visit www.bloomsbury.com
and sign up for our newsletters.

CONTENTS

Part Four: Atlantic Themes

LIST OF ILLUSTRATIONS

MAPS

PLATES

INTRODUCTION AND ACKNOWLEDGEMENTS

I was fortunate to do my doctoral studies at the Johns Hopkins University under Jack Greene and at the University of Pennsylvania with Richard Dunn just when the new historical subfield of Atlantic history was first coming into prominence in the mid-1980s. The study of Atlantic history has always had a certain generational aspect to it, with many of the early practitioners being people like myself, trained in the history of early modern colonial British America in the 1980s and 1990s whose horizons were turned by increasing conversation with scholars of other parts of the Western Hemisphere, who seemed to be doing very interesting things that scholars of colonial British America also ought to be doing. In one respect, Atlantic history is the formulation in books and articles of those conversations and experiences in mutual learning.

Atlantic history was also a way of studying history that spoke, as I note in Chapter 1 of this book, to the *zeitgeist* of the 1990s and 2000s, in the heady days after the fall of communism in Eastern Europe and the Soviet Union and before the disastrous invasions of Iran, Afghanistan, Libya and Syria which soured geopolitics from the mid-2000s. Atlantic history is a real subject, with themes of great historical importance but it also is a subfield that developed in response to contemporary affairs, notably the shared commitment of most people in the Western world to the reality and perhaps to the desirability of globalization as an irresistible force shaping human destiny. Whether there is such commitment or even belief in the world becoming increasingly globally linked as a good or at least inevitable process is questionable, given the sudden upsurge in populism and ethnic nationalism that the world has experienced from the mid-2010s. It is sobering that the leaders of the three largest democracies in the world – India, the United States and Brazil – are as I write men who are sceptical about a globally linked world and who each promote forms of ethnic nationalism that goes against almost everything that people studying Atlantic history find valuable and interesting. I suspect histories of the Atlantic World written later in the 2020s may reflect the changed environment of today just as current works build on the ambience of a very different world that existed just a few years ago and which some of us wish would urgently return. One of the primary reasons why Atlantic History has such a purchase at present on historical consciousness is because it is linked so closely to global or world history and has some of the assumptions and methodological underpinnings of this subject – one, also, that developed in its modern form out of intensive historiographical debate from the 1990s and 2000s.

This book is a short introduction to a vibrant subfield of history, the history of the Atlantic World from the mid-fifteenth century to the mid-nineteenth century. It is also about the birth of the modern world, a development that owes an enormous amount to what happened in the Atlantic World from Columbus onwards, but which became especially obviously Atlantic-inflected in the eighteenth century during the period of the Enlightenment and the Age of Revolutions. It is a challenging historical subfield to teach and research in, as it requires mastering a huge amount of information, envisioning expanding the scale and scope of historical investigation beyond what was customary in the past, mastering many languages (not my forte) and in assimilating many different historiographical traditions, from African history to European history to Latin American history to Caribbean history to North American history. It requires imagination and application to appreciate the connections that linked the peoples of four continents together over a very long period – what historians call the longue durée. I hope that readers of this book find this abbreviated account of some value in accessing this subfield and of coming to understand not just the temporal and spatial boundaries of Atlantic history but also its principal theme, which is how New Worlds in what are really Old Worlds attached to the Atlantic Ocean arise from the complicated but enthralling interaction involved in the movement of people, things and ideas over the Atlantic Ocean and within the lands with an Atlantic orientation.

This book, it is important to stress, is a synthesis rather than a textbook. What do I mean by this phrase? The difference between a synthesis and a textbook is that a synthesis does not attempt to deal exhaustively with all the events that made up the history of a field or subfield. In short, this synthesis is not encyclopaedic in form or function: it covers themes and main lines of historical interpretations in Atlantic history rather than providing an exhaustive, and very lengthy, summary of everything that happened in this geographical space over a long period. I have written about matters I believe show the underlying essence of Atlantic history, emphasizing some things that I believe are especially important or worthy of discussion while downplaying or ignoring other matters that other scholars might think need attention. I regret, for example, paying no attention, among other ignored things, to the history of the Danish Atlantic or to that quintessential Atlantic place, Bermuda, despite their obvious importance within this historical subfield. This book is thus an individual interpretation of aspects of Atlantic history, drawn from years of teaching this subject and reflecting about what students found interesting, important and controversial.

This book would have been impossible to write if I had not taught Atlantic history at numerous universities in Jamaica, Britain and New Zealand. I publish this book as I take up a position as Wilberforce Professor of Slavery and Emancipation and Director of the Wilberforce

Institute at the University of Hull. The work of this Institute reminds us that the consequences of the Columbian encounter and the creation of an Atlantic World reverberate still today. My first teaching position at the University of the West Indies at Mona, Jamaica, meant I had to teach a subject I had never studied before, which was the history of the Americas from Columbus to enslaved emancipation. My distinguished colleagues at Mona – Barry Higman, Verene Shepherd, Jonathan Dalby, Carl Campbell, Veront Satchell, Hilary Beckles (though he by then was in Barbados), Karl Watson, Kathleen Monteith, Swithin Wilmot, Michele Johnson and Brian Moore – helped me understand how central the Caribbean was to both Atlantic and world history and set me on research paths that continue to sustain me. I taught my first course on Atlantic history proper when at the University at Canterbury with Marie Peters and Glenn Burgess. Glenn is a very distinguished historian of seventeenth-century British intellectual history and now deputy vice-chancellor at the University of Hull. Glenn and his wife, Mandy Capern, also an outstanding British historian, have been firm friends and great supporters of my work (and much else besides) since we first met in pre-earthquake Christchurch, in 1990. I also taught Atlantic history at Brunel University, the University of Sussex and the University of Warwick, where my thinking on Atlantic themes developed in conjunction with teaching and research collaboration with Ken Morgan, Inge Dornan, David Ryden, Richard Follett, Richard Whatmore, Clive Webb, Richard Godden, Saul Dubow, Paul Betts, Naomi Tadmor, Rebecca Earle, David Lambert, Gad Heuman, Tim Lockley, Cecily Jones, Giorgio Riello, Tony Macfarlane, Roger Fagge and Mark Knights.

I have placed importance in this book on the historiography of the Atlantic World and in explaining what the appeal of the Atlantic history is and why it is a subject suitable for our times that expands our knowledge of the ways in which the past is written about. I have made frequent references to many distinguished Atlantic historians throughout my text, in part to alert readers to the wealth of great work in this field. One distinctive feature of this work is that at the end of each chapter I make specific reference to relevant articles in a terrific bibliographical resource, of which I am fortunate to be editor in chief. This resource is the Oxford Online Bibliography in Atlantic History (www.oxfordbibliogaphies.com). This ambitious and exciting project under the auspices of Oxford University Press is a compendious collection of selected and annotated bibliographies on almost every aspect of Atlantic history from 'the Abolition of Slavery' to 'Women Prophets'. There are nearly 250 separate entries at present, with more being added monthly. It provides a brilliant guide by experts to the best online, primary and secondary literature on assorted topics, especially designed for students, scholars and interested readers who want an authoritative online guide to resources that is better than the hit and miss recommendations of such online resources like Wikipedia.

Finally, I am not someone who grew up on or near the Atlantic Ocean. My ocean is the Pacific, the greatest ocean in the world, which lapped the shores of where I was brought up, in Dunedin and Invercargill in the South Island of New Zealand. The Pacific Ocean looked beautiful, but its waters were too cold to be really inviting. The Atlantic does not often compete with the Pacific in grandeur, but it has a history that is at least as interesting and probably in respect to the humans who have traversed its water is more historically important. Probably only the Mediterranean rivals the Atlantic as a place where human history has been made from ancient to modern times and no ocean, not even the Indian Ocean, plays such a role in the making of the modern world and in fashioning the early modern world. My career has taken me to many places that are Atlantic places, from Jamaica, to Britain, to France and to the United States. These travels have made me aware of how the Atlantic continues to be a highway connecting the world more than a barrier stopping global interactions. The study of it and the people on it has been very personally and intellectually rewarding.

My wife, Deborah Morgan, and my two marvellous children, Nicholas Burnard and Eleanor Burnard, have accompanied me on my journeys to some of the lands that rim the Atlantic, even if my concerns are not their concerns and Atlantic history does not often intrude upon their horizons. That does not lessen my thanks to them for how they ease my labours. The study of the Atlantic is a minority interest in the place where I now live but its history and culture does attract the interest of some terrific people and scholars. One person I continually learn from is my dear friend Deirdre Coleman, to whom I dedicate this book. She is an extraordinary literary scholar whose work on the Atlantic contexts of the early colonization of Australia; on the cultural and intellectual interplay between Africa, Europe and the Caribbean in the age of revolution; and on natural science, environment and knowledge in the eighteenth-century Atlantic always informs, entertains and enlightens. More than that, however, she is the firmest of friends, one of those rare people whose support is unwavering in bad times as much as in good times. I wrote this book during the most difficult period in my professional life. Deirdre's constant, life-affirming support has been vital to how my wife and I have got through a tough period. I cannot thank Deirdre enough but hope she appreciates this small offering.

Trevor Burnard, Hawthorn, Victoria, 16 August 2019.

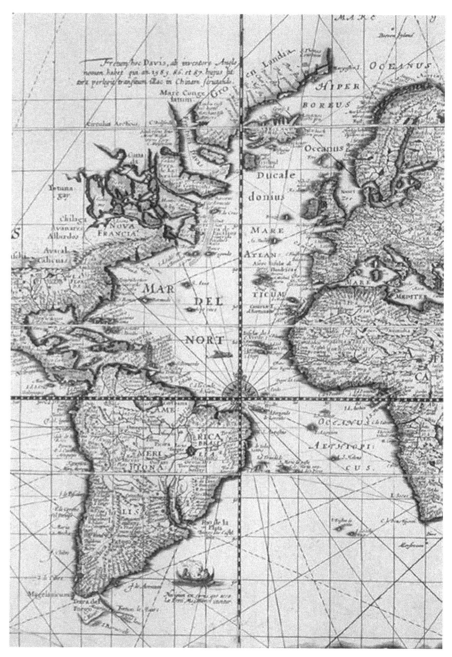

Map 1 *The Atlantic Ocean with bordering continental areas*, 1680.

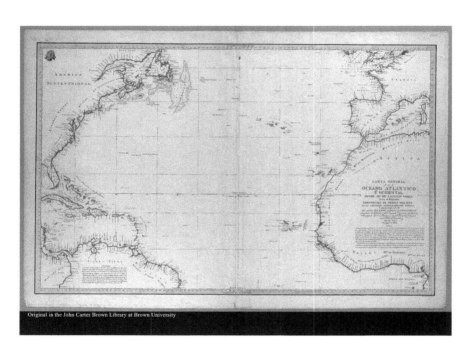

Map 2 *Carta general del Oceano Atlantico*, 1804. Courtesy of the John Carter Brown Library at Brown University.

Map 3 *European settlements in North America and the Caribbean,* 1733.

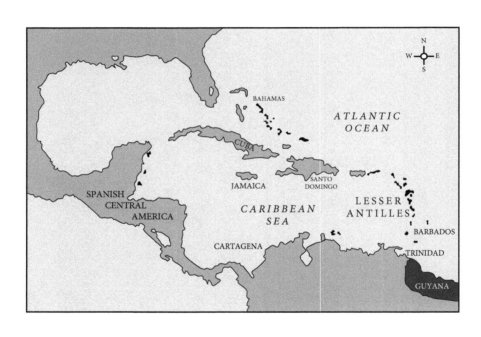

Map 4 *Caribbean, eighteenth century.*

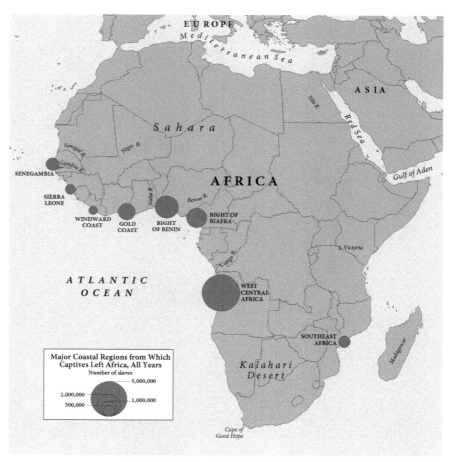

Map 5 *Major coastal regions from which captives left Africa.*

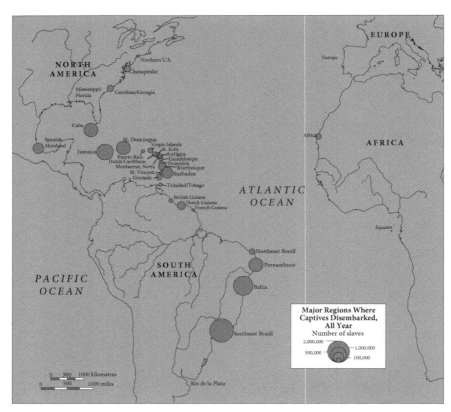

Map 6 *Major regions where captives disembarked.*

PART ONE

History and Historiography

1

ATLANTIC HISTORY AND THE ATLANTIC OCEAN

THE IDEA OF ATLANTIC HISTORY

This book looks at the historical connections between four continents – Africa, Europe, North America and South America – through the lens of one of the more exciting developments in the history of the early modern world – Atlantic history. Atlantic history, I believe, is not just a fashion nor merely a useful methodology through which to navigate one's way through institutional imperatives but is also an interesting and intellectually respectable way of looking at important historical processes. The institutional apparatus that has accompanied the advent of Atlantic history as one of the more important historiographical developments of recent times has not just developed because it met the needs of a generation of historians anxious to establish themselves in a dynamic new area. Atlantic history has real intellectual clout. Its principal theme – that the Atlantic from the fifteenth century to the present was more than just an ocean, more than just a physical fact but was a particular zone of exchange and interchange, circulation and transmission – is not only true in the sense that these exchanges and interchanges shaped profoundly the texture of life in at least four continents over a very long period of time but is also a conceptual leap forward, allowing historians to make links between place, people and periods that enrich our understanding of the complexities of a vital passage in the development of the world that we all inhabit. The idea of Atlantic history, as a field of historical enquiry that is more than the sum of an aggregation of several national or regional histories, is a very appealing one on intellectual terms alone.

If the Atlantic World could not have emerged and developed without an exponential movement of people, goods, capitals and ideas, it should not be confused with these connections *per se*. Most people who inhabited the Atlantic World, in Europe, in Africa and in the Americas, did not have a transatlantic experience; they did not move onwards from their places of birth and residence to reside a long distance from family and friends. Nevertheless, their lives could have been greatly affected by Atlantic dynamics even if they remained close to where they were raised. Thus, Atlantic history is something more than 'connected history'. It has an explanatory and interpretative dimension. The Atlantic paradigm postulates that one cannot understand the way societies on both sides of the Atlantic evolved and were transformed over time without taking into account the impact of Atlantic connections and dynamics, meaning not only transatlantic, but also hemispheric, regional and local connections. Indeed, it is important to play with all the possible scales to analyse which were the most influential, depending on the place, time and topic into consideration. As John Elliott underlines, it is also critical to avoid the 'natural temptation to exaggerate the extent to which one side of the Atlantic influenced developments on the other, perhaps in an effort to prove the writer's Atlanticist credentials'. As Elliot continues: 'but it needs to be recognized that there is no need to find a consistency, and still less a progressive development, of interaction over time and space. At sometimes and in some places the Atlantic component will figure strongly, while at others it may well occupy a subordinate position. Tracing and explaining the fluctuations in the degree of interaction between the whole and the parts is a necessary element in the writing of Atlantic history.'[1]

Hence, what characterizes most the Atlantic approach is its permissiveness, the fact that it has the potential to free historians from all historiographical boundaries, as Emma Rothschild notes.[2] Atlanticists have not tried to impose a new scale of analysis – the Atlantic scale – to the detriment of all other spatial scales. Rather, the introduction of this new scale has forced historians more generally to address and problematize the issue of spatial scale instead of working at the national, colonial or imperial scale by inertia or tradition. In this sense, Atlantic history is part of a more global spatial turn, an expression which has been used to describe several new historiographical trends, but which more generally underscores a new attention to space and territory, behind time, among historians. Thus, historians of the Atlantic World very often combine various scales from the local to the imperial or continental, to the Atlantic or the global, depending on what they analyse. Indeed, instead of promoting global, imperial or hemispheric history to replace Atlantic history, it is possible to play with all these scales to enrich and complexify our understanding of the past.

Cécile Vidal has argued that taking this approach raises the historiographical stakes considerably. She asks whether we should 'develop a more mobile and connective Atlantic history, which would mainly investigate the circulations and exchanges that led to the emergence and growing integration of the Atlantic world' or should we 'create a localised Atlantic history, which would focus on the impact of these connections on the internal evolution of the connected societies in a comparative perspective and mostly underline the diversity and fragmentation of the Atlantic world?'[3] What answer is chosen – the writing of a reasonably coherent and autonomous Atlantic World or writing connected histories the privilege the Atlantic scale but also open up to other scales of analysis, such as the global scale – will determine whether scholars see Atlantic history as a full-blown field of study that might encompass older fields based on the nation-state or on imperial formations or as a conversation among specialists of different places that allow them to put their works in perspective, while drawing attention to larger contexts. Atlantic history is a development that relates to a larger historiographical development – the so-called spatial turn in which historians have a new interest in space and territory as well as concerns about other traditional topics of historical enquiry that led to the New Social History of the 1960s.[4] But if geography is merely to replace society or culture as an unthinking category of analysis, we are not moving forward much. It might also form a barrier against connecting with colleagues in European or African history who are as interested in interiority as in large-scale spatial connections. This statement illustrates the perspective largely taken in this book: while there is some evidence that the Atlantic can be usefully looked at as the object of historical enquiry itself (there was such a thing as the Atlantic, if we define it carefully), it is more productive to see the Atlantic World as a simple unit of reference and frame of reference.

I think Atlantic history is an exciting way in which to have conversations with historians whose areas of interest previously did not intersect. But I am conscious of criticisms of Atlantic history as overly imperialistic and Eurocentric in its orientation. In my view, the rise of Atlantic history needs to be viewed alongside the development of hemispheric and continental history and the growing interest in world or global history as exciting new frames of reference that can supplant or supplement the traditional lenses of national or imperial history. All these frames of reference try to complement, overpass or suppress the nation as the most common unit of historical analysis; none corresponds to any kind of political entity. This makes Atlantic history not just different from national history but also different from imperial history, although the new imperial history increasingly consists of a global history of empires that compares imperial formations over time and space and studies their intra- and interrelations. Consequently, all these historiographical currents share in the rise of transnational and trans-imperial history. This work is part of the ongoing historiographical orientation. They differentiate themselves in their objects and in their chronological and geographical scales of comparison. Alan Karras sums up the promise of Atlantic history in a succinct way that underlines the principal premises of this book. He argues that many historical processes like trans-oceanic migration, long-distance trade, religious proselytization, democratic revolution and enlightened state building first appeared during the modern period in the context of the Atlantic World. Thus, these processes 'point to a significance for Atlantic world history that cannot be underestimated; without the Atlantic world's history, in fact, there would be no global history'.[5]

However, the fact that, already in the early modern period, the Atlantic World maintained close relationships with the Mediterranean world or Asia via the Philippines or via the Cape of Good Hope; the fact that the intercontinental slave trade linked the Atlantic and the Indian Ocean; the fact that, more globally, the Atlantic European trade was integrated into a world trade connecting most of the continents in the eighteenth century; and the fact that European colonial empires were world empires and not Atlantic ones should not mislead us in minimizing the singularity of the relationships uniting societies from both sides of the Atlantic and to question the Atlantic paradigm. What distinguished the Atlantic World from the sixteenth to the nineteenth centuries were: the development of a complex labour market after the demographical collapse of Native societies in the Americas; the beginnings of capitalism in Europe and its spread throughout the Atlantic World; the mass migrations of both Africans and Europeans to the New World; the economic exploitation of these various ethnic groups thanks to slavery, forced labour and other forms of labour; the creation of numerous settler colonies and the formation of new multiethnic and multicultural societies born from the encounter of Natives, Europeans and Africans in a colonial situation; and the formation of Atlantic colonial empires.

These Atlantic colonial empires were singular for three reasons: because they linked metropoles and settlers colonies; because in these settler colonies the colonized population was both 'autochtone'/Native (the Indians) and 'allochtone'/non-Native (the African slaves); and because the white settlers were in a potential position of being both colonizers towards the Indians and the African slaves and also colonized in their relationship with the metropole. All these phenomena had in return a series of very important impacts on the Old Worlds, both in Africa and in Europe, in the context of the imperial, labour and trade relationships linking the three continents. Thus, the specificity of the Atlantic World lay in the conjunction of these interrelated phenomena, whose entangled effects were not found elsewhere.

A NARRATIVE OF INTERCONNECTIONS

This book takes the above ideas about what Atlantic history as a subject might be about to construct a narrative of interconnections between peoples in the landmasses of the Atlantic basin and upon the Atlantic Ocean between the voyages of Columbus to the New World in the 1490s and the end of the Age of Revolutions around 1830 or 1840. Although it will address the question of how the development of an Atlantic World increased the global importance of Western Europe relative to other parts of the world, this narrative is not a modern version of older historiographies on the rise of the West and the triumph of Western civilization from the Enlightenment onwards. Rather, it stresses the interactive nature of encounters between various parts of the world, showing, for example, that Africa did not just march to a European beat during these centuries, that expansion into the New World was fiercely contested within Europe itself and even more contested outside Europe, and that the new societies developed by Europeans in contestation with Native Americans and African Americans in the Americas had their own ideas of what were the ideal relationships that should be established within a developing Atlantic World order from the seventeenth through the nineteenth centuries.

An Atlantic approach allows for a fresh perspective to be taken upon major historical events. Studying the Atlantic as an interconnected whole, both dynamic and complex at the same time, rather than focusing upon disparate national histories or individual incidents (though this work will use case studies of local areas and individual predicaments to exemplify larger themes), allows readers to discern better how larger historical patterns emerge from the movement of people, things and ideas across and within the Atlantic Ocean over a long historical period. It also encourages students and readers to think about multi-causal explanations of events and historical processes in ways that are both more accurate renderings of complicated situations and more intellectually satisfying in helping to examine problems with historical relevance and contemporary resonance. This book thus deals with traditional topics applying the techniques and approaches of Atlantic history outlined above. These topics include the age of discovery and the catastrophic consequences of the Columbian exchange; the Atlantic slave trade and the eventual campaign to abolish it; the repopulating of the Americas from the fifteenth to the nineteenth centuries; war as an increasingly global phenomenon, leading into wars between European empires for global dominance and liberation movements by settlers, slaves and indigenes during the Age of Revolution in the eighteenth and early nineteenth centuries; religious conversion and the development of new syncretic forms of religion in the various regions of the Atlantic World; changing ideas about governance and the relation of individuals to each other and to the state and the ambivalent nature of campaigns for freedom in highly unequal societies; nation-building and nationhood in ages of empires and colonization; the development of settler societies in multiracial and multiethnic societies; the development of Atlantic commerce as part of global trade and merchant capitalism; and the growth of intellectual movements such as the Enlightenment and Romanticism. At bottom, this text looks at how the modern world was born through an examination of the intersection of peoples and worlds colliding in a significant section of the world over a very long time. This work will form an important bridge between works of history that describe what historians sometimes call the world we have lost and works that describe how the world we live in has been shaped by long-standing historical events, themes and processes.

THE ATLANTIC OCEAN

One problem that immediately comes to mind when writing about Atlantic history is that the concept of Atlantic history is an ex-post-facto concept that makes sense to us today but made little sense to most people in the past. Few people living in Africa, Europe and the Americas before 1492 and not many more during the conventional boundaries that we use to date Atlantic history, roughly the mid-fifteenth century and the middle of the nineteenth century, saw themselves as 'Atlantic peoples', living in a space that was defined by the Atlantic Ocean. The idea of an Atlantic World predicated on common sharing of Atlantic boundaries would have been close to inconceivable to early modern people seeing themselves as parts of much smaller communities (families, tribes, nations and empires) than a semi-global community with linked concerns and interests. It is we, not they, who have a sense of global consciousness.

An Atlantic history is in part predicated upon identity formation – how peoples interacting with other peoples came to see themselves as Atlantic people and even more importantly how Atlantic interactions created the cultural change that historians describe as either creolization or ethnogenesis. The creation of an Atlantic World from the sixteenth century led to mixed ethnic and racial communities developing at the same time as Atlantic peoples tried hard to insist on their cultural autonomy and cultural distinctiveness. This contradictory set of urges reflects the 'disembedding' of individuals and institutions that was the special quality of the Atlantic World. As Jorge Cañizares-Esguerra and James Sidbury argue, what was key to Atlantic identity was how 'members of all groups, whether Amerindians struggling with the disembedding influence of the market through the chaos caused by epidemic disease, Africans facing the upheavals shaped by war, drought, and slavery, or Europeans seeking opportunity through migration, responded by seeking to re-embed themselves into communities, creating new identities rooted in the transformations that forged the early modern Atlantic world'.[6]

A central concept in Atlantic history is fluidity. It is seen most clearly in pre-contact Africa. Most of pre-colonial Africa was dominated by 'relatively small polities, and they often engaged in aggression with an eye less to territorial aggrandizement than to the acquisition of dependents, since the control of labour, not land, conferred wealth and prestige'. It made pre-colonial Africa characterized by the plasticity and multiplicity of socially constructed identities, which may have helped Africans adapt to horrible oppression in transatlantic slavery. Africans proved especially adept at reconstituting family networks in the Americas, sponsoring, as Herman Bennett notes, urban mutual-aid societies in Latin America or forming mixed Afro-Amerindian communities in the Guianas. What might be most important about African identity in the New World was not how it reached back to pre-contact African collective identities than to how it shared authentically African tendencies towards successful strategies of adaptation and reinvention in environments in which they were forced to conform to cultural practices not of their own making. What accepting fluidity and adaptation as key principles of African Atlantic identities reinforces is how futile it is to attempt to draw boundaries separating Old World and New World cultures.[7]

What is true for Africans in the Americas seems also true for Native Americans in the colonial borderlands of the Americas. These borderlands saw many new ethnic groups emerge in the wake of the demographic collapse and the interethnic wars that accompanied the arrival of Europeans. In Mexico and Peru, for example, catastrophic demographic collapse led to huge internal migrations in which entire populations of *forasteros*, ethnically unattached wanderers, formed new and ethnically diverse communities. These communities were 'further reshuffled by Spanish resettlement practices to bring the scattered survivors of the demographic collapse into new urban, civilizing spaces'. The result was a significant process of creolization, with new Native American cultural formations adopting a range of both Native American and European cultural trends. Nancy van Deusen and Jane Mangan have stressed how this cultural appropriation and reinvention were often done through the agency of Native American women marrying or cohabiting with Europeans or Africans. These women created families and networks with deep economic and emotional ties even within extremely vicious webs of oppression – the foundations of Iberian conquest were inherently violent, meaning that family and violence operated within a superstructure in which day-to-day resistance, as Michel de Certeau has argued, shaped the tactics of Native Americans' adaptation to European cultural hegemony.[8]

This process of ethnogenesis because of changes on peoples forced to deal with the consequences of European expansion into the Americas leaves Atlantic historians open to the charge of Eurocentrism. Seeing the histories of the many Europeans, Africans and Native Americans through the lens of the Atlantic relegates to the margins the experiences of most of these peoples who were only peripherally involved with the Atlantic. Yet it is undeniable that it was from Western Europe where many of the exchanges that led to Atlantic histories emanated and perhaps given their especially active agency in the making of an Atlantic World, some privileging of Europe might be warranted, if we do not revert to old ideas of active European agents and passive African and Native American recipients. One of the hardest parts of doing Atlantic history is acknowledging the role of European expansion in creating an Atlantic World without allowing

European historical experience to be considered normative. Stressing cultural fluidity and adaptability is to my mind an appropriate way of threading this needle, of appreciating European initiatives in shaping an Atlantic World and stressing the strengths of non-Europeans in resisting, changing and adapting to such initiatives while making actions of their own which changed trajectories of power and culture in an always evolving Atlantic history.

Indeed, it might be thought that conceptions of an Atlantic World became possible only when changes in transportation, finance and communication allowed the World to become so interconnected as to become truly global. That only occurred in the late nineteenth century. Bernard Bailyn, one of the principal proponents on the utility of Atlantic history as a means of understanding historical processes of global integration and disintegration, locates the 'ultimate source' of Atlantic history as a concept as recently as 1917 and to the writings of the journalist Walter Lippmann and his urgent advocacy of the United States entering the First World War on the side of what he called an 'Atlantic community'. Lippmann argued that the countries of Western Europe (and perhaps southern Europe), along with countries in North America, were part of an 'Atlantic highway' and that as members of 'one great community' these countries needed to join together to protect vital aspects of Atlantic civilization, such as democracy (though not, for an American interventionist, so much imperialism), from threats posed to such values by the Axis powers and from Bolsheviks in Russia.[9]

This sense of an Atlantic community was solidified in the decade after 1945 with the creation of transatlantic alliances such as the Marshall Plan, the Truman Doctrine, the North Atlantic Treaty Organisation and to a plethora of government and nongovernmental institutions that connected this putative community together. With movement across the Atlantic Ocean becoming ever easier and more commonplace, either by ship or by the twentieth-century invention of the airplane, it was easy to see from the second quarter of the eighteenth century onwards the Atlantic Ocean as a facilitative highway rather than as a barrier to expansion.

That was not how the Atlantic Ocean was seen at the start of our story – a story about the emergence of interconnected communities, the integration of those communities over the course of the seventeenth and nineteenth centuries, and the reconfigurations of the Atlantic World that occurred because of the Age of Revolutions from 1760 to 1840. Before the arrival in substantial numbers of Europeans on the coast of West Africa in the middle of the fifteenth century, few Africans paid much attention to the Atlantic Ocean, Atlantic ports in West Africa were few and most contacts with the non-African world were overland rather than by sea. That was true in West Africa but much less so in North Africa, which was closely involved with the Mediterranean World and had been for millennia, and in East Africa, where the connections with the Indian Ocean were equally substantial and of long duration.

In Africa, the absence of a sizeable interest in the Atlantic Ocean was in part a function of geography. As Philip Morgan notes, 'a combination of prevailing winds and currents, lack of sheltered seas, few natural harbours, treacherous offshore bars and heavy surf inhibited an indigenous seafaring tradition'.[10] West Africans' lack of interest in the sea was not because they were not without the skills to live maritime lives. Within West Africa, waterways were much used and African maritime technology was more than enough for the purposes intended. Whatever contacts there were with Europeans – and these were extensive well before an Atlantic World came into existence: the European advance into the offshore islands of the Canaries and into West Africa from the mid-fifteenth century was certainly no encounter between groups who had no previous knowledge of each other, as was the case for Europeans and Native Americans in the Caribbean in 1492 – occurred in that major crossroads region of the world, the Mediterranean. Africans did not have the relatively sophisticated boat building techniques of late medieval Western Europe, but they had no need for such technologies either. The Atlantic Ocean was thus for West Africans not a place they wanted to venture into. Eventually, of course, parts of West Africa, especially those involved in various forms of commerce with traders and sailors from Western Europe, became oriented to the Atlantic but for many West Africans the Atlantic Ocean remained a fearsome reality. For the millions of captives embarking on the Atlantic slave trade, for example, their experience of the Atlantic Ocean was that it was a place of death and disaster. The 'door of no return' in the whitewashed fort of Gorée Island, Senegal, now a major tourist attraction (Barack Obama visited in 2013 and Nelson Mandela in 1997), is a poignant reminder of the horror captives felt as they were pushed from the land to the sea. Entry through this door marked the end of their lives on the African continent and signalled a dreadful maritime voyage to an unpleasant future as enslaved people on American plantations.

The Atlantic Ocean was just as forbidding a barrier to people in the Americas as it was in Africa. If any Native American ventured far into the Atlantic, history has no record of their progress. As in Africa, connections between American people were frequent, but were either by land, by internal waterways or on the large but confined Caribbean Sea. Unlike Europe or even West Africa, the major places of Native American settlement were not on the Atlantic Coast but were inland or on the Pacific coast, with the great empires of the Americas, the Aztecs and Incas, being a long way from the Atlantic Ocean. Of the roughly 54 million people estimated to live in the Americas at the time of the Columbian encounter in 1492, about 3 million probably lived in the Caribbean and only a small proportion of the 3.8 million Native Americans in North America and the 8.6 million people in South American were on the Atlantic littoral. It is worth noting that for a very long time in Atlantic history, the main body of the Native American population of the Americas was mainly located outside European settlement and far from the Atlantic Ocean. The two greatest concentrations of Native American populations in 1492 were in Mexico, where 17.1 million Native Americans lived, and in the Andes, where 15.7 million Native Americans resided.[11]

Peter Wood, drawing on data presented by Douglas Ubelaker, reminds us that in 1700, after two centuries of Native American population decline in North America, especially within eastern and Atlantic coastal populations, the great majority of the 1.65 million people living in North America, including fewer than 300,000 people of European or African descent, all living very close to the Atlantic Ocean, dwelled away from the Atlantic. He estimates that more than three times the total number of people residing close to the Atlantic were Native Americans living in California, the Arctic, the Great Plains and the Pacific Northwest.[12]

It was different in Europe but not so different as to make the Atlantic Ocean an especially inviting place for European exploration. In 1400, no one in the Atlantic World, including Western Europeans, knew much about or even cared about deep-water navigation, crucial for moving across the Atlantic. As in the Caribbean and West Africa, mariners could comfortably sail moderate distances but had little ability to go beyond the sight of land. Except for deep-sea fishers, searching for cod in northern waters, sailors had little reason to risk for their lives in unexplored waters. Europeans, because of their pursuit of cod, had some experience in deep-water navigation and had sent fishing fleets out of various European ports to make temporary landings in Newfoundland, in the northeast of North America.

Western Europeans had made some tentative explorations of the Atlantic Ocean before the great age of exploration beginning in the fifteenth century. The first European contact with the Atlantic was with the Vikings and before them Irish monks who initially settled the Faroes and Iceland. Vikings had marvellous ships, the *knörr*, *halfskip* or *kampskip*, which can carry forty to fifty tons of cargo, allowing not just better navigation but also the capacity to carry substantial numbers of people and their possessions large distances. Sailing to the north and west, Viking ships used prevailing winds and currents to go to Greenland in the late tenth century and, probably because of accidental overshooting, to Newfoundland around 1000 CE. The first transatlantic voyage was made by a Scandinavian sailor called Bjarni Herjólfson in 986, who was blown off-course and made landfall on places we know as Labrador and Baffin Island. He returned to Greenland and few people thought much of what he had done until in 1002 Eric the Red, who had bought Bjarni's *knörr*, sent his son Leif Erikksson to retrace Bjarn's voyage and make a settlement in what the Norsemen called Vinland.

It was an unfortunate first encounter in the New World but very typical of the kinds of encounters between different peoples that were to make the making of the Atlantic World a very violent affair. The Norse killed eight of the first nine Native Americans they saw, fought among each other with much killing and had continually hostile relations with Inuit residents (whom the Norse called *skraelings* or wretches). Settlement efforts were quickly abandoned, and transatlantic exploration was relegated to memory. The next exploration of the rich fisheries in Newfoundland occurred only in the 1470s, when English cod fishermen were driven from Icelandic waters due to political and commercial considerations. Bristol ships discovered a rich fishery, possibly the Newfoundland banks and began fishing there, trading their produce with Spain and the Azores. Knowledge of this new Atlantic route was soon widely known and Portuguese, Basque, Breton and French ships soon joined the English in fishing cod and whales off Labrador and Newfoundland.

ALTERNATIVES TO EUROPEAN EXPANSION INTO THE ATLANTIC

The web of history could have turned out differently. In the early fifteenth century, it looked as if it would be Ming China, not Western Europe, that would expand its horizons into the world. China and India were easily the wealthiest and most populous regions of the world and had the resources to dominate other parts of the world. The Mongols had shown that world domination was possible from Asia in their incursions across Eurasia in the medieval period. Admiral Zheng took a vast fleet all the way to East Africa in seven state-sponsored voyages between 1405 and 1433. But the Chinese thought there was little to be gained by transoceanic exploration. The Ottomans were similarly uninterested in Atlantic exploration. Arab and Turkish merchants and mariners dominated the world's busiest and most lucrative trading routes. They had little reason to focus on the Atlantic. In short, major competitors to Europe left the seas to Europeans while concentrating on being triumphant on land. We need to appreciate that it was not strength but weakness that led to European expansion seawards. The first European nation to move west was Portugal, a nation with fewer than 1 million people and which was small, poor, short of good land and prone to famine. The Portuguese had good reason to expand overseas to find land, wealth and trade whereas the populous, rich and self-sufficient Chinese, Indians, Turks and Arabs did not.

Native Americans had no more reason to move outwards than did the Chinese. The period before the Columbian encounter was good times for humans in the Americas. Relatively warm climates between the tenth and the fourteenth centuries allowed growing seasons in temperate areas to be longer than in the past, allowing for an agricultural revolution, where maize, beans and squash cultivation spread northwards from Mexico into North America. It led to the development of new centres of Native American civilization, such as in the Chaco Canyon in what is now the Four Corners region of New Mexico, and greater settlements than before in the Mississippi

Valley. If we look eastward from Chaco Canyon rather than westward from the Canary Islands, we see Native Americans expanding their settlement of North America. That perspective is heightened if we look southward, to the flourishing and increasingly powerful and aggressively imperialist empires of the Aztecs in Mexico and the Incas in Peru.

The problem was that the warm weather did not last. In both Chaco Canyon and the Mississippi Valley, dense populations had been living on the edge of sustainability during the Medieval Warm Period. Daniel Richter speculates that 'perhaps the extraordinary religious fervor, political capital, and material resources devoted to agricultural ceremonies in both places shows a cultural recognition of just how unstable the balance was'.[13] Global cooling in the fourteenth through sixteenth centuries and the advent of the Little Ice Age in the seventeenth century wrecked these fragile ecosystems. Nevertheless, while great urban centres disappeared north of Mexico, core elements of previous cultures' settlement patterns remained, with most people in the Mississippi living in small hamlets. The agricultural revolution of corn-beans-squash was permanent, transforming Native American life except in areas where such production was impossible (Alaska, Canada, the Great Plains, the Great Basin of the Southwest and Patagonia) or the Atlantic and Pacific coasts where fishing was more important than farming. Most of these areas remained outside European contact until well into the eighteenth century. It was the farmers, not the hunter-gatherers or fishers, who encountered Europeans in the Atlantic World in the three centuries after 1492.

What is important to note is the variety of Native American societies that existed on the eve of European conquest. North American native populations were very different from the equally diverse populations of Central America and the Caribbean. And they had little lasting contact with each other. Desert separated Mexico and the Yucatan from North America, and it was hard for ships without sails to traverse the Caribbean seas. There were commonalities within Native American cultures, such as a common attachment to subsistence agriculture, matrilineal kinship, long-distance trade and (except for the Incas and Aztecs) decentralized chiefdom forms of political organization. But the differences were more obvious and important than the similarities as Native Americans were even more divided by language than Europeans and had endlessly varied local customs and beliefs, without the uniting features of Christianity, monarchy and bureaucratic forms of state-building that connected Western Europeans together. Indeed, it was the Spanish – the major European colonizers in the sixteenth century – who encountered the greatest diversity of indigenous societies in the Americas, ranging from the fully sedentary empires of Mesoamerica and the Andes to the small bands of hunters and gatherers scattered through the arid northern parts of Mexico and the grasslands of southern Argentina.

What did these Native Americans make of the strangers they encountered as the Medieval Warm Period morphed into the Little Ice Age? An abiding problem in Atlantic history is in the disparity of sources. We know a great deal about what Europeans thought of Native Americans. We understand little the other way around. Sources confound knowledge. It was only in Mesoamerica, and then only after the conquest, that abundant sources of writing in indigenous sources exist, like Nahuatl, Mixtec and Maya, using the Latin alphabet introduced by Europeans. Our only way of hearing Native American voices is generally one step removed – what Europeans thought that Native Americans were saying about them.

These constructions of Native American thinking about Europeans suggest that Native Americans viewed their invaders with amusement and contempt rather than with respect or even with fear. For example, Native Americans in seventeenth-century New Netherland (New York and Delaware) viewed Dutch settlers as 'brothers', 'scoundrels' or 'metal-makers'.[14] Space does not allow much explication of these notions, as complicated meanings attached to each construction. The first, 'brothers', tends to reflect Dutch hopes that Native Americans saw them as friendly and as like kin. It is more likely that Native Americans saw the Dutch as 'scoundrels' (a strong insult in Dutch). 'Metal-workers' was a more mixed description: it suggested that the Dutch, despite not being trustworthy, had skills Native Americans could use. What they did not value was Dutch culture, notably Christianity. Missionaries complained that when they attacked Native Americans for misbehaviour, according to Christian norms, using common European tropes that suggested the anger of God at seeing sinful humans, that Native Americans laughed at them and said that they did not rate the European God who seemed not to punish the Dutch even when there were many Dutch 'whores, thieves, drunkards and other evil doers'. Native Americans also adapted pejorative views of the Dutch which were common in European discourse: that they worked too hard, were overly avaricious, addicted to gossip and were hearty hypocrites. As connections between Native Americans and Europeans deepened and became more problematic and were shaped by frequent bouts of horrific violence, we stop getting these ethnographic descriptions of what Native Americans thought of 'the other'. A generation or two after conquest, Europeans became less interested in what Native Americans thought about them and more concerned about portraying Native Americans as irredeemable savages, prone to both cowardice and cruelty.

THE END OF ATLANTIC HISTORY

It is easy to work out when Atlantic history starts. It begins in the mid-fifteenth century with Portuguese explorations into West Africa and takes off with a bang when Columbus visited the Bahamas in 1492. It is harder to know when it ends, although in this book I make an argument in Chapter 15 that Atlantic history proper ends in the 1820s when for the first time we can see world history emerging out of the technical innovations of the Industrial Revolution, when the world could become connected and when Atlantic history becomes subsumed into global history. Historical periods don't end as easily as that, however, and scholars of the Atlantic World note that many of the features of Atlantic history continue well after the 1820s. One of the principal features of the Atlantic system, for example, lasted in the Western Hemisphere well after 1820. Slavery hardly ended in the 1820s and even with British abolition in 1834. It continued and grew in the American South until it ended after the US most violent conflict, in 1865, and continued in Cuba and Brazil until the 1880s, with the abolition of slavery in Brazil occurring only in 1888.

Indeed, some historians would argue that Atlantic history should be studied until at least the twentieth century. Alan Karras has made a powerful argument that one of Atlantic history's greatest failings has been its reluctance to move into the twentieth century. He notes that two of the big ideas that define world history – the expansion of religious proselytization and the increase in political engagement under the general rubric of democratization - expand out of the Atlantic World in the early nineteenth century into the world and take on most importance in an Atlantic context in the twentieth century. Decolonization, for example, may have started in the Americas in 1776 and in 1804 but its main manifestations came in the twentieth century. Karras argues that 'the world historical process of decolonization in the nineteenth and twentieth centuries needs to be more explicitly linked with the Atlantic's period of "revolution" in the eighteenth century. Not only will this show the prevalence and persistence of Enlightenment ideologies as motivating factors for these revolts, but it will also show the ways in which the Atlantic's history can be neatly fitted together – over a much longer period of time'. He argues that 'the Atlantic world needs to be pushed into the twentieth century, so that the region's transformation from a "new world" to one that became integrated in various ways into other, shifting, and sometimes opposing, regional blocks can be clearly articulated and explained, especially in relationship to existing national and world histories'. It is an ambitious brief, one that Karras himself admits that he could not do in his own 1992 co-authored book on Atlantic history, where his comfort zone only allowed for treatment of the Atlantic until the 1880s, when the last slave societies ended. And, as he admits also, while patterns and relationships characteristic of the Atlantic World continued into the twentieth century, the Atlantic had become increasingly integrated into global networks of exchange and into the ongoing narratives associated with world history. 'Its distinctiveness', he notes, 'faded, and its integration into a truly global economy continued apace.'[15]

What annoys Karras most about chronologies of Atlantic history is that he thinks they correspond too neatly to the concerns of early modern historians, and especially historians of early America. He goes so far as to argue that early Americanists have 'colonized Atlantic history' and in doing so 'have hijacked the field's internationalist tendencies and turned them upside down' in ways he finds 'deeply troubling'. Karras is very much of the school that wants to see Atlantic history as a unified field of study, and very sensitive to criticisms that Atlantic history is just a means of telling the history of the United States or other societies through an Atlantic lens. As noted above, I am less convinced that we get that far by insisting that Atlantic history must be 'integrated into a single, or singularly distinctive, historical narrative'.[16] To my mind this replaces one form of historical amnesia with another form of historical dogmatism. I am also not American so, as this book shows, the question of how Atlantic history is a means of internationalizing the history of the United States is not something that seems especially important to me, or, I think, to the readers of this book.

Nevertheless, I am a scholar of early British America without the deep immersion in Spanish, French, Portuguese, Dutch and Danish historical sources that may become someday the entry requirements for being considered a genuinely Atlantic historian. I have presumed in this book that most of the readers will be either English-speaking or fluent in English and thus have kept most of the references within the English language. Each chapter, however, contains at least one reference in another European language than English, to gesture towards the great work done in Atlantic history outside Anglo-American historical journals and books. It is not just in the United States but also in Britain where initial leadership in Atlantic studies began. In Britain, Euroscepticism (as so evident in the protracted debate over Brexit since 2016) has meant that the British have often (less in scholarly than in popular discourse) used the Atlantic as a counterpoint to Europe as it enabled them to convince themselves of British exceptionalism, of Britain's destiny, like its history, not being necessarily yoked to that of continental Europe and Ireland. Conversely, Cécile Vidal argues that the strong hegemony of national history and the difficult integration of imperial history into European national history explain why French historians (as one example of European-based historians) have been reluctant to use Atlantic history as an alternative to traditional historical narratives.[17]

My decision to end Atlantic history in the first third of the nineteenth century with just a few references to later development reflects above all my own experiences and skills. My knowledge gets less certain after the abolition of slavery in British and French America. What happens in the Atlantic after this debate leads into historical research on imperialism, decolonization and into reflections on contemporary, post-colonial societies in places that were once Atlantic societies in Europe, Africa and the Americas. It is quite possible that the new imperial history, which is increasingly a comparative and entangled history of empires over time and space and on a global scale, allows historians to connect early modern and modern imperialism and post-imperialism. Atlantic history has its limits as a tool of historical explanation. It might be that the 1880s suits better as an end of Atlantic history than the dates used in this book. It makes the end of slavery rather than the end of revolution crucial, thus putting Africa and Africans at the centre of the Atlantic narrative, which might be said to reduce Eurocentric bias. But this date has its own problems. It may be less Eurocentric but might be more American-centric, seeing the world since the 1880s as less post-colonial, as would be a common response to recent history in Europe and Africa, than post-slavery. It reinforces what Sylvia Frey underlines, that 'the emergence of racial ideologies and racial orders is one of the great fault lines, perhaps *the* great fault line in studies of Atlantic history'.[18] Finishing where I do may mean that parts of the Atlantic narrative remain unexplained, but it does mean that post-colonialism is not slighted as the consequence of the end of the Atlantic period of history in favour of a relentless focus on post-slavery. Outside the United States, the Caribbean and Brazil, racial questions are not so immediately linked to the legacies of slavery.

NOTES

1   J.H. Elliott, 'Afterword – Atlantic History: A Circumnavigation,' in David Armitage and Michael Braddick, eds., *The British Atlantic World, 1500–1800* (Basingstoke: Palgrave Macmillan, 2002), 240.
2   Emma Rothschild, 'Late Atlantic History,' in Nicholas Canny and Philip D. Morgan, eds., *The Oxford Handbook of the Atlantic World, 1450–1800* (Oxford: Oxford University Press, 2011), 634.
3   Trevor Burnard and Cécile Vidal, 'Location and the Conceptualization of Historical Frameworks: Early American History and Its Multiple Reconfigurations in the United States and in Europe,' in Nicholas Barreyre et al., eds., *Historians across Borders: Writing American History in a Global Age* (Berkeley and Los Angeles: University of California Press, 2014), 146. See also Vidal, 'For a Comprehensive History of the Atlantic World or Histories Connected in and beyond the Atlantic World?' *Annales: Histoire, Sciences Sociales (English)* 67 (2012), 279–300.
4   Matthias Middell and Katja Naumann, 'Global History and the Spatial Turn: From the Impact of Area Studies to the Study of Critical Junctures of Globalization,' *Journal of Global History* 5 (2010), 149–70.
5   Alan L. Karras, 'The Atlantic Ocean Basis,' in Jerry H. Bentley, ed., *The Oxford Handbook of World History* (Oxford: Oxford University Press, 2011), 529
6   Jorge Cañizares and James Sidbury, 'Mapping Ethnogenesis in the Early Modern Atlantic,' *The William and Mary Quarterly* 68 (2011), 184–85.
7   Ibid.; Herman Bennett, *African Kings and Black Slaves: Sovereignty and Dispossession in the Early Modern Atlantic* (Philadelphia: University of Pennsylvania Press, 2018).
8   Nancy Van Deusen, 'The Intimacies of Bondage, Female Indigenous Servants and Slaves and Their Spanish Masters, 1492–1555,' *Journal of Women's History* 24 (2012), 13–43; Jane E. Mangan, *Transatlantic Obligations: Creating the Bonds of Family in Conquest-Era Peru and Spain* (New York: Oxford University Press, 2016), 18–46; Michel de Certeau, *The Practice of*

Everyday Life, trans. Steven Rendall (Berkeley and Los Angeles: University of California Press, 1984).

9 Bernard Bailyn, *The Idea of Atlantic History: Concepts and Contours* (Cambridge, MA: Harvard University Press, 2005), 6–7.

10 Philip D. Morgan, 'Africa and the Atlantic, *c.* 1450–*c.* 1820,' in Jack P. Greene and Morgan, eds., *Atlantic History: A Critical Appraisal* (Oxford: Oxford University Press, 2009), 223.

11 Fifty-four million is from William Denevan, *The Native Populations of the Americas in 1492* (Madison: University of Wisconsin Press, 1992). Debates over the size of Native American populations in 1492 are fierce with very large disparities in estimates. The increasingly accepted estimates are those that suggest a range between 47 and 60 million. See Suzanne Austin Alchon, *A Pest in the Land: New World Epidemics in a Global Perspective* (Albuquerque: University of New Mexico Press, 2003), 150–71; and Linda Newson, 'The Demographic Impact of Colonization,' in Victor Bulmer-Thomas, John Coatsworth, and Roberto Contés Conde, eds., *The Cambridge Economic History of Latin America* (Cambridge: Cambridge University Press, 2006), 143–84.

12 Peter H. Wood, 'From Atlantic History to a Continental Approach,' in Greene and Morgan, eds., *Atlantic History: A Critical Appraisal* (Oxford: Oxford University Press, 2009), 284–85; Douglas H. Ubelaker, 'North American Indian Population Size: Changing Perspectives,' in John W. Verano and Douglas H. Ubelaker, eds., *Disease and Demography in the Americas* (Washington, DC: Smithsonian Institution Press, 1992), 173.

13 Daniel K. Richter, *Before the Revolution: America's Ancient Pasts* (Cambridge. MA: Harvard University Press, 2011), 30.

14 Daniel K. Richter, *Trade, Land, Power: The Struggle for Eastern North America* (Philadelphia: University of Pennsylvania Press, 2013), 45.

15 Karras, 'The Atlantic Ocean Basis,' 538.

16 Ibid., 530, 540–41.

17 Cécile Vidal, 'The Reluctance of French Historians to Address Atlantic History,' *Southern Quarterly* 43 (2006), 153–89.

18 Sylvia Frey, 'Beyond Borders: Revisiting Atlantic History,' in Cécile Vidal, ed., *Louisiana: Crossroads of the Atlantic World* (Philadelphia: University of Pennsylvania, 2013), 185.

BIBLIOGRAPHY

Oxford Online Bibliographies – The Idea of Atlantic History; Colonialism and Postcolonialism; Ideologies of Colonization; Oceanic History.

David Abulafia, *The Discovery of Mankind: Atlantic Encounters in the Age of Columbus* (New Haven: Yale University Press, 2008).

Bernard Bailyn, *The Idea of Atlantic History: Concepts and Contours* (Cambridge, MA: Harvard University Press, 2005).

Jeff Bolster, 'Putting the Ocean in Atlantic History: Maritime Communities and Marine Ecology in the Northwest Atlantic, 1500–1800,' *American Historical Review* 113 (2008), 19–47.

Barry Cunliffe, *Facing the Ocean: The Atlantic and Its Peoples 8000 BC–AD 1500* (New York: Oxford University Press, 2001).

Nicholas Canny and Philip D. Morgan, eds., *The Oxford Handbook of the Atlantic World 1450–1800* (Oxford: Oxford University Press, 2011).

Donna Gabaccia, 'A Long Atlantic in a Wider World,' *Atlantic Studies* 1 (2004), 1–27.

Alison Games, 'Atlantic History: Definitions, Challenges and Opportunities,' *American Historical Review* 111 (2006), 741–56.

Jack P. Greene and Philip D. Morgan, eds., *Atlantic History: A Critical Appraisal* (Oxford: Oxford University Press, 2009).

Martin W. Lewis and Kären E. Wigen, *The Myth of Continents: A Critique of Metageography* (Berkeley and Los Angeles: University of California Press, 1997).

Silvia Marzagalli, 'Sur les origines de l'Atlantic history: Paridgme interprétif de l'histoire des espaces atlantiques à l'époque modern,' *Dix-Huitième Siècle* 33 (2001), 17–31.

Joseph C. Miller, ed. *The Princeton Companion to Atlantic History* (Princeton: Princeton University Press, 2015).

David Northrup, *Africa's Discovery of Europe 1450–1850*, 3rd ed. (Oxford: Oxford University Press, 2014).

Kirsten A. Seaver, *The Frozen Echo: Greenland and the Exploration of North America* (Stanford: Stanford University Press, 1995).

2

WHAT IS ATLANTIC HISTORY?

'We are all Atlanticists now', declared David Armitage in 2002 in his introduction to a prolegomenon for Atlantic history, with blithe disregard for the perils of hubris. But advocates of an Atlantic approach to the history of the early modern Americas can be bullish about the now generation-old fashion for Atlantic history. The topic has developed the type of institutional and intellectual apparatus that signal that an intellectual movement is more than a passing fancy. Atlantic history has become a topic that carries some clout both in teaching and in research terms, almost enough that historians can claim to be specialists in Atlantic history rather than specialists in early American or Latin American or African history (European historians, with some notable exceptions, have not been as eager as Americanists and Africanists to jump on the Atlantic history bandwagon).[1]

At its best, Atlantic history offers a new global interpretative framework and coherent narrative to examine the making of the early modern world of the Americas, Africa and Europe. An Atlantic perspective allows historians to replace the older and Eurocentric narrative of European overseas expansion by a polycentric history of the encounters between Europeans, Natives and Africans in a conscious effort to get away from the 'paradigm of power that had dominated modern historical studies from the beginning'. In other words, Atlantic historians shy away from a focus on the single point of view of Europeans and, more generally, of white male elites. Atlantic historians are committed to avoiding any hint of a teleological narrative based on the transition from colony to nation.[2]

The adoption of Atlantic history as a way of seeing the past is based on more than its usefulness as a way of describing important phenomena that contributed to the making of the early modern and modern worlds. The practice of Atlantic history is older than the concept of Atlantic history, which is sub-discipline of history that emerged mainly in the 1990s. In the 1940s and 1950s, when Atlantic history had its first iteration as a way of describing a sort of transatlantic Western civilization, it was primarily European Europeanists who first wrote about the Atlantic 'community', 'civilization', 'space' and 'economy', in the context of the Second World War, the Anglo-American alliance, and then the Cold War and the creation of NATO. A few British historians who played a crucial role in the development of American studies in the UK were also influential. Except for Robert Palmer who conceived with Jacques Godechot the concept of 'Atlantic Revolution', most American-based historians did not take part in this debate. One generation later, the rise of the new Atlantic history has been the result of a tight collaboration between historians of the British Atlantic and early North America working on both sides of the Atlantic. Historiographically, the concept paralleled both Fernand Braudel's contemporaneous notion of a Mediterranean civilization and Herbert Bolton's interwar argument that the Americas shared a common history. Politically, the concept appealed to historians who agreed with internationalist arguments in America that Atlantic cooperation (by which they meant cooperation between the United States and Western European democracies) was crucial for the survival of freedom in an increasingly dangerous world. Institutionally, it led to a series of educational initiatives pioneered by the US government that led, among other developments, to the first concentrated teaching and research by Europeans into American history in American Studies programmes that started springing up all over Western Europe from the early 1950s.[3]

THE HISTORIOGRAPHY OF THE ATLANTIC WORLD

But this first flourishing of Atlantic history did not lead to any lasting interest in Atlantic connections. Indeed, the few proponents of Atlantic history met with a frosty response, notably in France, where the prevailing historiographical orthodoxy was Marxism. French historians thought of Atlantic history as an outgrowth of an especially reactionary political ideology of which they wanted no part. British historians, or at least those historians who formed part of the pioneering *Past and Present* generation (a leading, originally Marxist inspired, academic journal), were no more enthusiastic than their French counterparts in welcoming an emphasis on shared Atlantic values, ideas and institutional heritages between the Americas and Europe. Atlantic history was no new idea in Britain in the post-war period but was a variation on a well-worm theme, that theme being imperialism, and could be seen, and was seen, as an attempt by committed imperialists of a conservative bent to adapt the well-worn imperialist story to the demands of a new age where the outlines of the future decline of the

British empire to nothingness were all too clear. In general, Atlantic history, in Britain and France, was viewed with suspicion and was very much on the margins of historical discourse.[4]

The scholarship of the 1960s and 1970s was, in the main, leading away from a broadening vision where developments in a multitude of areas were brought together under an Atlantic history synthesis. The emphasis instead was on using the techniques of social history as developed in the famous French historical school publishing in the *Annales* journal to delve exhaustively into the social and economic conditions of small and well-documented populations, usually in Europe or North America. The work of scholars influenced by the *Annales* school was extraordinary, ushering in a golden age of scholarship from the 1960s onwards that has made the historical concerns of the present generation of historians indelibly different from the concerns of the generation of historians who preceded them.

One of the major failures, however, that accompanied the growth of social history in all its multitudinous varieties was a loss of focus. Historians concentrated so intently on the detail of small-scale communities in smaller and smaller geographical locales and over shorter and shorter temporal periods that wider boundaries became unclear. Historians coming into graduate school in the mid-1980s were confronted by a bewildering number of studies on small-scale communities in early America and seventeenth-century Britain, most of which were individually excellent, but which taken together generally led to contradictions and confusions. The logic of the subject did not appear to be leading towards Atlantic enlightenment but towards Balkanization and narrow parochialism where students of what should have been interrelated areas, such as Stuart England, the colonial Chesapeake and Hispanic America, could find little of common interest, even if they had the energy to try and master the ever-growing body of scholarship in fields cognate to their own area of specialization.

Leading historians lamented the trend towards narrowness of geographical and temporal outlook, even while applauding the increasing methodological sophistication and openness to developments in other disciplines, notably in the social sciences and literary criticism, which accompanied this shortening of perspective. Some of these calls were made by historians who can be numbered among the intellectual godfathers of Atlantic history. John Pocock, for example, a year before he published his magisterial work, *The Machiavellian Moment*, which established the lineaments of what Pocock termed 'the Atlantic republican tradition', made a clarion call in 1974 for historians to develop a 'new subject' of 'British history' that would unite the histories of the various nations that made up the early modern British archipelago and the extension of these histories across what David Armitage calls 'the maritime expanses of the Atlantic, Pacific and Indian oceans'.[5]

Pocock and other historians asking for the reappearance of larger narratives may have felt that they were, in Pocock's words, not only 'voice[s] crying in the wilderness' but also persons pointing out to disbelievers that 'there was a wilderness to cry in', but they will have been gratified that their clarion calls have been met with such a positive response by younger scholars who feared that continuing with current trends would lead to intellectual sterility.[6] If there is one thing that Atlantic historians most pride themselves on, it is that they study 'dynamic worlds in motion'. What has been especially noticeable about the types of studies that fall under the rubric of Atlantic history is that their notable contribution has been to extend the area and reach of history and to make connections between areas and periods that were usually left unconnected. The proponents of Atlantic history have been generally uninterested in demonstrating the type of methodological sophistication and technical skill that was so prized among practitioners of social and economic history in the 1970s.

The language used to describe Atlantic history is revealing about its appeal. The words that come up most frequently when Atlantic history approaches are described are 'movement', 'diversity', 'complex', 'networks', 'creation', 'negotiations', 'enlargement', 'dynamic', 'permeable', 'multiple', 'invention', 'exchanges', 'broadening' and, above all else, 'connections'. By contrast, other types of histories are 'narrow', 'technical', 'isolated', 'domestic' and 'static', I have listed them in this way, without attention to grammar, as might be done by speechwriters or New Labour politicians to capture the sort of ambience that politicians like Bill Clinton or Tony Blair try to create both reflecting and shaping the political and cultural tone of the post–Cold War world. Clinton's talk of 'triangulation' and Blair's evocation of a 'third way' are attempts in the political realm to create the sort of connections that Atlantic historians are trying to make in their work. It is interesting to speculate on whether this kind of language, so attuned to discourses of globalization in the first decade of the twenty-first century, will survive within Atlantic history as discontent with globalization becomes a major political trend in the end of the 2010s.

Of course, making direct linkages ('linkages' is another favourite word used by Atlantic historians) between the practice of history and contemporary politics (a politics now disturbingly different from the politics in operation as Atlantic history established itself in the 1990s and 2000s, as is clear in the rise of populism in the Western world and in India) is simplistic. Few historians are directly political in the sense of writing history that they believe speaks to contemporary political issues and historians of the early modern period are less directly political than modern historians, naturally enough given the distance of their period of study from the present day. The inner logic of scholarship is what drives new work rather than engagement with contemporary politics, which is just as well given the limited compass of most historians' political persuasions. But we cannot entirely divorce contemporary politics from the idea of Atlantic history, as Bernard Bailyn recognizes in his genealogy of how the subject came to be. Just as importantly, we need to explain how personal experiences made Atlantic history an attractive proposition for certain types of historians – the types of historians who find the words used above especially appealing and who were looking, like modernizing politicians of the centre-left in the 1990s searching for order in the post–Cold War world, for new ways of escaping from older conceptions of history while not abandoning those conceptions altogether.

For some historians, the motivation to do Atlantic history came from exactly the opposite motivation to that which Bailyn describes for the embryonic Atlanticists of the immediate post-war world. They found attractive what critics of Atlantic history usually consider the greatest weakness of the field, the amorphousness of the subject, the artificiality of locating the object of one's research in the middle of a large ocean rather than around a definable institution like a nation-state, and the absorptive capacity of Atlantic history to soak up all manner of different kinds of concern into one giant, perhaps soggy, very loosely interconnected system. Contra Bailyn, they did not want to return to a comfortable period when there was a narrative of Western history to which all historians could refer and did not want to put the story of the rise of the West back together again. The last thing that they wanted was a retreat into Eurocentrism, which seemed like a new way of promoting imperialism without mentioning its name. Instead, they wanted to foster movements that celebrated marginality rather than integration, that focused on disaggregation as much as aggregation.

We can see these impulses at work in the reminiscences of Jack Greene, as significant as Bailyn as a trainer of the current generation of Atlantic historians, about the origins of the first and most influential of all Atlantic programmes, the programme in Atlantic History, Culture and Society that flourished at the Johns Hopkins University in the 1970s and 1980s.[7] Greene wanted to move away from histories which barely concerned itself at all with the large portion of the globe that was not Western Europe. He was especially concerned with the lack of attention given to the black experience, which he knew was at least as important as the white experience in shaping the contours of early American life, the recapture of which was also an urgent political concern in the late 1960s and early 1970s.

NATION AND MODERNITY IN GLOBAL CONTEXT

An important feature of Atlantic history is that practitioners go past the modern nation as a principal analytical framework. Paradoxically, the field of Atlantic history is often divided into histories of the component imperial nations of Western Europe that participated in the Atlantic World. To critics, such a way of organizing Atlantic history is old-fashioned and obscures how people across the Atlantic did not solely act with other people in their own national territory, even though this is what their European governments expected them to act. This criticism is fair but elides how it is often impossible to go too far outside the framework of the nation-state, given how important it was in Europe in the early modern period and how tied up the concept of a nation is in the nineteenth-century invention of the modern historical method. And when we write about nations we tend to conflate nation with modern political nations, or nation-states, a conflation which reduces the complexities of the concept of nation. As Cécile Vidal argues, 'modern political nations did not exist before the Age of Revolutions proclaimed political citizenship, with its principles of rights and responsibilities'.[8] The eighteenth century saw the notion of nation change from an older ethnic conception of a nation as a people to being seen as a political entity based on place – a political community constructed with government intervention. Nevertheless, as Kathleen Wilson insists, 'in the eighteenth century, nation as a political-territorial entity continued to compete with older Biblical and juridical concepts of nation as a people, located in a relatively fixed spatial and cultural terrain, that was conceived of geographically and ethnographically (as well as ethnocentrically)'.[9]

The concept of a nation was not just a European invention. American societies, where tensions with the metropolis were a major pole of contention throughout the Atlantic period, were laboratories for the transformation of the concept of the nation, primarily because ethnic mixing made nations in the Americas distinct from how they were conceived in Europe. In a sense, European imperial identities were created out of the common identities developed from mixed migrant groups in colonial settings. Those national identities were always unsettled. European settlers in the Americas were insecure about their deeply held contention that they were properly European and Africans and Native Americans had to work out their collective identities in competition with domineering European cultural norms. Vidal argues that 'from these tensions emerged the idea that political and juridical incorporation required cultural assimilation' which 'paved the way for modern conceptions of national identity, and corresponding citizenship, as homogenous and exclusive'. Antonio Feros in relation to the creation of Spanish identity in the early modern period shows that Spaniards argued about national identity in an interconnected, imperial world, full of people with varying claims to Spanishness. To speak about Spain, therefore, meant talking about non-Spaniards. 'Spain' was created out of a conglomerate of different nations and many competing traditions, some recently invented.[10]

This formulation suggests that the Atlantic Ocean is intrinsically modern. Modernity is seen most obviously in labour relations where the people brought to the Americas by coercion were alienated from their homelands and excluded from making money from the lands they worked upon. These people made the Atlantic economy operate efficiently and represented the modern characteristics of production sites, separated widely from sites of consumption. Demographic disaster in sugar production (the most important product of the tropics) meant that even the biological reproduction of the labour force was outsourced to Africa through maintaining labour forces through the purchase of additional captives.

Modernity was especially evident in new understandings of how land could be acquired and sold. It was for Europeans no longer a matter of birthright but a matter of purchase (or appropriation). Land was purchasable by almost everyone, regardless of citizenship, and could be disposed of as people desired. Elizabeth Mancke argues that 'the intensified commercialization of land and naturalizing of the right of foreign ownership were critical mechanisms for introducing European modernity into the extra-ordinary European world'.[11]

Europeans liked to think that the historical processes they had generated in the Atlantic did little to change other societies. But they were obviously wrong: all societies in the Atlantic changed because of interacting with each other and none accepted change passively and without taking an active role in trying to shape change brought about by new interactions. As with world history, the growing importance of Atlantic history challenges ideas that Europe was a coherent historical unit – some parts of Western Europe were more familiar with the Americas than with southern or eastern Europe. Moreover, Atlantic history challenges simplistic notions that European inventions were the main factor changing the world. For example, the age of revolutions did not start from Europe as much as being part of a complex Atlantic nexus, in which places like Haiti and Venezuela played vital roles. The idea of human rights, for example, was less European than Atlantic. Practising Atlantic history is part of general historical processes that seek to provincialize Europe by denying that it was the source of all innovation and agency. As we seek for alternatives to Western-centric world views and hegemonic narratives, Atlantic history can challenge the idea of Europe as a coherent self-enveloping civilization, while acknowledging the force of European global interventions from the time of Columbus to the present.

PERIPHERY VS. CENTRE

Not surprisingly, Atlantic history conceived in this way, as a method of doing history that gave as great attention to developments in the peripheries as it did to machinations in the imperial centres, has proven especially attractive to people living in the peripheries – it is one reason why historians of British America (peripheral then even if its descendant, the United States is certainly not marginal now) took the lead in formulating the major lines of enquiry shaping Atlantic history investigations. Three reasons propel their interest in Atlantic history. First, it is a way of breaking free from the strictures associated with the histories of their own nations, histories which can seem absurdly introspective and inconsequential. Moreover, such histories can often seem part of a nationalistic agenda that historians of an Atlantic disposition feel wary about, an agenda, additionally, which is connected to exceptionalist theses that seem an intrinsic part of retailing the history of any nation-state. As Joyce Chaplin notes, Atlantic historians have an ambiguous relation with nation-state history and with exceptionalist history generally. They recognize the connections between their work and exceptionalist theses – very few Atlantic historians define themselves only as Atlantic historians and do not also reference themselves to the history of individual nation-states, whether these are Spain, Britain, or most commonly the United States. But it goes against Atlantic historians' instinctive interests to privilege the history of one nation over the connections between nations, peoples and events. The result is some uneasy contradictions at the intersections of several historiographical boundaries.[12]

Second, attaching oneself to Atlantic history was a way for historians to move, if not physically then mentally, from the narrow concerns of their small and insignificant homelands. Nicholas Canny makes this point very strongly on his autobiographical comments on how he got drawn into Atlantic history in post-war independent Ireland in the 1960s. Ireland nowadays may be the Celtic Tiger, with a self-proclaimed mission to be the gateway between the Americas and Europe, but it was, as Canny argues, a distinctive and dismal place for much of the twentieth century, the poorest country in Western Europe, priest-ridden and intellectually dormant. Canny describes his experience of how Irish history was taught to students in ways that would be familiar to many historians emanating from peripheral places. The choice for Canny was to devote himself to the study of Irish history, using books 'that might have been written in the nineteenth century (and some of them were)', en route to a secure but enervating career in the professions or in the still-powerful Catholic Church or was to break free, in the way that innumerable Irishmen had done for over a century in other arenas, by emigrating physically and mentally to the wider and more vibrant world where American or English history was part of the curriculum. As Canny puts it, he was 'drawn to the study of colonial American history for the simple reason that the writing on the subject seemed, from an Irish perspective, to be wide-ranging, innovative and venturesome' in a way that Irish history, described by Canny as 'narrow, linear' and nation-state focused, indubitably was not. It is an autobiographical journey that is familiar to many scholars of a similar background who come from small, relatively insignificant countries.[13]

The third impetus for historians of peripheral nations to do Atlantic history is that it is a way whereby historians from peripheral countries can connect the national stories of their own countries with a wider narrative. A notable example is the history of the Dutch republic and its twin empires in the Atlantic and Asia. Dutch historians, blessed by their educational system and their central place as a crossroads of central Europe with a command of European languages that is sadly missing among the historians of other national groups, notably in the Anglophone world, have both been attracted to the histories of their ancestors in places as diverse as

Brazil, New York, Curacao and Indonesia and have punched well above their weight as contributors to and facilitators of Atlantic history.[14] Scots, too, find in Atlantic history a useful way whereby the Scottish contribution to the making of the modern world can be celebrated and assessed and where Scotland is a nation that is not just a northern adjunct to the more significant history of England. In this respect, they follow the trajectory of the greatest Scottish historian, David Hume, whose eighteenth-century world, Emma Rothschild informs us, was an 'interesting illustration of how the Atlantic world of the 18th century extended ... into the interior of individual existence'. This 'oceanic world', she continues, 'was at the edge of the vision of almost everyone' in Scotland, including Hume.[15]

THE THEORY OF ATLANTIC HISTORY

A criticism sometimes made about Atlantic history is that one of its purposes seems to be to find the most insignificant places and then claiming earth-shattering importance for them. In a lot of ways this criticism is justified, because celebrating the peripheries as more important than is usually recognized is at the heart of the Atlantic project. Moreover, historians have argued that it is at the peripheries that the true lineaments of Atlantic history can be discerned, as it is there where the impact of the collision between various worlds can be most clearly measured. The sum of the connections, Atlantic historians contend, is greater than the parts. David Hancock, for example, has theorized Atlantic history using a spider's web approach that prioritizes multi-local interactions and non-metropolitan origins of authority and influences over a simple model of metropolitan giving and peripheries receiving. Hancock argues that the best way to see the Atlantic World is as a complex, non-linear and largely self-governing adaptive system. He draws on work in the physical and medical sciences and in economics which argue that the ordered behaviour of large-scale aggregates is the result of complex interactions among many smaller-scale elements that operate according to much simpler behavioural rules. As Hancock argues, 'large-scale conditions ... shaped the contours of the outcomes [of the net results of abundant, chaotic and decentralized interactions among self-regarding individuals], but the outline of specific outcomes was drawn by the individuals directly involved'. That the centre does not hold is something therefore to be celebrated and adumbrated rather than lamented.[16]

Atlantic history, in common with trends in history generally, is seldom theorized in the ways that Hancock has done for growing commercial links in the eighteenth century. The lack of theoretical explicitness about the assumptions underlying Atlantic history helps explain Atlantic history's diverse practices. Atlantic history has fewer programmatic principles: it has no agreed canon of problems, events and processes. For some of the more fervent advocates of the Atlantic approach, such wishy-washiness is problematic. If almost everything can be termed 'Atlantic', then does the term mean anything except capaciousness in historical interests at odds with a previous generation's narrowing of focus? That there were connections between places and people is not enough for some critics; what needs to be shown is the interconnectedness of the processes knitting an Atlantic World together. Having an agenda for Atlantic history, however, takes away one of the great advantages of doing Atlantic history, that it is little constrained by any larger impulse than being a means whereby specialists in one area can communicate with specialists in other areas, to the mutual advantage of all involved.

Atlantic history falls into three types. First, the most common type of Atlantic writing is detailed studies of places or themes that reference other parts of the Atlantic World as points of comparison. The comparisons, however, help clarify where a region is or is not distinctive rather than being a principal focus of historical investigation. Thus, the comparisons are neither deep nor unduly concerned about integrating these places into a wider world. The second type of Atlantic history is studies that concentrate on the interplay between a place or places and a wider interconnected world of which these places form a part. The stress here is less on comparing one region with another than on highlighting the interconnections between regions with the explicit aim of showing that it was the interconnections themselves that were the most dynamic and hence transformative aspects of these histories. The final type of Atlantic history concentrates on the Atlantic itself as the central unit of analysis. Historians doing this type of history (what David Armitage calls circum-Atlantic history) are especially interested in the interactions that occurred within the Atlantic, especially on the sea itself and on how the experience of being on the Atlantic Ocean and in contact with other people who criss-crossed continents.[17]

So how and why do historians choose what topics they study and what frameworks of historical inquiry they choose to use? There are always scientific and intellectual reasons to prefer one framework over another. For instance, historians of Native America have been especially critical of some of the principal assumptions undergirding Atlantic history. One reason for these criticisms is that Native Americans occupy a distinctive place among Atlantic actors since they did not take part in the transatlantic – free or forced – mass migrations which gave birth to the Atlantic World. Nevertheless, as Daniel Richter has underlined, Native Americans lived as much as Europeans and Africans in a 'New World': 'Native People, of course, did not literally travel to this "Indians' New World", but the changes forced upon them were just as profound as if they had resettled on unknown shores'.[18]

Among other things, these changes encouraged not only multiple movements of migration and resettlement within the Americas, but also some limited transatlantic mobility from the Western hemisphere to Europe. Still, some historians think that continental history is better suited than

Atlantic history to take into account Native American points of view: the fact that large parts of North America remained for a very long time Indian country or frontiers and borderlands where imperial rivalries allowed Indians to maintain their sovereignty and exercise their agency makes some practitioners dubious about employing an historical framework in which Europeans are principal actors forcing transformative change. Continental history also takes into better consideration than does Atlantic history the Pacific side of North America with its Spanish, but also Russian, colonies or settlements in the eighteenth century. These Pacific perspectives are hardly mentioned by Atlanticists – taking an Atlantic perspective often precludes taking a Pacific view of historical change in colonial contexts.[19]

CRITICISMS OF ATLANTIC HISTORY

Paradoxically, some historians have criticized Atlantic history as just a revamped form of older styles of imperial history, displaying some of the drawbacks of that mode of analysis, notably Eurocentric bias. Other scholars have underlined that the view of the Atlantic World as a world of 'entangled empires' leaves aside Africa and an alternative diasporic conceptualization of the Atlantic World. This tendency towards Eurocentrism is reinforced by the choice of many authors to stop Atlantic history at the independence of European colonies in the Americas, an independence obtained for the most part by the end of the 1820s, as noted in Chapter 7. Consequently, this historiography may overemphasize the White or Euro-American Atlantic. Nevertheless, even though the history of the Atlantic World cannot be reduced to the history of empires, even of entangled empires, empires mattered greatly within and outside the Atlantic World. National Atlantics were not identical to national Atlantic empires – English merchants, for instance, were active well beyond the borders of the English empire; a reconfigured French Atlantic survived the dismantling of the French Atlantic empire at the end of the Seven Years' War with migrations between the French metropole and its former colonies and between former colonies becoming more important in the late eighteenth century and during the nineteenth century.

Colonialism and Atlantic history have a complicated relationship. The latter was in part devised to escape the straitjacket of empire-colony dichotomies. Colonies were not always, however, subservient to empires. In the United States in the nineteenth century the former colonists became imperialists themselves. In Brazil, from 1808 when the Portuguese Crown moved to the south Atlantic colony, the relationship between empire and colony can be said to have been reversed, as the periphery became in effect the metropole. The United States complicates theories of colonialism within Atlantic history. While it is clearly a post-colonial state, it is also the nation against which other post-colonial peoples construct their identities and politics. Colonialism is something with which Atlantic historians continue to engage, as they analyse the development of processes of acceptance, emulation and resistance against imperial cultural hegemony. Indeed, Atlantic places were places that were deeply imbued with colonial prejudices born out of common cultural conditions. Consequently, Atlantic history embraces and rejects colonialism as a governing paradigm. It was a complex, plural and largely self-determining adaptive system, in which colonialism played only one part.[20]

One final point. Atlantic historiography is an exercise in making historical fields more consciously diverse. It moves decisively away from seeing the making of the modern world as being a story of active European expansion and passive acceptance of that acceptance by peoples in other parts of the world. Rather, it envisions the process by which Europe involved itself in African and the Americas as a much more complicated process in which Europeans did not always hold the upper hand, especially in West Africa. Nevertheless, the nature of the historical profession with its deep roots in scholarship and historical standards originating in Western Europe; the nature of sources, heavily biased towards European creators; and the encrusted legacy of history writing that celebrates European imperialism make Eurocentric perspectives often hard to avoid. Criticism of Atlantic history as implicitly influenced by European assumptions of their rightness to global superiority is not without justification. Europe gets more play than it should in most Atlantic-inflected histories.

One major achievement of Atlantic history is that it brings African history into the historiographical mainstream. The history of West Africa, of course, is more than just its role in the Atlantic World. Much of the continent was unaffected by Atlantic influences. Africa was bigger than the Atlantic Ocean in the early modern era. That Atlantic World was mostly a black Atlantic World: before 1820 more Africans than Europeans went to the Americas, mostly unwillingly in the case of Africans. Perhaps the single most important advance attributable to the Atlantic perspective has been its encouragement of the inclusion of Africans (less successfully Native Americans) into traditional historical narratives. Africans are noted not just as being the largest body of migrants to the Americas. What they did in the Americas was even more important than their numbers. Their labour produced the goods that made the Americas valuable to Europe and which hastened the eighteenth century of a commercial world based on the slave trade and on plantation agriculture. As Barbara Solow famously has noted, 'What moved in the Atlantic was primarily [African] slaves, the output of slaves, the inputs of slave societies, and the goods and services produced with the earnings on slave products'.[21]

The recognition within Atlantic history of the importance of Africans as active agents has encouraged historians of other places to take Africa seriously as a region incorporated into global patterns of exchange.[22] Africa has not yet been fully incorporated into the early modern world and much of what we know about Africa in this period and its place in the history of the Americas has been provided by historians of Africa translating Africa for Atlanticists than by Atlantic historians with a deep knowledge of African cultures. Yet what has become clear is how important Africa and Africans were in the making of this world. Africa was not a place that was acted on by Europeans, as in older historiographies, but was a part of the world where European control remained weak until after the Atlantic period was complete. Fully Atlantic perspectives help us see this region – and other regions in the continents adjoining the Atlantic Ocean – in their proper global historical context. These perspectives allow us to place European conquest, colonization and settlement as important but not determinative factors in significant historical processes of change, continuity and adaptation.

NOTES

1   David Armitage, 'Introduction,' in Armitage and Michael Braddick, eds., *The British Atlantic World, 1500–1800*, rev. ed. (New York: Palgrave Macmillan, 2002, 2009), 3; Cécile Vidal, 'The Reluctance of French Historians to Address Atlantic History', *The Southern Quarterly*, Special Issue: Imagining the Atlantic World 43 (2006), 153–89.
2   Cécile Vidal, 'Pour une histoire globale du monde atlantique ...,' *Annales: Histoire, Sciences, Sociale* 67 (2012), 391–413.
3   Bernard Bailyn, *The Idea of Atlantic History: Concepts and Contours* (Cambridge, MA: Harvard University Press, 2005).
4   David Armitage, 'Greater Britain: A Useful Category of Historical Analysis,' *American Historical Review* 104 (1999), 427–45.
5   Richard Bourke, 'Pocock and the Presuppositions of the New British History,' *Historical Journal* 53 (2010), 747–70.
6   J.G.A. Pocock, 'The New British History in Atlantic Perspective: An Antipodean Commentary,' *American Historical Review* CIV (1999), 490.
7   Jack P. Greene, 'Diversity at Hopkins: Some Reminiscences' Last accessed date – 14 August 2019. http:www.jhu.edu/~igscph/fall93jg.htm.
8   Cécile Vidal, 'Nation,' in Joseph C. Miller, ed., *The Princeton Companion to Atlantic History* (Princeton: Princeton University Press, 2015), 354.
9   Kathleen Wilson, *The Island Race: Englishness, Empire, and Gender in the Eighteenth Century* (New York: Routledge, 2003), 7.
10 Vidal, 'Nation', 356; Antonio Feros, *Speaking of Spain: The Evolution of Race and Nation in the Hispanic World* (Cambridge, MA: Harvard University Press, 2017); Gilles Havard, '"Les forcer à deviner Citoyen": État, Sauvages et citonyenneté en Nouvelle-France (XVIIe-XVIIIe siècle),' *Annales* 64 (2009), 985–1018.
11 Elizabeth Mancke, 'Modernity,' in Joseph C. Miller, ed., *Princeton Companion to Atlantic History* (Princeton: Princeton University Press, 2015), 342.
12 Joyce E. Chaplin, 'Expansion and Exceptionalism in Early American History,' *Journal of American History* 90 (2003), 1431–55.

13 Nicholas Canny, 'Writing Atlantic History; or, Reconfiguring the History of Colonial British America,' *Journal of American History* 86 (1999), 1093–114.
14 Wim Klooster, *The Dutch Moment: War, Trade, and Settlement in the Seventeenth-Century Atlantic World* (Ithaca: Cornell University Press, 2016).
15 Emma Rothschild, 'The Atlantic Worlds of David Hume,' in Bernard Bailyn, ed., *Soundings in Atlantic History: Latent Structures and Intellectual Currents, 1500–1830* (Cambridge, MA: Harvard University Press, 2011) 405–48.
16 David Hancock, 'Self-Organised Complexity and the Emergence of an Atlantic Market Economy, 1651–1851', in Peter A. Coclanis, ed., *The Atlantic Economy during the Seventeenth and Eighteenth Centuries* (Columbia, SC: University of South Carolina Press, 2005), 30–71.
17 Armitage, 'Introduction.'
18 Daniel K. Richter, *Facing East from Indian Country: A Native History of Early America* (Cambridge: Cambridge University Press, 2001), 41.
19 Paul W. Mapp, 'Atlantic History from Imperial, Continental, and Pacific Perspectives', *William and Mary Quarterly* 3d ser. 58 (2006), 713–24.
20 Trevor Burnard, 'Colonies and Colonization,' in Miller, ed., *Princeton Companion to Atlantic History*, 106.
21 Barbara L. Solow, ed. *Slavery and the Rise of the Atlantic System* (Cambridge: Cambridge University Press, 1991), 1.
22 Joseph E. Inikori, 'Africa and the Globalisation Process: Western Africa, 1450–1850,' *Journal of Global History* 2 (2007), 63–86.

BIBLIOGRAPHY

Oxford Online Bibliographies – Global History and Atlantic History; Native Americans and the Atlantic World; The Atlantic Ocean and India; The Pacific; Transatlantic Public Sphere.

Luiz Felipe de Alencastro, *O Trato dos Viventes: Formação do Brasil no Atlântico Sul Séculos XVI e XVII* (Sao Paulo: Campanha das Letras, 2000).

Bernard Bailyn, *The Idea of Atlantic History: Concepts and Contours* (Cambridge, MA: Harvard University Press, 2005).

Trevor Burnard and Cécile Vidal, 'Location and the Conceptualization of Historical Frameworks: Early North American History and Its Multiple Reconfigurations in the US and in Europe,' in Nicolas Barreyre et al., eds., *You, the People: Historical Writing about the United States in Europe* (Berkeley and Los Angeles: University of California Press, 2014) 141–64.

Nicholas Canny, 'Writing Atlantic History; or, Reconfiguring the History of Colonial British America,' *Journal of American History* 86 (1999), 1093–114.

Joyce E. Chaplin, 'Expansion and Exceptionalism in Early American History,' *Journal of American History* 90 (2003), 1431–55.

Jack P. Greene and Morgan, eds., *Atlantic History: A Critical Appraisal* (Oxford: Oxford University Press, 2009).

Ray A. Kee, 'Africa in World History,' in Jerry H. Bentley et al., eds., *The Cambridge World History: The Construction of a Global World, 1400–1800 CE* (Cambridge: Cambridge University Press, 2015), I, 243–70.

Gabriel Paquette, *The European Seaborne Empires: From the Thirty Years' War to the Age of Revolutions* (New Haven: Yale University Press, 2019).

Daniel K. Richter, *Facing East from Indian Country: A Native History of Early America* (Cambridge: Cambridge University Press, 2001).

John K. Thornton, *African and Africans in the Making of the Atlantic World, 1400–1800* (Cambridge: Cambridge University Press, 1992).

Cécile Vidal, 'L'Atlantic français,' *Outre-Mers: Revue d'histoire* 97 (2009), 7–139.

PART TWO

The Atlantic World over Time

3

THE COLUMBIAN EXCHANGE

CHRISTOPHER COLUMBUS

It is likely that Christopher Columbus, whose voyages to the Caribbean in the 1490s revolutionized world history, knew of the existence of North America from Bristol merchants, using such information as confirmation of his theories about the longitude of China and Japan. What Columbus 'discovered' in 1492 was indeed new, insofar as no European had previously knowingly sailed to and from the Caribbean. But it was not as new as Columbus insisted. Portuguese sailors had been sailing in the South Atlantic for many years, pushing down the coast of Africa in search of gold. They reached the Senegal and Gambia rivers by 1450, had crossed the equator by 1475 and had reached the mouth of the Congo by 1484. Their exploits meant that while the Portuguese did not know most of the physical geography of the Atlantic, they understood celestial navigation and wind systems. It is possible that some Portuguese seamen may even have got close to the coast of Brazil before Columbus's voyages, though the first known sighting of Brazil by a European was by Pedro Alvares Cabal in 1500.[1]

Columbus was not therefore sailing into entirely unknown waters in 1492. His voyage was informed by Portuguese explorers sailing down the west coast of Africa and English sailors going to Newfoundland. But he misunderstood what he learned. His Atlantic voyages were based on a misconception, one which he never understood or acknowledged. He thought he could get from the Canaries to Cipango (Japan) easily. He adopted the 'narrow Atlantic' theories of cosmographers who accepted Ptolemy's estimates that the Eurasian land mass extends over 180° of latitude (rather than 100°). From this, Columbus estimated Japan to be 2,400 miles (3,862 kilometres) rather than the actual figure of 10,600 (17,059 kilometres). Until his death, Columbus absurdly thought that he had reached Japan from Europe rather than just a series of islands. One reason why Columbus became derided before his death (aside from his vainglorious temperament and acquisitive greed) was that his navigational theories were quickly exploded as wrong. Experts in the Western Ocean (as it was then called) knew that the ocean was scattered with islands, just like those Columbus had discovered. After the initial excitement of Columbus's 'discoveries', observers placed Columbus's travels to islands within existing cartographic knowledge and downplayed the significance of what Columbus had found. In addition, Vasco da Gama's 1498 voyage to India not only gave Europe the practicable route to the highly desirable Indies that Columbus had not provided but allowed for an accurate estimate of the size of the world. This estimate destroyed Columbus's 'narrow Atlantic' fantasies. Columbus did make a major discovery on his third voyage in 1498, when after a classic miscalculation of the altitude of Polaris (the North Star is on the horizon at 0° at the Equator, making fixing latitude easy) he sighted the mainland of South America. He characteristically made ridiculous claims, principally that what he had observed from afar (the noisy mouth of the Amazon River) was the beginning of Paradise.[2]

Nevertheless, what needs to be stressed is that Europe avoided rather than explored the Atlantic Ocean for centuries after it knew that there was land in the west. The major impetus to Atlantic colonisation before Columbus was the Iberian conquest of the Atlantic islands off the coast of Africa, beginning with the Canaries, from the early fourteenth century. But this colonization activity was not a departure from past practices. It was conceived and implemented as an extension of the Mediterranean world, even if to reach these islands required new navigational techniques, notably fixing latitude at sea and working out tricky wind systems.

In general, Western Europeans before 1500 were as uninterested in the Atlantic Ocean as were Africans and Native Americans. It was thought of in ways first devised by the ancient Greeks, as a vast and dangerously mysterious barrier around the known world. It seemed to lead nowhere and to be of no value and not even a full ocean, like the Mediterranean. It was in changing this idea of a valueless Western Ocean that Columbus's main achievement lies. As Joyce Chaplin comments, 'Columbus would be the first person to transform the Atlantic from unknown barrier to physical entity although, significantly, he was not entirely aware he had done so.' But if Columbus did not recognize what he had done, others did. The shift can be seen, Chaplin continues, in comparing a map of the world that illustrated the 1508 edition of Ptolemy's *Geographia* to a 1477 edition. In 1477, the emphasis was on the Old World, with the Mediterranean at the centre. The 1508 edition, by contrast, 'is remarkable for its new sense that the Atlantic Ocean led outward, around Africa to the Indian Ocean, and to the west, toward the newfound lands and then beyond, a new route to the Orient'.[3]

To understand the start of the Atlantic World, one must appreciate that it was always an oceanic world. The Atlantic Ocean was the conduit – increasingly a highway, rather than a barrier – through which the movement of peoples, goods and ideas occurred, connecting and integrating together diverse peoples and places into a largely coherent single system. The Atlantic Ocean was the means through which this integration occurred. Sometimes this obvious fact is forgotten. As Alison Games notes, 'the Atlantic history that many historians produce is rarely centred around the ocean, and the ocean is rarely relevant to the project'.[4] The Atlantic Ocean is not the largest ocean in the world – it covers less than half of the space of the Pacific – but it is pretty large, considerably bigger than the coastal regions that funnelled people from one part of the Atlantic to another. It extends over 30 million square miles with complex patterns of surface winds and ocean currents that have always proved a challenge to navigators.

A DESIRE FOR EXPANSION

In the end, what initiated the Atlantic World was the sudden and to an extent inexplicable desire by some Western Europeans to extend the boundaries of Europe into Africa and the Americas. The leaders in this enterprise were the Iberians (Portuguese and Spanish), the British and to an extent the Dutch. The French, despite being a major maritime power, were surprisingly slow to get seriously involved in the Atlantic, with some exploration in the late sixteenth century but of a more limited kind than one would expect from the richest and most populous nation in Western Europe. Europeans were by no means the best sailors in the world in the mid-fifteenth century. That title probably belonged to Polynesians, whose mastery of the greatest ocean in the world was remarkable. Arabs and Indians were used to longer sea routes than Europeans and the Chinese had more money and better and bigger ships. It is possible, as N.A.M. Rodgers argues, that Europeans came from 'an intellectually curious society, in which sea voyaging might be associated with chivalry, honour and profit in this world or the next'.[5] They also were the first peoples to understand the complicated Atlantic wind systems, allowing navigators to not just leave their homeland but to return. This navigational discovery provided for the creation of a common seaborne culture in Western Europe and a system of graphic mapping practices in a world of sophisticated cartography that led to the growth of theoretical knowledge about the Atlantic Ocean that were used in practical sea voyaging. In this way, an emerging Atlantic World started to begin from the early sixteenth century.

COLUMBUS ARRIVES IN THE BAHAMAS

Atlantic history is customarily considered to have started on 14 October 1492. On that date, the Italian mariner and adventurer Christopher Columbus (1451–1506) made landfall at an island that the Native American inhabitants called Guanahani. Columbus, after having had his plans turned down by the kings of Portugal and England, was sponsored by Ferdinand and Isabel, the co-monarchs of Aragón and Castile, and began his journey much farther south than had been the case for Portuguese sailors who had previously headed west to discover nothing, as far as we know. Columbus started from the Spanish-controlled Canaries. This southerly point of departure allowed Columbus to pick up the Trade Winds heading west. He was carried across the Western Ocean at its widest point in a voyage lasting thirty-three days.

He found new lands, for Europeans at least, in the Caribbean Sea. Columbus took possession of the lands he found, starting with Guanahani, which he renamed San Salvador. He does not make mention in his journal of a ceremonial act, whereby Spain became the owner of this island, but he raised the standard of Ferdinand and Isabella and had the solemn declaration of their rights to the island duly notarized. The Spanish and the English accepted the Roman law of *res nullius*, whereby occupied land remained the common property of mankind, until used. The first user thus became the owner. Columbus claimed first use of these islands, which he considered waste land due to inadequate cultivation by the indigenous inhabitants. As he wrote in his journal when he arrived in other islands: 'I did not wish to pass by any island without taking possession of it, although it might be said that once one had been taken, they all were.'[6]

Of course, none of the places that Columbus visited in his four journeys between 1492 and 1504 and laid claim to on behalf of the Spanish Crown were *res nullius*. They were full of people and had been for millennia. In one of the great tragedies of history, the great majority of the peoples who inhabited those islands of the Greater Antilles disappeared from history within a few decades in a brief but brutal process of colonization and subjugation. What knowledge we have of these peoples comes mostly from archaeology and from the biased commentary of Spanish conquistadors from the early sixteenth century. The finding of new peoples, seemingly living in isolation, Columbus thought, since the Creation, was even more important than finding new lands. It introduced something new under the sun to European conceptions of the world, forcing writers to readjust their understanding of theology (Native Americans were unknown to biblical culture), nature (the environment of the Caribbean contained many things that had never been thought of in the European imagination), and of world geography and world cultures.

In many respects, however, this 'discovery' of new people was disappointing. After the initial excitement of news of the discovery of the Americas, hugely trumpeted by Columbus, wore down, the people Columbus had found seemed very unimpressive. They were 'meek and human people', as the chronicler Peter Martyr explained. They lived in a virtually naked state, which in European understanding suggested that they were extreme primitives and undeveloped versions of mankind. They were also unaccountably poor for being residents, Columbus thought, of land near

Japan. They had no cities or trading ports – key signs of civilization – and had little to recommend themselves to Spain, except perhaps as a body of people who might be led through Christ to salvation. More ominously, Columbus thought the Native Americans he encountered to be ideal servants and he brought several to Spain to be servants or slaves. Columbus also indulged in elaborate fantasies about the geography and make-up of the Caribbean. He based his views of Caribbean places he had not seen in part from cautious and uncertain conversations with the native inhabitants of Guanahani and other islands in the Greater Antilles and in part from his reading of late medieval texts such as those produced by Sir John Mandeville in the fourteenth century that speculated on what sorts of weird and marvellous people might exist beyond the western boundaries of Europe.

Columbus reported back to Isabel that in addition to the harmless people he had met and renamed as 'Indians', as if they were residents of Asia, one Caribbean island was inhabited by cannibals (Caribs); another by people with tails; and a third by Amazons, women warriors who lived in societies in which men were absent. Early explorers kept on looking for 'monstrosities' in the New World of the Americas. An early governor of Cuba, for example, instructed the conquistador, Hernan Cortés, to see if there were men with heads of dogs in his travels to the Yucatan and to Mexico. The late sixteenth-century English explorer Walter Raleigh was convinced that *acephali* – headless people with 'their eyes in in their shoulders and their mouths in the middle of their breasts' – lived somewhere in the Orinoco basin of northeast South America.

Such views of indigenous Native American diversity have had a long history. We do not believe, and have not believed for a long time, that monsters live in the forests of the Amazon or in the wastelands of Patagonia. But until recently scholars thought that Columbus was right to divide the indigenous residents of the Caribbean into several distinct ethnic groups called Tainos, Arawaks and Caribs. The consensus that has recently emerged is that while there were many ethnic groups in the Caribbean in 1492, 'nearly all of them' were speakers of 'mutually unintelligible' Arawakan languages.[7] These Arawakan peoples suffered first and worst from the Columbian encounter. Semi-sedentary peoples, influenced it appears by Mesoamerican civilization, they lived in towns of up to several thousand residents, although these towns did not have the sophistication of Mesoamerican societies in Central America and Mexico. Their semi-sedentary character exacerbated their harsh treatment under the Spanish, making enslavement and epidemic disease more prevalent. By the middle of the sixteenth century, the Native American population of the Greater Antilles had shrunk to such a point that the Spanish had to turn their attention to the mainland with its larger Native American population that even with diseases and warfare could provide plentiful labour for Spanish mining and agriculture. The indigenous inhabitants of the Lesser Antilles proved more able to resist disease and the ravages of colonization. Even though these populations hardly emerged unscathed from the Columbian encounter, they could offer considerable resistance to colonial powers over several centuries. More successful still were the native inhabitants of the Amazon, Orinoco and Atlantic Guyana. Spain did not try and colonize this region of northeast South America until the 1580s. The Amazon River continued to be tangential to Spanish and Portuguese colonization, meaning that the native population of this large region remained largely untouched by colonization until the 1630s and perhaps even into the eighteenth century outside the orbit of Portuguese slaving and missionary activities.

What happened on 14 October 1492 was the prime example in history of the 'shock of the new'. Abbé Raynal, the philosophe compiler of *Histoire des deux Indes* (1770), and a major advocate of the Black Legend, in which (following the incendiary 1552 work of Bartolomé Las Casas in *Brief Account of the Destruction of the Indies*) the Spanish were lambasted for their cruelty as conquerors, thought this day a dark one. He declared that it would have been best for humanity if Columbus had never reached the Americas. Yet, as stressed in Chapter 1, Columbus overstressed the novelty of what he had found in his 'discoveries'. He continued to brag unreasonably about what he had done to the increasing irritation of his long-suffering monarchical supporters. On his fourth voyage (1502–1504), Columbus was stranded in Jamaica due to worm-eaten and unseaworthy vessels. During his year's sojourn in Jamaica, he had a dream and wrote to Ferdinand and Isabel recounting what this dream told him. It was about the world significance of his life's work. He had apparently heard a voice that told him: 'The Indies, which are so rich a part of the world, He [God] gave thee for thine own ... Of the barriers to the Ocean Sea, which were closed with such mighty chains, He gave thee the keys, and thou wast obeyed in many lands and among Christians thou have gained an honourable fame.' By this time Columbus exhibited a strong Messianic streak, taking to sign his letters as Christopher Columbus 'Christ-giver', suggesting he alone had brought Native Americans to salvation.[8] Yet it was not the provision of salvation for pagan souls that motivated most Spaniards and their rulers in taking possession of Caribbean lands and peoples. What most attracted them was Mammon. The peoples of the Caribbean might be poor but in Hispaniola at least they had gold. Martyr wrote that in that large island 'they found gold, but in no great quantity, nor yet that pure. They make of it, certain breast plates and brooches, which they wear for comeliness.'

PORTUGUESE IN WEST AFRICA

The Iberian explorations of the west African coast had also been about the pursuit of gold, although it became quickly clear that West Africans knew very well the value of gold and silver, unlike the Native Americans Columbus imagined so deficient in imagination that they did not know they were sitting on riches in precious materials. Moreover, Europeans could not cheat Africans out of gold. Africans retained control of their lands and the direction of trade with Europe. That Africans retained their power to determine patterns of trade in societies that were under African control was a fundamental feature of Atlantic interactions between Africans in Africa and European supplicants from the mid-fifteenth century right through to the start of intensive European colonization of the continent in the mid- to late nineteenth century.

Gold dominated by value in transatlantic trade between West Africa and Europe until about 1700. Slaves leaving West Africa for the Americas only exceeded gold as a trading commodity for a century and a half between about 1700 and the 1840s. Moreover, the gold produced in Africa did not just end up in transatlantic trade. Gold exports from the various mines of the West African forest went across the Sahara to Egypt, where the bulk of it departed on shops for the trade of India, linking the forest mines of West Africa to the textile manufactures and spice plantations of Asia.[9] The Portuguese expeditions to West Africa were in search of gold, not slaves.

From the beginning, the Portuguese were eager to divert into the Atlantic World some of the gold trade that for centuries had crossed the Sahara to North Africa. They had little success in Upper Guinea, the region of West Africa that was least well integrated into the Atlantic economy, possibly due to political fragmentation and the strong influence of Islam on avoiding contacts with non-Muslims. They had much more success in West-Central Africa where in the Congo the Portuguese established a client state that was the only viable colony controlled by Europeans in the early modern era. In 1506, they persuaded the Kongo leader, Afonso, to become Catholic, thus cementing his power over his people through connections to Europeans. The problem with the Congo, however, was that it offered Europeans no gold. The Portuguese fared much better in the aptly named Gold Coast. By the first decade of the sixteenth century, there was an official gold trade of over 20,000 ounces per annum from the gold producing region of Mina, not accounting for gold smuggled illegally. Other European nations were also drawn to the gold in the area. West Africa before the early seventeenth century was the principal source of gold for Western Europe, exports averaging between 25,000 and 27,000 ounces a year from 1471 to 1600 and over 32,000 ounces per annum in the first half of the seventeenth century.[10]

It was this sort of trade (sugar in the Atlantic islands was another important product exploited by the Portuguese in the fifteenth century) that the Spanish wanted to replicate in their settlement of the Americas. It led them to extend what they had learned in their conquest of the Canaries between 1478 and 1493 to what became by the middle of the sixteenth century Spanish America. After 1492, Spain's possessions spread from a few isolated and unproductive Caribbean outposts to include the Aztec parts of Mexico, the Mayan lands of southern Mexico and Central America. By the 1530s, they had largely taken control of the Inca Empire (Tawantinsuyu).

They moved steadily south and north so that by 1600 they claimed possession of a vast region extending from the current southwest of the United States to the southern tip of Southern America.

The only significant parts of South America they did not lay claim to were Brazil and the Guianas. The latter stayed uncolonized until well into the seventeenth century. Brazil went to the Portuguese. Under the papally driven Treaty of Tordesillas (1494), the Spanish and the Portuguese divided the world along a pole-to-pole demarcation line 370 leagues west of the Cape Verde Islands (between 48°W and 49°W). Spain had access to all land west of the line and Portugal all land to the east. Of course, other Europeans rejected the idea of an Iberian *mare clausum* (or closed sea). Native American inhabitants of these lands so summarily given away by their supposed Christian protector to their enemies never agreed whatsoever to this grand division of land that did not belong to Iberian powers.

THE SPANISH CARIBBEAN

Initial colonization efforts by the Spanish in the lands Columbus laid claim to were unimpressive, even though it was in the Caribbean in which the Spanish established many of the features of Spanish American colonization that were to shape colonization in their empire until the age of revolutions disrupted everything in the early nineteenth century. Columbus emulated the Portuguese in how he tried to manage the lands he had seized between 1492 and 1504. He wanted to make Hispaniola the main centre of colonization for a Spanish empire in the Americas, viewing it as if it was a Mediterranean or African commercial outpost under his personal control with colonists serving as employees. It did not work, not just because Spanish colonists refused to accept Columbus's authority. One problem was health. Almost as soon as the Spanish set foot on Hispaniola, they began to die. The Spanish did not care for the new foods they encountered, and as the wine they brought disappeared, they drank parasite-filled water. The result was diarrhoea, cramps, dehydration, famine and death. Within two years, about two-thirds of the Spanish had succumbed to an alien Caribbean environment.[11]

A second reason was brutality. The Spanish came to find gold which they had been promised as being abundant when they joined Columbus's second expedition in 1693. The Spanish brutally forced the residents to serve them and tortured them to take them to the elusive source of the gold supposedly everywhere in Hispaniola. But gold was scarce. The Spanish turned to sending slaves from Hispaniola back to Spain. After a revolt against the tyrannical Columbus in 1497, Spanish colonists were humoured by being given control over indigenes in a kind of vassalage that eventually developed into the *encomienda*, a system of labour and tribute extraction from Native Americans that Spain later extended throughout Spanish America.

A final reason for the failure of early colonization efforts in the Spanish Caribbean was the lack of gold. What gold was in the Caribbean was obtained only through plunder or by using coerced Native American labour to mine under terrible conditions. These small amounts of gold disappeared within decades. The Spanish were forced to turn to developing a limited and not very profitable agricultural economy based on sugar, livestock and ginger. Sugar production, despite the example of the Canaries and Brazil, was unimpressive. In order, however, to cultivate these crops, the Spanish needed to import African slaves from Portuguese African trading posts. From 1520, African enslaved people supplanted and then replaced Native American workers on these embryonic sugar plantations.

Matthew Restall argues that the failure of the Spanish to establish a lasting economic presence in the early sixteenth-century Caribbean helps to explain the Spanish conquest of the American mainland, starting with the expeditions of Cortés to Mexico in 1519. He argues that 'had the Spanish presence in the Caribbean been truly dynamic, well-funded and driven hard from Spain', the centre of the Spanish empire would have rested in Hispaniola. But it was not dynamic, 'leading to continual Spanish exploration of the circum-Caribbean in search of people to make their colonies pay'. They found those people – Mesoamericans and Andeans – in the two great Native American empires, the Aztecs and the Incas. Restall notes that both empires in the 1520s were 'impressive examples of expansionist imperialism, driven by powerful political-religious ideologies and institutions of central control, supported by adaptable and deeply rooted organisational systems, arguably yet to reach their apex, let alone their decline'. The third empire in the region, the Spanish empire in the Caribbean, located in Hispaniola, paled in comparison, 'undermined from the very onset by the contradiction between colonial expectations and the realities of the natural and human environment on the island'.[12]

That it was a failure does not mean that the Spanish Caribbean was unimportant in the stages of imperialism in the Atlantic World. The forms and practices of Spanish government, fashioned around urban living, were first established in the Hispaniola city of Santo Domingo. Cities were Spanish and controlled the rural Native American countryside. The basic structures of civic and religious life, including the appointment of royal governors, the 1511 institution of a court of appeals, or *audencia*, and the arrival of missionaries and also in 1511 bishoprics, occurred in the Spanish Caribbean. The Caribbean was where the Spanish tested the transmission of Spanish culture and society into the New World, even if this culture 'was winnowed and screened by distance, local conditions, indigenous practices and eventually by earlier practices as successive groups of immigrants disembarked'. Stuart Schwartz concludes that 'what was crystallised in the Caribbean was a streamlined, innovative "conquest culture," that reflected a heavy dose of Andalusian and maritime influences and which incorporated local realities, vocabulary, and practices. This was then carried in the conquest to the rest of the Indies where it was again modified and reshaped by local human, geographic, and cultural realities.'[13]

SPAIN AND PORTUGAL ON THE AMERICAN MAINLAND

Spanish colonization in the Caribbean was thus a false start. If we want to date the 'real discovery of America' then a better date is 8 November 1519, the day Moctezuma, emperor of the Aztecs, met the conquistador Cortés on the causeway leading into Tenochtitlan.[14] Moctezuma delivered a speech that Cortés later represented to the king of Spain as being a statement of surrender. That statement entered folklore but is highly improbable to be true – the gap in status between the two men makes such a possibility so remote as to be impossible. It became part, however, of the mythology that was used to explain one of the more remarkable events in history, the relatively rapid takeover of a mighty empire by a group of brave but ragged and heavily outnumbered soldiers of fortune. What we do know is that Cortés achieved the impossible. By 1521, Moctezuma was dead, the great city of Tenochtitlan was in ruins and Cortés had completed an initial conquest of Mexico.

The conquest of the mainland was haphazard, usually organized locally, often as commercial ventures and by private individuals, acting usually with implicit state sanction. The conquistadors were a notoriously rum lot of adventurers, criminals and self-seekers. They concentrated their efforts on attacking areas of dense indigenous population and through taking major cities paralysing empires that were unusually centralized. That is what Francisco Pizarro did in his equally remarkable exploit in conquering Cuzco, the capital city of the Inca Empire, in 1533. In retrospect, what is most striking is just how rapid these conquests were. Between 1514 and 1540, Spanish conquistadors had explored and conquered much of two continents, as well as substantial parts of the Caribbean overcoming tremendous environmental challenges and the determined resistance of naïve inhabitants who vastly outnumbered their Spanish foes.

The Portuguese conquest of Brazil was less dramatic but was just as rapid and effective. Joâo III (1502–1557) established royal government in Brazil in 1549, setting in process the building of a capital in Rio de Janeiro, the construction of civil and ecclesiastical government, and plans to evangelize and pacify Native Americans (who lived more like Native Americans in the Guianas and the Caribbean than Native Americans in Mesoamerica). As in Spanish America, the pacification of Native Americans was brutal, especially in the northeast of Brazil in the 1570s, when settlers exterminated

Native Americans without mercy in a brutal war.[15] By 1570, Brazil was a full Portuguese colony; other European empires, notably France, had been excluded from Portuguese territory; the indigenous population had been pushed from the coast or brought under a subdued order by Jesuit priests; and port cities serving a developing sugar export economy, with nearly 200 sugar mills in operation by 1610 were flourishing.[16] A bishopric was established in Salvador, in the northeast, in 1551. The Portuguese carried their Atlantic island expertise to Brazil to create a mining and plantation colony, dependent on the large-scale importation of African slaves sourced from their African colony in West-Central Africa.

The two Iberian empires were both different from each other and had similar features derived from their common European experiences. Portugal and Spain were neighbours in southwest Europe, with similar socio-cultural roots (though Spain was much richer and more socially and economically complex). They each had fervently pro-Catholic monarchs at their helm, each of whom was receptive to colonization schemes masquerading as Christian crusades. The two European nations were connected through extensive familial ties and shared economic interests in Atlantic-oriented trade. Residents of both nations circulated throughout each American empire without much difficulty. Each was dependent upon a set of maritime networks that put metropolitan Iberians in contact with Atlantic markets. Most importantly, each Iberian nation shared a common imperial ideology that can be traced back to the Crusades and the Spanish Reconquista of southern Spain from Muslim control in the thirteenth through fifteenth centuries. Key monarchs such as Carlos V (1500–1558) of Spain and Manuel I (1469–1521) of Portugal saw themselves as universal monarchs ordained by God to spread the Christian faith into the creation of global empires.

For contemporaries, these similarities were less apparent than the differences. Portugal and Spain bickered and fought constantly in the crucial century of first colonization between 1430 and 1530, despite the apparent cordiality of the Treaty of Tordesillas. Structurally, the most important difference was that the Spanish Empire was mainly terrestrial and geographically coherent and contained, focusing on a large but generally contiguous body of land spanning North and South America. It was characterized by the possession of land, the extraction of resources and the extensive use of forced labour on mines and plantations. The Portuguese, also, relied on forced labour but their empire, split like that of the Dutch, English and French empires of the seventeenth century, into an Asian and an American empire, was maritime rather than terrestrial. Portugal also had a colonial presence in Africa, which differentiated it from every other European empire. The Portuguese Empire was dispersed and fragmented, focused on maritime trade and oriented towards maintaining control over the sea.

EXPLAINING THE CONQUEST

What explains the remarkable and world significant conquests of a huge continent and massive population by a small number of morally deficient Spaniards and Portuguese, done with an ease that in retrospect seems utterly extraordinary? The empires that the Spanish conquered in their colonial heartlands of Peru and Mexico were, by any measure, the equal in political sophistication, technological skill and imperial willingness to use violence against intruders to any European nation-state. How did they fall so easily? Why, moreover, was America so easily conquered when Africa proved resistant to such European attacks? Not surprisingly, this question has been raised repeatedly over the centuries. The traditional explanations can be easily dismissed. It is hard to believe, for example, that God favoured the Iberians and gave them victory, given how dissolute, sinful and brutally unchristian their behaviour had been in the half century since 1492. Just as unconvincing is the idea that European civilization was naturally superior to that of native Americans and that European technology was superior, or that somehow the Inca and Aztec empires were on the verge of collapse just as the Spanish fortuitously arrived on the mainland.

The major causes of the Spanish conquest were divisions among Native American populations and, of much greater importance, Native American demographic collapse through disease and the lethal epidemiological exchange of pathogens. These worked severely to the disadvantage of Native Americans and to the advantage of Europeans. In respect to Native American divisions, we need to remember that most of the wars in the early sixteenth century were between Native Americans with the conquistadors joining one side and contributing to rather than dominating warfare. In the case of the conquest of Mexico, internal divisions between sections of the Native American population were crucial. As Ross Hassig concludes, 'the Spanish conquest was not one of superior arms and wills but one that took advantage of existing cleavages within the system to split the empire, turn its members on the Aztecs and rend it asunder'.[17] Cortés succeeded because he joined with Tlaxcalan aristocrats who wanted revenge against the Aztecs. They believed that they had been the main people who defeated Moctezuma, not the Spaniards.

The Spanish conquistadors did play their part in the Conquest. Pizarro, for example, achieved a major coup on 15 November 1532, when he caught the Inca emperor Atahualpa in a trap. He captured him, ordered a huge ransom and terrorized the emperor's entourage through acts of random slaughter. But his bravado would not have worked if he had not arrived at the end of a great Civil War that had divided the Inca empire and caused divisions in the Inca ruling elite. He also arrived not long after a devastating epidemic started in the Caribbean because of Spanish contact with Native Americans. It devastated Peru in the late 1520s, several years before any Spaniard had arrived in the country.

It is important to remember, also, that the Spaniards' victory over the Aztecs and Incas was neither sudden nor complete. The coming of Spanish rule was through a series of incomplete conquests. It was also accompanied by Spanish accommodation with Native American ways and through an appropriation of cultural forms that reminded Native Americans of similar Native American conquests made in previous decades. The supporters of the Spaniards had no idea that these conquerors were different beasts to native American warriors and that eventually the Spaniards would edge native American rulers aside. By the time they realized that the Spaniards were different kinds of conquerors, it was too late. The conquest of the Incas, for example, only really was finished in 1572, when the successor to Atalhuapa, Túpac Amaru, was captured and executed. Even then, large parts of the Andes remained outside Spanish control and Inca nobles continued to be influential in policy making. As Henry Kamen insists, 'the so-called "conquest" was never completed. For Spanish power in America to become viable, it was essential to work out a system based on collaboration rather than "conquest."'[18] Cortés himself was determined that his conquest would not end in devastation. His philosophy was that 'without settlement, there is no good conquest, and if the land is not conquered, the people will not be converted. Therefore, the maxim of the conqueror must be to settle.' He was as good as his word, developing sugar plantations and long-distance trading ventures and in the process becoming immensely rich.[19]

DEMOGRAPHIC CATASTROPHE

The main reason why the Spaniards took control, eventually, of Spanish America was not by dint of arms or through anything that the Spaniards did themselves but came about through the agency of microbes. The arrival of the Spanish initiated the greatest catastrophe in human history when the population of the Americas dropped from 54 million in 1492 to just 13.5 million in 1570. Native Americans were not especially healthy before the arrival of the Spaniards. Maize was good for calories but poor in vitamins and niacin. They suffered from typhoid, syphilis and tuberculosis. Skeletal evidence does not suggest they lived long lives.

But what they did not have were 'crowd diseases' derived from Afro-Eurasian herd animals. Millennia of living cheek by jowl with domestic animals had given most Africans and Europeans partial immunity to the lethal disease that resulted from human–animal contact. These diseases included smallpox, influenza and measles – all which were to prove major killers of Native Americans from the earliest days of Spanish arrival in the Caribbean. The malign disease environment of the Americas after 1492 resulted from the movement of humans across the globe. It did not help Native Americans that the places where the Spanish and Portuguese settled were in the humid regions of the Americas. Microbes prefer warm and humid conditions to cold and dry ones.

The disease environment was also a syndemic – a term used by medical anthropologists to make sense of HIV/AIDS in the present, but which also fits the sixteenth-century Caribbean and South America. A syndemic occurs when two or more diseases form a cluster of epidemics affecting a given population in social contexts that perpetuate that disease cluster and exacerbate its effects. One recent development in explaining the catastrophic population decline of the early sixteenth-century Caribbean is to insist that it was not a blameless event. Of course, early modern Europeans had a limited understanding of biology and their medical knowledge was not sufficient to work out how diseases spread. But Spanish cruelty to Native Americans populations made a bad situation worse.

What is clear is that the extent of population declines in the Americas, especially in the Caribbean, where at least 99 per cent of the indigenous population died within a century of contact, was extraordinary. To take a worst-case example: the Spanish began colonization of Puerto Rico in 1508 when there were between 250,000 and 500,000 native inhabitants. By 1530 that population had reduced to 2,000 and by 1540 to only 50. The same sort of population declines happened on Hispaniola, Cuba and Jamaica. Not all Native Americans in the Caribbean disappeared, though most in the Greater Antilles did. In places which the Spanish left alone, like St. Vincent and Dominica in the Lesser Antilles, native populations survived, and survived to this day. By 1600 in the Greater Antilles, however, no-one who was biologically or culturally a Taino remained. Indeed, the work of scholars in trying to work out how disease operated in the Greater Antilles is greatly handicapped by the fact that few people living today have much Taino DNA in their genetic makeup.

Soon the population catastrophe that started in the Caribbean spread to the coasts of mainland South America. During a century, it had spread everywhere in the Americas where a Native population existed. In addition to disease, we must add the effects of violence and starvation to the situation Native Americans faced from European colonization. The health of Native American populations was compounded by stress and advanced by hunger, compromising an already weak immune system function. Spanish practices of labour coercion, which took men away from families, probably added to reduced fertility rates. Nevertheless, even if we attribute a high degree of responsibility to colonial mistreatment of Native Americans by European settlers, violence, reduced fertility and starvation account for only a small proportion of the deaths that resulted from the microbial invasion of the Americas that happened after 1492. Demographic decline would have been large even if the Spanish acted towards Native Americans with true Christian charity and good will.

Hispaniola experienced the true nightmare of a disease we can call a syndemic. Within a couple of days of Columbus's arrival in the island on his second voyage in 1493 with lots of men and, probably most ominously, eight pigs (ideal vectors for human-animal crowd diseases), influenza struck with great devastation. The Spanish priest, Bartolomé Las Casas, reported that one third of the native American population had died by 1496. Columbus probably brought malaria to Hispaniola in his fourth voyage, in 1502. In 1518, smallpox arrived, killing probably one-third of the population that still survived. Measles contributed to the disease mix, probably brought from Spain or West Africa in 1531. At this point, in the 1530s, several pathogens were working together to destroy the remnants of the Native American population of Hispaniola.

Not all places suffered as badly as the Caribbean. The high Andes probably lost in a century only 75 per cent of its population (still ridiculously high but not so high as to destroy the population entirely, meaning that Native American populations from the nineteenth century could start to increase). Cold and dry areas were healthier, and disease found it harder to thrive in these regions. So too areas remote from European colonization fared comparatively well. Patagonia, California and the Canadian Arctic seem to have had a more benign disease environment than areas where European settlers were living in large numbers. Genetic diversity (which seems to have been especially low in the Caribbean) also reduced the chances of a syndemic of diseases from occurring.

The result of this demographic catastrophe was a significant rebalancing in populations in the Atlantic World and changes in the composition of that population. In 1492, most of the world's population was in Asia. That remained true throughout the Atlantic period. Asia had 54 per cent of the world's population in 1400 (and the world population had been significantly reduced from 1200, due to plagues in Asia and Europe in the mid-fourteenth century) and 67 per cent in 1800. Europe and Africa both had 16–17 per cent of world population in 1400, with Europe increasing to 19 per cent by 1800 while Africa had declined to 11 per cent. The biggest change came in the Americas. It had 12 per cent of world population in 1500 but only 2.2 per cent of world population in 1600 and just 1.8 per cent by 1700. In 1800, American population was still just 2.5 per cent of the world population.[20]

Just as importantly, the composition of the American population had changed radically in a very short amount of time. The 54 million Native Americans of 1492 had reduced to 13.5 million by 1570 and to 8.5 million in 1820. Meanwhile, the European-American population had increased by the second half of the eighteenth century to 6.7 million and the slave population (comprising almost all the African-American population of the Americas) was 4.7 million. Together, migrants from Europe and Africa outnumbered native Americans by the time of the age of revolutions. At the same time, the population of Western Europe was rocketing ahead. In 1500, the nations of Western Europe had 29 million people; West Africa had 14 million people and Native Americans amounted to 54 million people. In 1700, Western Europe had a population of 42.7 million people and in 1800 had 69.3 million people. Europeans in the Americas and Europe thus had a population of about 77 million people in 1800, about nine times more than the Native American population in the Americas.

ANIMALS AND PLANTS

The Columbian exchange, as this dismal account of demographic catastrophe indicates, was a one-sided process. Europe received considerably more from the exchange than did the Americas. Perhaps syphilis went from the Americas to Europe, although the evidence about this transmission is unclear. But the amount of infections coming from Africa and Europe made this negative contribution by the Americas to European health rather minimal. The Americas received animals, mostly from Europe, but given that many of these were domesticated animals like horses, sheep, goats, cattle and pigs that carried crowd diseases many native Americans may have preferred that these animals had remained at home. Over time, these animals flourished in the Americas and proved useful to both Europeans and Native Americans. They were used for food and wool and, in the case of horses, facilitated a mobile military culture among native Americans in the southwest and Great Plains region of North America and the Argentine pampas. Mosquitoes found the Americas very appealing and caused havoc wherever they appeared, especially in the tropics where they felt most at home. One relief for residents in the Americas was that the world's most dangerous animal, the carrier of falciparum malaria, *anopheles gambiae*, did not get established across the ocean from Africa. But the mosquito breeds which did come were bad enough. They infected humans with yellow fever and malaria and were especially devastating for recently arrived Europeans living in the tropics, or, as soldiers and sailors sent from Europe to fight imperial wars. The mosquito greatly influenced the patterns of warfare in tropical America, as commanders realized that any prolonged period of warfare would lead to massive troop losses.

In addition to animals and people, the Columbian exchange meant the migration of crops and foodstuffs across the world. Once again, Europe and Africa seemed to get the better of the deal. Maize, potatoes, manioc, tomatoes, peanuts, cocoa and the drug tobacco were among the crops sent from America to Europe. Some, like potatoes, maize and manioc, produced substantially more caloric values per unit of land, allowing for improved health and the avoidance of famine. Maize and potatoes were especially important, Maize transformed agricultural production and cultural food-ways in southern Europe while the potato was massively important in heralding a nutritional revolution in cool and humid lands from Ireland to Russia. Maize was even more important in Africa where it quickly became a staple food stuff from Senegambia to Angola. Europeans and Africans took some time to adapt to American crops – people are conservative in how they eat – but by the seventeenth century the influence of American crops on

European and African cultures was immense. It is suggested that much of early modern European population growth can be attributed to the higher yields that maize and potatoes provided and their suitability to low-value soils. The same is likely to be true in Africa, though we don't have the data to substantiate such claims. Tobacco was a different kind of crop. It tended to be grown in the Americas and was then packaged for sale in Europe – in this respect being like sugar rather than to potatoes. Europeans took to tobacco instantly and did so less for its supposed medicinal properties as in the Americas because people enjoyed the good feeling that the nicotine in tobacco provided.

With crops there was a true exchange though some Old World plants failed to take hold in the tropical places where Europeans initially settled. But as settlement moved to temperate regions, then crops like wheat, barley and oats proved successful, while European fruits prospered. The most important crop from Europe was sugar cane. Sugar cane thrived in the climate of rich soil, heavy seasonal rainfall and warm temperatures. It needed lots of labour, which proved a problem until the Atlantic slave trade solved that issue, but sugar found a ready market in a European consumer culture where people had a sweet tooth. As early as 1520 sugar was being produced in Hispaniola and even more so in Brazil. The Spanish were not major sugar producers until the late eighteenth century. Nevertheless, the introduction of sugar was transformative for the Atlantic economy. It contributed to ecological transformations of an unprecedented kind, especially encouraging deforestation on a vast scale. As we will discuss in a later chapter, sugar meant the extension of the plantation system developed in the Mediterranean, Morocco and the Atlantic islands into the New World. The beginnings of sugar cultivation were helped by the demographic disaster of Spanish arrival. Native Americans before 1492 had routinely burned vegetation to establish gardens and fields. As Native Americans died, this burning ceased, allowing the growth of tall forests – thought of as being there from time immemorial but in fact of recent invention. These forests provided rich nutrients that provided high rates of crop yield in the initial tricky times of planting.

CONCLUSION

The establishment of sugar plantations from the 1520s pointed the way forward whereby the Americas could be made profitable, and thus valuable to European colonisers. They marched in step with the demographic decline of Native American populations, leading to the largest and most significant movement of people across the Atlantic – the 12 million Africans brought unwillingly to the Americas to serve as bonded labour, usually on sugar, coffee, tobacco and rice plantations. Sugar was to be one foundation of a prosperous Atlantic World by the seventeenth century. The other source of wealth which confirmed to the Iberians that colonization was worthwhile was the discovery of vast silver mines in upper Peru, at Potosi. The start of mining at Potosi came in 1545. It secured the profitability of the Spanish empire in the Americas, just as sugar did for the Portuguese empire. The values of this silver wealth, minted in coins valued at eight Spanish reales, overwhelmed even gold as the financial basis for the Atlantic. It made Spain fantastically rich and able, at least in the sixteenth century, to finance European wars that augmented its status as a major European power. With the mountains of silver at Potosi, the value of European colonization in the Americas was made clear, meaning that for Europeans at least the destruction of the Indies had been a necessary working out of a providential plan to increase European wealth and power in the world.

NOTES

1   Felipe Fernández-Armesto, *Before Columbus: Exploration and Colonisation from the Mediterranean to the Atlantic, 1229–1492* (London: Macmillan, 1987).
2   Idem, *Pathfinders: A Global History of Exploration* (Oxford: Oxford University Press, 2006), 156–64.
3   Joyce E. Chaplin, 'The Atlantic Ocean and Its Contemporary Meanings, 1492–1808,' in Jack P. Greene and Philip D. Morgan, eds., *Atlantic History: A Critical Appraisal* (New York: Oxford University Press, 2009), 38–39.
4   Alison Games, 'Atlantic History: Definitions, Challenges and Opportunities,' *American Historical Review* 111 (2006), 745.
5   N.A.M. Rodger, 'Atlantic Seafaring,' in Nicholas Canny and Philip Morgan, eds., *The Oxford Handbook of the Atlantic World 1450–1850* (Oxford: Oxford University Press, 2011), 85.
6   J.H. Elliott, *Empires of the Atlantic World: Britain and Spain in America 1492–1830* (New Haven: Yale University Press, 2006), 30–31.
7   Samuel L. Wilson, *The Indigenous Peoples of the Caribbean* (Gainesville, FL: University Press of Florida, 1997), 7.
8   William D. Phillips and Carla Rahn Phillips, *The Worlds of Christopher Columbus* (Cambridge: Cambridge University Press, 1992).
9   Ralph Austen, *African Economic History: Internal Development and External Dependency* (London: James Currey, 1987), 34.
10   David Northrup, 'Africans, Early European Contacts, and the Diaspora,' in Nicholas Canny and Philip D. Morgan, eds., *The Oxford Handbook of the Atlantic World 1450–1800* (Oxford: Oxford University Press, 2011), 44.
11   Noble David Cook, 'Sickness, Starvation, and Death in Early Hispaniola,' *Journal of Interdisciplinary History* 32 (2002), 349–86.
12   Matthew Restall, 'The Americas in the Age of Indigenous Empires,' in Jerry H. Bentley et al., eds., *The Cambridge World History: The Construction of a Global World, 1400–1800 CE* (Cambridge: Cambridge University Press, 2015), I: 235.

13 Stuart Schwartz, 'The Iberian Atlantic to 1650,' in Nicholas Canny and Philip Morgan, eds., *The Oxford Handbook of the Atlantic World 1450–1850* (Oxford: Oxford University Press, 2011), 151.
14 Hugh Thomas, *The Real Discovery of America: Mexico, November 8, 1519* (Mount Kisco: Moyer Bell, 1992).
15 H.B. Johnson, 'Portuguese Settlement, 1500–1580,' in Leslie Bethell, ed., *Colonial Brazil* (Cambridge: Cambridge University Press, 1987), 1–38.
16 Stuart B. Schwartz, *Sugar Plantations in the Formation of Brazilian Society: Bahia, 1550–1835* (Cambridge: Cambridge University Press, 1985).
17 Ross Hassig, *Aztec Warfare: Imperial Expansion and Political Control* (Norman: University of Oklahoma Press, 1988), 267.
18 Henry Kamen, *Spain's Road to Empire: The Making of a World Power, 1492–1763* (London: Penguin, 2002).
19 Elliott, *Empires of the Atlantic World*, 21.
20 Massimo Livi-Bacci, *A Concise History of World Population*, 5th ed. (Chichester: Wiley Blackwell, 2012), 25.

BIBLIOGRAPHY

Oxford Online Bibliographies – Death; Disease; Environment and the Natural World; Spanish Colonization to 1650.

Suzanne Austin Alchon, *A Pest in the Land: New World Epidemics in a Global Perspective* (Albuquerque: University of New Mexico Press, 2003).

Alfred Crosby, *The Columbian Exchange: Biological and Cultural Consequences* (Westport, CT: Greenwood Press, 1972).

Noble David Cook, 'Sickness, Starvation, and Death in Early Hispaniola,' *Journal of Interdisciplinary History* 32 (2002), 349–86.

J.H. Elliott, *Empires of the Atlantic World: Britain and Spain in America 1492–1830* (New Haven: Yale University Press, 2006).

Herbert S. Klein, 'The First Americans: The Current Debate,' *Journal of Interdisciplinary History* 46 (2016), 543–61.

William D. Phillips and Carla Rahn Phillips, *The Worlds of Christopher Columbus* (Cambridge: Cambridge University Press, 1992).

Matthew Restall, *When Montezuma Met Cortés: The True Story of the Meeting that Changed History* (New York: Ecco, 2018).

Stuart B. Schwartz, *Sugar Plantations in the Formation of Brazilian Society: Bahia, 1550–1835* (Cambridge: Cambridge University Press, 1985).

Samuel L. Wilson, *The Indigenous Peoples of the Caribbean* (Gainesville, FL: University Press of Florida, 1997).

4

THE IBERIAN LAKE

SILVER, SUGAR AND THEIR EFFECTS

The discovery of silver at Potosi was transformative for Spanish America and Spain. Sugar was similarly transformative for Brazil and Portugal. Both commodities made Iberian expansion into the Americas worthwhile and in the sixteenth century created what we can term an 'Iberian lake' in the Atlantic, connecting Africa with South and Central America and with Europe. It allowed for the changes started in the early sixteenth century by Spain and Portugal to be institutionalized and reduced the massive and rapid changes of early settlement into predictable patterns. By 1570, the general character of the two Atlantic empires established by Spain and Portugal were fully formed. The Portuguese in Brazil had established an extractive and plantation colony dependent on slave labour, producing silver and even more importantly sugar for consumption in Europe. This empire formed part of a worldwide maritime empire, with bases in Africa and Asia as well as America. Spain, by contrast, had established a landed empire in the Americas, stretching far into the south of South America and into the southern regions of North America. This empire was firmly based upon silver and upon the exploitation of indigenous labour. It was less dependent on African labour than in the great European maritime empires. By 1570, the period of rapid indigenous depopulation had largely ended, at least in the two main centres of Spanish colonization, in Mexico and Peru. It became a period of relative political stability and demographic equilibrium, especially when compared to the tumults of the first seventy years of Spanish colonization in the Americas.

By the early seventeenth century, both empires were economically prosperous. The sugar boom in Brazil that occurred between *c*. 1580 and *c.* 1630 was producing a healthy 120,000 tons of sugar per annum, mostly exported to Europe. This boom enabled the creation of a South Atlantic system that integrated African ports in Angola providing slaves to Brazil which used those slaves to produce sugar to be sent to Europe. Luanda in Angola was the lynchpin of this system in Africa, sending 10,000 slaves to Brazil per annum during this period. Silver made Spanish America rich. By 1600, Spain was producing 85 per cent of the world's silver, of which 15–20 per cent went to Asia, thus making Spain a central part of a developing global economy.

Silver was a mixed blessing for Spain and sugar may have been just as a mixed blessing for Portugal. In 1500, the two countries were the most advanced countries in Europe and the first to expand into the Atlantic. Three centuries later, however, the economies of both countries ranked among the most backward in Western Europe. The impact of Spanish trade with the New World on the Iberian economy was limited, as Spain exported little to its colonies except some textiles and alcohol and even some of these were re-exports from more economically advanced European economies that were paid for by the floods of silver coming from Spanish America. The principal effect of silver in Spain seems to have been negative, encouraging the Spanish to embark on ongoing and expensive wars with rival European powers over hegemony in Europe and, ironically, over protecting Spanish access to its valuable markets of precious metals.

What it did not do was provide means and motivation to diversify a moribund and increasingly eclipsed local economy. As noted below, Spain and Portugal did not participate except marginally in the capitalist transformations of Europe in the sixteenth through eighteenth centuries that pushed Western Europe to the forefront of global prosperity, leading countries like Britain and France to overtake China and India as the world's leading economies. The fact that the floods of silver that flowed into Spain and the head-start that the development of plantation economies in Brazil gave Portugal did not lead to lasting economic growth in Europe is a sobering reminder that we should not overestimate the importance of Atlantic trade in long-term patterns of European economic growth. Studies by economic historians have shown repeatedly that the profitability of Europe's Atlantic activities was not especially extraordinary, had only a limited connection with the early stages of industrialization, that industrialization did not really need much capital anyway to develop, and that domestic commerce and national markets were always more important than Atlantic commerce in making industry fundamental to the European economy. The time lag involved between the start of Atlantic commerce and the advent of industrialization was also considerable: Spain and Portugal were among the last Western European countries to industrialize.

Such conclusions would have seemed implausible in the sixteenth century as silver imports rapidly increased. The mines of Potosí seemed inexhaustible, with official output increasing from 340,000 pesos in the 1520s to 100 million pesos in the 1580s to 129 million pesos by the 1630s. There was also contraband silver which was perhaps 17–20 per cent of the value of official silver imports. After the 1630s, silver production in Spanish America started to fall, so that it was 112 million pesos in the 1720s, with just 27.4 million pesos coming from Potosí with the centre of silver production beginning to move from Peru to New Spain (Mexico). Gold from Minas Gerais in Brazil surged in this period, meaning that silver and gold remained central to the Iberian economies until well in the eighteenth century. This mountain of silver may have been wasted by Spain in ineffectual wars but was much more important in Spain's colonies. Legal and contraband precious metals allowed Spain to penetrate Asian markets and to integrate its economies throughout Spanish America. In New Spain, market exchanges linked the Caribbean port city of Veracruz to Mexico City and to the northern mining town of Zacatecas. Similarly, silver connected almost all of Peru, from Lima to Bolivia to Potosí, and extended north to Quito and south to Chile. Unlike Spain, silver and gold production was accompanied by a gradual diversification of economic activity in the late seventeenth century. As Kenneth Andrien explains, investment capital from colonial merchants and the Catholic Church flowed from mining enterprises to agriculture, textiles and artisan production. This diversification combined with economic decline in seventeenth-century Spain strengthened the peripheries against the centre. By the early eighteenth century, regional economies in Spanish America were economically, if not quite politically and bureaucratically, autonomous, meaning that the balance of power between Spain and its colonies had shifted.[1]

The ambivalent effect of silver on the Spanish economy made Spaniards start to doubt whether its adventures in the New World were worthwhile. The historian Juan de Mariana wrote in the 1580s that Spain seemed to be worse off than it was before silver arrived as 'the sustenance we used to get from our soil, which was by no means bad, we now expect in large measure from the winds and waves that bring home our fleets; the prince is in greater necessity than he was before, because he has to go to the defence of so many regions, and the people are made soft by the luxury of their food and dress'. It seemed that Spain was in 'decline' and that silver was to blame. Martin González de Cellorigo lamented that 'our Spain has its eyes so fixed on trade with the Indies, from which it gets its gold and silver, that it has given up trading with its neighbours; and if all the gold and silver that the nations of the New World have found, and go on finding, were to come to it, they would not make it as rich and powerful as it would be without them'. Bullion, in this view, was a fortuitous windfall with deleterious long-term effects as it prevented efforts to improve national productivity, assumed to be got through cultivation of Spanish soil.[2]

In Brazil, sugar proved an ideal crop and Brazil benefited from being closer than any other Atlantic sugar-producing place to the point of labour supply in Africa, utilizing its extensive slave trading infrastructure in its

African colony of Angola. Between 1580 and 1680, the Brazilian northeast became the world's largest sugar producer, enjoying exponential growth in which the proportion of Africans in the workforce increased from one-third in 1570 to nearly one half just thirty years later. By the seventeenth century Brazil was a majority African population. Its planters made good money from sugar planting. They were handicapped, however, by Portuguese weakness. Portugal found it hard to monopolize slave trading in Angola because it offered fewer, poorer quality and more expensive manufactured goods than other European nations, notably the Dutch, who targeted Angola as a market for slaves at exactly the same time as they set their sights on sugar-producing north-western Brazil, rampaging in Bahia in the 1620s and occupying between 1630 and 1654 captaincies from Pernambuco to the Maranhão.

The main problem that Brazilian planters faced, however, was lack of access to capital and credit from Portugal's ill-equipped mercantile sector. When prices for sugar slumped in the 1620s, as attacks from the Dutch increased and as slave rebellion started to become a significant issue, Brazilian prosperity declined. From rapid growth, the mid-seventeenth-century Brazilian sugar industry moved into a long period of stability around low profits. This relative decline meant that British and French planters with more sophisticated plantation systems overtook Brazil as major sugar producers. Brazil's golden age (for planters, at least) ended just as Barbados's began, in the 1650s. The Dutch played a vital role in Brazil's decline, showing how by the mid-seventeenth century the Atlantic had become an arena for European competition. They learned the techniques of sugar cultivation and played a possibly important role (historians debate the matter) in passing on knowledge about sugar making to English and French planters in the eastern Caribbean and in providing what Brazilians lacked, which was the capital needed to invest in sugar mills. War between the Dutch and the Portuguese in the 1640s also disrupted Atlantic commerce, which may have led to a rise in sugar prices at a very propitious time for Barbadians moving to sugar production.

THE SUBJUGATION OF NATIVE AMERICANS

By 1650, both the Portuguese and Spanish American empires were relatively settled into patterns that were to last until the second half of the eighteenth century. The major Native American populations had been subjugated; market economies had been established; and these economies were increasingly diverse, regionally integrated and self-sufficient. The population mix was also stable, with growing numbers of African slaves brought to work in cities, mining and on plantations, added to Native

American populations that had finally outlasted a century and a half of demographic disaster. Emigration from Spain was constant, with 158,000 European migrants arriving in Spanish America between 1640 and 1700 and a further 193,000 coming between 1700 and 1760. Such migration was much less than the numbers going to British America and less in the eighteenth century than migrants moving to Brazil, but it did mean that a stratified Spanish society atop of a racially diverse population of native Americans, Africans and increasingly large numbers of mestizos (mixed race descendants of unions between whites and Indians) was transplanted to the Americas.

But that stability had emerged out of trauma, as outlined in Chapters 2 and 3. Spaniards were forced to contemplate what they had done in the New World to Native Americans just as they began to wonder whether the floods of silver had brought decline rather than real wealth to the kingdom. There was heated debate in the first half of the sixteenth century over the rights, if any, that native Americans had. The debate was initiated in 1512 by King Ferdinand, resulting in the Laws of Burgos which decisively declared for Native Americans having rights Spaniards had to consider and as people who should be brought to salvation through membership of the Catholic Church. In 1550, Charles V convened a debate between the two principal intellectual proponents of different views about Native American rights. The Dominican friar, Bartolomé Las Casas, author of the polemical indictment of Spanish colonisation, *Brief Account of the Destruction of the Indies* (1552), which established for European nations the notion of the Black Legend – that the Spanish were naturally cruel and vicious colonists – was pitted against the king's chaplain, Juan Ginés de Sepúlveda. Sepúlveda argued that Native Americans were naturally suited to enslavement and were not capable of becoming full citizens or proper Catholics. Las Casas argued the opposite and his views prevailed. From the 1550s, Native Americans were considered 'brothers' but with the legal status of children – free people capable of becoming citizens and who could be made to serve the Crown as labourers and pay it extensive taxes.

Thus, from 1550 onwards Native Americans occupied a clear and subordinate position in an organic, hierarchical and multiracial society, governed by Spanish-appointed bureaucrats and closely monitored by representatives of the Catholic Church. The suppression of Sepúlveda's views also spelled the end for the exploitative *encomienda* system in which conquistadors had iron control over Indian labour. Demographic decline made the *encomienda* system increasingly hard to maintain but its abolition was just as much about ending the rule of conquistadors – who had proved fractious and troublesome for a Crown wanting to impose order over large territories. Replacing the power of the *encomenderos* was an extensive Crown bureaucracy, ruled by viceroys. The sixteenth-century viceroyalties – New Spain and Peru – were huge and complex and relied on an elaborate system of law enforcement enforced by rural magistrates (*corregidores de indios*) who dealt mainly with issues of labour and relations between Spaniards and Native Americans and city magistrates (*corregidores de españoles*) who tended to regulate civic matters and local affairs.

Relations between Spaniards and Native Americans were better, or at least more regulated, than in the period of conquest but there were tensions aplenty and Spaniards struggled to keep Native Americans under control. One area where they faced difficulties was in religion. Native Americans became Christian but often under their terms and in ways that offended Catholic priests determined on orthodoxy. The religions that were established in native American communities in the Americas were syncretic in nature, in other words had elements of several religions in them rather than conforming to what the Pope decreed to be the Truth. When Native Americans accepted Christianity, they adapted Christianity into their own evolving cultural forms, adapting and changing those forms in the process. This process was viewed by suspicion by priests who worried that a vast anti-Christian underground lurked beneath the appearance of Native American piety.

They were especially concerned that Indians were worshipping the Devil rather than God. Such suspicions sometimes led to regimes of persecution. In the 1560s, for example, the Franciscan friar, Diego de Landa, orchestrated a campaign of imprisonment, torture and execution among the Maya of the Yucatan in pursuit of his zealous uncovering of idolatry. His investigations painted a picture of native Americans adding Christian doctrine alongside and often on top of pre-existing religious practices. It was not unusual, for instance, for Native Americans to use a Spanish priest in an essentially shamanic role to fend off an epidemic or halt a drought. That Native Americans used Christian practice selectively and for their own purposes is hardly surprising, given that they were excluded from the priesthood and tended to encounter Christianity piecemeal rather than as an integrated authoritarian whole.

The Iberians had one weapon, inherited and adapted from Europe, that they could deploy to keep Native Americans in line religiously. That was the Inquisition, a powerful weapon of investigation with potentially very serious consequences. It was employed to control both Native American and African religious impulses. Thousands of both groups were accused in the sixteenth and seventeenth centuries of practising witchcraft or forbidden religious rites, like African religions like obeah or vodou. Some priestly orders, notably the Franciscans, were especially keen on rooting out witchcraft and in punishing Native American 'sorcerers'. The Inquisition allowed for torture and in some cases large communities were persecuted and whole families were put to death, often painfully through burning at the stake. These ceremonies were made in public, to enforce the solemnity of accepting Catholic religion. The condemned were marched in special clothes, the *sanbenitos* (later hung up in church to remind relatives of the infamy of the accused), to their places of execution.

The efforts of the Catholic Church to enforce religious orthodoxy were only partially successful. While it is true that eventually everyone in Spanish and Portuguese America became Catholic and that over time Catholic practices became regularized and brought more into conformity with European customs, religious belief could be remarkably flexible. Case studies of people brought before the Inquisition suggest that many ordinary people rejected the exclusive validity of the Church to determine who could or could not attain salvation. Moreover, ordinary people were much more inclined to toleration of other religions than the Church allowed. They accepted that even Muslims, Jews, Protestants and pagans might reach heaven along with orthodox Catholics. Despite the Church's attempts to view deviations from what it considered proper practice as evidence of Native Americans' tendency to devil-worship, local clergy could not destroy Indian religious traditions and seldom even tried to do so. Local inflections of Catholicism appeared everywhere and over time became incorporated into what was always a living religion.

Religious issues sometimes led to violence. Native Americans had little choice but to accept their subordinate status within Spanish American society but they occasionally rebelled, sometimes seriously and violently. One of the greatest rebellions in Spanish American history came in northern Mexico in 1680 in the Pueblo Revolt. The Pueblo Indians of this region launched a concerted attack on the Spaniards of this region with some success. The Pueblos, under attack by the Comanche and Apaches, were suffering from drought-induced losses of stock and harsh treatment from Spaniard settlers who demanded excessive amounts of labour from them. These settlers numbered only 3,000 and were vulnerable to attack from a larger and more determined, if less well-armed, force of Native Americans. Their rebellion was a cry of protest by a people whose traditional ways of life were being eroded by Spanish attempts to make them adopt Spanish culture and to accept a subordinate position in a colonial hierarchy. The rebellion was planned in secret and took the Spaniards by surprise. They surrendered their capital Santa Fe in present-day New Mexico, and retreated to El Paso. The rebellion quickly spread to the whole northern frontier and briefly destroyed Spanish rule in the region. The area, however, was too important to New Spain to be left to the Pueblo rebels. In the 1690s, Spanish forces were sent to New Spain's northern borders and little by little they wore down Pueblo resistance until at last an accommodation was reached and relative calm restored.[3]

The greatest rebellion in Spanish American history came exactly a century later, this time in the very heartland of the colonies, in Peru. Spain had entered the American Revolution and needed funds and made increasingly harsh tax demands on its Native American inhabitants, including for the first time a tax on coca, which Peruvian Native Americans depended upon to cope with the cold of mountainous areas. José Gabriel Condorcanqui Noguera, a well-educated elite Native American, assisted by his merchant wife, Micaela Bastidas, who claimed descent from Inca royalty, took up the peasants' cause, adopting the name of Tupac Amaru, to suggest he wanted a restoration of the Inca Empire. Hundreds of thousands of Native Americans joined him in a serious assault on Spanish power. He laid siege to the key inland city of Cuzco but after fierce fighting the rebels failed to defeat Spanish American forces, augmented by thousands of troops coming from the colonial capital of Lima, on the Pacific coast. Tupac Amaru retreated into the Andes but again lost a crucial battle, in April 1781. The Spanish were vindictive in victory. They executed Tupac's wife and son in the central plaza of Cuzco and subjected the rebel leader to hanging, drawing and quartering. The rebellion carried on for two years after Tupac's death, but the Spanish eventually overcame the last rebels. By the end of the war in 1783, over 100,000 Native Americans and 10,000 Spaniards had perished.

A POLYGLOT EMPIRE

Why did Spaniards move to the New World? For most, it was about making money. One way of getting rich was in cultivating pearls, one commodity which, unlike chocolate and tobacco, was as highly valued by Native Americans as by Europeans. Columbus, on his 1498 voyage, saw Native Americans wearing pearls and news of this in Spain led adventurers to try their luck in the rich oyster beds of the Venezuela coastline. They did so with the occasional support of the Crown. Pearl fishing was a mixing of individual and royal initiative and the reckless quest for jewels took its toll not only on oyster beds but on local flora and fauna. Ecological devastation was as much part of the Atlantic World as was demographic disaster.

It was also a trade dependent upon Native American assistance though European settlers caused chaos and dislocation through their violent displacement of Native Americans as it sought a labour force to dive for oysters in the middle of extensive disease and death. Eventually, labourers had to be obtained as slaves from Africa. Pearl wealth embedded the Pearl Coast of Venezuela in networks of commerce that spanned the Atlantic and extended into the Indian Ocean. The violence led to blistering condemnation from the Spanish missionary, Bartolomé Las Casas, who characterized the fisheries as violent and lawless with a horrible labour regime that transformed Native American divers into terrifying monsters. He wrote of pearl fishing that 'no hell and hopeless life on this earth may be compared with it, however bad and terrible taking out the gold in mines might be'.

For Spaniards, the agony that Native Americans faced as disposable divers, with their skin breaking out in sores, being beaten by Spanish overseers and dying from the bends in cold water diving, was worth it as the riches from pearls were astounding. They reached 600 pounds of pearls sent to the Spanish Crown in the peak year of 1527. More and more divers from more and more far-flung places were needed and were made to work through enslavement. But few Europeans buying such luxury goods were aware of, or cared about, how pearls were collected. As Molly Warsh notes, 'on a hem, around a neck, traded for food or wine or passage, pearls bore no traces of the lives altered and lost through enslavement or the submarine pillaging of the reefs that brought them to light'.[4]

The ecological costs of pearl fishing were enormous. Probably 1.2 billion oysters were harvested in less than three decades. Pearls soon became rare. The end to the good times came in spectacular fashion in 1541 when a tsunami wiped out the main beds in the principal town of Cubagua, a small and now mainly uninhabited island off the Caribbean coast of Venezuela. French pirates then attacked in 1543 what remained of the settlement, carrying off pearls and people to Panama and Peru. Nevertheless, pearls had entered the European imagination, while they had been briefly affordable outside the ranks of the very rich in the booming first three decades of Spanish settlement. They offered a way for Europeans to explore the diversity of the world, both in the Atlantic and in the Indian Ocean, where pearls were abundant.

The movement of Europeans and Africans to Spanish America produced a polyglot society that cannot just be described through Native American subjugation and African enslavement. Thousands of free blacks of Old Christian heritage (in other words, from Catholic regions of Africa) settled across Spanish America and became integrated into Atlantic economies through working in a diverse range of occupations. What they did in Spanish America complicated Iberian understandings of racial purity. Blackness, it seems, was not quite as irredeemable for status in this period of ethnic fluidity as historians once thought – we are finding lots of evidence that free blacks forced their ways into social positions they were not meant to be allowed to enter. Many Africans from Seville and elsewhere in Spain claimed that they were Old Christians from Guinea and that their religion marked them out more than did their race. David Wheat has shown that some of these black migrants became significant settlers, especially free black women who married white men.[5] The lives of such women could be startlingly complex as with a *mulata* (or mixed race) woman called Mariá Gerónima, a servant who travelled from Seville to Cartagena, then to Nueva Veracruz, then to Mexico and then back to Nueva Veracruz. She worked as a servant, innkeeper and healer, the latter causing her to be investigated in Mexico City for witchcraft. The indictment forced her into poverty, begging in the streets. The evidence, however, suggests that she had a degree of autonomy, albeit forced upon her by unfortunate circumstances, in how she shaped her life as a servant and migrant settler and then as an indigent. What harmed her in her quest for full membership in the community was less her colour than her poverty. Both went together, of course, but class divisions continued to be very important within as well as between racial groups during the whole of Spanish colonization in the Americas.

SLAVERY AND SLAVE TRADE

If the first century of Spanish engagement with the New World was very much about the subjugation of Native American peoples, the subsequent centuries saw slavery and the slave trade become central. Slavery was a vital part of the Spanish Empire even before Spain began colonization in the Americas. The story starts in the Canary Islands as fifteenth-century Castilian monarchs and the Catholic Church developed a frighteningly effective logic about enslavement where African enslavement was justified more, initially, on the grounds of religion more than on the grounds of race. Spain was jealous of what Portugal was able to achieve in West Africa in establishing a slave trade (from which Spain was excluded) and envisaged from the beginnings of Columbus's arrival in the Caribbean that one goal of colonization was to set up a transatlantic slave trade in imitation of what the Portuguese had done in West Africa. Thus, African slaves arrived in Hispaniola as early as 1505.

The religious justification for African enslavement was accompanied by racist ideology tinged with biblical interpretation, notably the Curse of Ham, an obscure text from Genesis when Noah cursed Ham's son Canaan to be a 'servant of servants'. Canaan was supposed in biblical genealogies discovered by Islamic scholars to be the ancestor of sub-Saharan Africans. That interpretation, which was accompanied by denigrations of Africans' physical appearance as being bestial and descriptions of black sin as being associated with the Devil, had long-lasting influences upon European and American racial thinking as a means of explaining and justifying ideologies of African difference, inferiority and 'natural' aptitude for enslavement. As James Sweet argues, this curious racial ideology was how 'the sub-Saharan African emerged as the son of Ham, destined to perpetual servitude'.[6] We do need, however, to be careful not to make simplistic assumptions that the Curse of Ham justified the enslavement of black Africans in Africa and then in other places. This reading of the Curse of Ham was a misreading of early rabbinic literature, as the great North African historian, Ibn Khaldun, noted. Khaldun preferred to base colour difference and racial inferiority on climate. In the late medieval period, thinkers tended to see the Mediterranean and North Africa as having ideal climates, and that people living south (Africans) or north (Western Europeans) of that region were deficient in body and character.

It is important to note, however, that explicitly racist doctrines of African inferiority developed in the Spanish Empire only in the late sixteenth century, after settlement was well advanced in the Americas. Before then, a racially diverse Spain tended to base African subjugation upon people not being Christian, rather than on them being African. Emily Berquist Soule argues that the increasing association of perpetual slavery with blackness came from Spanish competition with Portugal in Africa and came from distinctions, drawn from ancient Rome, that there were differences between 'peaceful' natives, who accepted Christianity and 'rebellious' groups whose resistance to Christian power made them eligible for enslavement. Thus, it became geography as much as race or religion that came to justify the enslavement of Africans. Spanish understandings of slavery were, as Toby Green argues, 'mediated through experiences first developed in Africa'.[7]

Once African slavery was justified, it was quickly transformed into an active slave trade which sent Africans to Spanish and Portuguese Americas from the sixteenth century onwards. The numbers of Africans sent to Iberian America were considerable. Portugal started the Atlantic slave trade earliest and finished last and thus was easily the largest European slave carrier in the trade taken as a whole. Between 1519 and 1867, it imported 5,074,000 Africans, or 45.9 per cent of all Africans transported across the Atlantic, with 1,401,900 arriving between 1826 and 1867, when other European nations, notably the British, had ended their slave trades. Spain, which never had its own slave trade except briefly, imported many fewer Africans directly – just 517,000, almost all after 1800. It was, however, the direct recipient of many more African arrivals through transfers from other European traders. It received 1,222,200 slaves from 1519 with the great majority (718,300) arriving after 1800 in the Spanish Caribbean, in the years when Cuba was the sugar-producing powerhouse of the world.

In Brazil, the slave trade was more constant and more geographically diverse: 876,000 Africans were sent to northeast Brazil; 1,008,000 to Bahia; and 2,017,900 to southeast Brazil.[8] By 1759, gold and silver mining in Minas Gerais had surpassed sugar production as the leading employer of slaves. Most Brazilian slaves worked for small-scale industrialists, with fewer than ten slaves, meaning that in Brazil slaves were more able than elsewhere to gain manumission. The result was that by the early nineteenth century Brazil had a large population of free people of colour in addition to one of the Western Hemisphere's largest concentration of slaves. The nineteenth century saw slavery expand rapidly in Brazil. Between 1806 and 1830, seven in ten slaves landing in the Americas disembarked in Brazil.

The relatively low numbers of Africans imported into the Spanish American mainland do not mean that slavery was marginal in the region. On the contrary, slave labour was essential to the day-to-day running of homes and businesses in mines, cities, cattle ranches, maritime trade and in plantation agriculture. The slave trade was also a major source of revenue for the Spanish Crown – outsourced before the late eighteenth century to other slave trading nations in a process called the *asiento*. The ending of the *asiento* after 1750 formed part of what historians call the Bourbon reforms of the second half of the eighteenth century. As profits from silver declined, the revenue from the *asiento* became correspondingly more important. In the middle of the eighteenth century, the Spanish Crown tried to increase profits from the slave trade, briefly creating a Spanish slave entrepot in the

West African islands of Fernando Po and Annabōn. In 1789, Spain declared a policy of 'free trade' in slaves, which allowed slave traders in a few select locations the right to purchase slaves from any foreign dealer. The result was a fivefold increase in Africans coming to Spanish America, mainly to Cuba, between 1761 and 1820 from trading patterns between 1701 and 1760. This increase was one that rapidly changed the population dynamics of Spanish America to be more obviously African and was an increase that depended not just on increased demand in a period of growing sugar and coffee production in Cuba and Puerto Rico in the Spanish Caribbean but a better supply system, exploiting the advantages that other European nations had in their vibrant slave trading businesses.

Brazil was the major destination for Africans transported to the Americas, as noted above. Africans were carried there in numerous ways by chartered companies, by merchant groups, by individuals and through illegal trade. Slaves mostly worked on sugar plantations in the sixteenth and seventeenth centuries, but by the eighteenth-century Brazilian slavery was becoming increasingly diverse. Slaves were found in the burgeoning gold industry in Minas Gerais (a highly profitable trade that brought Brazil back into the considerations of the Portuguese government after half a century of neglect). They were also present in cities, notably in Rio de Janeiro which, despite not having a plantation infrastructure to rival that of the northeast, had become Brazil's most important city and which had the largest, liveliest and most diverse slave community in the Americas.

What made African slavery in Brazil distinctive was its close connection to one originating region – Angola. More than in any other part of the Atlantic World, African migrants to Brazil from this single region were able to establish African-American cultures that had strong and persistent ties to African cultural formations, reinforced by a constant supply of new people from Angola brought over in the slave trade who could reinvigorate Afro-Brazilian culture through direct experience of Angolan culture. African slaves referred to people from their own nations as 'relatives', thus noting the formation in Brazil of a symbolic kinship band rooted in African inheritance. Its members met in Catholic black brotherhoods, especially in urban settings, and in Muslim and other African religious communities. They tended to interact with each other and marry within their own communities and participated in revolts led by ethnic leaders.

Brazil's slave regime was brutal, especially in the northeast sugar plantations where slave gangs tended to be larger than in coffee plantations in the southeast. Sex ratios among African slaves tilted strongly towards males, birth rates were low and mortality rates were high. These demographic factors meant that enslaved populations did not increase naturally, except for Minas Gerais from the late eighteenth century. Slave resistance was frequent, with enslaved people escaped from slavery in their hundreds to form *quilombos*, or Maroon communities of runaway slaves, pursued by private armies of slave catchers. The most famous such *quilombo* was Palmares, in northeastern Brazil. Palmares was a confederation of villages, containing 11,000 people, including Native Americans, poor whites, Portuguese deserters as well as a majority population of Angolan-born Africans. It flourished as a state-within-a state for nearly a century until a large Portuguese army in 1694–1695 routed it. Until then, it resisted successfully multiple attempts by Dutch and Portuguese soldiers to overcome it. It did so through the help of a complex political and social order and under the inspired leadership of men such as Ganga Zamba and the legendary Zumbi.

Until the middle of the eighteenth century, sugar was the predominant plantation crop of Brazil. In the nineteenth century, coffee produced in southeast Brazil came to supplement and indeed overtake sugar as Brazil's most important export. Indeed, it was in coffee production that Brazil for the first time since the late sixteenth century came to have a dominant share in world production of an important commodity and thus a considerable amount of power in shaping global coffee markets. Coffee and sugar involved quite different processes of production and use of labour. Coffee was far less capital intensive a crop than sugar and needed fewer slaves to make the most of land. It was thus an ideal crop for small, cash-poor planters. The work involved, while onerous, was less heavily regulated by plantation operatives forcing slaves to work in lock-step discipline as was done in sugar and the relationship between master and slave was more personal and thus the terms of slavery were more varied and more individually negotiated. Sugar, on the other hand, required not just more enslaved people but more skilled labour and much greater investment in fixed equipment and buildings, such as *engenhos* (mills and boiling houses).

The reinvigoration of slavery in nineteenth-century Brazil also reinvigorated slave resistance. Before 1800, the main source of slave resistance was running away and the formation of *quilombos*. In the eighteenth century, colonial authorities in Minas Gerais reported around 160 *quilombos*, at least one of which, the Prolho *quilombo* of Mato Grosso, survived between 1740 and 1795. These communities tended to act as safety valves in slave society, adapting to slavery through forming alternative communities rather than challenging it directly. Runways did point, however, to how slavery was an endemically unstable social system and, like bandits in European and Asian countries, runaways proved to be disruptive presence in societies which prided themselves as being based on organic hierarchical social orders, where the poor automatically accepted the rule of the elite. There were occasional slave revolts or plots for rebellion. In Minas Gerais in 1719, for example, slaves plotted an Easter uprising (Easter and Christmas were favourite times for rebellion throughout slave communities in the Atlantic World, suggesting not only that enslaved people took advantage of European festivities when masters were off-guard but there was often a religious aspect to rebellion). The plot failed, mainly because the leaders belonged to two different African nations – Angola and Mina (slaves from the Bight of Benin) and they disagreed over who would take command. One reason why slave rebellion was so seldom successful was that plots were very difficult to keep secret until implementation.

Slave resistance increased in intensity in the nineteenth century, especially in the northeastern captaincy of Bahia. Bahia saw a massive increase in African slaves after 1800, including numerous Muslims. They were a restless and rebellious population. Some slave revolts in the region were small local affairs, undertaken by young African warriors who disliked the harsh conditions of sugar cultivation. Other slave revolts were more calculated affairs, designed to overturn the colonial system. Serious plots for rebellion were discovered in Bahia in 1807, 1814 and 1816. The most important revolt came in 1835, the Malê or Muslim revolt. Bahia was a centre of revolt because it had many Nagôs with recent experience in wars linked to the spread of Islam in their homelands. They were joined by Hausas, many of whom were Muslim. In 1835, these groups combined in a revolt, scheduled to take place at the end of Ramadan. Rebels took to the streets of Salvador, wearing Islamic garments and amulets containing passages from the Quran. It was not just, however, a religious revolt designed to turn Salvador into an Islamic place. There is some evidence that rebels also drew on the iconography of the Haitian Revolution for inspiration. The revolt was put down with the usual ferocity that slave owners showed to slave rebels but the revolt and its aftermath showed to many white Brazilians, many of whom were increasingly nervous about how slavery compromised their safety, that increased slave importation was likely to bring about more serious rebellions.[9] The connection with Haiti was especially ominous for white Brazilians. Although the experience of Saint-Domingue was not repeated in Bahia, fears of another cataclysm were not just political propaganda nor fevered nightmares but had a basis in reality, as slaves from Bahia had repeatedly made violent challenges to the white slave regime. The influence of the Haitian Revolution on the ideology of slave resistance was an important signal of how by the nineteenth century the Atlantic World was an integrated place, a region where words spread as easily as did people.

CAPITALISM

The 'Spanish Lake' ended around the mid-seventeenth century when the Atlantic became crowded with European competitors determined to reduce Iberian, especially Spanish, power. Spanish America, however, remained very powerful in the Atlantic World, fruit of the considerable wealth that Spanish Americans made from their extensive trading networks. Nevertheless, increasingly Spain found it hard to compete in the Atlantic against richer and more aggressive rivals from England, France and the Dutch Republic. What was noticeable about these rivals, especially the English and the Dutch, is that they were much more capitalist in orientation than was Spain. Spain was among the slowest Western European states to adopt capitalism as a mode of economic organization, retaining a strong element of feudalism until at least the end of the seventeenth century.

The absence of a capitalist system and perhaps a capitalist profit-making system in Spain reduced its influence in an Atlantic World particularly attuned to capitalist rhythms. As Mark Peterson notes, 'Capitalism made the Atlantic World go around, from the ships that moved people and goods from one coast to another, to the silver dug from the mountains of Mexico and Peru and minted with coins, to radically commodified labour in the form of enslaved persons forcibly transported from distant places and turned en masse to producing commodities from which their alienation was total'.[10] Definitions of capitalism vary but in general they have one thing in common. Authors talk about capitalism to outline economic practices in their own time that they identify as modern, new and different than what happens in more traditional societies and in former times. Calling a society 'capitalist' is thus often a shorthand for talking about the processes of modernization and identifying differences in economic activity. In this context, calling the Atlantic World inherently 'capitalist' suggests it was also inherently 'modern'.

For historians of the Atlantic World, the most protean definition of capitalism comes from the famous French historian Fernand Braudel, who sharply distinguished 'capitalism' from 'market economy'. All societies had the latter; only Western Europe after 1500 had the former. He tended to reserve the term 'capitalism' for the businesses of a relatively narrow and exclusive superstructure of influential merchants, bankers, shipowners, entrepreneurs and financiers who competed against each other and sometimes colluded together for profit and power. For Braudel, the key moment in the transition of Western Europe to a capitalist world economy came in the sixteenth century. His definition of capitalism was not that of Karl Marx who saw capitalism in linear terms as one stage in a process of change from feudalism to socialism but was closer to that described by the eighteenth-century Scottish Enlightenment writer, Adam Smith. Smith argued that capitalism existed where there was a system of production for sale in a market for profit and an appropriation of this profit based on individual and collective ownership.

Smith was not just the founder of political economy but was a principal theorist of colonization. It raises the question of whether capitalism did not just make the Atlantic World go around but was a major consequence of the rise of an Atlantic economy after 1500. Some scholars such as Immanuel Wallerstein, founder of world system theory, expand on Braudel and Smith to argue that a pre-capitalist Europe expanded into the Atlantic after 1492 and that its predatory behaviour, leading to a systematic exploitation of indigenous peoples and their land, produced the necessary capital accumulation to establish capitalism. Sven Beckert is a prominent proponent of this line of interpretation. He argues that 'in vast swathes of the New World enterprising Europeans entered lands emptied of Native populations ... with the newcomers ... then able to invent a radically new world of commodity production, with low initial costs and huge profits. This violent and radical transformation of the social structure and ecology of the American countryside was thus one of the most important factors in Europe's rise towards global economic supremacy by the nineteenth century'. He concludes that 'commodity trades laid the foundations for modern capitalism by extracting land and labour by violence, by accumulating capital as a result, and by enabling well-financed merchants to create globally integrated networks of production, using innovations in finance, insurance, banking, bookkeeping and personnel management. These Atlantic, and eventually global, commodity markets also financed the fiscal-military states that would become increasingly important in the unfolding of industrial capitalism in Europe itself'.[11]

The timing of the Columbian exchange and European transitions to capitalism is intriguing but ultimately unconvincing. Internal developments in Europe provided the main impetus for capitalist transformation especially in the English countryside and in the Dutch republic. Importantly, these transformations in England preceded rather than followed English intrusions into the Americas. The most we can say is that European merchants channelled foreign technology and overseas profits into a more productive European domestic economy. What is most important is that once capitalism was established in the sixteenth- and seventeenth- century Western European economies, it made European empires especially adept in using the exploitation of the New World for economic advantage. Merchants were key figures in how New World wealth was assimilated into European economies. Their activities in the Atlantic furthered commercial expansion in Europe. Smith commented in *Wealth of Nations* (1776) that 'one of the principal effects of those discoveries [of Columbus] has been to raise the mercantile system to a degree of splendour and glory which it never could have attained to'. A century previously another British commentator, Sir Josiah Child, in *A Discourse of Trade* (1668) explained the success of the Dutch Republic was in part due to its skilled merchants operating in overseas trade, to its excellent ships, to a government that left commerce alone, and to a well-regulated and helpful banking and financial system. Like Smith, Child thought that overseas commercial success fuelled domestic demand for agriculture and manufacturing: 'the repute of their said commodities abroad, continues always good, and the buyers will accept of them by marks, without opening'. The overseas merchant was a significant maker of Europe's mercantile system which itself was a means that facilitated what Karl Polanyi just after the Second World War described as the transformation of societies with markets into market societies – places in which social relations are embedded in market relations rather than those social relationships governing how markets operated. That many places in Western Europe by the seventeenth century were market societies helped Europeans take advantage of the multiple market opportunities that advancement into the Atlantic afforded.

When looking at how the New World had an impact on the market societies of the New World, we need to look at both production in the Americas and consumption in Europe, Africa and Asia. Sugar is an ideal example of how production and consumption intertwined and intersected. It was a commodity itself which was well known in Europe. Indeed, it was a European crop, first cultivated in the Mediterranean and then in the Canary Islands before being transported to the New World. Its successful implantation in the New World depended upon readily available of tropical lands suitable for sugar planting and the adoption of African slave labour through an increasingly efficient slave trade to make labour cheap enough to ensure that sugar could be produced at cheap enough prices for European purchase. Here the Portuguese presence in West Africa in the fifteenth century was highly fortuitous. It was easy for the Portuguese to use their links with African merchants to start the Atlantic slave trade with slaves bought at very low cost, an indirect subsidy that eased the costly transition to intensive capital investment in sugar production. The next century saw Dutch and English merchants invest greater amounts of capital in plantations in the Caribbean, where all the functions of production were contained in one place, allowing for substantial economies of scale in production.

Sugar started off as a luxury good but over time became an everyday commodity. Luxury goods had limited markets. What investors needed were mass markets for affordable products. Sidney Mintz's classic study of sugar as a commodity describes how a mass market for sugar arose in Britain as consumers became accustomed to using sugar in all aspects of cooking and eating. By the eighteenth century, sugar was crucial to British identity, a daily necessity employed in food and a marker of pleasure in the form of cakes and puddings that were not just foodstuffs but markers of celebration. Other commodities went through a similar process where they were turned from luxury goods into everyday products through manipulation of consumer demand. David Hancock, for example, has shown how merchants in the Americas and Europe worked with producers, consumers and government (who received customs money for products transported within the Atlantic World) to create a market for Madeira wine in North America and the Caribbean. Similarly, Giorgio Riello has shown how cotton from India was used by merchants to fashion goods suitable for African consumption that purchased slaves who eventually came to produce cotton in the Americas which was sent back to Britain and used to develop new cotton products that came to become very popular among consumers and helped displace India from its position as the leading world producer of cotton. As Mark Peterson concludes, 'the development of reliable mass markets, in which the locations of high-investment commodity production were separated from the places of their consumption over oceanic distances, increased the anonymity of production, the expansion of production for exchange rather than for use, and the alienation of the producers from the returns on their labour – all significant aspects of the gradual transformation of capital and its investment from linking local producers and consumers into the "market" integration eventually understood as "capitalism."'[12]

As Peterson intimates, slavery was a key feature of this Atlantic capitalism. Indeed, in some respects enslaved people are best seen as themselves forms of commodities, 'produced' for a growing mass market. Slaves were liquid capital, priced rigorously as types of human capital, and used to satisfy debts and moved around to suit varying production schedules. The profits these slaves generated and the commodities they produced and sometimes consumed were key in advancing the demand for workers to be paid in wages rather than in kind so they could purchase New World slave-produced commodities, such as sugar. Thus, as Peterson argues, 'slave labour on a grand scale in the tropical Americas made wage labour on a grand scale possible in parts of Europe and North America'. 'Despite their seemingly oppositional character', he continues, 'wage and slave labour were complementary parts of an integrated broader system of capital, in which enslaved human beings produced the commodities and secured the credit that financed the relative economic autonomy of the "free."' By the eighteenth-century, 'the proliferation of investment in production, mass markets, mobile and uprooted labourers, and flexible forms of private ownership made "capitalism" easy to latch onto anywhere in the Atlantic World by those with the resources to do so, and increasingly difficult for everyone else to avoid'.[13]

NOTES

1   Kenneth J. Andrien, *Crisis and Decline: The Viceroyalty of Peru in the Seventeenth Century* (Albuquerque: University of New Mexico Press, 1985).

2   J.H. Elliott, *Empires of the Atlantic World: Britain and Spain in America, 1492–1830* (New Haven: Yale University Press, 2006), 26.

3   David J. Weber, *The Spanish Frontier in North America* (New Haven: Yale University Press, 1992), 137–41.

4   Molly A. Warsh, *American Baroque: Pearls and the Nature of Empire, 1492–1700* (Chapel Hill: University of North Carolina Press, 2018), 48.

5   David Wheat, *Atlantic Africa and the Spanish Caribbean, 1570–1640* (Chapel Hill: University of North Carolina Press, 2016), 166–80, 207–15.

6   James Sweet, 'The Iberian Roots of American Racist Thought,' *William and Mary Quarterly* 54 (1997), 149.

7   Emily Berquist Soule, 'From Africa to the Ocean Sea: Atlantic Slavery in the Origins of the Spanish Empire,' *Atlantic Studies* 15 (2018), 16–39; Toby Green, *The Rise of the Transatlantic Slave Trade in Western Africa, 1300–1589* (Cambridge: Cambridge University Press, 2012), 184–85.

8   The latter figures are underestimates, as 1,463,000 Africans arriving in Brazil cannot be assigned to a region of arrival. For figures, see David Eltis, 'The

Volume and Structure of the Transatlantic Slave Trade: A Reassessment,'
William and Mary Quarterly 58 (2001), 43–46.

9   João José Reis, *Slave Rebellion in Brazil: The Muslim Uprising of 1835 in
    Bahia* (Baltimore: Johns Hopkins University Press, 1993).

10 Mark Peterson, 'Capitalism,' in Joseph C. Miller, ed., *The Princeton Companion
    to Atlantic History* (Princeton: Princeton University Press, 2015), 71.

11 Sven Beckert, 'Commodities,' in Joseph C. Miller, ed., *The Princeton
    Companion to Atlantic History* (Princeton: Princeton University Press, 2015),
    116–18.

12 Peterson, 'Capitalism,' 75.

13 Ibid., 76–79.

BIBLIOGRAPHY

Oxford Online Bibliographies entries – Brazil, Iberian Atlantic World, 1600–1800;
   Iberian Empires, 1600–1800; Markets in the Atlantic World; Mexico. Peru;
   Portuguese Atlantic World.

Jan de Vries, *The Industrious Revolution: Consumer Behavior and the Household
   Economy, 1650 to the Present* (Cambridge: Cambridge University Press, 2008).

Robert DuPlessis, *Transitions to Capitalism in Early Modern Europe* (Cambridge:
   Cambridge University Press, 1997).

J.H. Elliott, *Empires of the Atlantic World: Britain and Spain in America, 1492–
   1830* (New Haven: Yale University Press, 2006).

Fernando Novais, *Portugal e Brasil na crise de antigo Sistema colonial, 1777–1808*
   (São Paulo: Editors Hucitec, 1979)

Gabriel B. Paquette, *Enlightenment, Governance, and Reform in Spain and Its
   Empire, 1759–1808* (London: Palgrave Macmillan, 2011).

Stuart B. Schwartz, *All Can Be Saved: Religious Tolerance and Salvation in the
   Iberian Atlantic World* (New Haven, CT: Yale University Press, 2008).

Stuart B. Schwartz, *Sugar Plantations in the Formation of Brazilian Society: Bahia,
   1550–1835* (Cambridge: Cambridge University Press, 1985).

Emily Berquist Soule, 'From Africa to the Ocean Sea: Atlantic Slavery in the
   Origins of the Spanish Empire,' *Atlantic Studies* 15 (2018), 16–39.

Stanley J. Stein and Barbara H. Stein. *Silver, Trade and War: Spain and America in
   the Making of Early Modern Europe* (Baltimore, MD: Johns Hopkins University
   Press, 2000).

Stanley J. Stein and Barbara H. Stein. *Apogee of Empire: Spain and New Spain in
   the Age of Charles III, 1759–1789* (Baltimore: Johns Hopkins University Press,
   2003).

Daviken Studnicki-Gizbert. *A Nation upon the Ocean Sea: Portugal's Atlantic
   Diaspora and the Crisis of the Spanish Empire, 1492–1640* (Oxford and New
   York: Oxford University Press, 2007).

Sanjay Subrahmanyam, 'Holding the World in Balance: The Connected Histories
   of the Iberian Overseas Empires, 1500–1640,' *American Historical Review* 112
   (2007), 1359–85.

5

OLD WORLDS RESPOND

THE EXCITEMENT AND DISAPPOINTMENT OF COLUMBUS'S VOYAGES

Columbus's voyage to the Caribbean in October 1492 was a sensation. Reports of what he had found percolated quickly around Spain and around Europe. Columbus had high hopes that what he had done would lead to more than just the establishment of an overseas trading base, like what the Portuguese had been doing in fifteenth-century Africa and which both Iberian powers had been doing in the Atlantic islands off Africa. 'Be sure', he wrote in his journal, addressing the Spanish monarchs, Ferdinand and Isabella, 'that this island [Hispaniola] and all the others are as much your own as is Castile, for all that is needed here is a seat of government and to command them to do what you wish'. As John Elliott notes, Columbus was arguing for a programme we might think of as being that of the archetypal colonial regime. Columbus suggested that Spain establish government (immodestly he thought it should appoint him as governor) in the West Indies and work out ways to rule indigenous populations, so that they produced commodities suitable for Europe, with a side role in missionary activities to a pagan population.

The Spanish were receptive, in ways the Portuguese, Dutch, English and French initially were not, to an approach to the Americas that was based on conquest and subjugation rather than on the establishment of a string of trading enclaves. Columbus's voyages fell within a Spanish context of Reconquista – the successful taking back land by Christians in Spain from the Moors, a process which also concluded in 1492 when Ferdinand and Isabella made a triumphal entry into the Moorish city of Granada in January 1492. Columbus 'participated in, and turned to his own advantage, the euphoria generated by this climactic moment in the long history of the Reconquista. From the vantage point of 1492 it was natural to think in terms of the continuing acquisition of territory and of the extension of the Reconquista beyond the shores of Spain. Across the straits lay Morocco; and, as Columbus would soon demonstrate, across the Atlantic lay the Indies'.[1]

It became clear very soon, however, that the great things Columbus promised were mostly in his mind. His voyages produced little tangible for the Spanish Crown and the Spanish court soon tired of Columbus's megalomania, troublesome character and tendency to create havoc wherever he went. His greed to establish a dynasty for his family whereby he would become immensely wealthy soon made him and his family unwelcome. But the West Indies was not the East Indies. It offered no lucrative trading network; had no gold or silver to speak off; and if it was to be exploited, it would have to be done by the Spaniards themselves rather than by indigenous vassals. The New World, at least until silver was found in great quantities in Peru (modern day Bolivia), was a great disappointment. To make a twentieth-century parallel, it appeared to Europeans before 1540 like the US moon launches were in the 1960s and 1970s to people today – seemingly massive advances in global knowledge and national prestige that produced little of lasting value except hype and huge wastage of money and which by the early twenty-first century seemed more important as mid-twentieth century cultural moments than as a lasting change in human history.

The limited benefits early colonization in the Americas brought to Spain and to Europe in general were one reason why other nations in Western Europe did not follow the Iberians into the Atlantic for a couple of generations, at least. By the 1520s, only 100 ships a year sailed from Spain to the Americas, carrying 9,000 *tonelados* of carrying capacity (each *tonelado* being 1.42 cubic metres). It was only in the late sixteenth century that this level of shipping doubled, with carrying capacity increasing fourfold. The European 'discovery' of the New World had even less impact on Atlantic Africa than on Europe, at least until the Atlantic slave trade developed fully in the mid-seventeenth century. For most Europeans and Africans, therefore, the impact of the New World was relatively small for the first century of the Columbian Encounter.

The biggest impact was ecological and was, for Africa and Europe, mainly positive. The encounter with the New World introduced important new crops which transformed life in both Old Worlds. In Europe, the crops with the most influence were maize and the potato, although clover was also important, and tobacco was highly desired. Potatoes suited ideally the soil and climate conditions in northern Europe, from Ireland to Russia. In the former country, the potato became so central that a blight on potatoes in the 1840s created one of the world's worst famines. The planting of potatoes was easy; it was harvested with ease through family labour and potatoes could be stored excellently. Its arrival and spread allowed for considerable population growth in northern Europe, helping to supply manpower for overseas colonization and for the Industrial Revolution. Its implantation required clover, which also came from the Andes. Clover provided the nitrogen which potatoes as a nitrogen-hungry crop needed. It was also an excellent fodder crop, providing the means whereby cattle populations could grow, raising milk and meat consumption in northern Europe.

Maize was probably even more influential. It transformed much of southern Europe's food production, notably in Italy. It allowed new lands to be put under production and prospered where grains and tubers failed. It helped increase population growth in southern Europe and provided a buffer against famine. Its yield per acre and per labourer was high. It was easy to plant and produced bumper crops – two crops a year in the right conditions – in land from sea level to mountain valleys. Its most significant impact was in Africa, where it became the staple crop for much of the continent, including areas away from the Atlantic coast. Its main impact, however, was on the Atlantic coast, from Senegambia to Angola. It was important as an agricultural crop, storing very well and able, as in Whydah, to form part of seasonal crop rotations. It had significant social effects, as well. It was ideal for the sustenance of slave ships and migratory caravans. Farmers along long-distance trade routes were especially inclined to adopt maize.

It may have encouraged the rise of larger states than had existed before because its portability helped armies from maize regions range further than before, build states and extend the power of forest kingdoms like the Asante. This kingdom expanded in the 1670s, greatly helped by armies who could carry their maize-based provisions on distant campaigns. Maize became central to Atlantic African culture, especially for the Yoruba, who used maize in religious and political rituals. Cassava (or manioc) was another important American crop that flourished in Atlantic Africa and with maize helped offset population losses from the slave trade by providing people with more reliable diets, making them less prone to malnutrition and thus more fertile. Cassava served much the same purpose in Africa as potatoes did in Europe, helping peasantries to flee and survive war raids. It was more complicated to grow than maize, as one variant, bitter manioc, is poisonous. Harvesting manioc and making it edible was skilled and laborious work, most of which fell to women.

Culturally, however, the impact of the New World upon Old Worlds was either unimpressive or where important was very troubling. In particular, it added to the violence of a world that, especially in Europe, seemed to be getting more rather than less violent, wracked as it was in Europe by devastating wars of religion as a previously unified Christendom cracked into two antagonistic religious divisions of Protestant versus Catholic. Violence, to a lesser extent, may also have increased in Africa. There, wars and the social dislocation brought about by the biggest change to affect

Atlantic Africa, which was the development of a vibrant but violent Atlantic slave trade, which was important from the mid-seventeenth century until the mid-nineteenth century, meant that large-scale violence within states and non-states became more prevalent.

VIOLENCE

For most people outside Europe, the contacts established during the period of encounter were invariably violent. The European invaders, especially in the Americas, brought with them monotheistic religions and alien political structures that they wanted to impose upon indigenes, whom they envisaged as people to conquer and dominate rather than people who they could live alongside in terms of equality. The most noticeable feature, therefore, of how the different peoples of the world interacted with each other, therefore, was through violence. That was hardly surprising, given how violence was fundamental to each of the societies involved in the Atlantic and was a feature of social and political life that increased in frequency and intensity, especially in Europe, during the period when the Atlantic World was being formed. In Africa, by contrast, where African rulers retained control of most political and commercial processes until the mid-nineteenth century, the relationship between Europeans and Africans was mostly one of wary negotiation rather than actual violence.

The birth of the Atlantic World saw an increase in European violence. The late fifteenth and early sixteenth centuries saw great violence in the civil wars that devastated England, France, Iberia and Flanders. Wars of religion arising from the Reformation were even more devastating, sundering a previously untied Christendom. Despite the optimism of the Renaissance and an increasing belief in rational thinking, the first two centuries of the Atlantic World saw in Europe a growth in intolerance and a readiness to engage in vicious warfare. Moreover, ferocious penal codes and the institution of the Inquisition meant that the numbers of individuals subjected to punishment, torture and execution were greater than before. One radical novelty was that Europeans came to believe that violence in Africa and the Americas mirrored European violence, blurring the line between 'civilized' and 'savage' people. It seemed to many people that the world was entering a new dark age, where the only solution, as Thomas Hobbes argued in his political masterpiece, *Leviathan*, was to rely on state protection, no matter how authoritarian, from the possible violence of everyday life – life itself being nasty and brutish. Episodes of extreme violence were common. One example was the Elizabethan invasion of Ireland in the late sixteenth century which led to Protestant English settlement on confiscated Catholic land. When the native Irish rebelled, as they did in the 1590s and in the great uprising of 1641, they were subjected to a retaliatory ideology of extermination, in which violence was glorified. Sir Humphrey Gilbert in the 1590s reportedly lined the approach to his camp headquarters with the heads of rebels, providing a grisly sight for the kin of such executed people, as they were forced to walk past them. The experience that English colonists gained in treating Irish Catholics with extreme barbarity was transferred to their dealings with Native Americans. Fifty years later, the British Isles was convulsed by the most violent conflict in its history: 86,000 people were killed in battle and 100,000 were killed by other means in the British Civil Wars of the 1640s, a rate of death per capita greater than in the Great War of 1914–1918.

Europeans brought such violence with them to the New World. When Pánfilo de Narváez landed in present-day Tampa, Florida, in April 1528, the reputation of the Spanish as violent men had already reached Native American ears. They stayed away from the Spaniard. But Narváez was relentless in making sure that Native Americans were aware of him. Using methods of intimidation employed by the Spanish in the Caribbean, he terrorized the local population, setting fire to the village where the Tocobaga lived and sending in snarling mastiffs to attack the *cacique's* (chief) mother. He then amputated the nose of Hirrihigua, the *cacique*, a painful insult that in Spain was a mark of extreme dishonour. The Tocobaga were no pacifists. They bided their time and then extracted vengeance by killing all except one of a search party sent from Cuba to find Narváez and tortured Juan Ortiz, the sole survivor, flaying him over a fire for hours. Amazingly, Ortiz survived and escaped to a rival Native American village. This early and violent contact demonstrates that along with trying to learn each other's language and bartering clumsily for goods, both Spaniards and Native Americans used their mutual traditions of violence to connect with each other. 'Extravagant violence', Fitz Brundage tells us, 'became a means of communication, complementing the broader negotiation, exploitation, violence and theft that accompanied the European conquest of North America. Torture became one of the most emphatic forms of cultural exchange between these wary interlocutors.'[2] Native Americans inherited a culture of vengeance. Violence had to be avenged, otherwise the honour of the victim's blood relatives would be harmed, amity in tribes would be destroyed and the journey of the souls of the dead to the afterlife would be hampered. Trapped in the world of the living, these tormented souls would insist on their living relatives getting either retribution or compensation.

Violence also helped to knit together Atlantic America. The region was a remarkably underinstitutionalized world full of unassimilated populations who had little more to unite them than mutual fear and cultural misunderstanding. The threat and application of force and the acceptance of a level of violence in relations with the enslaved and with indigenous people marked the peripheries of empire as savage and outside the normal experience of Europeans, themselves not unused to brutality. One sign of that violence was the frequency of war and massacre. British America, for example, was mostly at war during the seventeenth and eighteenth centuries, either with each other, as in the Civil Wars of the 1640s, or with France and Spain, as was almost constant between 1688 and 1815. Wars in the Americas were especially brutal and unlike war in much of continental Europe, outside of the Thirty Years' War (which was notoriously vicious), the objectives of these Atlantic conflicts were not just to defeat an enemy but to destroy by any means, including torture and genocide, the civilizations of people characterized as alien.

It is a difficult question as to whether violence declined over time. It probably became less ferocious in respect to Native Americans, although violence on the frontier in French and British America could be devastating. Pontiac's War (1763–1764) in the Great Lakes region of North America, Tupac Amaru's rebellion (1780–1781) in Upper Peru and the Haitian Revolution (1791–1804) were all notoriously bloody. But some of the bloodiest episodes occurred earlier in Atlantic history, as in Brazil in the 1570s, when settlers decimated Native Americans in the coastal northeast in brutal war, enslaving those who survived. The general view is that the barbarous years of the seventeenth century, when white colonists led stunted lives in ramshackle buildings and in heavily undeveloped and basic social and economic conditions and where relations with Native Americans, African Americans and poor white people were marked by extreme brutality and lack of compassion, were followed by greater gentility in the eighteenth century. Social relations deepened and became more predictable and the consumption of European goods within denser and more urban populations made white colonists seem increasingly similar in wealth, cultural orientation and political sophistication to metropolitan European societies. That white prosperity was founded, however, on a slave system was much more brutal in the first half of the eighteenth century than in the seventeenth century.

When planters and ordinary whites behaved callously towards enslaved people and described them in harsh language, often comparing them to beasts, or giving enslaved people classical names as a form of bad joke, it was not because, as is sometimes suggested, that they were displacing their fear into emotions like anger. They acted so badly to enslaved people because they despised them, often for reasons of a pernicious racism that accompanied the beginnings of chattel African slavery in the sixteenth century and which deepened and became more pervasive as an ideological feature of Atlantic life in the eighteenth century. In the heyday of the plantation system, before abolitionism encouraged planters to temper their disdain towards blacks, between 1720 and 1780 in French and British America, planters revealed what they truly thought about Africans and enslaved people. It is an ugly picture. Sadistic cruelty was so normal as to be unexceptional.

When cruelty was commented upon, it was so egregious as to demonstrate that ordinary day-to-day violence was unremarkable. The slave ship captain and later abolitionist John Newton related a story from 1748 or 1749 in which a slave ship captain called Richard Jackson punished rebellious slaves by having them 'jointed', which involved dismembering each man limb by limb until finally their heads were cut off. Jackson threw the bodies into the sea for the sharks to feed upon. Then, in front of the 'trembling slaves', gathered on the foredeck, he placed a rope around the head of some captives and squeezed hard with a lever within the rope until 'he forced their eyes to stand out of their heads'. Newton noted that in the slave trade there was 'a savageness of spirit [that] infuses itself into those who exercise power [which] is the spirit of the trade, which, like a pestilential air, is so generally infectious that but few escape it'.[3]

Some indication of the customary violence in slavery within plantations can be seen in the copious journals of Thomas Thistlewood, an English-born overseer and small planter in western Jamaica, who detailed how he punished slaves in graphic detail for the years between 1750 and 1786. Thistlewood was cruel but there is little evidence to suggest that he was anything out the ordinary in respect to his violent personality for this place and time. In a region where slaves outnumbered whites by at least 12 to 1, Thistlewood found it was essential to use violence to keep enslaved people at bay. Some of the methods he used were sadistic. He whipped slaves (most men under his employ were whipped at least once), rubbing salt, lime juice or pepper into their wounds. He made one slave defecate in another's mouth and then gagged that mouth shut. He forced slaves to urinate in each other's eyes and cropped the ears and slit the nostrils of enslaved people who ran away. He chained others in stocks and branded them with his initials. He forced enslaved women to have sex with him, having sex by his own accounts with 138 women over thirty-seven years.

Slaves responded to such violence by running away, by committing suicide, by acts of sabotage and, eventually, by revolt. Thistlewood gives a vivid account of a slave revolt in Westmoreland Parish, where Thistlewood lived, in 1760, where hundreds of slave rebels, under the leadership of an ex-warrior prince from the Gold Coast, burned down plantations, killed perhaps sixty whites and came close to overcoming white rule in the region. The slave revolt failed, leading to retaliation on a massive scale, that was noticeable for its cruelty. Rebels were burned to death by slow fire, were gibbeted alive until they starved to death and were transported by the hundreds into exile in British Honduras in Central America. Europeans and North Americans may have prided themselves that by the eighteenth-century they were living in more Enlightened and 'polite' worlds but the savagery of New World slavery showed that this politeness masked societies willing to govern through ferocious violence. So too, ordinary people, hanged in great numbers in eighteenth-century Britain and France, belied the notion that European life was becoming gentler over time.

Whites found ways of justifying such violence through suggesting that Africans were so naturally barbarous that the only way to rule them was, as Daniel Defoe argued, with 'a Rod of Iron, beaten with Scorpions, as the Scripture calls it, and they must be used as they do use them, or they would rise and murder all their Masters'. Nicholas Lejeune, a sociopathic planter whose depravities against his slaves – burning women to death for virtually no reason – were so outrageous that the authorities in slave owning Saint Domingue put him on trial for murder, to the outrage of local planters, who believed no white should ever be punished what he did to a black person, echoed Defoe's matter-of-fact practical defence of planter tyranny. The intendant of Cap Français argued that Lejeune needed to be tried because 'what will happen if our common impotence in this affair is publicly demonstrated and if at the same time the tribunals join with the barbaric planters to oppress these unfortunates? For one hundred years these cruelties have been exercised with impunity; they are committed right before the slaves because it is known that their testimony will be rejected'. But Lejeune was absolved of all guilt (while being obviously a sadistic torturer) by the highest court of Saint-Domingue. He crowed to his supporters on acquittal in 1788 that 'the unhappy condition of the Negro leads him naturally to detest us. It is only force and violence that restrains him … It is not the fear and equity of the law that forbids the slave from stabbing his master; it is the consciousness of absolute power that he has over his person Remove this bit, he will dare anything'.[4]

ATLANTIC SLAVE TRADE

In many ways, Africa was not especially affected by the integration of Old and New Worlds that Columbian contact started. As detailed in Chapter 8, the Atlantic World's impact on most of Africa was relatively slight. Yet Africa also enjoyed (or, better, suffered) the most striking developments between the mid-seventeenth and late eighteenth centuries compared to Europe and the Americas if we move from looking at changes within continents because of the Atlantic encounter to examining changes in the nature and size of connections. Those connections were manifest in one of the great crimes in human history, the Atlantic slave trade. This trade is probably the quintessential event or process in Atlantic history and deserves a detailed treatment as a major consequence for an Old World of the discovery of the so-called New World.

This chapter will discuss the slave trade mainly in macro-historical terms – its size, scale, magnitude and social, demographic and political consequences – but we need to keep in mind micro-history as well: the individual, quotidian experiences of individuals enmeshed in the horror of the slave trade. For those Africans caught up in the slaving machine (the mechanical metaphor was one constantly used in describing the trade), being a captive was a deeply personal tragedy. Unfortunately, our sources on the Atlantic slave trade are limited, although Aaron Fogleman has shown that there are more sources than we once realized.[5] The best-known account is also one that is particularly problematic. Forty years after his enslavement in Africa and shipment to the Americas, Olaudah Equiano, or Gustavus Vassa, 'the African', published a best-selling autobiography in 1789, recounting his kidnapping in inland Africa, his journey to the Atlantic coast and then to America, his employment and manumission in the West Indies, and his conversion to Methodism and to the cause of antislavery in England. His book contains the most vivid description of the Middle Passage extant, although recent research has suggested, inconclusively, that possibly Equiano was not African but had been a slave in South Carolina.[6]

The basic facts of his life are detailed in the autobiography. He was born in modern southeast Nigeria, a long way from the sea. He was kidnapped at age ten, and after a harrowing six-month journey, he arrived at the coast, was sold to English traders, and was shipped to Barbados and then reshipped to Virginia. His *Narrative* relates the brutality of his kidnapping and how he was force-fed and marched to the coast. He describes his 'astonishment, which was soon converted into terror' on seeing a slave ship. He was convinced that he was 'in a world of bad spirits' and that he would be killed and eaten. After being flogged for not eating he contemplated suicide though 'not being used to the water, I naturally feared that element to the first time I saw it'. He described at length the 'absolutely pestilential' state of life below decks with the 'galling of the chains', the 'filth of the necessary tubs' and the 'shrieks of the women, and the groans of the dying', all of which showed the slave ship as 'a scene of horror almost inconceivable'. Arrival brought no relief, as he was separated from his country-people and left alone and isolated – a fate most West Africans, especially teenage boys like Equiano, viewed as almost as bad a fate as becoming enslaved. His *Narrative* provides a rare African perspective on the Atlantic crossing, even if qualified by his sympathy for abolitionism, which helped shape how he structured his account, and by his temporal distance from the events he described. His life also demonstrates that captives were not just passive victims of their country people's and European villainy but exercised some agency in how they survived the Middle Passage (the second of three stages in the so-called Triangular Trade, the first being the voyage to Africa where ships were laden with textiles and other goods, like firearms which were desired by Africans; and the third being the return from Brazil or the Caribbean, where 95 per cent of ships went to, carrying either bills of exchange or tropical commodities). His story also shows how in a few cases African captives could build a meaningful life under slavery and even gain their freedom and become cosmopolitan Atlantic travellers.

The Atlantic slave trade was just one of several large oceanic migrations. In Africa alone, the total volume of the slave trade in the longer-lasting slave trade in the Indian Ocean world probably equalled and perhaps exceeded the volume of captives in the Atlantic slave trade. If we look at slaves who moved in or out of Africa between 1400 and 1900, of 37 million enslaved migrants, 12.6 million were in the Atlantic slave trade and 18.5 million migrated within Africa. It was only in the eighteenth century that the Atlantic slave trade, with 6.5 million captives involved, came close to internal slavery (7.8 million slaves).[7]

Yet the Atlantic slave trade was distinctive in several ways. At bottom, as David Eltis and David Richardson argue, the result of the trade was one whereby 'relatively small improvements to the quality of life of a people on one continent [Europe] ... was made possible by the removal of others from a second continent [Africa], and their draconian exploitation on yet a third [the Americas]'.[8] It was not just an economic event. It was a crime and an arena of dramatic social transformation, the most visible indication of how the Columbian encounter opened a virtually unconstrained form of capitalism, in which morality was placed below economic gain, and where slave traders devised new and ingenious ways in which to reduce people to the status of commodities. The Atlantic slave trade, Stephanie Smallwood argues, was where 'individual paths of misfortune merged into the commodifying Atlantic apparatus – the material, economic, and social mechanisms by which the market molded subjects into beings that more closely resembled objects – beings that existed solely for the use of those that claimed to hold them as possessions'.[9]

One curiosity about the Atlantic slave trade is that Europeans travelled to Africa to get labourers when they might have met their New World labour needs from transporting and then enslaving the lower social strata of European society, strata that caused European rulers no end of problems and members of which, when criminals, they had little compunction in torturing and executing. David Eltis suggests they did not do so because Europeans saw Europeans, but not Africans, as members of their own moral community and thus not eligible for enslavement.[10] In this respect, Christians adopted what was also the case for Muslims, who believed that Islamic law banned the enslavement of believers. Nevertheless, Europeans had fewer problems in using indentured labour to put Europeans to work, showing they were not opposed to coercion for members of their own communities. More urgent reasons against the enslavement of Europeans were that it was likely that such actions in the mid-seventeenth century would have led to massive popular revolt in France and Britain by poor people who were convinced that they had as much right to liberty as rich people. Africans had no such problem, outside Islamic areas, in enslaving their own country people – whom they seldom saw in such terms. Africans had long experience with slavery and thought of slaves as a source of wealth and as a common form of currency. When Europeans sought slaves in return for European goods, African merchants were happy to oblige, especially as they tended to control the terms under which the trade operated.

The Atlantic slave trade was organizationally complex. It was inherently risky for merchants, as it involved myriad business decisions in distant places that could easily unravel. Merchants required large amounts of capital to enter the trade as private individuals, giving an opportunity before 1700 for government companies like the Dutch West India Company and the

English Royal African Company to monopolize the trade. Private trading only became very important in the eighteenth century. Climatic concerns and agricultural cycles in Africa and the Americas shaped when and where slaves were delivered to plantations. Traders wanted their cargoes to arrive in the most profitable markets outside the hurricane season and during the dry season harvest (between December and February in Jamaica and Brazil). In this period, planters had money to buy captives and crops to send back to Europe in payment. African ecological patterns were even more important. In Old Calabar in present-day southern Nigeria, for example, the best time to buy slaves was during the four-month yam harvest.

Other places had different preferred seasonal times for purchasing slaves. One reason why the British proved so adept at slave trading in the eighteenth century is that they were masterful in controlling these complex African ecological rhythms, thus reducing risk in a time-dependent trade. They relied, as all Europeans did, on having good relations with the African merchants who controlled the trade in West Africa. They did this by paying duties, giving preferential prices and participating in palavers, or meetings, with extensive rounds of gift giving. They sent small ships to politically decentralized coastal markets with intermittent slave supplies and large ships to politically centralized ports which had extensive commercial infrastructures supporting large-scale slave shipments. The Windward Coast was an example of the former; Bonny and Ouidah exemplified the latter.

The most notorious section of the Triangular Trade was the Middle Passage. Hundreds of traumatized men, women and children were sent, naked, on tightly packed, foul-smelling ships on a four- to six-week journey on the sea. Henry Smeathman, a late eighteenth-century natural scientist, described what the ships were like in vivid fashion, like that of Equiano. He lamented the ship as a 'scene of misery and distress' with 'the clanking of chains, the groans of the sick and the stench of the whole'. He noted how there were 'two or three slaves thrown over-board every day dying of fever, flux, measles, worms all together'. The Africans who endured this horror were controlled through extreme force by a larger-than-normal crew of badly paid and unappreciated seamen – the slave ship was a floating prison, full of weapons that were often used on the approximately 10 per cent of voyages that experienced a slave revolt. The very real possibility of slave revolt meant that slave ships were overmanned on the Middle Passage and sailors were then cut adrift when they arrived in the Caribbean or Brazil. Seamen learned while on board slave ships the technologies of power that were used from the late seventeenth centuries to subdue plantation slaves on large estates. It is no accident that the rise of very large West Indian plantations, with over 100 enslaved people coincided temporally with the transformation of the English slave trade in the late seventeenth century and the evolution of more military relationships among seamen aboard slave ships. Slave ship sailors could easily transition in the Americas into being overseers on plantations.

Seamen seldom had a pleasant experience on ships. But the real victims of the Middle Passage were the African captives who were degraded by the horrors of what they underwent at sea. Some historians argue that this degradation made captives 'socially dead' – people who had lost their contacts in their native land and whose experience aboard ship involved so much ritual dishonouring that it resulted in close to complete disempowerment. The conditions aboard ship were certainly terrible. Describing slaves as 'socially dead' goes too far, however, as it underestimates the means that captives had in overcoming their dehumanization, such as forming links with other fellow sufferers. These 'shipmates' formed quasi-kin relations and were often important in establishing linkages between slaves on plantations.

One historical fact that has been established through extensive work in archives over the last fifty years is the volume and distribution of the trade. The best estimates we have are that between 1501 and 1866, 12,521,336 captives left Africa in the trade and 10,702,656 are known to have disembarked. The trade increased in volume during the seventeenth and eighteenth centuries, reaching its peak in the latter half of the eighteenth century, when 3,440,981 captives were transported out of Africa, with the British alone carrying 1,580,658 captives and the French, especially to their West Indian colony of Saint Domingue, 758,978. In the eighteenth century, most captives went to the Caribbean while in the nineteenth century, after the abolition of the slave trade in 1807 by the British and the implosion of Saint Domingue after 1791, Brazil became the major destination for slaves, with 2,367,329 arriving in Brazil between 1801 and 1850. The largest provenance region over the entirety of the trade was West-Central Africa, from where 5,694,574 captives left. But other places also provided many slaves: 2 million from the Bight of Benin and 1 million each from Biafra and the Gold Coast.

The slave trade was brutal but not genocidal, mainly because the aim of the trade was to get as many captives as possible in a healthy state to American plantations where they could be sold for profit. The transformation of captives into slaves is the least studied part of the triangular trade. The sale of slaves usually led, as Equiano noted, to a dispersal of slave cargo through a process that included being treated like livestock on arrival; being conducted to a merchant's yard where they were herded together 'like so many sheep in a fold'. Slaves were then sold and 'seasoned' on plantations. By this last stage in the process, the commodification and dehumanization of enslaved people were close to complete. As Smallwood suggests: 'if in the regime of the market, Africans' most socially relevant feature was their exchangeability, for Africans as immigrants the most socially relevant feature was their isolation, their desperate need to restore some measure of social life to counterbalance the alienation engendered by their social death.'[11]

The Atlantic slave trade left many legacies. It may have contributed to African underdevelopment. It may too have played a role in encouraging British industrialisation. The linkages between the slave trade and European wealth tended to be indirect. Private fortunes made in the trade had limited effects on metropolitan capital accumulation, both in Britain and in France. What the slave trade did do economically, however, especially in Britain, where business practices were most sophisticated, was to accentuate demands in the New World and Africa for manufactures and to help improve and make more efficient long-term credit banks and insurance. The most important legacy was undoubtedly cultural. It brought to the Americas not just Africans but African culture. It is somewhat perverse to envision the slave ship as a place of cultural creation when it was such a place of terror, violence and death. But creative elements of Atlantic culture could emerge even from such dreadful environments. It created a neo-Africa in the Americas. The slave ships carried not just people but malaria and yellow fever, which devastated European populations in the tropics. They brought West African rice, the cultivation of which may have been greatly influenced by African knowledge, crops which became dominant in South Carolina, Georgia and Surinam. By the eighteenth century, a neo-Africa existed from the Chesapeake to Bahia. Most people in this region were of African descent and their cultural forms, such as music, dancing and emotional religious expression, formed the building blocks of Atlantic culture in the plantation zone. African foodstuffs and African knowledge systems (slaves' knowledge of plants and healing were extensively exploited by Europeans) travelled widely. Nevertheless, this neo-Africa differed in one very important respect to what happened in neo-Europe in the northern regions of North America. Up until the Haitian Revolution (1791–1804), when for the first time a black republic was established with the rulers being formerly enslaved people, nowhere in the Americas were people of African descent in control of any aspect of society. By contrast, in neo-Europe, the descendants of Europeans came to exercise dominance, even if constrained by colonial obligations.

NATURE AND CULTURE

Not all the reactions to the European discovery of the New World and African complicity in establishing a trade in people to exploit the lands that had been supposedly discovered were as antagonistic and conflictual as war, violence and the slave trade. The Atlantic World was essential in the process by which Europeans changed their view of the world, from one that pivoted on religious explanations to one that was explicit with reference to natural phenomena. Changes in understanding nature emerged largely due to the start of an Atlantic community when for the first-time far-flung people met each other. When Europeans and Americans encountered each other, they not only exchanged plants and commodities. They also shared ideas about both the seen and the unseen. These encounters, Peter Mancall contends, were decisive in moving Europe from a medieval to a modern mindset. Europeans' appropriation of the natural resources of the Americas reshaped human and nonhuman communities. Perceptions about nature changed. To take one poignant example: in Mexico in 1576, Nahua artists who had studied the work of Pliny embraced his ideas in their depiction of indigenous plants at a time of a great epidemic in Mexico, thereby, Mancall notes, 'creating a memorial to their world in a visual language used by early modern Europeans to explain phenomena known in ancient Rome'. New ideas about nature swirled in a culture in which the marvellous nature of the new mixed with established notions from the past about what natural phenomena were meant to be.[12]

The most important impact of the 'discovery' of the Americas on European consciousness is that it disturbed established ideas of what knowledge was. For David Hume in the mid-eighteenth century, the Columbian encounter was when modern history started. He linked it with the Reformation and the Renaissance, the invention of printing and gunpowder, global commerce and new forms of government. It was now a period of rapid change, a time in which, William Robertson, Hume's contemporary, decreed, 'when Providence decreed that men were to pass the limits within which they had been so long confined'. It also meant that new areas in the world had been brought, as Europeans saw it, into history. As Bartolomé Las Casas put it, the great contribution of Columbus had not been to bring the Spanish to America (Las Casas thought that a very bad thing) but to bring 'so many countless people' into history and thus having 'broken the locks that had held the Ocean Sea fast ever since the Flood'.

That these people were not in the Bible was troubling. It suggested that ancient wisdom was wrong, or at least incomplete. People were not meant to live in 'the Torrid Zone' of the Tropics but clearly they did. The discovery of America seriously undermined European classical geography and traditional Christian accounts of the creation and subsequent peopling of the world. It also undermined humanistic ideas about natural philosophy, the idea that all knowledge was in the texts of ancient commentators, notably Aristotle. If they were wrong about the geography of the world, what else might they be wrong about? That was what the Jesuit historian Jose de Acosta thought in the mid-sixteenth century when on a ship to America and finding himself cold at midday with the sun directly overhead – an impossible situation according to ancient meteorology. He 'laughed and made fun of Aristotle and his philosophy'.[13]

The discovery of America was linked very closely to the Reformation. Both contributed to the collapse of the late medieval intellectual order and respect for the authority of the ancient world. Both phenomena showed that received authority could be overthrown. They showed that the current view that the law of nature was a set of universal and binding principles no longer held. Natural law had only a limited foundation in fact in nature. Natural law was only a matter of collective opinion, pretending to be definitive certainty. As the great nineteenth-century natural historian Alexander von Humboldt opined, before Columbus's voyages Europeans thought of time and how people moved through time as a set of responses to 'external circumstances'. After Columbus, there was 'a new and active state of the intellect and feelings, bold wishes, and hopes scarcely to be restrained' that 'gradually penetrated into the whole of civil society'. Since Columbus, the European mind 'produces ... Grand results by its own peculiar and internal power in every direction at the same time'. Humboldt's great claims are perhaps purposefully vague, but they do point to a feeling, developed increasingly over time, that the New World could even be a replacement for the Old. Georg Friedrich Hegel, for example, writing in 1830, saw History as starting in the East; being perfected in Europe; and was now moving across the Atlantic, mostly to the new United States, 'where in the ages that lie before us, the burden of the World's History shall reveal itself'.[14] These strongly aspirational views by leading European intellectuals in the nineteenth century fed into the exceptionalist ideologies of the United States, still evident today, of a New World set in motion to rescue the Old World from its excesses, with the United States have a special, even God-ordained, role in shaping global interactions. Possibly the whole enterprise of Atlantic history fits within this exceptionalist reading of the moral duty of the United States to the rest of the world.

NOTES

1   J.H. Elliott, *Empires of the Atlantic World: Britain and Spain in America 1492–1830* (New Haven: Yale University Press, 2006), 18–19.
2   W. Fitz Brundage, *Civilizing Torture: An American Tradition* (Cambridge, MA: Harvard University Press, 2018), 13–14.
3   Marcus Rediker, *The Slave Ship: A Human History* (London: Penguin, 2007), 218–20.
4   Trevor Burnard and John Garrigus, *The Plantation Machine: Atlantic Capitalism in French Saint-Domingue and British Jamaica* (Philadelphia: University of Pennsylvania Press, 2016), 260.
5   Aaron Fogleman, 'Ideologies of the Age of Revolution and Emancipation in Enslaved African Narratives,' in Trevor Burnard and Sophie White, eds., *Hearing Slaves' Voices: African and Indian Slave Testimony in British and French America, 1700–1848* (New York: Routledge, 2020).
6   For disputing views, see Vincent Carretta, 'Olaudah Equiano or Gustavus Vassa? New Light on an Eighteenth-Century Question of Identity,' *Slavery & Abolition* 20 (1999), 96–105; and Paul E. Lovejoy, 'Olaudah Equiano or Gustavus Vassa – What's in a Name,' *Atlantic Studies* 9 (2012), 165–84.
7   Pier M. Larson, 'African Slave Trade in Global Perspective,' in John Parker and Richard Reid, eds., *The Oxford Handbook of Modern African History* (Oxford: Oxford University Press, 2013), 60.
8   David Eltis and David Richardson, 'A New Assessment of the Transatlantic Slave Trade,' in Eltis and Richardson, eds., *Extending the Frontiers: Essays on*

the Transatlantic Slave Trade Data Base (New Haven: Yale University Press, 2008), 45.

9   Stephanie Smallwood, *Saltwater Slavery: A Middle Passage from Africa to American Diaspora* (Cambridge, MA: Harvard University Press, 2007), 63, 182, 187.

10 David Eltis, *The Rise of African Slavery in the Americas* (Cambridge: Cambridge University Press, 2000), 63–84.

11 Smallwood, *Saltwater Slavery*, 189.

12 Peter C. Mancall, *Nature and Culture in the Early Modern Atlantic* (Philadelphia: University of Pennsylvania Press, 2018), xii–xiii.

13 Cited in Anthony Pagden, 'The Challenge of the New,' in Nicholas Canny and Philip Morgan, eds., *The Oxford Handbook of the Atlantic World 1450–1850* (Oxford: Oxford University Press, 2011), 459.

14 Ibid., 460–61.

BIBLIOGRAPHY

Oxford Online Bibliographies – Dreams and Dreaming; History of Science; Sex and Sexuality; Slave Rebellions; The Atlantic Slave Trade; The Slave Trade and Natural Science; Violence.

Trevor Burnard, *Mastery, Tyranny, and Desire: Thomas Thistlewood and His Slaves in the Anglo-Jamaican World* (Chapel Hill: University of North Carolina Press, 2004).

Vincent Carretta, *Equiano, the African: Biography of a Self-Made Man* (London: Penguin, 2005).

Jacques de Cauna, François Hubert and Christian Block, *Bordeaux au XVIII siècle: Le commerce atlantique et l'esclavage* (Paris: Feston, 2010).

David Eltis, *The Rise of African Slavery in the Americas* (Cambridge: Cambridge University Press, 2000).

David Eltis and David Richardson, 'A New Assessment of the Transatlantic Slave Trade,' in Eltis and Richardson, eds., *Extending the Frontiers: Essays on the Transatlantic Slave Trade Data Base* (New Haven: Yale University Press, 2008), 1–60.

Toby Green, *The Rise of the Trans-Atlantic Slave Trade in Western Africa, 1300–1589* (Cambridge: Cambridge University Press, 2012).

Pier M. Larson, 'Horrid Journeying: Narratives of Enslavement and the Global African Diaspora,' *Journal of World History* 19 (2008), 431–64.

Peter C. Mancall, *Nature and Culture in the Early Modern Atlantic* (Philadelphia: University of Pennsylvania Press, 2018).

J.R. McNeill, 'The Ecological Atlantic,' in Nicholas Canny and Philip Morgan, eds., *The Oxford Handbook of the Atlantic World 1450–1850* (Oxford: Oxford University Press, 2011), 289–304.

Kenneth Morgan, *Slavery and the British Empire: From Africa to America* (Oxford: Oxford University Press, 2007).

Brian Sandberg, 'Beyond Encounters: Religion, Ethnicity, and Violence in the Early Modern Atlantic World, 1492–1700,' *Journal of World History* 17 (2006), 1–25.

Stephanie Smallwood, *Saltwater Slavery: A Middle Passage from Africa to American Diaspora* (Cambridge, MA: Harvard University Press, 2007).

6

SETTLER WORLDS

'A WIDOWED LAND'

Eighteenth-century thinkers like William Robertson in Scotland and Abbé Raynal in France thought the opening of the Americas a moral monstrosity, costing the lives of 20 million Native Americans (we know today that the numbers were much larger) in return for relatively modest improvement in science, a quickening of transatlantic commerce and some useful if not essential tropical commodities such as sugar, tobacco and potatoes. The educated view was that early America was a catastrophe – a horror story, John Murrin exclaims, not an epic, as customarily described in nationalistic celebrations of the pioneer spirit in Hollywood westerns and Latin American patriotic narratives.[1] What the philosophes omitted, however, and which led to furious responses from Creoles in the Americas, including Thomas Jefferson in Virginia, is that one achievement that had occurred by the middle of the eighteenth century was the establishment of viable, flourishing and influential settler colonies, full of happy, contented and prosperous whites of European descent. As economic historians Peter Lindert and Jeffrey Williamson have comprehensively shown, at least in British North America white settlers lived in materially better conditions and in more egalitarian societies (if only whites are considered) by the 1770s than any population on earth. Settler prosperity in the eighteenth-century Atlantic World, even if founded on the mistreatment and displacement of others, was a massive achievement that contributed greatly to the consolidation of European and then American hegemony in the world in the nineteenth century and which might have helped Europe overcome a Malthusian dilemma of too many people chasing too few resources.[2]

DISPLACEMENT AND NATIVE AMERICAN RESISTANCE

Settler achievement, of course, was founded on Native American displacement. Native Americans found it nearly impossible to understand what was happening to them during the maelstrom of change that saw first them experiencing a highly disadvantageous Columbian exchange and then the taking over of their lands and power by Europeans decisively and permanently in the eighteenth century. They could not work out how the Europeans they thought weak and cowardly for their inability to withstand, as Native American warriors were proud to do, torture while being executed, could win every war and come to prevail over them. It seemed that the weak were beating the strong. But as detailed in Chapter 3, Europeans had disease on their side. By the end of the seventeenth century, Native Americans were in retreat in most of the areas in which Europeans had settled most intensively. They had, of course, their occasional triumphs. Mistreatment on the missions of New Mexico led to Pueblo Native Americans revolting in 1680 in the most successful Naïve American revolt in North America. Missionaries and Spanish settlers were killed or expelled, not returning to the region for a decade. Elsewhere, however, Native Americans were losing the long battle to prevent European domination, with thousands being enslaved in British and French America in ways that brought Native American slavery closer to the model of African-American slavery developing at the same time from the mid-seventeenth century. The rest of Native Americans in European-controlled land were either driven from their homes or were forced to assimilate in ways that caused immense damage to their self-esteem and to the cultural coherence of their long-standing ways of life.

Such degradation was seldom enough for their European opponents. They wanted Native Americans to not be just humiliated, but to be destroyed. As Governor William Berkeley of Virginia argued in 1666, 'I thinke it is necessary to Distroy all those Northerne Indians for ... twill be a great Terror and Example of Instruction to all other Indians'. As John Murrin again notes, 'until the arrival of pacifist Quakers in the Delaware Valley after 1675, the English colonies were all founded by terrorists'.[3] That terrorism extended past Native Americans to African Americans, whose arrival in great numbers in the Americas from the mid-seventeenth century transformed a population of white and red into one that had increasing numbers of both whites and blacks and diminishing numbers of Native Americans. The crucial story of the Atlantic World between 1600 and 1800 is that the American continents saw the most remarkable shift in relative shares of population by different ethnic groups in the history of mankind, save perhaps, and on a smaller scale, in nineteenth-century New Zealand and Australia.

MIGRATION

By the end of the Seven Years' War in 1763, the Americas were full of people of European and African descent, with Europeans in control and thus much more easily able to influence the cultural directions of these new settler societies. What these descendants of European migrants wanted to do was to improve their material conditions and live a life better than was possible for them in Europe, with the acquisition of land and the achievement of a 'competency' or independence within patriarchal systems of government a major ambition. They also wanted to recreate as much as possible Europe in the Americas, which is why they named their colonies as being fresh versions of European societies – New England, New France, New Netherlands and New Spain, for example. That ambition was seldom achieved in the 'barbarous years', as Bernard Bailyn calls them, of the seventeenth century. But in the eighteenth century, societies in which the rulers were no longer immigrants of sometimes uncertain heritage but Creoles, or native-born men with roots in their localities and inherited position from membership in wealthy families, white settlers pursued with much more success than before policies of Anglicization or Hispanicization that turned their societies into more exact political and cultural models of metropolitan homelands. Everywhere, from the second quarter of the eighteenth century, settler societies in the Americas started to exhibit the same internal complexity and external similarities as European societies and settlers could more persuasively be argued to be conforming to European models of behaviour that meant they could not any longer be dismissively characterized by metropolitans as uncouth barbarians living in societies with no pretensions to European sophistication.

This increasing conformity to European norms was most apparent in British North America, after nearly a century where, except in New England, white population was only able to increase through migration, not natural growth, demographic normality was finally achieved. Sex ratios changed from being heavily biased towards male-majority populations to being nearly equal between men and women. Slave populations in British North America became demographically self-sustaining a generation later than did the European population and soon started to multiply rapidly. This made the American South slave system exceptional within the Atlantic World as having a demographically self-sustaining enslaved workforce. By the 1760s, planters in the American South no longer needed to rely on the transatlantic slave trade, meaning that abolition in 1808 was largely an empty gesture. It also meant that the American slave population had far fewer influences from Africa than less demographically successful slave populations in the Caribbean and in Brazil.

To understand how completely the Americas were changed by the migration of Europeans and Africans to replace Native Americans as the dominant population groups, we need to turn to numbers. The most significant numbers are the overall numbers of migrants – 2.5 million Europeans between 1500 and 1820 and 8.8 million Africans. There were 1,263,000 Europeans who arrived between 1640 and 1760 alongside 3,962,000 Europeans. Of Europeans, the most numerous were the British – 1,257,000 moved to the Americas before 1820, initially in the seventeenth century more often to the Caribbean and in the eighteenth century to North America. British migrants were dominant as settlers between 1640 and 1760 when 592,000 (47 per cent of all European migrants) left for the Americas. Iberians came closest to the British in total numbers – 460,000 moving between 1640 and 1760 and 1,250,000 between 1500 and 1820. In the eighteenth century, a substantial number of Germans – 97,000 between 1640 and 1760 and 148,000 before 1820, almost all from 1700 onwards – moved to the Americas, mostly to British America, though some went in the seventeenth century to Dutch America. The contrast between British migration and French and Dutch migration is immense. France was easily the most populous nation in Western Europe but just 96,000 French came to the Americas between 1640 and 1760 and a mere 18,000 Dutch. Both European empires suffered for the unwillingness of their residents to move to the Americas. European migration mattered less in tropical regions, where labour needs could be made up by enslaved Africans, but it limited colonial expansion in the northern regions of North America, even considering that in New France a small number of French migrants multiplied rapidly to make population levels reasonable.[4]

Aaron Fogelman has done pioneering work on total migration patterns to the Americas that deepens our knowledge of some fundamental features of both European and African migration. He shows conclusively that in the seventeenth and eighteenth centuries most people brought to the Americas did not come willingly or as free people. Between 1492 and 1699, 59 per cent of migrants arrived as slaves, 1 per cent as convicts or prisoners of war, 10 per cent as indentured servants and 30 per cent as free people. In the eighteenth century before the American Revolution, the dominance of unfree migrants in migration statistics was even more pronounced. Of the 4,480,600 people who crossed the Atlantic in that period, 80 per cent were slaves, 2 per cent were convicts, 3 per cent were indentured servants and 16 per cent were free people. If we confine ourselves only to migration to the thirteen colonies of British North America, the percentages of convicts and indentured servants increase markedly (they comprised 28 per cent of migrants between 1700 and 1775), as does the percentage of people who arrived as free people. That percentage arriving as free people, however, declined from the seventeenth century, when they comprised 37 per cent of all migrants, to the eighteenth century, when they were 28 per cent of all migrants. The United States proclaims itself as the home of the free but that was untrue for the colonial period when just 236,000 people from migration of 779,100 (30 per cent) were free people on arrival. It was only after 1810 in the United States and after 1830 in the Atlantic that free people became the majority percentage of migrants.

Fogeleman also has some interesting data on migration by gender. We know that English women were more reluctant migrants than English men. Unsurprisingly, therefore, it was even more likely that any woman who came to the Americas from Africa or Europe was unfree than was the case for men. Only 20 per cent of women arriving before 1700 came as free people, and in the eighteenth century this percentage dropped to 14 per cent. In that century, males also became significantly less likely to arrive as free people, primarily because of a boom in the Atlantic slave trade, meaning that this notable gender difference in migration disappeared. It appears that in the formative period of colony-building before 1700, Europeans were more prepared to bring in unfree females to work for them than to consider migrating with wives or other free women to build their projects. Moreover, since many of the females arriving as free people were children and a few were single women or widowed, relatively fewer migrants across the Atlantic came as married couples before the age of revolutions. In addition, we must ask whether free women were actually 'free'. Men made the decision to migrate and many women who came to the Americas probably did so at the choice of their husband or father. As Fogelman notes, 'reluctant migration in fulfilment of the obedience prescribed by the marriage bond were a factor that many women and virtually no men experienced'. As he continues, 'historians normally stress male interests in the colonies when addressing the reasons for the male surplus in free and indentured migration, but from the female perspective it could also mean that European women did not want to go or that patriarchal restrictions prevented them from leaving if they wanted to'.[5] Legal servitude characterized the status of most women and slightly fewer men before 1775.

What kind of people moved to the New World? In seventeenth-century British America, the largest group of migrants were indentured servants, contracted to serve between four and seven years, mostly as agricultural workers, in return for their passage, board and lodging and some privileges on gaining freedom, including in the earliest days of settlement access to land. English opinion of indentured servants tended to be poor. They were described as petty criminals, prostitutes and vagrants. But over time indentured servants appear to have come from respectable service and artisan backgrounds. Few 'destitute and unskilled slum dwellers and uprooted peasants'[6] came to America, although there were always a substantial number of convicts from unskilled backgrounds coming to Maryland and Virginia between 1718 and 1775. Free settlers were, of course, better resourced than the unfree. They had generally some money, useful friends and applicable skills that enabled them to get good positions on arrival and to prosper more than their less fortunate counterparts.

One notable feature of migration to British America, especially to the Middle Colonies of Pennsylvania and New York, was that after the mid-seventeenth century, relatively fewer migrants came from the metropolitan heartland of southern and midlands England. Instead, British migrants in the eighteenth century tended to come from northern England, Scotland and especially from Ulster. These migrants from the 'Celtic fringe' settled in the interior regions of the Ohio Valley, moving southward down the Appalachian Mountains into western Virginia and the Carolinas. They took their experiences of living within Ulster, where Protestants and Catholics lived in apprehension of each other, to their new homeland, giving those regions, in the views of some historians, a distinctive culture marked by fierce independence and a readiness to use violence against anyone they felt was taking their liberty from them. In addition, Germans and Swiss migrated in large numbers to the places where the Irish and the Scots had also moved, making those places multiethnic and multicultural if racially homogenous.

These movements need to be placed within a larger context of a Europe where people were frequently on the move. Europeans moved not only west to the Americas but east to Poland, Prussia, Hungary and Russia. Eastward movement was usually more substantial than westward movement. Europe, no less than Africa and the Americas, was a continent where migration was frequent. Migration was seldom a one-step process: most of the people moving to the New World had already moved away from their birthplaces well before departure overseas.

Changes in migration patterns over time were less extreme elsewhere in the Atlantic World. It was only in parts of British North America that saw sizeable migration of people who qualified as aliens or as foreigners. Some changes in Spanish migration, however, happened over time. Before 1650, most Spanish migrants to the Americas came from Andalusia and southwest Spain. After 1650, however, Spanish migrants were more likely than before to come from poor parts of the north coast, from eastern Spain and from the Canary and Balearic Islands. The relatively fewer French people who left for the Americas came from the northwest provinces of Brittany and Normandy and from the Atlantic ports of Rouen, Saint-Malo, Nantes, Bordeaux and La Rochelle.

Because migrants were people on the move already, it was difficult for them to transfer regional customs and identities directly to the New World. As D.W. Meinig explains, 'the Midlands labourer who had spent decades in London before emigration was already an Englishman in a larger sense; the Glaswegian agent bound for the Potomac who had done a tour of duty in the British West Indies was already in some degrees a British American; the man who in his youth had left a Tipperary cottage for the docks of Kingsale … was no longer an Irish peasant'.[7] As James Horn and Philip Morgan expand on this point, 'mobility and sustained contact with other peoples and cultures led to the evolution of new identities that frequently coexisted alongside older ones. Settlers took on multiple identities that embraced both inherited Old-World traditions the development of new forms of cultural expression in America.'[8]

LABOUR

Slavery and how it became a major social and economic institution in the Atlantic are dealt with elsewhere in this book, but it is important to note in a chapter on settler worlds that it was not an institution that sprung up without any connection to labour relations inherited by settlers from Europe. We can take seventeenth-century British America as an example. Slavery became a distinctive American institution, but it was an institution with thoroughly English roots. It was those roots that enabled English planters in the early seventeenth century in Barbados and the Chesapeake to have the tools that enabled them to brutalize English-born indentured servants and plantation workers in ways that paved the way for even greater mistreatment of African slaves.

The question of how masters might control 'unruly' poor labourers was an urgent question in Tudor and Stuart England. Vagrancy and the issue of 'masterless men' were a major social problem in a society where population was exploding, where pernicious forms of early capitalism were emerging to transform the rural landscape, and where growing ranks of such 'masterless men' and the occasional unsupervised woman seemed to pose a serious threat to social order and good government. Of course, the real threat was the other way around. England was in the throes of remarkable social change in which a modernizing gentry class of agricultural landlords abandoned long-standing customs derived from a commonwealth understanding of shared communal values to extract as much surplus profits as they could from intensively worked land. These ruthless class warriors posed an unprecedented threat to the welfare of ordinary people as they systematically went about destroying traditional understandings of patriarchal government where deference towards authority came not from insistence to obedience and from the use of state power, including a large increase in executions of people condemned for offences arising from need and necessity rather than from criminal intent but from belief that deference was underwritten by protection and fairness of treatment in work and in social relations.

The institution that English masters used and tried to reform to suit their own needs and to keep troublesome labourers in check was in-service husbandry, or indentured servitude. Being in service was a rite of passage for most young people, with perhaps 60 per cent of people in sixteenth-century England who were aged between 15 and 24 being servants. In theory, service-in husbandry provided servants with legal protection (usually only possible if servants had parents or influential kin to intercede on their behalf – many did not) and was a stepping-stone, if all worked well, to independence and possibly even to wealth. But the practice of indentured servitude was different. Bound labourers were subject to the authority of their masters and masters could be brutal or insensitive and get away with mistreatment without meeting with punishment for violating servant rights.

In England, laws existed to protect servants and they were sometimes employed to keep servants from the worst abuses. Law and order depended in part on the governors respecting the wishes and dignity of the governed. Systematic and excessive abuse of masters' powers over servants risked the breakdown of the entire system, which was something masters feared knowing how volatile England was and how ready ordinary people were to turn to violence, very often with success, if they felt their rights were being trampled upon. One reason why the dire conditions of servitude which led to African slavery coming into being in mid-seventeenth century Barbados and Virginia were not replicated in England is because English rural labourers from the fourteenth century onwards were willing to protest violently against designated authority when they felt that authority did not meet with community approval. Moreover, unlike most enslaved people, indentured servants both in England and in America had access to firearms, which they showed themselves willing to use and were supported in their protests by many 'respectable' people socially below rulers but above indentured servants being oppressed.

Restraints on masters' power were much less in English America than in America. Barbadian planters, as Simon Newman explains, were often drawn from the middling ranks of English society and brought with them an understanding of how to compel and control labour, which they did with increasing ferocity and success in the second quarter of the seventeenth century. More indentured servants went to Barbados than anywhere else and they faced an exhausting work regime and limited prospects. Newman notes that 'the social, economic and political situation of the British Isles aligned neatly with the needs of the developing Barbadian sugar economy'.[9] The Wars of the Three Kingdoms which ripped the British Isles apart during the 1640s and 1650s accentuated Barbadian disdain for servant rights, as many servants in this period did not come voluntarily but came as people who were kidnapped or 'Barbadosed' or came as prisoners of war or convicts. It was easy for planters to think of white servants as being people different to themselves and as people not entitled to English liberties and perhaps as people politically if not culturally akin to African slaves. That they might be thought of as being slaves was of intense concern to mistreated indentured white servants who shared the common racism of the English towards Africans that can be seen in the works of William Shakespeare (less in *Othello* than in *Titus Andronicus*).

It was a short step for the English coming to the islands to be caught up in a system that seemed internally logical and perfectly natural. Planters began to treat labourers as being close to chattel, meaning that the real gap between how servants were treated, and the brutal punishments and ferocious discipline meted out to enslaved Africans (who often worked in the fields alongside white servants and convicts) became smaller and smaller. Planters had a fresh sense of 'bound labourers as a new kind of work force, inferior and contemptible, composed of commodities to be utilised rather than free-born individuals with rights'.[10]

Servants were not slaves, but they often compared their condition unfavourably to Africans. Moreover, the implicit bargain that servants had with masters – that after serving their time they would become free people able to compete on near equal footing with their former employers so as to acquire a central ambition for seventeenth-century Englishman of attaining a 'competency', or a measure of economic prosperity and independence from compulsion – disappeared over time as planters became richer, land became dearer and opportunities became more limited. Unsurprisingly, few ordinary English people wanted to share in this misery as conditions in Barbados became increasingly publicized in the 1650s and 1660s.

But the move by the 1660s to a full-fledged plantation system staffed mostly by enslaved Africans meant that the dire situation of ordinary white people in Barbados proved to be just a temporary phenomenon, albeit one with serious consequences. Those servants who did come to Barbados in the last quarter of the seventeenth century were in a much better situation than their counterparts coming a generation earlier. The move to a plantation system based on chattel slavery in Barbados, followed by its adoption in the Leeward Islands, Martinique, Jamaica, Saint-Domingue, the Chesapeake and the Carolinas by 1700 meant that planters needed white men not as servants but as plantation managers. They needed men tough enough and willing enough to discipline slaves so that enslaved people did not revolt. The whites who came to British America in this period were often inured to violence through their service in British and European wars. They were not scared of angry black men in the ways that previous generations of whites without military experience had been. The bargain that ensued was that ordinary white men would work for wealthy white planters as long as they received both financial reward in the form of high wages and psychic comfort in having their claims to superiority over Africans assured by colonial societies accepting doctrines of white supremacy as a fundamental political value. If poor white men and their families received both forms of reward, the result was to be acquiescent to a political system that largely excluded them. Black inferiority was the acceptable price to pay for white happiness. Thus, plantation America was transformed in the early eighteenth century into being both a profitable and socially stable form of social and economic organization, increasingly organized along caste lines (whites being always considered superior in custom and in law to blacks, whether blacks were free or enslaved) rather than along the class lines that had proven so potentially destructive in the middle of the seventeenth century.

That Americans 'invented' doctrines of white supremacy to overcome the possibility of poor whites combining with blacks on class lines rather than siding with wealthy whites is too simplistic. Throughout the eighteenth century, in both plantation and non-plantation societies, ordinary whites were prepared to stand up for their rights and challenge richer whites when they felt their rights were being violated. One example of this intra-racial conflict came in 1789–1791 in Saint Domingue when 'petit blancs' (poor whites) who were generally Royalist contended with 'grand blancs' (wealthy planters and merchants) who favoured Republicanism as a mechanism for gaining the local control they thought necessary to dominate a restive enslaved population. Without this conflict between classes of whites, with free people of colour challenging both sides, the slave rebellion of 1791 would probably have led to marronage, or the creation of communities of ex-slaves claiming autonomy in how they lived, rather than Revolution. A lack of unity among whites gave rebellious slaves the opening to turn discontent into an actual revolution. The lesson was not lost on whites elsewhere – white supremacist doctrines kept them safe from slave revolt.

HOUSEHOLD GOVERNMENT AND SEX

The settler societies that developed after 1600 can be analysed in many ways, from how increased settlement led to the development of political structures that satisfied the basic demands of white citizens; to the establishment of religious institutions that allowed for an increase in not just religious but civic life; and to the growth of cultural formations that both linked these settler societies to their originary places of departure and which indicated intellectual engagement with the new places, new peoples and new experiences that were entailed in becoming Atlantic citizens. One way of examining the peculiar character of Atlantic societies that is especially rewarding is to see settlement and 'improvement' (a key Enlightenment term) through the lenses of continuity and change in household government. How men and women and parents and children interacted with each other was the most important bond in settler societies, especially given how under-institutionalized such societies were, even in the later eighteenth century. Studying changes and variations in Atlantic household government is a primary way of looking at change over time in settler societies, and how such societies varied from those that existed in Africa and Europe.

Northwest Europe had a distinctive household system that was not replicated elsewhere in the early modern world and which was sharply differentiated from the other major European household system, that existing in the Mediterranean world, where extended rather than nuclear families were the norm. The principal features of the northwest household system which European migrants tried to recreate in the New World were that it involved a bilateral system of descent with brides coming into marriages, at least if from well-off backgrounds, with a dowry which became controlled and owned by the husband and then was devolved mostly on male children of the marriage. In its strictest form, occurring within English aristocratic families from the late seventeenth century, what was called the strict settlement kept the great majority of wealth within the hands of the eldest son, under the principle of primogeniture, meaning that younger sons and all daughters were disadvantaged but allowing great estates to be passed down largely intact over time, with fortunate heirs heavily restricted on how they could dispose of the wealth that came fortuitously into their hands.

In general, lineage principles in northwest Europe heavily favoured males and made patriarchy a principal organizing principle for family relationships. Such patriarchal principles were easily extended into political relationships, where the relationship between kings and subjects was often likened to being like and justified by the patriarchal bargain between husbands and wives – husbands provided while wives were obedient. William Shakespeare in *The Taming of the Shrew* is a wonderful guide to how patriarchy worked and how its harshest edges were meant to be softened through mutual, if unequal, negotiation. The northwest household pattern was conspicuously different to that pertaining in most Native American societies, which had matrilineal systems of descent, where the relationship of mothers to children determined family relationships, even if was accepted that males were in control of daily life and major decisions.

Another distinctive feature of the northwest household system was that individuals postponed marriage later than any other people in any society that has been studied. Women married for the first time customarily in their mid- to late-twenties while men married somewhat later, in their late twenties and sometimes into their thirties. Moreover, a large percentage of people, perhaps 15–20 per cent of the population, never married at all. Late marriages and no marriages depressed fertility, limiting the size of families even more than relatively high infant mortality did. Late marriage also meant that European couples were a little less dependent than in other household systems on patronage and support from parents, as many men were able to marry when they had established themselves in life and had acquired their own property. Couples also moved out of their paternal households and formed new households separate to and often reasonably distant from where they had been born or raised. One reason for late marriage and for relatively low incidences of marriage was that having the resources to set up an independent household was not easy. The household structures established were resolutely nuclear in form – it was not common for households in northwestern Europe to contain other people more than parents, children and, if households were well-off, one or two servants. Grandparents and more distant kin formed their own households rather than joined extended kin.

By the middle of the eighteenth century, Americans such as Benjamin Franklin celebrated the American family that had formed in northern

North America as a better variant upon the northwestern European model. Abundant land, acquired from Native Americans and thus cheap and available for white families, allowed young couples to marry earlier than in Europe (though we need to remember that the age of marriage of women was also declining in Britain at the same time, leading to an explosion in population in the late eighteenth and early nineteenth centuries. In the absence of effective contraception, women marrying in their early twenties rather than in their mid-twenties meant a few extra years of fertility, leading to one or two additional children. Good health and excellent nutrition also pushed out the years in which women could have children, adding perhaps another one or two children to family sizes. In these circumstances, natural population growth was strong and families of six or more surviving children common. In addition, the incidence of marriage, Franklin argued, was more frequent, meaning that perhaps only 5 per cent of people aged under 40 did not marry. Better mortality rates also meant fewer deaths of children in childhood and fewer marriages broken by the death of one partner.

But such happy analyses of marriage as made by Franklin belie a lot of variety in populations and hence in household patterns throughout the Americas. The nuclear household that Franklin celebrated may have been dominant in Pennsylvania, but it was not as dominant in Jamaica, Mexico or Brazil. Fertility, mortality, incidence of marriage and likelihood of family breakdown were quite different in tropical as opposed to temperate America. For much of the eighteenth century, population stagnated in plantation zones as rampant disease made forming viable families very difficult. In eighteenth-century Jamaica, for example, the average marriage lasted for only five or six years and the numbers of surviving children produced on marriages were very small, well under the number needed to allow for natural population increase. And white population increase was affected by white men's tendency to engage in sexual relationships with non-white women. In mid-eighteenth-century Kingston, one in nine children in baptism registers was of mixed parentage. In plantation America, high sex ratios, high infant mortality and high numbers of people choosing not to marry but to enter casual relationships, both between whites and between whites and other races made for different household patterns than in Pennsylvania. Other whites, such as indentured servants in the Chesapeake, were forbidden to marry or thought marriage unattractive or expensive.

Moreover, it was only in the northern colonies of British and French America where the nuclear household of parents and dependent children formed both a familial and an economic unit, working together on family forms or in urban occupations. In plantation America, households were very large but that size was misleading as most members of households were not white people related to each other but enslaved people who were either not considered proper members of families, as in those parts of the American South where paternalistic doctrines were promoted that suggested that the relationship between master and slave was familial in origin, or were not thought of in familial terms at all, as in Jamaica, Cuba or Saint-Domingue, where slaves were seem through the lenses of being liquid forms of capital. In these households, enslaved children belonged officially to masters rather than to parents. This meant that masters could easily usurp the authority of parents in controlling, disciplining or protecting enslaved children.

Even in northern North America, households may not have been as stable as Franklin argued. Unlike England, which in the 1750s tightened up its marriage registration system and which had an effective church structure which governed how marriages were made and recognized, American recognition and regulation of marriages and hence family formation were very loose. British America's religious pluralism, lack of an established church and the inability of church building to keep pace with population growth and westward expansion, especially in borderland areas, meant that a significant number of couples lived together outside marriage, making the dissolution of marriage ties comparatively easy.

Indeed, the propensity to marry that Franklin celebrated was not a pronounced feature of settler societies. The realities behind what Carole Shammas calls 'marriage-challenged zones' come from the ethnic mix in Atlantic populations.[11] In the early 1770s, it was only in Canada and in northern British colonies that the percentage of Europeans was over 90 per cent. In the American South, 57 per cent of the population was European while in Latin America and the Caribbean the proportion slipped to 23 per cent in Brazil and around 15 per cent elsewhere. Overall, 48 per cent of the Atlantic populations in 1774 were Native Americans, 25 per cent were European, 21 per cent were African and 6 per cent were mestizo, or mixed-race Native American-European.

Neither Native Americans nor African-Americans had much chance to marry and those who could marry, as in Iberian America, where the Catholic Church was prepared to marry slave couples and baptize their children, often did not want to do so. Both peoples had different cultural traditions about marriage than Europeans, lacked the means to effectively form households and, in the case of enslaved Africans, risked losing loved ones through master caprice when families were broken up and slaves were sold away from families and their homes. In French, British and Dutch America, slave marriages were strongly discountenanced as in some ways harming the influence of the master by providing slaves with other sources of support and authority. Enslaved people did, of course, make informal marriages, formed families (which recent research has confirmed were sometimes polygynous, as in Africa) and looked after and loved their children. Nevertheless, slave families, without the protection of the law and outside Iberian America removed from the oversight of the Church, were inherently weak as social institutions. Slave marriages could be easily broken up, either by the master, with white planters and their servants considering the exploitation of enslaved women as one of the perks of being a white man, or by enslaved people themselves. We should not underestimate the extent to which the much-lauded slave community was riven by conflict between, often newly arrived 'saltwater' slaves and more established Creole slaves, and was inherently unstable, as enslaved men and women found it difficult to find lasting relationships, given the traumatic conditions of their lives.

Sexual exploitation was a constant threat to slave autonomy and slave dignity. The sexually frank diaries of Thomas Thistlewood, a migrant from Lincolnshire, England, to Jamaica in 1750, demonstrate just how much risk African and African American women were in from predatory white men. Thistlewood had sex with almost every female slave who was not very young or in old age that he controlled, detailing sex with 138 different women in thirty-seven years. Many of these encounters were rapes; most of the rest were non-consensual, with women choosing to have sex with him either for financial gain or because of fear of punishment if they refused. The only enslaved woman who might be said to have exercised some degree of autonomy in her sexual life was his long-term partner, the creole slave housekeeper, Phibbah. She chose when, or when not, she had sex with Thistlewood and did not get punished for her refusals. As in all times and places, evaluating the exact nature of sexual relationships is fraught with difficulty. Not all interracial relationships were either coerced or unhappy. But any honest evaluation of these relationships, especially when one person was a master and the other a slave, would place more emphasis on the impropriety and sordidness of such relationships than on how they might lead the individuals involved towards happiness. Neither Thistlewood nor any other white man in Jamaica, for example, respected the integrity of enslaved relationships or tried to encourage either slave marriage or enslaved reproduction. Children were mostly nuisances whose upkeep, minimal though it was, was a plantation expense that planters preferred not to have. In the American South, planters encouraged women to have children, as these children could then be sold in the domestic slave trade and thus augment planter wealth. In Jamaica, where children were more likely to die than thrive, planters resented women getting pregnant, as it deprived them of workers, and did little to encourage nursing of infant children. And these planters lived in worlds where family relationships were derided. The Jane Austen world of churches, weddings and the business of parish life is absent from the world of Thistlewood and his slaves.

The Atlantic World diverged considerably from household patterns in Europe mainly because Atlantic populations were not European populations. American populations were less likely than European populations, for example, to be composed of free people and less likely to be enfolded within religious systems that promoted marriage and punished irregular expressions of sexuality. Even in those parts of the Americas that most closely resembled Europe, such as mainland North America, household government evolved away from patterns established in northwestern Europe. Lower age at marriage pushed couples into the interior where policing marriage and sexuality and preventing households from dissolving as people pleased were difficult. In plantation America, Shammas contends, household patterns were very different from those of Europe. It had a 'patriarchal figure presiding over a family core, surrounded by others, often matrifocal, domestic sub-units, a structure not so dissimilar from African patrilineal polygynous households, except that polygyny was not instituted and African men had no lineage to help them acquire wives. Whites were household heads. In short, what evolved in the Americas offended almost everyone.'[12]

Household government was not unchanging, even though some of the essential principles, notably that husbands ruled wives and that children had to respect, in different ways, the authority of both fathers and mothers, remained constant in the northwest family system throughout the whole of the Atlantic period. But in the eighteenth century, changes in the relative ways in which this authority occurred, with marriages increasingly becoming thought of as affectionate (people marrying for love rather than just as a way of preserving family wealth and transmitting that wealth to future generations) and sexual relations loosening considerably. It is going too far to say there was a sexual revolution among Europeans in Europe and North America but there was a long period in which rules and expectations of intimate behaviour were transformed. There was more sexual behaviour practised outside marriage in the eighteenth century and more acceptance of different forms of sexual expression, including a tolerance of though not an acceptance of certain kinds of homosexual behaviour. Indeed, historians often argue that it was only in the Victorian age that repressive attitudes to irregular sexual activity (in other words, sex that was not religiously sanctioned and which occurred outside marriage) really developed.

The major influence on beliefs about marriage and sexuality came from the sea-change in ideas about the world that emerged during the Enlightenment, from seeing the world, and gender relations especially, as part of a fixed and hierarchical order in which male rule over women was ordained by God and essential for the orderly functioning of society. Enlightenment thinkers drew from science a new conception of the world, one that was fluid and dynamic and subject less to God but to man in how society was ordered. If humans ordered society, they could order it in any ways that they wished. Maybe this meant that male superiority over women, the naturalness of the rule of the rich over the poor and various forms of racial subordination were not immutable but instead could be altered if people wanted different and better ways of 'pursuing happiness'. This new view of the world underlay all the reform movements that emerged in Europe and America in the late eighteenth century. One aspect of reform was around women's rights and about the regulation of and practice of sexuality. These changes, it need to be emphasized, preceded the age of revolution and came out in part from a consideration of the different ways in which household government operated in the Americas as opposed to Europe. These changes happened everywhere but were most important in cities such as London, Boston,

Paris, Philadelphia and Cap Français in Saint-Domingue. Cities were the electric motors of social changes. Their growth in the urban renaissance of the eighteenth-century Atlantic underlaid rapidly changing patterns of sexual behaviour which eventually forced institutions like family, church and marriage to change with them.

By the middle of the eighteenth century, some men and a few women rejected notions that marriage was for life (divorce was very hard to achieve and was usually reserved for the very rich, and was done under male rather than female terms, but it happened with increasing frequency during the eighteenth century, thus breaking down the religious assumption that marriage was everlasting). They also started to reject ideas that sex was only possible during courtship or marriage – illegitimacy rates soared in colonial America from the middle of the eighteenth century, as did rates of venereal disease. About one-third of European British North American women were pregnant at marriage. Casual sexual relationships, prostitution and tolerated adultery became more accepted parts of the sexual landscape of urban areas. An even more dramatic change was that in an age where sensibility and sentiment were increasingly considered important in fashioning relationships, some people started to think of sex as not just a means of procreation but a form of self-expression within partnerships based on emotion rather than economic utility.

Benjamin Franklin, always at the forefront of changing attitudes, mocked the old order which ruled that illegitimacy was immoral in his witty tale of Polly Baker. Polly was a Connecticut woman, repeatedly brought before the courts for having bastard children. She defended herself by stating that instead of being punished for sexual irregularity she should be rewarded for bringing forth children who added to the population and thus increased the wealth and prosperity of a colony that needed additional inputs of white children (Franklin's support of increased population was very racially specific: he wanted the white population to increase so that it overwhelmed what he thought were inferior African, Native American and German populations). His own life mirrored that of his fictional creation: he fathered an illegitimate son, William, whom he not only acknowledged and supported but who achieved Franklin's most desired ambition, which was to become a governor of an American colony.

It is good to end this chapter on Franklin, the first home-grown American celebrity because in his numerous and always witty publications he formulated a vision of an America that joined with Europe in adopting policies of 'improvement' and which by the mid-eighteenth century could be 'improved' or (to use another loaded eighteenth-century term 'civilized'. Franklin was an active participant in lively debates over modern commerce, the role of the cosmopolitan intellectual thought in shaping individual behaviour on such matters as sex, family and civic life, and, less positively, was a major voice in arguing for the necessity of white supremacist policies if the Americas were to improve further. In his person he exemplified much that was good about the settler societies that had developed in the Americas, most conspicuously on the Philadelphia that he graced in such a distinguished fashion, and some of the bad about those societies as well.

NOTES

1 John Murrin, 'Beneficiaries of Catastrophe: The English Colonies in America,' in Eric Foner, ed., *The New American History* (Philadelphia: Temple University Press, 1997), 4.
2 Peter H. Lindert and Jeffrey G. Williamson, *Unequal Gains: American Growth and Inequality since 1700* (Princeton: Princeton University Press, 2016).
3 Murrin, 'Beneficiaries of Catastrophe,' 13.
4 James Horn and Philip D. Morgan, 'Settlers and Slaves: European and African Migrations to Early Modern British America,' in Elizabeth Mancke and Carole Shammas, eds., *The Creation of the British Atlantic World* (Baltimore: Johns Hopkins University Press, 2005), 19–44.
5 Aaron Fogelman, 'The United States and the Transformation of Transatlantic Migration during the Age of Revolution and Emancipation,' in Patrick Spero and Michael Zuckerman, eds., *The American Revolution Reborn* (Philadelphia: University of Pennsylvania Press, 2016), 251–69.
6 Bernard Bailyn, *Voyagers to the West: A Passage in the Peopling of America on the Eve of Revolution* (New York: Alfred Knopf, 1986), 160.
7 D.W. Meinig, *The Shaping of America: A Geographical Perspective on 500 Years of History* vol. 1, *Atlantic America, 1492–1800* (New Haven: Yale University Press, 1986), 218.
8 Horn and Morgan, 'Settlers and Slaves,' 40.
9 Simon Newman, '" In Great Slavery and Bondage": White labour and the Development of Plantation Slavery in British America,' in Ignacio Gallup-Diaz, eds., *Anglicizing America: Empire, Revolution, Republic* (Philadelphia: University of Pennsylvania Press, 2015), 68.
10 Ibid.
11 Carole Shammas, 'Household Formation, Lineage, and Gender Relations in the Early Modern Atlantic World,' in Nicholas Canny and Philip Morgan, eds., *The Oxford Handbook of the Atlantic World* (Oxford: Oxford University Press, 2011), 372–74.
12 Ibid., 379.

BIBLIOGRAPHY

Oxford Online Bibliographies – Colonial Governance; Colonial Government in Spanish America; Continental America; Iberian Empires, 1600–1800; Marriage and Family; Native Americans in the Atlantic World; Settlement and Region in British America; Sex and Sexuality.
Susan D. Amussen and Allyson M. Poska, 'Restoring Miranda: Gender and the Limits of European Patriarchy in the Early Modern Atlantic World,' *Journal of Global History* 7 (2012), 342–63.

Bernard Bailyn, *The Barbarous Years: The Peopling of British North America – The Conflict of Civilizations, 1600–1675* (New York: Vintage, 2013).

Juliana Barr and Edward Countryman, eds., *Contested Spaces of Early America* (Philadelphia: University of Pennsylvania Press, 2014).

Jack P. Greene, *Pursuits of Happiness: The Social Development of Early Modern British Colonies and the Formation of British Culture* (Chapel Hill: University of North Carolina Press, 1988).

Allan Greer, *Property and Dispossession: Natives, Empires, and Land in Early Modern North America* (New York: Cambridge University Press, 2018).

Gilles Havard and Cécile Vidal, *Histoire de l'Amerique française* (Paris: Flammarion, 2003).

James Horn and Philip D. Morgan, 'Settlers and Slaves: European and African Migrations to Early Modern British America,' in Elizabeth Mancke and Carole Shammas, eds., *The Creation of the British Atlantic World* (Baltimore: Johns Hopkins University Press, 2005), 19–44.

Wim Klooster, *The Dutch Moment: War, Trade, and Settlement in the Seventeenth Century Atlantic World* (Ithaca: Cornell University Press, 2016).

Simon Newman, *A New World of Labour: The Development of Plantation Slavery in the British Atlantic* (Philadelphia: University of Pennsylvania Press, 2014).

Carole Shammas, *A History of Household Government in America* (Charlottesville: University of North Carolina Press, 2002).

Douglas Winiarski, *Darkness Falls on the Land of Light: Experiencing Religious Awakenings in Eighteenth-Century New England* (Chapel Hill: University of North Carolina Press, 2017).

7

THE AGE OF REVOLUTIONS

INTRODUCTION

The most dramatic period in the history of the Atlantic World is the tumultuous years from the second half of the eighteenth century to around 1825 in the first half of the nineteenth century. These years are commonly called the 'Age of Revolution' and were a period in which we can say that we saw, as C.A. Bayly argues, the birth of the modern world, fashioned through a series of political revolutions and no less so through major social and cultural changes.[1] This period saw major political and sometimes social convulsions on two sides of the Atlantic (Africa was comparatively little directly affected by revolutionary impulses), all at the same time as what in world historical terms might have been the biggest convulsion of that time, the Industrial Revolution.

This non-political revolution is commonly called the Industrial Revolution, although increasingly historians term it an industrious revolution, in order to emphasize that this revolution was more a gradual change than a sudden rupture in economic organization and was connected to wide social changes in consumption and working practices, that themselves were influenced by Atlantic concerns, notably the increasing consumption in Britain of slave-produced tropical commodities like sugar and eventually cotton. This massive change in economic activity happened first in Britain from the beginning of the eighteenth century and then spread in the late eighteenth century to continental northern Europe and to the northern part of North America. It occurred first in Britain as a successful response to a developing global economy, in which Atlantic commerce was a vital part and due to internal factors in Britain, notably high wages (that allowed people to buy manufactures) and cheap energy (due to the fortuitous presence of lots of coal). Consequently, the breakthrough technologies of the Industrial Revolution such as the steam engine, the cotton mill and the use of coal in making metals were easier to invent in Britain, especially as Britain encouraged a knowledge economy in which technological invention and scientific experiment were encouraged and, most importantly, were 'useful knowledge' which might lead to profit for the inventors. The Industrial Revolution will not be touched on except briefly in this chapter, but it deserves a chapter as it heralded the start of the rise of Western Europe and the United States to a global economic and political dominance in the nineteenth and twentieth centuries that no part of the World have ever previously attained. It also signalled the start of a new age – the Anthropocene age – in which the activities of one animal – homo sapiens – for the first time in the geological history of the world changed the environment in major ways, leading in our time and in the future to massive biological and environmental consequences, including possibly irreversible climate change.

Even without considering the political revolutions which customarily are considered to comprise the Age of Revolutions – the American Revolution (1763–1789); the French Revolution and Napoleonic counterreaction (1789–1815); the Haitian Revolution (1791–1804); and the Latin American Revolutions and Brazilian Independence (1808–1825) – the economic and environmental effects of the Industrial Revolution that started in a country (Britain), customarily thought not to have had a 'revolution', still live with us. It will probably determine in the long term the future of Atlantic World as much as the results of the political revolutions after the Declaration of American Independence in 1776 have shaped the political culture of the last few centuries by putting forward agendas promoting human equality that led eventually to the beginning of democratic politics.

The Age of Revolutions is generally thought of now in quite different ways than was thought of by people who lived through this period. We are struck more by continuities than by changes in social and political organization in all the societies experiencing revolution, save Haiti where the repercussions of revolution are inescapably profound, if contradictory in their implications for advancing democratic politics. For people at the time, the Atlantic Revolutions signified a complete break with the past in ways that they deemed revolutionary. John Adams, for example, the second president of the United States (1796–1800), a participant in what is generally considered the most conservative of the Atlantic Revolutions, argued in a letter of 1818 that the major effect of the American Revolution was not in the bloodiness of the conflict or even in the constitutional and political changes that resulted in an independent republic in the New World but was in 'a radical change in the principles, opinions, sentiments, and affections of the people, was the real American Revolution'.

In short, Adams argued, in place of the old hierarchical bonds that constituted British society, Americans had created after 1776 new fraternal ones (brotherly amity was a theme of importance in all revolutionary ideology), linking human beings in a common political system. What was true, he argued, for the American Revolution was even more true for the French Revolution, where, instead of a political regime based on absolute monarchy, the French after 1789 proclaimed themselves devoted to principles of 'liberty, equality and fraternity' and, most dramatically, was true for the Haitian Revolution where occurred what in the mid-eighteenth century was literally unthinkable – a republic governed by black ex-slaves where the plantation system that had made the colony the wealthiest place on earth for fortunate owners was effectively destroyed and where people of African descent declared that they were the equal of Europeans and as much the inheritors of Enlightenment values as the philosophes of Paris. Adams's views expressed a common opinion in the nineteenth century: that the Age of Revolutions marked a decisive caesura between old assumptions – the 'ancien regime' – and a modern, liberal and democratic world.

Few historians would accept Adams's characterization as easily as his correspondents did in 1818, even though remarkable ideological changes clearly occurred between the start of the Seven Years' War in 1756 and the end of Spanish rule in most of Latin America by 1825. Old ideas about pre-revolutionary societies being archaic, stultifying hierarchical, non-democratic, unchanging and so tired that they were ripe for revolution are too simplistic. The Old Regime, especially in Western Europe and British and French America, was dynamic, modern and constantly changing to adapt to new circumstances and fresh ideas. As the example of Britain and its transformation into an industrial society in the early nineteenth century shows, it was possible to combine massive economic and social change within an oligarchical and monarchical political structure. Revolution was not necessary for social and economic change to occur. That is especially true for such things as an expansion in female rights or the growth of antislavery, which were as strong or stronger in non-revolutionary Britain as in revolutionary France.

THE ENLIGHTENMENT

The century before the Age of Revolutions, after all, was the period of the Enlightenment. This broad and all-encompassing intellectual movement reshaped the Atlantic World in ways that were probably more profound than the Age of Revolutions which the Enlightenment helped inspire and which, to an extent, was a natural outgrowth from the ferment of ideas about the proper order of things and how old ideas might be abandoned that flourished in the eighteenth century. The Enlightenment is hard to analyse. It is either a series of specific intellectual changes, mostly in Scotland and France, that can be traced to the writings of specific philosophically inclined intellectuals or, as most historians now prefer, a description of a whole range of ideas about religion, culture, commerce and politics that was more the 'spirit of the age' than a definable movement. How we think about the Enlightenment is shaped from a famous essay by Immanuel Kant in 1784, 'What Is the Enlightenment?' He declared that modern man (he meant Western European man and did not extend his thoughts to women, let alone to non-Western peoples) was by this time freed from the accumulated misery of prejudice and superstition that arose from the dictates of organized religion, and the inhumanity and ignorance of past ages. He argued that the 'new' age applied the doctrines of reason derived from philosophers such as Spinoza, Locke, Diderot, Montesquieu, Voltaire, Hume, Smith, Rousseau and himself and the findings about the natural world discovered by scientists, notably Isaac Newton, not just to the study of physics and biology but to studies of the human condition in order to transform society and politics. The primary belief of the Enlightenment, apart from an assumption that the present age had cast itself intellectually loose from the traditions of truth and authority that had distinguished and disgraced the past, was a belief in progress. By progress, Enlightenment thinkers thought that change was possible, desirable, achievable and beneficial for society and the individual.

The stirring words of Thomas Jefferson in the Declaration of American Independence on 4 July 1776, that the new nation brought into existence by this document and which sought recognition for its existence from other nations, were dedicated not just to Americans having rights to life and liberty but to 'the pursuit of happiness'. That phrase was a paean to Enlightenment ideology which nodded to a whole corpus of political ideas that suggested that inherited authority (as in the authority of kings) was wrong and that the purpose of political organization was to maximize the opportunities of individuals to find personal fulfilment in societies devoted to propositions that 'all men are created equal'. The Enlightenment found its fruition in Europe, but it had significant New World roots. As Sankar Muthu writes, 'the discovery of the New World ... promoted crucial advances in moral thought because its diverse practices enabled thinkers to discern that the roots of political injustice, economic exploitation and social ills were not divinely sanctioned or historically inevitable but "only the product of time, ignorance, weakness and deceit"'.[2]

HISTORIOGRAPHY

Among the plethora of works on the Atlantic World and the Age of Revolution, three from the last sixty years stand out as especially influential. The Princeton historian, R.R. Palmer, and his Paris co-writer, Jacques Godechot, wrote a paper in 1955 that introduced Atlantic history into Western European historiography. That paper met with little favour – indeed it was fiercely criticized by Marxist historians for pandering to American internationalism at a time of great Cold War tension. Undeterred, however, Palmer wrote *The Age of Democratic Revolution* (2 vols., 1959, 1964), a work that has proved enduring. His argument was that the Age of Revolutions should be about the advent of popular politics which in its purest form, in France in the early 1790s, warranted being considered properly democratic in form and intent. Palmer and Godechot concentrated their attention on Western Europe and North America, ignoring the Haitian Revolution entirely and downplaying the importance of events in Latin America. In their view, the revolutions started and were most important in Western Europe and North America with the Caribbean, Latin America and the rest of the world having to wait until the twentieth century to get their turn at political enfranchisement. As David Armitage and Sanjay Subrahmanyam note, Palmer's conception of the Age of Revolutions was that 'it was a gift from the North Atlantic world to other peoples who had apparently contributed nothing to its original emancipatory potential'.[3] Such a view fitted well with a mid-century American and NATO view where the West, especially the United States, was the mechanism through which the world could be led to liberal democracy and economic prosperity. That was so despite the uncomfortable fit that existed due to the difficult fact that it was the empires of Western Europe and the United States which though colonization and the expropriation of indigenous land had most handicapped other parts of the world from becoming model democratic states.

Palmer argues for more than this, however. He considered that the American Revolution 'dethroned England and set up America as a model for those seeking a better world'. Thus, the ideas of the American Revolution were highly influential in creating a new kind of politics. Scholars following the lead of J.G.A. Pocock and Bernard Bailyn outlined a political system brought into being in the United States in 1787–1788 through the American Constitution which they characterized as being a specific kind of political ideology that goes by the short-hand term of 'radical' or 'country' republicanism. What is meant by 'radical republicanism' is that it was a comprehensive belief system adopted by people inherently suspicious of the likelihood of those people with power to act corruptly so that they could amass more power and reduce the populace through tyranny to a state of slavery.

One reason why the American Constitution is distinguished by having systematic checks and balances in multiple and competing parts of government (executive, judiciary and legislature) is that the Founding Fathers were more concerned about making sure that any one group or person's exercise of power could be limited than about creating effective and efficient forms of government. The republican beliefs that were shared by many Americans and French people in the 1760s through the 1780s insisted that people were motivated to political action by a conviction that corruption was a perpetual danger to the integrity of the state and the liberty of free citizens. Thus, ensuring the safety of the state's citizens necessitated a constant vigilance on the part of independent, virtuous and patriots so that liberty could be secured, and abuses of power prevented.

The second great survey from the early 1960s was Eric Hobsbawm's *The Age of Revolutions, 1789–1848* (1962). It was more European focused than Palmer's. It concentrated upon the Industrial Revolution and the French Revolution as 'the twin crater of a regional eruption' from which 'world revolution spread outwards'. Europe was the actor and the rest of the world was the often-unwilling recipient of a 'European expansion in and conquest of the rest of the world'. It was a powerful and influential thesis, whereby Hobsbawm argued that what Western Europe had taught the rest of the Atlantic World was how to eventually roll back the European hegemony that the Age of Revolution had established.

His Marxist-inflected account made a direct link between capitalism and colonial expansion, which has been built upon by Kenneth Pomeranz, who has argued for what he sees as 'the Great Divergence', whereby the customary leading global position of the East was overtaken by the growth of Western European economic prosperity exactly during the Age of Revolutions. The rise of the West, he argues, was facilitated by 'ghost acres' in the Americas – a hinterland of underused resources expropriated from Native Americans that could be added to European lands to make the production of foodstuffs more abundant. European seizure of land and labour through the expansion of the plantation system gave Europe a bonus of massive amounts of land that could be used to feed Europe's growing population and allow Europeans to concentrate their attentions on increasing manufactures rather than having to devote most of their resources to food production. In addition, Western Europe was able to export to the Americas its surplus population as population levels surged in the late eighteenth century, thus providing Europe with a safety valve and a solution to the Malthusian problem of food production not meeting the demands of a rising population, leading (as in Ireland in the 1840s) to famine, destitution and likely revolt from poor and starving populations. The Atlantic World thus was vital for explaining why the revolutions of the late eighteenth and early nineteenth centuries did not continue into the second half of the nineteenth century.

What Hobsbawm's account did not do was allow for alternative explanations of world history than one that was exclusively around European expansion and non-European responses to that expansion. Robert Travers, referring to India but in an argument also applicable to Africa, Latin America and the Caribbean, argues that Hobsbawm's notion that there had been four centuries of complete European domination of the entire world was 'conjured up by a number of historical sleights of hand'.[4] In short, Hobsbawm tended to assume that as early as 1750 the West had vast technological and military superiority over other places when, in fact, as John Darwin notes, the regions of the world were more nearly in balance than Europe being dominant.[5] Hobsbawm also implied that anti-colonial revolts, such as that led by Tupac Amaru in 1780, were 'medieval' or 'Homeric', if they did not conform to a rather rigid model of 'Western' revolutionary nationalism.

'THE WORLD CRISIS'

The interpretive model that has currently replaced these earlier synoptic accounts is C.A. Bayly's *Birth of the Modern World* (2004). Bayly places the Atlantic Revolutions within a broad global framework, arguing that there was a 'world crisis', starting around 1700 and intensifying about 1720 when multiethnic agrarian empires in Asia started to fragment and decentralize. This collapse of multiple great empires (Ottomans, Safavids, Mughals and Mataram) provided an opportunity for expanding European empires to break into Asia after having made incursions into the Americas and, from 1770, into the Pacific. It also drew them into worldwide conflicts which placed (except perhaps for Britain who had in its fiscal-military state worked out how to tax its wealthy subjects sufficiently to pay for an administrative apparatus that enable it to fight wars effectively) enormous stress upon state finances, as discussed in Chapter 6. Bayly argues that 'it is the global interconnectedness of the economic and political turbulences of this era which is so striking'. John Darwin, another British historian with a global understanding of imperialism, agrees, arguing that 'the Eurasian Revolution was in fact three revolutions in geopolitics, in culture, and in economics'. The coming together of commercialization, warfare, social crisis and 'the growth of uniformity between societies and the growth of complexity within these them' made the Age of Revolutions global, as much as they were Atlantic, given how the force of revolutionary events 'ricocheted around the world'.[6]

Jeremy Adelman has built upon Bayly to argue that a worldwide revitalization of empires around the time of the Seven Years' War, now occurring in Europe rather than Asia, led to Atlantic disturbances that were more imperial crises than democratic revolutions.[7] The imperial nature of these revolts was most apparent in the Iberian empires. They were parts of interlocking systems of imperial competitions that they could not escape from and to which they had to adapt. But adaptation from the metropolis was not enough. Neither Spain nor Portugal could keep their empires intact when global competition (especially between Britain and France) escalated. Global imperial competition led to a series of crises in the Atlantic World. Unlike Bayly, Adelman returns, with some fresh twists, to Palmer's notion that the Atlantic Revolutions in the New World were reactions to metropolitan European tensions.

He argues that European states struggled with notions of 'sovereignty'. There was no such thing in reality in the eighteenth century as 'the state' as an entity with definable and coherent powers but, as Lauren Benton argues, states functioned as legally pluralistic organisms and usually within multiethnic and constitutionally diverse empires – there were in eighteenth-century states a multitude of political and economic arrangements that did not rely upon any single creed or practice but upon syncretic, or mixed, forms of governmental organization.[8] As Adelman concludes, 'we might treat statehood as an amalgamation of practices locked in equivocal conjunctions, and are thus more about relationships between powers – exemplified by Montesquieu and Madison's image of "balance" – than their natural or coherent features'. He insists that European empires were not 'backward and brittle systems cracking under the pressure of global competition and confrontation'.[9]

There was no inevitability about imperial collapse. Britain, for example, understood the loss of the thirteen colonies that became the United States less as a fatal blow to their imperial policies than as part of the high price of their remarkable imperial success around the mid-eighteenth century. Britain emerged from the American Revolution with its imperial ambitions intact and being perhaps a stronger and more adaptable polity, able to quash calls for reform in Britain and able to advance its imperial reach in South Asia, the Antipodes, Africa and the Caribbean. Nor were empires cracking from within in the late eighteenth century – in this way European empires can be differentiated from their Asian counterparts earlier in the eighteenth century.

One interpretation of why the American Revolution occurred is that after the end of the Seven Years' War, the British government looked at its huge and diverse global empire and tried to bring the North American part of that empire more fully into an increasingly rationalized system where local differences had been ironed out in favour of common policies imposed on colonies by metropolitan dictate. As Eliga Gould writes, 'for all their cocksure certainty, the British saw their actions towards the colonies as fundamentally pacific'.[10] They had no intention of forcing American colonists to break with empire – the opposition of Americans to what they thought were gentle and reasonable initiatives such as the Stamp Act in 1765 took British statesmen greatly by surprise, as they had been reassured by constant American exultations of delight in being in a victorious empire as signs that they would be willing to pay a larger price for maintaining the security needs of that empire. What they wanted to do, instead, was make the empire more harmonious and safer through instituting policies that brought all parts of the empire into common submission to a supposedly beneficent British parliament. The exception to this rule was Iberian America where metropolitan implosion caused by the Napoleonic invasion of the peninsula in 1807 set up a crisis of sovereignty. The internal collapse of sovereignty in Iberia 'forced colonies to amalgamate older practices with newer ones to shore up legitimacy as politics grew increasingly polarised and social systems imploded'.[11]

Why then did such empires break up if we are not just to see Atlantic revolutions as 'the consequence of circumstance'? Adelman provides the answer: it 'lies in the ways in which global conflagration provoked local contestation and the slide from negotiations over how to handle a mounting imperial crisis to a civil war and from civil war to revolution'. Perhaps we need to think less about causation, he argues, than about sequences: 'the change of sovereignty, the demise of older systems and the emergence of successors was a *process* that has often eluded triumphalist nationalist narratives, or those which insisted that old regimes – among them, empire – were doomed because they were outmoded'.[12] In short, the Atlantic Revolutions occurred because the 'world crisis' starting with the decline of Asian agrarian empires led to European overreach and incessant warfare that in turn provoked problems within empires that in turn led to local opposition which eventually led to revolution, regimes change and a few social and cultural transformations that may not have otherwise occurred. In some places, it helped advance a general push in the late eighteenth century for politics based on deference to inherited or ascribed authority to be replaced by democratic politics and new institutions of the state.

If there was one big winner from the Age of Revolutions, it was the state. State power increased dramatically from the middle of the eighteenth century to the middle of the nineteenth century and has kept on increasing until the present day. The Atlantic state became larger, more powerful internally, more willing to extend itself externally, militarized, intrusive and increasingly able to cope with revolutionary unrest. That was a major consequence of the French Revolution – the Napoleonic state was able to crush revolutionary opposition in ways that France under the ancient regime had found impossible. There was to be no second French Revolution.

The new state was grasping and intrusive. It worked best in Britain where the tax-gathering and war making functions of the state worked sufficiently well compared with Western European fiscal-military states. It was the state that was the winner in the Age of Revolutions. This fact is seen most clearly in Britain, which had no revolution, but which fought the French Revolution relentlessly and eventually, in the Battles of Trafalgar (1805) and Waterloo (1815) overcame their European opponent. The main result of the French revolutionary and Napoleonic wars in Britain was a substantial increase in taxation to maintain the most powerful navy in the world and a strong army, including the first income tax. Britain was able to use war and revolution to strengthen their grip in Ireland; to force Canada to be more submissive to imperial authority than had ever happened in colonial British America; and to use its moral, economic and military power to force the abolition of the slave trade on the West Indies. The exception to this strengthening of the state may have been the United States. The American Revolution remained a 'revolution against the state' in part because America was involved in fewer wars between 1783 and 1861. It was only in the American Civil War that the strengthening of the state that had occurred in the late eighteenth century in Britain and France accelerated in the United States. Nevertheless, even in the United States, the state was stronger after the revolution than before. One of the ironies of the American Revolution was that the rebellion started over British requests that Americans should pay a small amount of additional tax on a very low tax burden. The results of an expensive war and Alexander Hamilton's financial reforms in the 1790s meant that the average American paid much more in taxes in 1800 than their predecessors had paid in 1750. That tax increase was especially true in the South, the region of the United States which never regained after the revolution its position as the wealthiest region of colonial British North America.

THE AMERICAN REVOLUTION

What, then, about the individual revolutions that made up the Age of Revolutions in the Atlantic World? Space precludes more than the briefest discussions of each conflict. In the case of the American Revolution, the simple causes of the event, its course and consequences are easily told. The British tried in the 1760s to impose taxes upon American colonists which Americans, imbued with 'radical' republican sensibilities interpreted in a close to paranoid fashion, saw as attempts to take away American liberty. The main furore was set off in 1765 with the Stamp Act, which led to violent protest in North America and some parts of the British Caribbean. Further attempts by the British to find a way to tax Americans in ways that Americans thought acceptable, while insisting that Americans adhere to accepting that the authority of Parliament over British and colonial subjects was absolute, failed. An attempt to solve one problem of empire – the parlous financial position of the East India Company, the major importer of tea into Britain and America – by addressing another – the unwillingness of Americans to accept parliamentary sovereignty – failed dismally, as seen in the Boston Tea Party of 1773.

By 1775, Britain and thirteen of its twenty-six colonies were at war (the West Indies and Canada remained loyal) and from 1776, with the Declaration of Independence, until 1783, with the Peace of Paris, Britain and America were involved in a messy, complicated and violent war, which is best described as not just a civil war, but a series of civil wars, in which allegiances were often uncertain and where local grievances often shaped whether Americans were 'Patriots' or 'Loyalists' more than commitment to a unified ideological position. In North Carolina, for example, fierce disputes in the early 1770s, termed the 'Regulator' disputes, led to the losers in this dispute keeping themselves out of the conflict. The men who drove the Regulator movement became 'neutral' in the war because they saw the war as a project of Carolinian elites who had crushed their aspirations. We need to be careful not to privilege the anti-colonial contest of American revolutionaries over local skirmishes. Poorer white Americans often felt silenced during the American Revolution, thought that the levies placed on them to fight were nothing less than theft and in post-revolutionary rebellions, such as Shay's Rebellion of 1786 in Massachusetts and the Whiskey Rebellion in western Pennsylvania in 1794, opposed the federal union as a result of 'sense of alienation, authoritarianism and violence' that was everywhere in the backcountry in the late eighteenth century.[13]

American troops under the leadership of George Washington, later the first president of the United States (1789–1796), held out against great odds from British assault between 1776 and 1778, encouraging the French to join in the world on the American side. In 1779, Spain joined France and America and in 1780 the Dutch reluctantly, and because of British pressure, also took part in the conflict. The decisive Battle of Yorktown in Virginia in 1781, which was won by Washington, in part because the British navy had stopped a blockade of the American shoreline in order to chase the French and Spanish fleet which was planning an attack on British possessions in the Antilles, ended any hopes that Britain had of retaining the thirteen colonies, ensuring American independence; the formation of a new nation; and, after many travails due to inadequate forms of government, to the adoption of a federal constitution in 1789, under which constitution the United States has constantly operated.

Britain, however, did not do badly out of the war as it retained the valuable possessions of the West Indies after defeating the French in April 1782 at the Battle of the Saintes, acquired Gibraltar and Minorca because of peace negotiations in Paris in 1783, and was able to continue its imperial activities unimpeded in India and South Asia. In 1788, it even extended its presence to the far side of the world when it established a colony in Australia – an imperial adventure directly resulting from the American Revolution, as one result of American independence was that Britain could no longer send its convicts to Virginia and especially Maryland. The loss of America was more a matter of national embarrassment than economic disaster. Britain retained an 'informal' empire in America after 1789 that was in many ways easier to deal with than a formal empire and a good deal more profitable.

We used to think, following Palmer, that the American Revolution, with its uplifting rhetoric about equality and liberty, set off a wave of radical reform throughout the Atlantic. That is how the importance of the American Revolution is still celebrated in American popular and political culture. And it reflects the optimism of Thomas Paine, a radical rabblerousing writer, who composed not just a key text of the American Revolution – *Common Sense* (1776) – but a major text of the French Revolution – *The Rights of Man* (1791). Paine argued in *Common Sense* that 'the cause of America is in great measure the cause of mankind'.

Historians now tend to dismiss such utopian thoughts about the worldwide influence of the American Revolution. Its most important influence was indirect: the cost of supporting the American rebels between

1778 and 1782 was so great that it contributed to a financial crisis in France, leading to the calling of the Three Estates that in 1789–1790 provoked the French Revolution. But its ideological influence was surprisingly small. Its ideals had some international influence, but mostly as debating points in London and Paris. It was important for the evolution of republican thought among some Latin American elite Creoles, like Simon Bolivar, who were important in Latin American rebellions.

But even before the American Revolution, one of the principal contradictions in the American creed had become clear. As the conservative writer Samuel Johnson declared in the 1760s, 'why is it that we hear the loudest yelps for liberty from the drivers of slaves?' American revolutionaries wanted liberty for themselves – and were willing to extend political participation further down the ranks of white men than in colonial times – but they were not prepared to give the same privilege for enslaved African-Americans. Furthermore, one result of the Revolution, after a spate of manumissions in the 1770s and 1780s and the ending of slavery in the northern colonies and a ban on its extension to new territories in the American midwest, was that slavery became further entrenched, especially where it was strongest, in the plantation South, and was able to spread easily westward into the cotton and sugar producing states of the Deep South. Unsurprisingly, neither slaves in the United States nor in the British Caribbean were inspired by the words and actions of slave owners such as Thomas Jefferson, James Madison and George Washington. Slave revolts in the British West Indies in the early nineteenth century owed nothing in inspiration to the ideals of the American Revolution. The Haitian Revolution owed immensely more to the French Revolution than to the American Revolution. The limits of American commitment to equality can be seen in its hostility to Haitian independence in 1804. The Haitian government did not gain recognition from its northern neighbour until the 1860s.

Indeed, Gary Nash argues that because of southern commitment to slavery in the nineteenth century, Americans themselves did not wish to export their revolution to other countries because they feared that talk of universal and undeniable rights might spark slave rebellions within the American South. Enslaved people understood how quickly revolutionary principles turned into conservative certainties and understood how shallow the commitment of men like Jefferson and Madison to antislavery was (though George Washington was willing to free his slaves, though not those of his wife, at his death). They were inspired by the example of Haiti when thinking of ways to freedom. Even more so, and ironically, they looked to antislavery forces in Britain and its province of Canada as their best hope for redemption. The War of 1812 laid bare some American pretensions as thousands of slaves flocked to the British army, where they were promised freedom. And slaves knew that it was the British navy, not the American government, who played the main role in enforcing an international ban after 1808 on the Atlantic slave trade.[14]

Another reason why the example of the American Revolution did not reverberate widely in the world was because the first colonial revolt against an imperial power did not really lead to a rejection of imperialism. Instead, it led to a new, and to Native Americans more pernicious, kind of imperialism, directed at making the land of North America available for white settlers. The new nation that emerged in 1780 was as contingent, as negotiated, and as devoted to white supremacy and to imperialism as the British empire from which it broke. As Eliga Gould comments of American settlers heading westward, they 'drew on notions of sovereignty that were new and innovative, re-enacting in each territory the home rule proclaimed in 1776 and asserting rights of conquest and self-government that went well beyond those of American settlers still subject to the British Crown'.[15] The United States carried on the same imperial agenda as Britain had done, with white Americans on Native American territory motivated by land hunger, profit seeking and an eagerness to exploit new resources. Thus, the American Revolution was no radical rupture between a colonial past and a republican future. As Serena Zabin notes, 'the Revolution laid the foundation for the creation of a neo-imperial past through the appropriation of Indian land, the solidification of white power and the persistence of patriarchy'.[16]

A final point is that the American Revolution was a world war as much as a struggle for America's future, especially after 1778. It meant that the war was fought in the Caribbean, Asia and West Africa as well as in North America. The threat of invasion in Ireland by France – always a touchy point for Britain, given the large and repressed Catholic population that seemed ever ready to rebel and which indeed did so in 1798 – was very real and led to troops that might have gone to North America being kept in readiness within Britain and Ireland. France was less interested in advancing American liberty than it was concerned with reducing the power of its principal rival in Europe and the Caribbean. They were very interested, for example, in regaining ground lost in Asia – an objective that they did not achieve. In many respects, and ironically, the French were the great loser of the American Revolution. They did not stop Britain from its imperial and European advances, did not restore French territory and prestige, and weakened their finances to the extent that the events that convulsed the country in 1780 were advanced and which led to the loss of their richest colony, Saint-Domingue (later Haiti), and a decline in their imperial role in the world.

THE FRENCH AND HAITIAN REVOLUTIONS

The study of the French Revolution is generally an internalist one – the focus is on events in France and the effects on French society and politics. Unlike the American Revolution, however, the influence of the ideas of the French Revolution had a lasting global impact. The world historical significance of the ideas emerging after 1789 was immediately apparent, even to conservative thinkers. Edmund Burke, for example, in 1790, declared that 'all circumstances taken together, the French Revolution is the most astonishing that has hitherto happened in the world'. Radicals everywhere were highly enthusiastic about its Atlantic relevance and as an example for colonial revolt, as seen in Ireland in 1798.

The Atlantic reverberations of the French Revolution are too complex and substantial to cover here. But two consequences of the conflagration with Atlantic consequences might be highlighted. First, as Lynn Hunt argues, the French may have invented the concepts of human rights in the 1790s. The French Revolution, in this view, was a vehicle whereby the transmission of new ideas about the 'the rights' that individuals and peoples were transported around the world. A small group of proselytizing intellectuals called the Physiocrats, either directly because of the French Revolution (Hunt) or as re-statement and re-invigoration in the 1790s of intense but mostly academic discourse from mid-century (Dan Edelstein), advocated for universal rights to be considered part of human existence.[17] These rights were linked directly to the individual. A popular French opera of 1793 opened with a song celebrating how this new age saw 'the empire of liberty, established on the rights of humanity'.

Human rights talk had a harsh edge. Natural law theory was especially hostile to 'enemies of the human race', who violated the laws of nature and who must be destroyed. That was the underlying logic of the Terror of 1794, when the French Revolution descended into tyranny and totalitarianism. French revolutionaries had no difficulty in suppressing individual liberty in the name of collectivity and the interests of the nation-state. What can be said is that the French Revolution marked a turning point in history, when notions of individual and collective rights became the foundation of politics. Rights went from being a political theory to becoming a political practice. As Dan Edelstein comments, however, rival conceptions of rights had contradictory results: 'the enlightened theory of individual rights revealed itself to be less than universal, its protections vanishing for those deemed "unnatural"; while the constitutional theory of natural rights became in the troubled years of 1792–94, a judicial and political instrument of repression'.[18] The language of human rights was a means whereby the 'rights' of women, enslaved people, Jews and foreigners could be discussed, even though the language of French revolutionary discourse narrowed down the political nation very much to white men.

Second, human rights talk had practical effects in one area: efforts to end slavery. As the Marquis de Condercet argued in 1781, before the Revolution, in using natural rights to attack slavery, 'it is impossible that it always benefits a man, and moreover a perpetual class of men to be deprived of the natural rights of humanity'. Hunt insists that human rights had practical effects, arguing that 'the bulldozer force of the revolutionary logic of rights can be seen even more clearly in the French decisions about free blacks and slaves ... France granted equal political rights to free blacks (1792) and emancipated slaves (1794) long before any slaveholding nation'.[19]

A difficulty on accepting this argument is that having abolished slavery, France under Napoleon (whose wife was from a Martinique slave holding family) was also the first nation to reinstate slavery. What liberty enslaved people gained during the French Revolution came largely from their own efforts. The most notable example of enslaved people gaining freedom came in Haiti (formerly Saint-Domingue) between 1791 and 1804. The events of the Haitian Revolution are fiendishly complex, being several revolutions in one and involving whites, free people of colour and enslaved people in three different regions of the colony (all which had quite different experiences of the Revolution), and involving three outside powers – France, Britain and Spain. It intersected with the events of the French Revolution at every point and in complex ways. At bottom, however, the underlying issue of the Haitian Revolution was simple. It was a revolt by enslaved people against colonial authority to emancipate themselves from slavery and break down an oppressive plantation system. Napoleon was determined to reconquer the colony and was prepared to waste the lives of thousands of his best soldiers, who died in droves from tropical disease, in a fruitless attempt to force ex-slaves to return to slavery and to plantation agriculture. His main efforts to do this were in a dramatic war conducted between 1802 and 1803, following the capture of Haiti's charismatic leader, Toussaint L'Ouverture and his subsequent death while imprisoned in rural France. Toussaint was replaced as leader by the man who had betrayed him, Jacques Dessalines, who led Haitian forces to victory in an immensely bloody, chaotic and brutal war. Perhaps 40,000 French and over 100,000 Haitians perished in this conflict, making it one of the deadliest events in the whole period of the French Revolution and Napoleonic counter-reaction, 1789–1815.

Atrocities became normal in these dreadful years as the French military adopted strategies that were close to genocidal against rebels, including the use of attack dogs to tear people limb from limb. Haitians reacted by adopting a scorched-earth policy that was remarkably successful in denying the French army access to necessary resources and in destroying the plantation economy the French were there to preserve, as well as practising guerrilla warfare which the French found difficult to deal with. French earlier crimes encouraged Dessalines to issue his notorious order to 'avenge' his country against Europe on the declaration of independence on 1 January 1804 by massacring virtually all of the several thousand whites who had decided to trust their luck to the new regime. To be Haitian, he declared, was to be black. Dessalines's actions presaged a grim future for the ex-colony as a volatile mix of black and mixed-race politicians jostled for power with little concern for the rights and liberties of the mass of the population who were once slaves and were now peasants.

Thus, the result of the Haitian Revolution was ambiguous. The main result was positive: the destruction of France's most valuable colony and the permanent end of slavery in that colony, as well as the finish of the slave trade to the new nation. The example of Haitian revolutionaries proved inspirational to enslaved people elsewhere, especially in the United States and Cuba, and served as a stark warning to slaveholders of the risks they faced from the slaves they pretended to themselves would be faithful and dutiful. But it did not end Atlantic slavery. It only pushed it into different places. Cuba, Brazil and the United States pushed up their production of slave-produced commodities to take up the slack opened by the destruction of the plantation economy of Saint-Domingue and, eventually, by the decline of the older colonies of the British West Indies, like Jamaica, after the abolition of the slave trade in 1808.

Moreover, one of the most important consequences of the Haitian independence was that it partly encouraged Napoleon to abandon French ambitions for a tropical American empire centred on the Greater Antilles. The loss of Saint Domingue and the costs of war in Europe made him sell France's massive landholdings in the middle of North America in the Louisiana Purchase of 1804, all at bargain prices. This sale was the greatest real estate deal in American history. It facilitated westward expansion and the further expropriation of Native American land. It also allowed the expansion of slavery into the American South and what scholars call 'second slavery', a nakedly capitalist increase in plantation agriculture, mostly involving the production of cotton for Britain's cotton mills, with the labour for cotton production being native-born African-American enslaved people.

In Haiti, a real revolution occurred. There was not just regime change in Haiti but the whole basis of society was altered. While from a European perspective it looked as if the wealthiest place on earth had become one of the poorest, for ex-slaves their standard of living was much enhanced, as well as having the immense psychological benefit of no longer being enslaved. Most important, independence without major social change – the aim of the North and South American Founding Fathers – was not the central goal in Haiti. What Haitians wanted was emancipation from slavery. That was given to them by the French in 1794, but the reality of emancipation was only achieved by the determined efforts of ordinary men and women to resist any attempt at re-enslavement or, as Toussaint wanted, any return to debilitating plantation labour over which they had no control over how they worked. Toussaint and Dessalines aspired to dictatorship and were far from being the principled leaders that naïve accounts of the Haitian Revolution sometimes depict them as being. But they never dared alter the fundamental achievement of slave rebellion, which was to abolish slavery immediately and forever.

LATIN AMERICAN REVOLUTIONS

The Latin American Revolutions which followed in Haiti's wake were, by contrast, relatively pacific in their aims if not in their execution – as in Haiti, the violence in the many Latin American revolutions was extreme. These multiple colonial rebellions between 1808 and 1826, along with Brazilian independence in 1822, did not arise from anti-colonial sentiments wanting to create new polities and revolutionary systems of government. Instead, what was at stake in Latin America was not an escape from empire but complicated local decisions, based on local circumstances and historical contingencies, made by strategically placed elites who were determined to retain and increase their power because of political change. What these elites wanted to do was to reconstitute in the Americas on new foundations the empire that Spain and Portugal had lost due to Napoleonic invasion. As Adelman argues, 'under the carapace of decomposing empires what emerged was not the idea of a singular nation born of oppression but a plethora of ideas about sovereignty that followed the fracturing of the political spaces once outlined by empires'.[20]

The conservative nature of these revolutions can be seen in the determined efforts leaders of revolution made to preserve the rights of the Catholic Church, the interests of merchants and most of all the power of Creole elites, who replaced Spanish imperial officials while for the most part continuing Spanish imperial policies. What remained constant was the exclusion of Native Americans from any access to wealth and power and the solidification of rigid racial caste systems. Indeed, racial relations probably became more restrictive for non-whites in the nineteenth century than under the Old Spanish regime, a regime that after 1750 had been actively promoting unpopular political, economic and social reforms designed to bring Latin America more in line with the more progressive empires of Britain and France. Unsurprisingly, given this conservative trend, the most successful adaptation to the new order was in Brazil where an alliance of planters and merchants consolidated their oligarchical powers in a racially divided and socially retrogressive polity in which an expanding slave trade and a revitalized plantation and mining sector kept this elite wealthy.

Latin America independence has a curious place in the history of the Age of Revolutions, mainly because the results of independence were very inconclusive. That slavery in Latin America continued and solidified after 1830 is not perhaps surprising – slavery was strengthened in the places where it was important in the United States after 1776. But independence in many parts of Latin America did not lead to a noticeable increase in freedom for non-whites or to an increase in democratic politics or, more consequentially, to stronger and more independently viable economies. It was during the Latin American Revolutions that the gap in economic performance between

North America and South America and the Caribbean became unbridgeable (as it remains today). It was also during this period that British influence in Brazil, Argentina, Chile and elsewhere made Latin America subject to new forms of dependence. As early as 1830 Simón Bolivar, the totemic figure of Latin American revolution farewelled Columbians with a lament that 'I blush to say this: Independence is the only benefit we have acquired, to the detriment of all the rest'.

As in the United States, understanding the process of independence has been made more complicated by a long history of celebrating founding fathers as personifying some sort of national spirit. The first treatments of Latin American independence came as the discipline of history established certain norms of history writing, notably that an object of enquiry needed to be the nation-state. For nineteenth-century writers on South American revolutions, creators of new nations had a collective past, shared a cathartic and bonding experience in toppling an old order and were thus likely to have a future in common. Thus, independence in Latin America was written about as national sagas dominated by the martyred efforts of great men, Bolívar foremost, but also José de San Martin and Miguel Hidalgo. We can see the modern culmination of this focus in John Lynch's classic synthesis of 1973.[21] Lynch's enduringly popular book follows the careers of 'great men' as symbols of 'incipient nationalism' among Creole whites who, in Lynch's opinion, not only created nations but fostered political styles and habits that continue to torment modern Latin American politics. That unfortunate continuation of poor governance occurred because the nations that Latin American nationalists imagined were incipient, not mature, and thus struggled between democracy and autocracy. The idea of revolutions in Latin America as flawed national sagas appealed to novelists as well as historians, with Gabriel Garcia Márquez, Carlos Fuentes, Mario Vargas Llosa and Jorge Luis Borges all writing tales about the travails of revolutionary leaders.

Octavio Paz was one novelist who saw the Latin American Revolution as a failed revolution or perhaps not even a revolution at all. As he argued in 1959, 'the newness of the new Spanish American nations is deceptive: in reality they were decadent or static societies, fragments and survivals of a shattered whole'.[22] Recent work by historians such as Jaime E. Rodríguez O. has seen the Latin American Revolution as a civil war among Spaniards, only some of whom lived in the Americas. He argues that there was friction but no colonial identity ready to be unleashed waiting for men to lead Creoles into nationalism. Instead, the Latin American Revolutions were not heroic manifestations of nationalism but diverse responses to a problem thrust on colonials by problems in the metropole – the implosion of the Spanish monarchy because of Napoleonic invasion. Rodríguez's argument was that colonies did not secede as much as they were forced to react to a prolonged metropolitan crisis in what had been in the eighteenth century a multicontinental cosmopolitan empire. There were fewer underlying structural problems in the Spanish Empire that required revolutionary outcomes and in part these outcomes worked out relatively poorly because the crisis in imperial relations was not foreseen and not the result of a pre-existing propensity.[23]

As in the United States, the main revolutionary achievement in Latin American revolution was constitutional change. Between 1810 and the late 1820s, juntas, assemblies and congresses wrote foundational laws and constitutions to provide a framework for government. Following explicit declarations of independence, constitutional republics quickly emerged as the favoured form of government in New Granada and Venezuela. Some people favoured constitutional monarchy, with Manuel Belgrano advocating a figurehead Inca monarch for the province of Río de la Plata. In the end, however, all new Latin American nations, even Mexico, which created an empire in 1821, quickly adopted a federal republic. The notable exception was Brazil, which received the royal court of Portugal in 1808 with John VI, king of Portugal and Brazil from 1816, deciding to remain in Brazil. John VI only returned to Portugal in 1821. It seems clear that events in Portugal destabilized Brazil by subordinating Brazil's economic interests to those of Britain. This subordination was orchestrated by General William Carr Beresford, chosen to govern Portugal in the absence of John VI. Brazil was independent in 1822.

By 1826, Spain retained only Cuba, Puerto Rico and the Philippines from its once great empire. Cuba, however, was a valuable acquisition, the 'ever faithful isle', and a booming plantation colony that took over from Saint Domingue the mantle of the leading producer of coffee and sugar in the Caribbean. Cubans liked their colonial status especially as they saw mainland independent nations struggle with economic devastation, fiscal insolvency and political stability. Its wealthy elite thought its relationship as a colony of Spain to be beneficial until the 1860s. It was slavery that convinced white Cubans to remain within the Spanish Empire; it was slavery that eventually caused problems. After essentially uninterrupted economic growth in the first half of the nineteenth century, economic downturn after 1860 led to division within elites about the colony's economic and political future. The result was a separatist war that had striking parallels with the earlier Latin American revolutions, 1808–1826. It led to antislavery becoming more important, often led by enslaved people themselves.

What made this combination of national revolution and antislavery distinctive in Cuba was that it coincided with a crisis of slavery in North America and to an extent in Brazil. The American Civil War destabilised Cuba, as the US government had given it and Brazil diplomatic and military cover, which from the 1860s was suddenly withdrawn. Once again, events in Europe were pivotal. Abolitionism in Spain was linked to liberalism and thus when a liberal revolution in Spain succeeded in 1868, abolition of slavery in Cuba became for the first time a real issue. Spain established the Moret law in 1870 which provided for partial emancipation. Nationalist rebellions also occurred in Cuba at this time, quickly turning into civil war, in part over the future of slavery. Enslaved people themselves became increasingly rebellious, supporting arguments by abolitionists that slavery was inherently problematic and dangerous in a multiracial and multiethnic society.

The course to independence and the abolition of slavery was tortuous. In Cuba an insurgency took root after 1868 in the eastern part of the island and lasted until 1878. The rebellion's leaders declared slavery to be abolished, in part as a response of runaway enslaved people flocking to the insurgents' army. That infuriated conservatives in Havana and the surrounding plantation countryside who were determined to preserve both slavery and colonialism. Conservatives managed to delay emancipation until 1886. But slavery had been dying for years – the number of enslaved people peaked at 370,000 in 1860 and was 230,000 in 1878. Slavery had already been replaced by a *patronato* system, like apprenticeship as practised in the British Caribbean in the mid-1830s. Enslaved people increasingly fled the plantations, were freed by masters in return for agreeing to be wage workers or themselves bought their freedom. When slavery was abolished, it affected perhaps just 25,000 enslaved persons. Cuba finally became independent only after a violent war, in which the United States played a major part, between Spain and Cuba from 1895 to 1898.

CONSEQUENCES

The effects of the Atlantic Revolutions were globally profound. One frequent comment by historians is that the revolutions were all interconnected. But this interconnectedness can be overemphasized. The differences between the revolutions – a conservative American Revolution; a radical French revolution with a dramatic counter-revolution that returned France to a more conservative position; a truly radical Haitian revolution; and a diverse and variegated set of revolutions in Latin America that led to only occasional revolutionary changes – are more pronounced than the similarities. What was structurally similar about the Atlantic Revolutions was that they each began as local reactions to imperial problems. They each are best viewed in terms of process rather than causation – contingency was vital in shaping events in every case. The Revolutions also resulted in limited social change, except in Haiti, and Haiti was essentially a pariah state within the international states' system for most of the nineteenth century. Most social and cultural change that occurred in the Atlantic World in the late eighteenth and early nineteenth centuries, especially regarding household formation and changes in the relationship between men and women and children and parents, would have happened with or without revolutionary political change. Non-revolutionary Britain changed as much socially as revolutionary France in fundamental aspects of social and cultural organization in the early nineteenth century. Indeed, the effects of the Industrial Revolution probably meant that Britain saw more changes in social and economic organization than any part of the Atlantic World except Haiti after 1800.

To an extent, the accumulated revolutions in this period led to an Atlantic World that was integrating around common themes in the early eighteenth century becoming disintegrated, although Bayly insists that modernity in this period meant that Atlantic societies became increasingly similar insofar as each was growingly complex. We need to remember, however, that many Atlantic societies, such as Cuba and Brazil in the Americas; most of West Africa except perhaps Sierra Leone; and most notably Britain within Europe, were mostly impervious to the ideologies and actions advanced during the Age of Revolutions. The nineteenth century did not see the end of empire but rather imperial intensification. It did not see a diminishment in the state or a democratic politics in which ordinary men (let alone ordinary women) had any power. Aristocrats ruled as firmly in 1850 as they had done in 1750, and they did so in states that were much more powerful than in the Old Regime. And while in some places and times revolutionary principles about equality, liberty and fraternity led to the abandonment of that central Atlantic institution of the slave trade and slavery, overall slavery and unfreedom were as constant after the Age of Revolutions as before those events. They may have even advanced in importance. That the age after the Age of Revolutions is commonly termed in Anglo-American literature as the Victorian Age is telling: naming the world imagined by revolutionaries after a female monarch with decidedly conservative and imperial views suggests that the impact of revolutionary change after 1756 did not alter fundamental assumptions about hierarchy, authority and patriarchy in the Atlantic World.

NOTES

1   The first section of this chapter is heavily indebted to C.A. Bayly, *The Birth of the Modern World 1780–1914* (Oxford: Blackwell, 2004).
2   Sankar Muthu, *Enlightenment Against Empire* (Princeton: Princeton University Press, 2003).
3   David Armitage and Sanjay Subrahmanyam, eds., *The Age of Revolutions in Global Context, c. 1760–1840* (Basingstoke: Palgrave Macmillan, 2010), xvii.
4   Robert Travers, 'Imperial Revolutions and Global Repercussions: South Asia and the World, *c.* 1750–1850,' in ibid., 145.
5   John Darwin, *After Tamerlane: The Rise and Fall of Global Empire* (London: Bloomsbury, 2007).
6   Ibid., 162; C.A. Bayly, *The Imperial Meridian: The British Empire and the World, 1780–1830* (London: Longman, 1989), ch. 6.
7   Jeremy Adelman, 'An Age of Imperial Revolutions,' *American Historical Review* 113 (2008), 319–40.
8   Lauren Benton, *Law and Colonial Cultures: Legal Regimes in World History, 1400–1900* (Cambridge: Cambridge University Press, 2002).

9   Jeremy Adelman, 'Iberian Passages: Continuity and Change in the South
     Atlantic,' in David Armitage and Sanjay Subrahmanyam, eds., *The Age
     of Revolutions in Global Context, c. 1760–1840* (Basingstoke: Palgrave
     Macmillan, 2010), 61, 69.
10   Eliga H. Gould, 'Fears of War, Fantasies of Peace: British Politics and the
     Coming of the American Revolution,' in Gould and Peter Onuf, eds., *Empire
     and Nation: The American Revolution in the Atlantic World* (Baltimore: Johns
     Hopkins University Press, 2005), 20.
11   Adelman, 'Iberian Passages,' 59.
12   Ibid., 69–70.
13   Patrick Griffin, *American Leviathan: Empire, Nation, and Revolutionary
     Frontier* (New York: Hill and Wang, 2007), 222–23.
14   Gary Nash, 'Sparks from the Altar of '76: International Repercussions and
     Reconsiderations of the American Revolution' in David Armitage and Sanjay
     Subrahmanyam, eds., *The Age of Revolutions in Global Context, c. 1760–1840*
     (Basingstoke: Palgrave Macmillan, 2010), 4.
15   Eliga H. Gould, 'The Question of Home Rule,' *William and Mary Quarterly*
     64 (2007), 258.
16   Serena Zabin, 'Writing to and from the Revolution,' *William and Mar
     Quarterly* 74 (2017), 763.
17   Lynn Hunt, 'The Long and the Short History of Human Rights,' *Past & Present*
     233 (2016), 323–31; Dan Edelstein, 'Enlightenment Rights Talk,' *Journal of
     Modern History* 86 (2014), 530–65; idem, *On the Spirit of Law* (Chicago:
     University of Chicago Press, 2018).
18   Dan Edelstein, 'Nature or Nation? Rights Conflicts in the Age of the French
     Revolution,' in David A. Bell and Yair Mintzker, eds., *Rethinking the Age of
     Revolutions: France and the Birth of the Modern World* (Oxford: Oxford
     University Press, 2018), 40.
19   Lynn Hunt, *Inventing Human Rights* (New York: W.W. Norton, 2008), 160.
20   Adelman, 'Iberian Passages,' 76.
21   John Lynch, *The Spanish American Revolutions, 1808–1826* (New York:
     W.W. Norton, 1973).
22   Octavio Paz, *The Labyrinth of Solitude: Life and Thought in Mexico*
     (New York: Grove Press, 1961), 161.
23   Jaime E. Rodríguez O, 'The Emancipation of America,' *American Historical
     Review* 105 (2000), 147.

BIBLIOGRAPHY

Oxford Online Bibliographies – The American Revolution; The Black Atlantic
     in the Age of Revolutions; Empire and State Formation; Latin American
     Independence; Nation, Nationhood and Nationalism; Republicanism; The
     French Revolution; The Haitian Revolution.
Jeremy Adelman, *Sovereignty and Revolution in the Iberian Atlantic* (Princeton:
     Princeton University Press, 2009).

Robert C. Allen, *The British Industrial Revolution in Global Perspective* (Cambridge: Cambridge University Press, 2009).

David Armitage and Sanjay Subrahmanyam, eds., *The Age of Revolutions in Global Context, c. 1760–1840* (Basingstoke: Palgrave Macmillan, 2010).

C.A. Bayly, *The Birth of the Modern World 1780–1914* (Oxford: Blackwell, 2004).

David A. Bell and Yair Mintzker, eds., *Rethinking the Age of Revolutions: France and the Birth of the Modern World* (Oxford: Oxford University Press, 2018).

Yves Benot, *La revolution française et la fin des colonies* (Paris: La Découverte, 1988).

Stephen Conway, *The American Revolutionary War* (London: I.B. Tauris, 2013).

Suzanne Desan et al., *The French Revolution in Global Perspective* (Ithaca: Cornell University Press, 2013).

Caitlin Fitz, *Our Sister Republics: The United States in an Age of American Revolutions* (New York: Liveright, 2017).

David Geggus, 'The Haitian Revolution in Atlantic Perspective,' in Nicholas Canny and Philip Morgan, eds., *The Oxford Handbook of the Atlantic World 1450–1850* (Oxford: Oxford University Press, 2011), 533–49.

Wim Klooster, *Revolutions in the Atlantic World: A Comparative History* (New York: New York University Press, 2018).

Anthony Macfarlane, *War and Independence in Spanish America* (London: Routledge, 2008).

Janet Polasky, *Revolution without Borders: The Call to Liberty in the Atlantic World* (New Haven: Yale University Press, 2015).

Jeremy D. Popkin, *A Concise History of the Haitian Revolution* (Oxford: Wiley-Blackwell, 2011).

Alan Taylor, *American Revolutions: A Continental History, 1750–1804* (New York: W.W. Norton, 2016).

PART THREE

Atlantic Places

8

WEST AFRICA

AFRICA AS AN ATLANTIC PLACE

Nearly sixty years ago, the Oxford historian Hugh Trevor-Roper, in a moment of notorious condescension, declared on BBC radio that 'perhaps in the future, there will be some African history to teach. But at present there is none ... there is only the history of the Europeans in Africa. The rest is darkness'. The statement is unfortunate but probably not as ethnocentric as it appears. His point was not that African did not do things interesting to 'sociologists and anthropologists'. The point he was making was that Africa was not part of the discipline of history because it had few to no written records and it did little 'to discover how we came to be where we are', which for Trevor-Roper was through European ideas and European history.

We know better now that Africa does indeed have a history, but we still face a problem, especially as Atlantic historians, in that African history only seems to exist if Europeans are somehow involved in it and that internal African history is hard to make relevant to other concerns. That statement is too baldly Eurocentric to defend but statements like these reflect long-standing ideas of Africa as being a place without history, as somehow a timeless and unchanging continent. Conventional world history metanarratives, for example, construct the Sahara Desert as an unhistorical wasteland and an impenetrable barrier between North Africa and sub-Saharan Africa. Below that barrier, so this narrative went, lay a whole host of small-scale societies that seemed to have an unchanging character. Studying these societies may not have been, as Trevor-Roper, in a phrase more deserving of denigration than the one so far quoted, merely about the 'unrewarding gyrations of barbarous tribes in picturesque but irrelevant parts of the world', which we only condescend to examine because, perhaps aware that he was talking at the new and radical University of Sussex rather than Balliol College, 'undergraduates, seduced, as always by the changing breath of journalistic fashion, demand that they be taught the history of black Africa'.[1] African history in this telling is not really history, but is anthropology, timeless and unconnected to wider historical patterns. It reflects the argument made by G.W. F. Hegel in the late eighteenth century that Africa has no history because it represents human society before the purposive movement of historical events.

That there are still echoes of this view of 'timeless' Africa in part derives from the uneasy relationship between Africa and Atlantic history, the latter which since the end of the fifteenth century has been seen to be one of the principal motors of history. Of all the four continents in the Atlantic World, Africa was the least affected by the movements of goods, peoples and ideas across the ocean. Most of Africa except for a sliver of the continent located on the shores of the Atlantic Ocean was relatively little affected by Atlantic integration. It was not that these areas unaffected by Atlantic history were isolated by Atlantic currents and cut off from contact with other peoples. On the contrary, Atlantic Africa was the last major area of Africa to establish overseas connections – North Africa was closely linked to the Mediterranean basin and East Africa had centuries of close contact with the Indian Ocean World. Indeed, the people of the Sudan Belt and North Africa in the first millennium were more urbanized and more deeply intertwined economically with other world regions than were Western Europeans of the same period. Ironically, however, the continent least affected internally by Atlantic connections was also the continent that was most influential shaping the Atlantic World as the original home of the Atlantic slave trade, the institution which along with the Catholic Church had the most impact on Atlantic integration.

The slave trade made, as described often in this book, an out-of-size impact on the Atlantic World. That Africa was affected least by being involved in the Atlantic but was the most influential part of the world in making the Atlantic World what it was helps us understand the ambivalence of including Africa in patterns of world history. Yet, as David Eltis argues, if we switch our focus from immediate impacts to changes in the nature and size of connections in the Atlantic World, then the most striking developments in the Atlantic between the 1640s and 1770s occurred in Africa. By this statement, he prioritizes the importance of the Atlantic slave trade and economic activities over internal African development and takes the risk, as so often happens in writing on Africa in the Atlantic World, of conflating African history with the presence of Europeans in the region, as Trevor-Roper did but also as do Africanists like Joseph Inikori and G. Ugo Nwokeji, who tend to disagree with Eltis about the limited economic impact within Africa and who stress how the Atlantic slave trade had long-term negative repercussions on African development.[2]

The Africa that the Portuguese and Spanish encountered in the mid-fifteenth century was one that was well used to foreign visitors. It just was one that was not that interested in the Atlantic Ocean. The Sahara was not, in fact, a wasteland but was one of the world's principal cross roads, a space of cultures and cross-cultural ventures, and a resource base for salt, copper, dromedaries and gemstones. It supported towns and trade and was the means whereby Africa became a central part of Mediterranean exchanges. Similarly, south of Atlantic Africa was a region that historians call Greater Zambezi, a resource-rich space with lots of human activity and cross-cultural interactions. Africa was not a place of disconnected villages but quite cosmopolitan. Travel throughout Africa was constant; indeed, there was a culture of travel that was especially strong in Muslim Africa, predicated in part on the need to make a pilgrimage once in one's life, if possible, if one was a believer to Mecca. Believers travelled in search of knowledge, to trade, to experience a sense of adventure and to satisfy one's curiosity about the wonders of the world.[3]

Nevertheless, the involvement of a small part of the African continent in the Atlantic World led to comparatively important changes for Africa as a whole. Before the arrival of Europeans, seaborne contact with the rest of the world was limited on the western side of the continent. The Atlantic Ocean in Africa is not a welcoming place, generally having unfavourable winds and currents, a lack of sheltered seas and treacherous offshore bars. West Africans were accustomed to the water but used the extensive river and lagoon system in the region using canoes rather than building ships for ocean sailing. Moreover, Africans saw little reason to venture offshore. Population pressure was minimal, meaning there was enough land to go around on the continent without needing to find new lands to settle. There was no West African attempt, for example, to colonize the offshore islands of the Atlantic.

By the start of the nineteenth century, it was a very different situation. Large parts of Africa had been pulled firmly into the Atlantic orbit. From Senegambia to Kongo-Angola, ports were founded and grew during the Atlantic period, linking West Africa to Western Europe and the Americas. The most distinctive architectural embodiment of this new set of relationships was a series of European fortified trading stations belonging to chartered companies created to trade for gold or enslaved people. These ports provided the mechanisms by which 12 million Africans were shipped to the Americas and were the spatial locations whereby European merchandise was imported into West Africa's payment for slaves. The establishment of this system of forts helped create a vibrant, if narrowly focused, elite cultural landscape on the African Atlantic coast, with palaces, royal courts, public gardens and libraries, cosmopolitan markets and a multi-faith religious environment. One sign of the cosmopolitan nature of these ports was the proliferation of West African languages alongside creole adaptations of European languages, notably a pidgin mixture of Portuguese and African languages. Raymond Kea notes that 'that landscape, with its normative structures, epitomized an upper-class social imaginary of order, efficiency, predictability, prosperity and reason, and the achievement of personal capacity and spiritual agency'. But, he also notes, 'from the point of view of the countryside, this landscape was realized at great social cost'. That was especially true in the eighteenth century when predatory slave-raiding states such as the kingdom of Dahomey used the doctrine of *asuwada* (a dialectical philosophy that emphasized hierarchical order and authority and which stressed that there was a difference between free and non-free with the non-free person being a 'thing belonging in cords and deprived of liberty') to enforce obedience to a tyrannical political regime that used terror against ordinary people as a weapon of choice. The ports were where affluent merchants lived, using Atlantic goods to emphasize their high social standing. These merchants were instrumental in lowering the standard of living of almost everyone except themselves and in reducing many rural people to conditions of servitude, either in Africa or as slaves through the Atlantic slave trade.

It is important to emphasize the dominant role of merchants in African ports because one of the major historiographical findings of the last generation has been to insist that, unlike in the Americas, Africans were in control of Atlantic processes, with Africans calling the tune in commercial and cultural relationships, even if Europeans may have benefited overall the most from their involvement with Africans and Africa. One principal reason why Africans remained in control was the limited intrusions Europeans made into the African interior before the early nineteenth century. They were susceptible to the malign African environment, suffering such massive mortality that West Africa became known as the 'white man's graveyard'. Europeans did not come as colonists, let alone as settlers, and there was no significant European presence in the continent except for a small Dutch community in South Africa and a few Portuguese living in the colony of Angola.

Europeans came as merchants, selling Africans textiles, metals, alcohol, tobacco and firearms, as noted elsewhere in this book. Textiles were the most important item of sale, amounting for nearly one half of West African imports. In return, African merchants exchanged gold – the main basis of exchange before 1700 – and some African goods, like ivory, trades and dyewoods. Europeans were initially keener on buying gold than in buying slaves. Sometimes they had to accept slaves as payment when what they really wanted was precious metals. They then took these slaves who they had purchased and sold them within African markets. Eventually, slaves came to dominate African-European trade. By the 1780s, which was the peak decade in the Atlantic slave trade, when 866,000 Africans were put onto the Middle Passage to the Americas, slaves comprised over 90 per cent of the value of all West African exports.

It is important, however, not to exaggerate the connections between Africa and the Atlantic. The slave trade looms large in any discussion of Atlantic history and it is impossible to write about this topic without stressing the indispensability of African slaves in shaping the economies and societies of the Americas. The most well-known African contribution to the New World was in music but they made other contributions that we are only starting to recognize. It was only recently, for example, that historians became aware that the Brazilian martial arts tradition of *capoeira* is drawn from similar traditions in the seventeenth-century Kasanje kingdom in Angola.[4] But this does not mean that the effects of Atlantic involvement were so great within Africa itself. It was not even the largest slave trade in Africa itself, as detailed elsewhere. The per capita impact of Atlantic commerce was small, except in West African port cities. Most Africans remained within their own domestic economies rather than trying to enter the specialized and often-difficult trade. Moreover, the Atlantic diaspora of Africans was just part of a larger movement of Africans, often coerced, internally within Africa or to the Mediterranean or Indian Oceans. As Philip Morgan concludes, 'in the early modern era, Africans were more important to the Atlantic world than the Atlantic world was to Africans'.[5]

PORTUGAL AND AFRICA

The only European nation with any long-lasting presence in Africa was Portugal. Indeed, Portugal was not just the first European nation to settle in Africa; it was also the last to leave, abandoning its colony in Mozambique only in 1975. Its first significant involvement in Angola came in 1482–1483 with the arrival of Diogo Cão at the River Zaire, initiating exchanges between the Portuguese and Kongo courts. The Portuguese thought the Kongo was a field for conversion and potentially a means of coming closer to the land of the legendary Christian ruler, Prester John, in Ethiopia. The Prester John legend had been a potent source of information and misinformation about Africa in late medieval Europe. More prosaically, they wanted access to precious metals and minerals.

But few Portuguese merchants followed the royal lead. By the end of the sixteenth century, Portugal realized that the Kongo had little to offer it except slaves and ivory. The initial enthusiasm of the Kongolese for Portuguese goods and military assistance also faded, though Portuguese evangelization was successful enough to lead to a lasting Christian enclave being founded in Central Africa. Conflict ensued in the seventeenth century. In the Battle of Mbwila of 1665, the Portuguese routed the Kongolese army and killed the Kongo king. The result was that Kongo became a sort of Portuguese protectorate. Few Portuguese ever went to the Kongo, however, except as slave traders. Much Atlantic commerce remained in the hands of Africans, especially merchants of mixed race.

What did happen was that the Portuguese military aggression in the first half of the seventeenth century lessened as it realized that evangelization returned meagre returns and that disease killed large numbers of Europeans. The conversion efforts even when they worked resulted in what to the Portuguese were unsatisfactory results as the Kongolese adapted Christian religion to their own belief systems, assimilating missionary teachings to their inherited assumptions. For example, the Kongolese prophetess, Dona Beatriz Kimpa Vita, claimed to be possessed by St. Anthony and criticized both witchcraft and European slave trading. She revised the Catholic liturgy to suit her views and taught her disciples that Jesus and Mary had been black Kongolese, striving to fashion a Christianity that met the needs of her society rather than one which conformed to the dictates of Rome. Her movement attracted fervent interest in the 1690s but dwindled after 1706, when political and church authorities in the colony executed her for practising witchcraft and violently suppressed her followers.

Angola never really became a Portuguese colony in the sense that the Portuguese exercised control over local populations. The Portuguese imprint on the region, outside the slave trade, was in the end slight. The one period when Angola was an effective Atlantic possession came after the expulsion of Jesuits in 1759, thus ending missionary activity which had created considerable tension for the ruling Kongo elite. The new governor, Sousa Coutinho, was an Enlightenment administrator and encouraged agricultural production for the Atlantic market and even some industrial activity in the form of iron production and shipbuilding. His efforts did not meet with long-term success, as vested interests in the slave trade stopped attempts at economic diversification, making Angola becoming reduced in the early nineteenth century to being solely a provider of labour to Brazil. Angolan-Brazilian links were otherwise very limited, as neither colony had much interest in what the other colony had to offer, except for the vital industry of the slave trade.

The cultural links between Portugal and Africa were stronger than for other European empires. The slaves from this region who went to the Americas often spoke fluent Portuguese and were baptized in the Catholic faith and thus at least nominally attached to that religion. The Portuguese were more inclined than other Europeans to enter traditional client relationships with local chiefs, often marrying strategically into their hosts' households. These *lançados* provided wealth to the African widows and Euro-African children who then became entrepreneurs within the Atlantic environment. These children spoke their own language, Crioulo, a mixture or Portuguese and African languages.

The Christianity Africans adopted in Portuguese areas separated out these people from Africans elsewhere – it was only the Portuguese, not the French, British, or Dutch, who promoted actively their religion in West Africa. Perhaps the most important Portuguese importations, as elaborated elsewhere in this book, were domestic animals and American cultigens, like sugar cane, pineapples and especially maize and cassava. The Portuguese even introduced tobacco to the Gold Coast, although Dutch traders played a greater role in making tobacco available. Few of these adaptations, however, did more than add a European aspect to enduring African identities. Even in Portuguese Africa, West Africans resisted extensive colonization or creolization in ways that their compatriots transported to the Americas were unable to do.[6]

LABOUR RELATIONS

What was it like for ordinary Africans involved in the Atlantic World? The contact most Africans had with Europeans was small. In 1700, no more than a few thousand Europeans were stationed on the entire West African coast of some 3,000 miles extent. Most of these Europeans were in forts on the Gold Coast, trading first in gold, ivory and spices but increasingly in slaves. To assist Europeans in these forts were free and enslaved Africans and a growing number of mixed-race Africans who liaised with Europeans while developing families and trading business in nearby African ports. Without African labour the Atlantic slave trade Europeans conducted would have been impossible. This labour, however, was African labour and did not follow European rules.

'Company' slaves were enslaved people, so their lives were far from ideal, but the conditions of enslavement were relatively good, especially compared to those of the unfortunate millions shipped to the Americas. They were in general protected against transportation to the Americas unless they committed a crime or got irretrievably into debt. They enjoyed a fair degree of agency in their daily lives, able to form families without interference from slave owners and to receive what was in effect wages for their labour while being able to place conditions on their terms of service. They also expected to be treated with respect. They were often skilled tradesmen, learning European trades and working alongside whites, together playing an important role in maintaining forts. Women seldom did such work and led less comfortable existences, always being likely subject to sexual exploitation from European men who thought unfettered sexual access to African women one of the rights they were entitled to. Mixed-race children listed in records indicate the degrees of familiarity that were common in slave forts.

The labour of company slaves was supplemented by the labour of pawns. Pawnship was a long-standing West African practice that expanded alongside the expansion of the Atlantic slave trade as coastal societies became more commercial and where debt bondage became more institutionalized. It was a system whereby individuals were held in debt bondage as loan collateral with the labour of the pawn constituting interest on debts and with this labour covering the subsistence needs of the pawn. Pawns tended to be local and free-born people because the system could only work if the pawned person was valued enough for a debtor to want to redeem the pawn. Pawns also tended to be women, facilitating male sexual access to such females as well as being a means to gain their labour. One consequence, however, of Africa entering the Atlantic World was that when pawns worked for Europeans they were more likely than when they worked for Africans to be treated like slaves. Overall, however, the presence of pawnship within European forts showed less European intervention into African customs than showed how Europeans were necessarily drawn into respecting local economic traditions and arrangements.

These company slaves and pawns were important in another way in shaping Atlantic slavery. They were the group who formed what Ira Berlin has termed 'Atlantic creoles' and who played a disproportionate role in creating African-American culture in the crucial formative stages of creolization in British North America.[7] Many such slaves working in British forts on the Gold Coast had been born in Gambia before moving south. They lived in a liminal setting, physically located, as Simon Newman notes, between Europeans and the people of the Gold Coast. They operated in the interstices between African and Atlantic slavery. Those who went to the Americas as slaves brought their understanding of the fluid nature of African slavery to counteract within African enslaved communities in the Americas the rigid nature of the slave system developing there in the mid-seventeenth century.[8]

An especially interesting group of Africans who worked for Europeans on the Atlantic coast of Africa were canoemen. These men were highly skilled boatmen who transported virtually all freight and people between shore and ship. They were fishermen and sea workers who found it profitable to work within the Atlantic slave trade, usually at high wages. Large forts regularly employed almost 100 canoemen to navigate the highly dangerous surf on Gold Coast beaches. Canoemen were highly proficient sailors, with skills that apparently few European sailors ever mastered.

Their skill made them indispensable. The canoemen knew this and insisted both on high wages and on not doing menial labour. When they wanted to, they worked very hard, and very efficiently and fast. They operated in a tight-knit group of proletarian-like workers, with strong collective ties. Jobs were passed from father to son in ways that showed that canoemen were firmly in control of the labour process. They controlled with an iron fist the movement of any goods into and out of coasts – if canoemen did not agree to goods being moved, they stayed where they were. Europeans appreciated their skills but resented their agency and collective control over work conditions. A Portuguese governor complained after one labour dispute that the canoemen 'have once again refused to work, and all our efforts to punish them have made them more objectionable'. But Europeans learned to work with, rather than against, this group of workers. A later Portuguese governor admitted that if treated 'correctly', canoemen would faithfully 'work long hours and carry out the work with skill and care'.[9]

A few of these men became sailors in the Atlantic slave trade, replacing Europeans who had died while waiting for slave cargoes to be filled. Black sailors were always a presence on slave ships plying the Atlantic, although they tended to be concentrated in the coastal rather than in transatlantic trade. As sailors, Africans had less protection than when they worked as canoemen on the Gold Coast and they faced the same problems as did white sailors in the slave trade, generally the least privileged of all white seamen. Over time, the problems endured by Gold Coast sailors on the Atlantic Ocean caused tension between local communities and Europeans and reduced the number of men willing to be black sailors in a white man's trade.

Atlantic trade gave opportunities to both Europeans and Africans. It created new groups of workers tied directly to Europeans living in Africa, such as mixed-race people serving as intermediaries between the two sides of their heritage. The activities of such men and canoemen meant that the coastal regions of Atlantic Africa – remote and insignificant backwaters before European arrival – became wealthy and cosmopolitan. Africans were in control of these coastal regions, as seen in what Europeans lamented as 'spirited independence'. An eighteenth-century British observer argued that Africans had a 'spirit of liberty' in their dealings with Europeans who linked them with 'the meanest wretch in London Streets, for in all countries this kind of liberty is chiefly confined to the lowest class of men'.

Sean Hawkins and Philip Morgan have observed that 'no people were more uprooted and dislocated; or travelled more within the [British] Empire by both sea and land; or crested more of a trans-imperial culture' than Africans and their descendants.[10] Such a statement is only partially true for the Africans who remained in Africa. These were the people who facilitated such a transformative exchange but who resisted such transformations in their own lives. On the Atlantic coast, a few Africans were intimately connected to the Atlantic World as merchants, rulers and workers, but even the latter did not have to alter their lives all that much to accommodate Atlantic rhythms.

SLAVERY AND THE SLAVE TRADE

The Atlantic age in Africa was conditioned by temporality. We can divide this age into three separate time periods. The first period lasted from the mid-fifteenth to the mid-seventeenth century and brought prosperity to many Africans on the Atlantic coast and to the ports they lived in. The advent of Atlantic commerce on the Atlantic coast of Africa made these regions more part of the most dynamic parts of Africa, connecting them with the inland cities near the Saharan crossroads. Merchants in this Sudan Belt were able to gain new outlets for their commodities through Atlantic trade. The arrival of the Atlantic age helped end the medieval age of empires in the western Sudan Belt, as a greater diversity of products and more centres of commercial production undercut the power of any one polity to concentrate wealth and power to itself. The result was the decline of empires and the rise of many middle-sized kingdoms.

The next stage in the Atlantic age in Africa lasted until the early nineteenth century. It was a period in which the Atlantic slave trade dominated all other commerce, with some new states like Dahomey and Oyo rising due to their ability as predatory regimes to conduct warfare to acquire captives for transportation to the Americas. The third period came after 1800 and saw a simultaneous move towards abolitionism by Europe and a dramatic expansion in internal African slaveholding. Merchants and rulers had to seek other commodities to make up for a gap in their import-producing power. A fall in the price of slaves made it easier for Africans to buy them while a greater commitment to commodity production in West Africa created labour demands that only enslavement could supply. Thus, one of the terrible ironies of the nineteenth-century Atlantic age in Africa was that the abolition of the slave trade *out* of Africa led to an increase in slavery *within* Africa. The Islamic world of the Sudan Belt faced a crisis in this period. Jihads replaced the rule of largely secular elites with that of clerics from Senegambia to Lake Chad. Another irony was that these clerics' efforts to insist that the enslavement of Muslims had to stop led to more non-Muslims than ever before becoming enslaved within Atlantic Africa.

What happened in the second Atlantic age, the period of slave trade dominance, has attracted fierce historiographical controversy. The arguments revolve around three questions: was slavery always part of West African culture or did it greatly intensify from around 1700? Did the Atlantic slave trade lead to African underdevelopment from the eighteenth century, with lasting consequences until the present? And did the slave trade destabilize West Africa, by increasing the levels and intensity of warfare as nations competed to provide captive labour for the Americas?

Slavery has always existed in Africa. It commenced early, ended late and played a key role in the development of global modernity. The internal slave trade was overall the largest, with 18,522,000 slaves traded within Africa between 1401 and 1900, compared to 12,521,336 in the Atlantic slave trade. It was only in the eighteenth century when 6,495,000 Africans crossed the Atlantic that this trade approached the numbers in the internal slave trade, which were still larger at 7,810,000 in that century. The Atlantic trade was dominant in Africa's external slave trade, accounting for 68 per cent of the total. Africa was thus a net provider of labour to the globe. It probably was in this role because Africans themselves both capable and willing to sell other Africans to strangers which, for a variety of reasons, never happened to such an extent in East Asia and Western Europe.

Yet it is unclear whether slavery was central to African social and economic structures before the mid-seventeenth century, when the Atlantic slave trade accelerated in importance. John Thornton thinks that slavery was widespread everywhere in West Africa before 1450, primarily because the absence of public ownership in land left slaves as the only form of private, revenue-producing property recognized in African law.[11] Certainly, slavery was common in Islamic Africa, where the conquests of non-Islamic peoples in the seventh and eighth centuries had produced significant numbers of slaves, though this slavery tended to be confined to the Sudan Belt. What was especially significant about Islamic slavery, apart from its existence, was its racial aspects, which eventually became part of the European justification for slavery. In Islamic Africa, where the so-called curse of Ham had considerable purchase, there developed an ideological association between blackness and slavery (and also, to an extent, an association between whiteness and slavery – both sub-Saharan Africans and northern Europeans were considered to be naturally inferior due to the fact that they did not live in an ideal climate, which was considered to be that of the Mediterranean and North Africa). Dark-skinned Africans formed an increasing majority of slaves in the Islamic world, well before Atlantic slavery became racially based.

A second strand of historians think that slavery was unlikely to be widespread in West Africa outside Islamic regions and with the very important exception of the Gold Coast. They argue that in most parts of non-Islamic West Africa markets slave produced commodities were so small that they could not support an extensive slave system, especially as slaves were often purchased or owned as much to display status as for their money-making potential. Paul Lovejoy, who has written the most comprehensive and authoritative study of slavery in West Africa, connects the growth of slavery in the region directly to the development of overseas trade, which alone, he argues, provided the economic foundation through which widespread slavery was possible. Thus, he suggests, while slavery was practised everywhere it was not that significant an institution until the mid-seventeenth century, when demand for slaves for export made slavery acceptable everywhere in West Africa.[12]

The Gold Coast was different, as in this area slavery was extensive throughout the early modern period, including the 200 years before the Atlantic slave trade became fully established. In the Gold Coast, there was a vibrant market economy where slave-produced commodities could be sold. Alone in non-Islamic West Africa, the Gold Coast imported slaves to work for slave owners from other areas and never became just a slave-exporting region. The presence of slavery from early times on the Gold Coast is a factor that needs to be taken into consideration when evaluating the long-term presence of slavery in West Africa, as the Gold Coast was one of the primary areas where Europeans involved themselves with Africa. But the presence of slavery in the Gold Coast needs to be balanced against a wider trend where slavery developed mostly because of Europeans creating a market that had previously not existed for both transatlantic and local slavery. It is noticeable, for example, that it was wealthy African merchants in the

Atlantic slave trade who became the largest slave owners in West Africa. Slavery became economically profitable during the heyday of the Atlantic slave trade in ways it had not been before European arrival.

An even more contentious issue is whether the slave trade led to lasting African underdevelopment. The strong argument was made by Walter Rodney nearly fifty years ago in a series of polemical works in which he argued that it was the Atlantic slave trade that made Africa lastingly poor.[13] The novelty of this argument was that it moved backwards in time the usual reasoning for why twentieth-century Africa was lagging behind in the world economy from nineteenth-century colonization to events centuries earlier. Historians who support Rodney's analysis have narrowed down his indictment of the slave trade's effect on African underdevelopment to the seventeenth and eighteenth centuries – the middle stage of Africa's Atlantic age – when trade in African slaves to the Americas dwarfed all other export activity. Joseph Inikori suggests that the slave trade had far-reaching adverse effects for West Africa, halting what was until then a flourishing of markets that was leading to economic diversification which, he argues, was providing a means in the sixteenth century for Africa to be integrated into Atlantic and global economies. Gold, unlike slaves, had knock-on effects within the domestic economy, even allowing for some embryonic industrialization, as Ray Kea shows.[14]

Inikori states that after the mid-seventeenth century the slave trade stopped the commercializing economy of Africa dead in its tracks, with domestic manufacturing sidelined in the single-minded pursuit of gaining captives to sell to Europeans and with Africans importing most manufactures from Europe instead of developing its own industries. In addition, the seeking out of captives led to a huge increase in the purchase of firearms with which African warlords in the Gold Coast and the Bights of Benin and Biafra conducted prolonged and widespread warfare in the interiors. African ports with slave trading business prospered; everywhere else declined, with ordinary people oppressed and naturally fearful that they might be captured and enslaved.[15] It is a powerful argument, though one that needs to be tempered by the realization that overseas trade was probably too small in relation to the domestic economy to make as much difference as Rodney and Inikori suggest. Thornton argued that the slave trade was not that vital to the African economy and that 'African manufacturing was more than capable of handling competition from preindustrial Europe'.[16] And Philip Curtin in 1975 suggested that the export trade in slaves from Senegambia was not as important as other economic and non-economic activity. Indeed, he argued that Senegambian states produced slaves for political more than economic reasons, meaning that for the elites of the region the advent of the Atlantic slave trade was not all that much a break with the past as adherents of 'world-systems' theory have argued.[17]

Slavery in Africa might be linked to the Atlantic slave trade, but it was very different in character to American slavery. Its most distinctive attribute was that slavery was neither perpetual nor hereditary. In a classic article, Igor Kopytoff and Suzanne Miers termed African slavery as a mechanism for the incorporation of outsiders, with women especially prominent as outsiders who needed to be accommodated within kin systems.[18] There were limits, however, to this ideal of social incorporation. Slaves seldom reached the point where they became equal to free people and ancestry from a slave was a matter of embarrassment, stopping people of slave descent from becoming political leaders.

Another distinctive feature of early modern African slavery was that slaves were important in trade and riverine work, activities that led to them being largely unsupervised, and except in the Gold Coast, which was once again exceptional, did not feature heavily in agricultural work. That was especially true for male slaves: female slaves, acting according to West African custom, worked in such agricultural activities as milling and grinding maize. Gender was crucial in shaping slave structures, with women generally favoured in most places over men. Women provided important domestic services and were also desirable as marriage partners. Marrying an enslaved woman gave a man the ability to acquire her labour and have unimpeded control over their jointly parented children – slave women could not divorce and thus return property to the matrilineal line. Sandra Greene notes regarding gender roles on the Upper Guinea Coast that free women sought slave wives for their polygamous husbands as these slave women could do the work in the household that they would otherwise have to do.[19]

As everywhere, slaves were badly treated. Their treatment was probably better than on American plantations as slaves and masters were tied together in complicated webs of obligation occasionally enforced in law that gave enslaved people some small protection. Historians have modified Kopytoff and Miers's assertion that becoming a slave in Africa was always a traumatic loss of status and led to socially demeaning feelings of shame that were heartfelt in societies built on a shame-honour ethos. Slaves were not as removed from civil society as that statement suggests and were not shunned by others to the extent that they became non-persons. Slaves in West Africa had active religious lives, for example, and many kin connections with free people that were not ended when a slave became enslaved. In short, enslaved Africans lived in relatively 'open' slave systems compared to the 'closed' systems of southeast Asia and the Americas. Just as people could become slaves as a substitute for being executed for murder, adultery, theft or witchcraft, so too enslaved people could be freed because of socially approved good behaviour, such as killing an enemy. Once again, conditions were different on the Gold Coast where, for example, women were less favoured than men as slaves. It was one of only two regions (the Bight of Biafra before the mid-eighteenth century being the other) where more women than men were sent into the Atlantic slave trade, signifying that male slaves were more desirable than female slaves in the local economy.

Warfare accompanied enslavement in the middle period of the African Atlantic age. In Benguela, for example, in western Angola, military campaigns between the 1680s and the 1720s provided the slaves that traders sent to Brazil. But these military campaigns were only sporadically successful, raiders meeting fierce resistance from individuals and communities that did not want to be enslaved. It meant that the numbers of slaves brought to the coast to be put on slave ships were insufficient to meet Brazilian demand. Nevertheless, slave traders persisted in pitting Africans against each other in interior communities to get enough captives to fuel the transatlantic slave trade. As well as warfare, there was kidnapping, which was an especial threat to ordinary Africans. Mariana Candido relates the story of Dona Leonor de Carvalho Fonseca, a free mulatto woman and widow of a Portuguese trader, who in 1811 was on a business trip in the Mbailundu state in the Benguela highlands who was ordered by the ruler of the state to be enslaved and who was sold and then transported to Luanda. She petitioned the Portuguese governor that she should not be enslaved as she was a mulatto and a vassal of the Portuguese Crown, as a widow of a Portuguese citizen. The governor agreed, and she was released. She was fortunate – for the Portuguese, unlike other European empires, recognized certain attributes, like skin colour and vassalage, as denoting freedom. As Candido argues, 'the same legal system that promoted violence against and the enslavement of some Africans offered a legal space for those seen as insiders … to regain their freedom'. But her ordeal, even though it turned out happily for her, shows how vulnerable free blacks were to mistreatment in the early nineteenth century.[20]

NINETEENTH-CENTURY TRANSFORMATIONS

Slavery did not end quickly in Africa. The number of slaves probably increased in the nineteenth century and only slowly declined in the twentieth century. Ironies abound. Sierra Leone was founded, for example, as a refuge for those freed from slavery by the British navy. But when slavery was abolished in the British Empire, it continued in Sierra Leone, which was considered a 'protectorate' rather than a colony. The legal status of slavery did not end until 1896, meaning that a slaveowner could no longer claim the return of a runaway, and slavery was not finally prohibited until 1928. Nevertheless, Sierra Leone saw some interesting developments as a place of great attention for abolitionists who were keen to try and use Sierra Leone as an experimental location for providing alternatives to slavery. The Sierra Leone Company was established in 1787 to try and solve the perceived problem of a free black population in Britain. It was reformed in 1791 to promote commercial agriculture using the labour of free blacks returned from Canada and the West Indies. It didn't work but other attempted economic alternatives were more successful, such as growing palm oil. This product eventually became central to the West African economy, being grown along the entire coastal forest area of West Africa, from Sierra Leone to Angola. Groundnuts were another crop that became a vital part of African international trade.

One consequence of this shift from slaves to palm oil as the principal trade of West Africa was that the region turned its transatlantic trade from the Americas to Europe. By the 1840s, this agricultural trade for the first time probably exceeded in size and profitability the Atlantic slave trade. It was meant to be a means whereby slavery was upended by a commodity trade produced by small farmers but in fact slavery became integral to palm oil production with most palm oil being grown by slaves on large plantations. And while African trade to the world increased in the nineteenth century, it did so at half the rate of total world trade, meaning that Africa became increasingly marginal in the world as the Atlantic period came to an end. Africa also entered from mid-century a period of dependency which was a new thing on the continent. European colonization of Africa began in earnest after 1850 and became intense during the Partition of Africa in the 1880s.[21] Thus, as the Atlantic period of African history came to an end, African agency over politics and economics within West Africa came to an end, steadily declining as European influence and political power increased. In many ways, the Atlantic period in African history may have marked the last time in which a few Africans could exercise control over their lives, though doing so when many of their compatriots were sacrificed to having their lives disrupted and controlled by Europeans and Americans through becoming enslaved in the New World.

NOTES

1 Hugh Trevor-Roper, 'The Rise of Christian Europe,' *The Listener* 70: 1809 (28 November 1963), 871–75.
2 David Eltis, 'Africa, Slavery, and the Slave Trade, Mid-Seventeenth to Mid-Eighteenth Centuries,' in Nicholas Canny and Philip Morgan, eds., *Oxford Handbook of Atlantic History* (Oxford: Oxford University Press), 271–72. See also Joseph E. Inikori, *Africans and the Industrial Revolution in England: A Study in International Trade and Economic Development* (Cambridge: Cambridge University Press, 2002) and G. Ugo Nwokeji, *The Slave Trade and Culture in the Bight of Biafra: An African Society in the Atlantic World* (Cambridge: Cambridge University Press, 2010).
3 Ray Kea, 'Africa in World History, 1400 to 1800,' in Jerry H. Bentley et al., eds., *The Cambridge World History* vol. VI, part 1 (Cambridge: Cambridge University Press, 2015), 244.
4 T.J. Desch-Obi, *Fighting for Honor: The History of African Martial Art Traditions in the Muslim World* (Columbia: University of South Carolina Press, 2008).

5   Philip D. Morgan, 'Africa and the Atlantic, *c.* 1450 to *c.* 1820,' in Jack P.
    Greene and Morgan, eds., *Atlantic History: A Critical Appraisal* (New York:
    Oxford University Press, 2009), 241.
6   James H. Sweet, *Recreating African Culture, Kinship, and Religion in the
    African-Portuguese World, 1441–1770* (Chapel Hill: University of North
    Carolina Press, 2005).
7   Ira Berlin, 'From Creole to African: Atlantic Creoles and the Origins of
    African-American Society in Mainland North America,' *William and Mary
    Quarterly* 3d ser. 53 (1996), 252–88.
8   Simon Newman, *A New World of Labour: The Development of Plantation
    Slavery in the British Atlantic* (Philadelphia: University of Pennsylvania Press,
    2013), 164–65.
9   Ibid., 176.
10 Sean Hawkins and Philip D. Morgan, 'Introduction,' in idem, eds., *Black
    Experience and the Empire* (Oxford: Oxford University press, 2004), 1.
11 John Thornton, *Africa and Africans in the Making of the Atlantic World,
    1400–1680* (New York: Cambridge University Press, 1992).
12 Paul E. Lovejoy, *Transformations in Slavery: A History of Slavery in Africa*, 3rd
    ed. (Cambridge: Cambridge University Press, 2011).
13 Walter Rodney, *A History of the Upper Guinea Coast, 1545–1800* (Oxford:
    Oxford University Press, 1970).
14 Ray A. Kea, *Settlements, Trade, and Politics in the Seventeenth-Century Gold
    Coast* (Baltimore: Johns Hopkins University Press, 1982).
15 Joseph E. Inikori, 'Transatlantic Slavery and Economic Development in
    the Atlantic World: West Africa, 1450–1850,' in David Eltis and Stanley L.
    Engerman, eds., *The Cambridge World History of Slavery* vol. 3 AD 1420–
    AD 1804 (Cambridge: Cambridge University Press, 2011), 667–72.
16 Thornton, *Africa and Africans in the Making of the Atlantic World*, 44, 125.
17 Philip D. Curtin, *Economic Change in Precolonial Africa: Senegambia in the
    Era of the Slave Trade* (Madison, WI: University of Wisconsin Press, 1975).
18 Igor Kopytoff and Suzanne Miers, 'Slavery as an Institution of Marginality,'
    in Miers and Kopytoff, eds., *Slavery in Africa: Historical and Anthropological
    Perspectives* (Madison, WI: University of Wisconsin Press, 1977), 3–81.
19 Sandra Greene, *Gender, Ethnicity, and Social Change on the Upper Slave Coast*
    (Portsmouth, NH: Heinemann, 1997).
20 Mariana Candido, 'African Freedom Suits and Portuguese Vassal Status: Legal
    Mechanisms for fighting enslavement in Benguela, Angola, 1800–1830,' *Slavery
    & Abolition* 32 (2011), 447–59.
21 Robin Law and Kristin Mann, 'West Africa in the Atlantic Community: The
    Case of the Slave Coast,' *William and Mary Quarterly* 56 (1999), 307–34.

BIBLIOGRAPHY

Oxford Online Bibliographies – Africa and the Atlantic World; African Ports;
    African Religion and Culture; Benguela; Bight of Biafra; Creolization; Europe
    and Africa; Portugal and Africa; Sierra Leone; Slavery in Africa; the Atlantic
    Slave Trade.

Ralph Austen, *Trans-Saharan Africa in World History* (Oxford: Oxford University Press, 2010).

Mariana Candido, *An African Slaving Port and the Atlantic World: Benguela and Its Hinterland* (New York: Cambridge University Press, 2013).

Walter Hawthorne, *Planting Rice and Harvesting Slaves: Transformations along the Guinea-Bissau Coast, 1400–1900* (Portsmouth, NH: Heinemann, 2003).

Linda Heywood and John Thornton, *Central Africans, Atlantic Creoles and the Foundations of the Americas, 1585–1660* (Cambridge: Cambridge University Press, 2007).

John Illiffe, *Africans: The History of a Continent* (Cambridge: Cambridge University Press, 2007).

Joseph Inikori, 'Africa and the Globalization Process: Western Africa, 1450–1850,' *Journal of Global History* 2 (2007), 63–86.

Robin Law, *The Slave Coast of West Africa, 1550–1750: The Impact of the Atlantic Slave Trade on African Society* (Oxford: Oxford University Press, 1991).

Paul E. Lovejoy, 'Islam, Slavery, and Political Transformations in West Africa: Constraints on the Trans-Atlantic Slave Trade,' *Revue d'Histoire Outre-Mer* 336–37 (2002), 247–82.

James C. McCann, *Maize and Grace: Africa's Encounter with a New World Crop* (Cambridge, MA: Harvard University Press, 2007).

David Northrup, *Trade without Rulers: Pre-Colonial Economic Development in South-Eastern Nigeria* (Oxford: Oxford University Press, 2008).

G. Ugo Nwokeji, *The Slave Trade and Culture in the Bight of Biafra: An African Society in the Atlantic World* (Cambridge: Cambridge University Press, 2010).

Olivier Pétré-Grenoulleau, *Les traits négrières d'histoire globale* (Paris: Gallimard, 2004).

Matteo Salvadore, 'The Ethiopian Age of Exploration: Prester John's Discovery of Europe, 1306–1458,' *Journal of World History* 21 (2011), 593–627.

1 *Philanthropic Consolations after the loss of the Slave Bill,* (1796). Courtesy of Alamy

2 Samuel Jennings, *Liberty displaying the Arts and Sciences* (1792). Courtesy of Alamy

3 Dominic Serries, *The Capture of Havana* (1762). Courtesy of Alamy

4 John Singleton Copley, *The Copley Family* (1771). Courtesy of Alamy

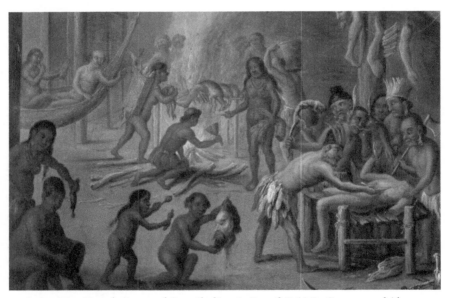

5 Jan Van Kessel, *Scene of Cannibalism in Brazil* (1644). Courtesy of Alamy

6 Louis Freret, *Arrivée des Européens en Afrique* (1795). Courtesy of the John Carter Brown Library at Brown University.

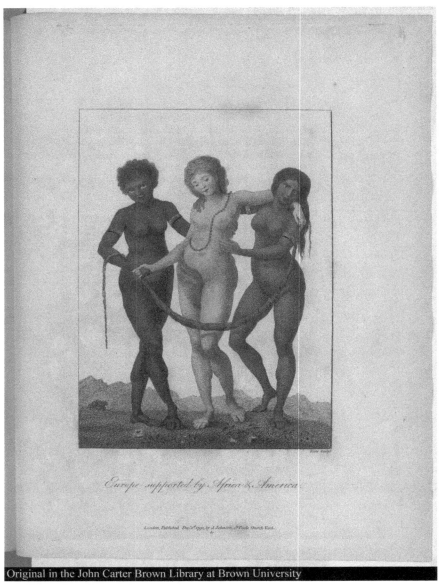

Europe supported by Africa & America

London. Published Dec.1.1792, by J. Johnson, St Paul's Church Yard.

7 William Blake in John Gabriel Stedman, *Narrative of a Five Years' expedition against the Revolted Negroes of Surinam* (London, 1792), 'Europe supported by Africa and America'. Courtesy of the John Carter Brown Library at Brown University.

8 Jean Baptiste du Tertre, *Sucrerie* (1667) in *Histoire generale des Antilles habitées par les François* … (Paris, 1667). Courtesy of the John Carter Brown Library at Brown University.

9 Agostino Brunias, *A Negroes Dance in the Island of Dominica* (1779). Courtesy of the John Carter Brown Library at Brown University.

10   Henry T. De La Beche, *Jamaican Negroes Cutting Canes in their Working Dresses* (1825) in *Notes on the Present Condition of the Negroes of Jamaica* (London, 1825). Courtesy of the John Carter Brown Library at Brown University.

11 John Mawe, *Negroes Washing for Diamonds, Gold* (1823) in Mawe, *Travels in the Interior of Brazil* ... (London, 1823). Courtesy of the John Carter Brown Library at Brown University.

12 Theodore de Bry, 'Native Americans are Burned at the Stake' (*c.* 1590; 1707).
Courtesy of the John Carter Brown Library at Brown University.

13 *The Buildings of Maran Estate in the Island of Grenada, the Property of Thomas Duncan, esq.* (1822). Courtesy of the John Carter Brown Library at Brown University.

14 'Pirates terrorize Hispaniola', in A.O. Exquemelin, *De Americaensche Zee-Rovers* (Amsterdam, 1678). Courtesy of the John Carter Brown Library at Brown University.

15   Henry Koster, *A Sugar Mill (Brazil)* in Koster, *Travels in Brazil* (1816). Courtesy of the John Carter Brown Library at Brown University.

16 *Een plantaadje Slaven kamp, Surinam* (1860–1862). Courtesy of the John Carter
Brown Library at Brown University.

17   Richard Phillips, *Two Female Domestics of Lima, Native, Who Have Adopted the Spanish Dress* (1805). Courtesy of the John Carter Brown Library at Brown University.

MEXICAN GENTLEMEN.

18 *Mexican Gentlemen* (1826). Courtesy of the John Carter Brown Library at Brown University.

19 *The Manner of propagating, gathering and curing cochineal in the Bishopric of Guaxaca in the kingdom of Mexico in America* in Hans Sloane, *Voyage to the Islands, Madera, etc* (London, 1707). Courtesy of the John Carter Brown Library at Brown University.

9

WESTERN EUROPE

FROM MEDITERRANEAN TO ATLANTIC

As is possible when writing the history of Africa, it is perfectly easy to write the history of Europe with little reference to the Atlantic Ocean. Indeed, it is frequently done. The great European themes of Renaissance, Reformation, General Seventeenth Century Crisis and Enlightenment can be outlined as if they were entirely internal European matters. Instead of the Atlantic Ocean, the Mediterranean can be the focus of attention and the centre of action. Seeing Europe from the vantage point of the Mediterranean – traditionally one of the crossroads of world history since antiquity – makes perfect sense. Its greatest historian, Fernand Braudel, insisted that the Mediterranean was not just the centre of European history but had a fundamental unity that transcended political and cultural boundaries. Studying that unity is an essential entry point into European history.

The rise of the Atlantic in European consciousness after 1492 challenged the primacy of the Mediterranean as the shaper of European history. The traditional view is that Columbus's discoveries and Vasco da Gama's nearly simultaneous voyages around Africa to India were a symbolic turning point in European history. The Mediterranean world faced a twin challenge around 1500 of Ottoman advances against it from the East and European discoveries of a New World in the West. The dual challenges to the normal European order suggested that the cradle of European civilization was being increasingly irrelevant as northwestern powers previously marginal within European history, at least when compared to Italy and the Holy Roman Empire, were coming to dominate the world, with the new routes they forged across the Atlantic eclipsing the significance of cultural and trade patterns in the old sea.

Of course, such a statement is overblown. It was not until the growth of the Russian empire in the late eighteenth century and Napoleon's incursions into Italy, causing the collapse of the 1,000-year Venetian Republic in 1797, that the status of the Mediterranean relative to the Atlantic was truly challenged. If there was a crisis in the Mediterranean – then it took an interminably long time to come to a head. The traditional interpretation is that European expansion across the Atlantic and Indian Oceans turned the Mediterranean from the centre of the European economy into being on the periphery. Such a view is nowadays thought to be too Eurocentric. Instead of seeing the shift in the early modern period as one of one-way westerly displacement, we should note how the rise of the Atlantic after 1492 combined with the vitality of the Mediterranean and with Ottoman expansion in the sixteenth century to highlight the growing interconnectedness of the globe in the sixteenth and seventeenth centuries.

What the opening of the Atlantic to European exploitation did do, however, was allow for new opportunities to be made for interactions with distant regions on an unprecedented scale. Genoa, for example, not only gave Columbus to Iberia but financed Spain's expeditions to the New World and participated in its profits. Indeed, Europe's move to the Atlantic probably also intensified its relations with an expanding Ottoman Empire. That empire was largely self-sufficient in raw materials and foodstuffs but was very interested in American precious minerals. The late sixteenth century also saw an intensification of trade between the Mediterranean and northern Europe. Rather than seeing the Mediterranean as being provincialized, the rise of the Atlantic turned the Mediterranean and Europe in general into more globally connected places. Between 1400 and 1800, Europe experienced a new global economic and cultural framework which people from many places came into regular contact with each other. As Filippo de Vivo argues, 'the export of manufactured goods from the Old to the New World shaped consumer habits in the Americas just as the ability to turn exotic luxuries into products for mass consumption lay at the heart of a consumer revolution in the Mediterranean'.[1]

WHY EUROPEANS WENT INTO THE ATLANTIC WORLD

By 1800, if one looked at a map of the world, the greatest share of overseas empires belonged to what John Elliott calls the three 'conquest societies' of late medieval or sixteenth-century Europe: Portugal, Spain and England.[2] Portugal and Spain had been shaped in the early modern period by their long medieval war with Islam which had turned each Iberian kingdom into militant, crusading states, with an ideology shaped indubitably by ideas that they were fighting a holy war, first on the peninsula and then globally. Their incursions into the New World were a rational extension of their Reconquista histories. England, too, was an aggressively expansionist country, even if under the early Tudors, especially during the disastrous reign of Henry VIII (1491–1547), they had contracted rather than expanded their territorial ambitions. By the sixteenth century, England's long involvement in and aggression towards the French Crown had ended in dismal failure. But within the British Isles, it continued to be a colonizing power. It had established its title to Ireland early on, as part of the Normal offensive of the twelfth and thirteenth centuries, and had long ago conquered Wales, which was consolidated firmly into the English empire by the accession of the Welsh Henry VII (1457–1509).

It was only in the mid-eighteenth century, as overseas expansion by the Europeans was beginning to have world historical significance, that European intellectuals started to theorize about why Europeans wanted Atlantic empires. The most important theorist was the Scottish philosopher and political economist Adam Smith (1723–1790). He noted that 'the establishment of the European colonies in America and the West Indies arose from no necessity'. His bald statement was a salvo in an eighteenth-century debate about the utility of empire. Smith moved on from critics of European involvement in the Americas like Abbé Raynal to question whether empire itself was economically worthwhile: perhaps, he suggested, Europeans would have been materially better off if they had resisted the siren lure of overseas conquest and stuck to developing commerce within their own countries. That debate, of course, about the purpose of European or American empire when there are problems at home continues to the present day. The example of an empire that withdrew from the world was China, which decided in the mid-fifteenth century that maritime expansion was not a good geo-political strategy.

Smith also made an explicit contrast between 'projects of commerce' (which he falsely thought were characteristic of British overseas involvement) and 'projects of conquest' (which he rightly attributed to Iberian colonization efforts). We often tend to elide the differences between these two differing reasons for overseas activity by Europeans, combining both together into a single process called 'imperialism' which are better kept separate, as we will see when looking at the Dutch involvement in the Atlantic World. What Smith was also arguing for was that at least until when he himself was writing, in the early 1770s, Europe did not need to move to the New World to avert a Malthusian crisis of overpopulation intruding upon inadequate resources. Europeans went to the Americas collectively, if not individually, by choice. As Elliott argues, 'the seizure of territories resulted from a complicated variety of motives, springing partly from aspirations and predispositions that had developed in Europe, and especially Mediterranean Europe, during the Middle Ages, and partly from local circumstances in the overseas territories themselves'.[3]

Spain and Portugal also embarked on Atlantic invasions because they were part of a competitive European state system, where windfalls such as New World silver had immediate repercussions on the European balance of power, as least as European monarchs saw it. If one country gained an advantage, the idea was that this meant that other countries had somehow lost something. Ferdinand (1452–1516) and Isabella (1451–1504) themselves sponsored Columbus to respond to the overseas success in Africa of the Portuguese monarch, Manuel I (1469–1521). Portugal responded to Spain's success by solidifying its hold on Brazil. Portuguese and Spanish involvement in the Americas in turn led to Francis I of France (1494–1547) refusing to accept the papal decision to divide the Atlantic World between Spain and Portugal, his actions informed by a highly territorial consciousness. England also responded, although belatedly, in the second half of the sixteenth century to what it saw as danger to its position in Europe if it had no Atlantic presence and little Atlantic trade, starting a long involvement with Atlantic settlement with an abortive expedition to North Carolina in 1587. England was a more determined imperialist than France and more successful in its efforts than the richest country in Europe in establishing an overseas empire by the seventeenth century. That success was probably due to it being a 'conquest society' as it had models to draw on for how to conduct itself in the Americas from its lengthy and violent repression of Irish Catholics in Ireland from the twelfth to the late sixteenth century.

English colonization in the New World, despite its late start, was especially purposeful. Colonization and settlement were never secondary aims, as they were for the Spanish, but were primary ambitions. When they settled in Jamestown in 1607, they established a base from which it was hard to dislodge them and that allowed them to eventually expand their territory into the new colony of Virginia. In short, the English did not leave ravaged landscapes once they had plundered them, as the Spanish did but stayed and set to work to transform landscapes into as close as approximations of the English landscape as they could manage. The English developed quickly an ideological justification for colonization that led to successful implantation of colonists in land that they believed looked like the English countryside, even when in tropical regions. The principal feature of their colonizing ideology was 'improvement', a seventeenth-century doctrine that conferred ownership of land onto people who turned that land into something resembling the agricultural landscape of England, with towns established to confirm the presence of 'civilization' in the New World. English colonization proceeded therefore in tandem with the simultaneous capitalist transformation of the English countryside by 'improving' landlords who acquired for themselves land that had previously been common property used by everyone and converted land to profit-bearing units that could be bought, sold or used as individual capitalist farmers desired.

As has been repeatedly emphasized in this book, European dreams of acquiring Atlantic land and converting them into European possessions were always contested, often successfully by Native Americans. Europeans did not even try to colonize West Africa, wisely, given that until the nineteenth century their chances of success in colonization efforts without African assistance (which they seldom received) were minimal. Why did Europeans succeed as well as they did in the Americas? Disease was their most important weapon, as noted in Chapter 3. But they also had some technological advantages over Native Americans that facilitated conquest. The development of the gun-carrying sailing ship was important. The Spanish were able to destroy the Inca Empire of Atahualpa (1502–1533) by bringing in men and supplies over an ocean the Inca had thought impassable. Guns were useful also on land, especially when combined with the use of horses. Cavalry was a major weapon that the Spanish had, and which Native Americans initially did not. Warfare on horses provided the Europeans with the capacity to change tactics with speed and to extend the range of warfare quickly and effectively.

But conquest was not the only option available to Europeans determined to make money from Atlantic endeavours. The most successful European state in the seventeenth century was the Netherlands and their Atlantic activities, at least after they lost Brazil in 1654 and New Netherlands in 1660 (turned into New York by the English), worked on a quite different model than that which pertained to the Iberian empires and to England. Indeed, the distinctiveness of Dutch Atlantic involvement has led historians, like Benjamin Schmidt and Pieter Emmer, to claim, surely wrongly, that by the early eighteenth century that there was no such thing as a Dutch Atlantic, their argument being that the Dutch engaged with the Atlantic in a supranational and global way with considerably less emphasis than in other empires on colonization and settlement.[4] The Dutch involvement in the Atlantic was distinctive, however, in being more about commerce than conquest. They mainly operated in both the Atlantic and Asia through state-sponsored trading corporations through which they inserted themselves into existing trading relationships and considered profit rather than colonization the main game. Of course, commerce was not easily separated from conquest, or at least separated from warfare. As Jan Pieterszoon argued in 1614, 'trade cannot be maintained without war, nor war without trade'.

Sir John Elliott's summary of what drove Europeans overseas is worth quoting in full, as it neatly shows how European movement overseas was indeed conducted not out of necessity, as Smith rightly argued but purposively. Europeans eagerly wanted to advance their interests in the wider world, whatever the damage to the people they encountered along the way. One famous interpretation of European imperialism in the nineteenth century was that is arose almost by accident. Europeans did not want colonies, in this reading, at least colonies that were not settler colonies, but had to acquire territory and assert political control over that territory because they were forced to intervene in the affairs of other peoples when European trade overseas was disturbed by local politics.[5] The early modern empires of early modern Europe in the Atlantic did not arise in this accidental way. The movement of Europeans overseas was deliberate and the colonies they acquired were not gained in a haphazard way but as parts of general European patterns. As Elliott argues, European imperialists in the early modern period were themselves 'implicit in the very preconditions that sent them overseas'.

He concludes: 'Consumed by the lust for profits, driven forward by a strong territorial imperative which made concepts of empire and sovereignty as natural to them in their dealings with non-Europeans as in their dealings with neo-Europeans as in their dealings with themselves; and arrogant, and increasingly self-confident, in their attitude to the non-Christian peoples of the world, they would prove incapable of observing or preserving a distinction between the pursuit of trading relationships and the exercise of power.' He makes a final, essentially moral, observation: 'If, in consequence, they were sucked into a quagmire, they went into it with their eyes half open and they made it for themselves.'[6]

THE SEVENTEENTH-CENTURY CRISIS

Some accounts of the rise of Western Europe from relative poverty at the start of Atlantic history in the mid-fifteenth century to undisputed economic global dominance after the 'Great Divergence' had been completed by the early nineteenth century see the process as smooth and uninterrupted. Yet Europe faced significant issues during the over 300 years from Columbus to the 'Great Divergence', a term coined by the historian of China and the world Kenneth Pomeranz to describe when the West became for the first time in history richer and more geo-politically important than the East. Jack Goldstone argues that the sixteenth century was generally a period of relatively good times for Europe, following a fifteenth century which saw violent disorder all around the world. A warm interval interrupted the 'Little Ice Age' of the fourteenth and fifteenth centuries and the Columbian exchange brought new crops to Europe which expanded nourishment. Goldstone's analysis is possibly true for Asia and Europe, as the growth of centralized administrations that provided security to merchants allowed trade to flourish more than at any other time in recorded history, but it is rooted in economic rather than cultural explanations, ignoring, for example, the tumult of the Reformation which led to Christendom tearing itself into two warring religious camps of Protestants and Catholics. It is also Eurocentric: the fifteenth century, as Chapter 3 outlines, saw the greatest tragedy in human history, the demographic disaster that befall Native Americans following European contact.[7]

It does seem clear, however, that whatever one's view of the sixteenth century as a period of relative prosperity or disaster, the seventeenth century was a more challenging time for most parts of Europe. It seemed that the four horsemen of the apocalypse were riding all at once through the continent. The years around mid-century saw a peak in warfare, disorder, death and famine. It confirmed for many Europeans that disaster was the natural human condition. In 1651, the English political thinker Thomas Hobbes wrote his masterpiece, *Leviathan*, a brilliant and enduringly influential treatise on the need for people to obey duly constituted authority for their own protection. Writing in the aftermath of the English Civil War and the calamitous Thirty Years' War, in which perhaps 35–40 per cent of the population of the Holy Roman Empire perished from death or disease, he claimed that 'There is [now] no place for industry ... no arts; no letters; no society. And, which is worst of all, continual fear and danger of violent death; and the life of man, solitary, poor, nasty, brutish, and short'. The Welsh historian James Howell echoed Hobbes in a lament two years previously, just after the English had executed their king in an action which shocked Europeans everywhere as being contrary to natural and religious laws, that 'God Almighty has a quarrel lately with all mankind, and has given the reins to the ill spirit to compass the whole earth'.

In 1954, Eric Hobsbawm, who thereafter turned to the study of nineteenth- and twentieth-century Europe, used explicitly Marxist theories of history, notably the use of the dialectic, to suggest that the various bad things that happened in Europe in the seventeenth century were not accidental but were part of a pattern which he termed the 'General Crisis of the Seventeenth Century'. The Oxford historian Hugh Trevor-Roper challenged Hobsbawm's mainly social and economic approach by arguing that the crisis was more one concerning the standing of political elites than an economic calamity, providing a non-Marxist explanation of the crisis, while agreeing that there was such a thing as a General Crisis in the mid-seventeenth century, as Hobsbawm had suggested. Amazingly, the idea of a 'General Crisis' still survives as an historiographical issue of debate nearly seventy years after Hobsbawm initiated the debate. In one way, the debate has circulated back to its origins. Hobsbawm linked the solving of the crisis in Europe to precocious colonization. He argued that '*the* major achievement of the seventeenth-century crisis is the creation of a new form of colonisation', namely the plantation economies of Atlantic America, which gave Europe 'several precious decades of dizzy economic expansion from which they drew inestimable benefits'. Recently, there has been a return in the debate to emphasizing the importance of colonial adventuring across the Atlantic and in Asia to solving the crisis. Kenneth Pomeranz, for example, argues that colonialism 'did more to differentiate western Europe from other Old-World cores than any of the supposed advantages over these other regions generated by the operation of markets, family systems, or other institutions within Europe'. Europe had overseas colonies; China did not. Possibly Europe's global aggressiveness allowed it an easier route out of the crisis than was possible in either China or the Ottoman Empire.[8]

The seventeenth-century General Crisis in Europe was real. Between about 1640 and 1680 a fundamental reorientation took place in Europe that was more transformative than anything Europe had seen since the early Reformation or was to see again until the French Revolution. The most broadly accepted characterization of the crisis is that a long era of economic expansion, starting from the end of the Black Death in the fourteenth century, ended and gave way to either economic depression or economic stagnation. Economic problems were accompanied by demographic decline. The population of Spain, mostly in Castile, declined by 14 per cent between 1600 and 1650 and that of Italy by a little more. Population decline in Europe overall was around 5 per cent, with the only exceptions to decline being in England and the Netherlands. Nevertheless, England's population also started to decline, by about 5 per cent, in the fifty years after 1660. It appears that the main reason for such population decline in Europe was a significant rise in mortality rates, possibly meaning that there was a Malthusian process of population having to readjust to declining agricultural resources. The crisis was accentuated by what Geoffrey Parker has posited as 'the Little Ice Age', a period of colder temperatures in which harvests regularly failed. The reason for colder temperatures was not man-made but was due to sunspot frequencies, volcanic eruptions and resulting volcanic ash, and perhaps a long-lasting El Niño effect. Parker insists that 'no convincing account of the General Crisis can now ignore the impact of the unique climactic conditions that prevailed' in this dire century.[9]

We can see the effects of crisis most clearly in Spain, but also in France. Spain's trade with the New World was in decline by 1621 and it compounded its problems through constant and expensive warfare. The current explanation for this decline is that a more self-sufficient New World economy, one more resistant to Spanish fiscal exactions, led to trade volumes of 30,000 tons of shipping capacity in the 1610s dropping to 13,000 tons in the 1640s, with the money thus going to the state in customs duties taking a very big hit. Population decline and less New World trade combined with rising fiscal pressure to undermine agricultural production and thus to economic depression. Germany was very much worse off than Spain, as its connections to the Atlantic economy were very slight and given the devastation of biblical proportions that had occurred in the area during the Thirty Years' War. Politics exacerbated economic problems, even as economic issues encouraged costly and ideologically and religiously charged warfare. People blamed the Devil for their woes. Germany and Scotland experienced huge increases in witchcraft prosecutions. In the fraught drought and war-ridden famine years of 1649–1650 more witches were executed in Scotland for sorcery than at other time.

France suffered less than Spain, but it too experienced a sharp crisis of productivity in its agricultural sector between 1625 and 1650. Social unrest also increased markedly. Popular revolts in Aquitaine and Provence, for example, increased from 155 events between 1590 and 1634 to 438 between 1635 and 1660 (or from 3.4 events per annum to 12.6). Because France was the richest and most populous country in Europe, its difficulties had a disproportionate impact. The General Crisis may have encouraged it to adopt policies of protectionism known as mercantilism, policies it continued essentially unchanged until the French Revolution. In France, and in Europe in general, the Crisis saw agricultural stagnation, the collapse of urban industry and the dislocation of financial institutions.

THE DUTCH MOMENT

The one area of Europe that seems to have benefited from economic shifts elsewhere was the Netherlands. That shift was decisive, moving the centre of European financial life from the Mediterranean to the North Atlantic, with Amsterdam becoming the leading money centre of Europe until displaced by London around 1750. Population changes heralded the change. In the first half of the seventeenth century, the population of northwest Europe rose from one-half to three-quarters of the Mediterranean population. It is significant that this is the period in which the Atlantic loomed large as an area of expansion for northwestern Europe. And the increase in size and wealth of northwestern cities like London and Amsterdam resulted in population increases that outstripped such population increase in general, meaning that for the first time Atlantic cities came to approximate or exceed Mediterranean cities in population and in scale.

The economists Acemoglu, Johnson and Robinson argue that the General Crisis fostered a newly vigorous capitalist economy focused on the Atlantic. They argue that the rise of Atlantic trade strengthened merchant communities in European Atlantic ports, that urban centres became more able to bargain with territorial states to devise their own institutional needs, and that what resulted were states with effective constitutional constraints on state power. This led, they believe, to the creation of governments favourable towards economic growth.[10] As Jan de Vries explains, 'their model supposes that the Atlantic trades, by themselves, were sufficiently large to account for the long term economic growth of Europe but that the opportunities of these trades, acting as a lever, forced the development of political institutions in a few states, which then enjoyed the concentrated benefits of intercontinental trade plus the generalized benefits of efficient economic institutions'.[11] Their model is disputed but their argument does provide a compelling case for the Atlantic economy to be considered the driving force for accumulated political and economic change in northwestern Europe. Britain was the biggest beneficiary of the new Atlantic economy after 1660 with 37 per cent of its merchant fleet involved in Atlantic trade as early as 1683, a percentage that kept on increasing during the eighteenth century.

Jacob Soll has shown that Atlantic trade was facilitated by advances in finance developed in early seventeenth-century Amsterdam. Dutch

merchants' knowledge of finance became increasingly sophisticated as their
merchant empire expanded to include luxury goods from the Americas and
Asia. Moreover, it has functioning information exchange that allowed for
the assessment of the world's merchandise and how to sell and dispose of
it. The Dutch were great accountants and the foremost practitioners of
gathering and dispersing commercial information. Jan de Vries and Ad
van der Woude place what might be called the 'Dutch miracle' in a wider
European context. They argue that the General Crisis led in the Netherlands
to a permanent change in the rules of European economic life. Crisis led to
disruption and then to productive economic change which eventually gave
northwestern Europe its edge over its rivals in the Atlantic World in the
eighteenth century with market-driven labour and a facilitative state with
strong fiscal resources. They argue that the seventeenth century allowed
'labour, but also foodstuffs, raw materials and capital' to be 'liberated'
from local economies to be used in 'large-scale regional and international
economies'. In short, crisis allowed the very structure of European society
to be altered so that an Atlantic economy could be formed. The Netherlands
thus became the first modern economy. The Dutch did not industrialize in
the seventeenth century, but they did develop new production processes,
increased productivity rates, invested heavily in human capital and
encouraged innovation. All these advances led to strong economic growth
in a period of general economic stagnation.[12]

The mid-seventeenth century was the European moment of political
economy, led by the Dutch. The best students of the Dutch were the English.
Samuel Pepys (1633–1701), the diarist and naval administrator, adopted
Dutch methods to help England fight the Dutch army in the Anglo-Dutch
Wars of the 1660s. William Petty (1623–1687), an Anglo-Irish founder of
English political economy and an accomplished mathematician, copied and
expanded on Dutch examples to devise measures of national income and
taxation. His main contribution was to invent the practice of cost accounting
which involved setting a budget and determining the cost of operations
and landholdings to project future management. Along with the financial
innovations that were initiated in England in the aftermath of the Glorious
Revolution of 1689, this ability to accurately predict future earnings of any
economic project greatly aided England's and Europe's ability to exploit
Atlantic resources ever more effectively.

Jonathan Israel has looked at the Dutch experience of the early
Enlightenment in the late seventeenth century and argues that the General
Crisis in that century was a key turning point in history. It was more
transformative, he argues, than the Renaissance and Reformation, which
were 'really only adjustments and modifications to what was essentially still
a theologically conceived and ordered regional society, based on hierarchy
and ecclesiastical authority, not universality and equality'. His argument
is provocative, teleological insofar as it presumes a direct link between
what happened in the Netherlands under the intellectual direction of

Baruch Spinoza, a leading philosopher of rationalism who made significant contributions to new understandings of the self. Israel argues that these new understandings of the 'self' led to a radical and rational Enlightenment. His critics argue that he is presumptuous in seeing a direct link between the late seventeenth century early Enlightenment and the birth of global modernity. But his argument does provide a useful way of conceptualizing how Europe used the crisis of the seventeenth century to develop new conceptions of the self, a more equal politics, less deferential social interactions, and even a challenge to the unchanging nature of patriarchal and monarchical power. It is the seventeenth century, it seems, that provides the necessary link between European encounters in the early Atlantic World and to what used to be called the 'rise of the West' and which we would now discuss under the terms of the 'Great Divergence'.

SCOTLAND IN THE ATLANTIC

Some parts of Western Europe benefited disproportionately from their involvement in the Atlantic World. In France, for example, the Atlantic port towns of Nantes, Bordeaux and La Rochelle flourished because of their involvement in Atlantic trade. So too the English towns of Bristol and Liverpool during the eighteenth century oriented themselves firmly, to their advantage, to Atlantic commerce. The growth of cotton manufacturing in the late eighteenth and early nineteenth centuries connected the new town of Manchester to the slave cotton-producing regions of the American South in a lasting transatlantic relationship. London, as the capital and commercial hub of England, used its political and commercial strength to create a coherent Atlantic system in the late seventeenth century which gave it a prominent role in promoting overseas expansion and in designing a regulatory framework designed to reward its powerful merchant class so that it benefited more than any other place in Europe from burgeoning Atlantic trade in the eighteenth century.

But if we are to examine a nation that tied itself in especially successfully to the Atlantic World, then Scotland is an ideal case study. The contrast in its fortunes before and after it became involved with the Atlantic World (roughly before and after 1720) is remarkable. Scotland went from being among the poorest regions in Europe to becoming a booming industrial region of Britain, with many of the major inventors of the Industrial Revolution hailing from its excellent practical educational system. In the sixteenth and seventeenth centuries, however, Scotland was a poor country. The northern region of the nation – the Highlands – was especially benighted, being considered by contemporaries as notably backward and uncivilized. Sixteenth-century visitors to the Americas, such as John White who sketched Native Americans of North Carolina in 1587 and who also included some representations of ancient Picts in warlike pose, made explicit comparisons between 'barbaric' Native American savages and Scottish Highlanders, usually to the disadvantage of the latter.

During the seventeenth century, despite its royal house becoming also the royal house of England and Wales in 1603, Scotland was distinguished by its poverty, religious extremism (it was strongly Calvinist) and its sufferings. It fared badly in the War of the Three Kingdoms that raged in the British Isles in the 1640s, losing large numbers of its inhabitants in warfare, experiencing massive religious dissent and floundering economically. It hardly involved itself in any Atlantic endeavours. Perhaps no more than 200 Scots settled in the English colonies before 1640, with a few people going to New France and New Netherlands. Scotland preferred to do business with northern and central Europe, where it had long links. Moreover, when people migrated they tended to go to Ulster – 16,000 Scots had moved there by the 1630s, greatly complicating the ethnic and religious mix in that English plantation colony.

Scotland was a prime example of a country affected badly by the General Crisis of the seventeenth century. It is an excellent example of the role of climate in producing catastrophe. Civil War broke out in 1637, the driest year in two decades, when food became very scarce. A decade of cold, wet summers, ruining one summer after another, explains why the Scots were so keen in the 1640s to invade England to steal their resources. Scotland feared starvation; so, it opted for revolution.

Atlantic activity picked up after 1660 but it was still rather limited and was undertaken by private interests rather than under the aegis of the state. Nevertheless, increased commercial activity led to one of the greatest disasters in Scottish history, the ill-fated expedition to Darien, in the Panama Isthmus in Central America in 1692. The key promoter of the plan, William Paterson (1658–1719), was a founder of the Bank of England, a good financier and a skilled political operator. He persuaded the Scottish state to invest a large proportion of its wealth into the ambitious scheme, which was intended to take advantage of Spanish imperial weakness to intrude Scotland into the lucrative Spanish American trading network. Paterson was very familiar with the Caribbean and Central America. The plan to establish a Scottish trading post at Darien came out of previous Scottish attempts at colonization made in the 1680s in South Carolina and East New Jersey. As Douglas Watt argues, the scheme failed due to managerial incompetence, Spanish hostility and English indifference, while the unfortunate Scottish migrants who went to Darien nearly all died from disease.[13] The result was a national humiliation, making the country close to bankrupt. Combined with dearth and famine in the 1690s due to bad harvests, Darien helped force Scotland to enter a political union joining itself with England and Wales to form Great Britain.

Becoming part of Great Britain eventually proved highly beneficial to Scotland. That was not initially the case, however. Scotland was a troublesome part of Britain in the first half of the eighteenth century, with the Highlands under the leadership of powerful clan leaders being openly rebellious and conspicuously poor. It was a centre of Jacobite opposition to the Hanoverian kings of Britain, supporting the Catholic son and grandson of James VII and II (1633–1701) as the rightful heir to the British monarchy. In 1716 and 1745, the Highlands rose up in rebellion. In 1745–1746, the rebellion was ruthlessly put down by the royal brother of the king, the Duke of Cumberland (1721–1765), after a massacre at the Battle of Culloden.

Yet in the next hundred years, Scotland became a different country, turning from internal rebellion to being an enthusiastic partner in empire, including the Atlantic World. As Andrew Thompson notes, 'Of all the peoples of the United Kingdom, it is the Scots' contribution to the British Empire that stands out as disproportionate. They were the first peoples of the British Isles to take on an imperial mentality, and possibly the longest to sustain one. In the spheres of education, engineering, exploration, medicine, commerce, and shipping the Scots earned a particularly strong reputation for empire building.'[14] Thompson includes here Scottish empire building in Asia but until the nineteenth century it was the Atlantic which occupied most of the Scottish intention when they contemplated the wider world.

There were two areas where Scots were especially involved in the Atlantic World: commerce and the military. During the eighteenth century, traders in Glasgow became prominent in the tobacco trade with the Chesapeake. Tobacco made up 40 per cent of Scotland's total imports and exports in 1773, most of which was re-exported to the European continent. The period of most impressive growth in the tobacco trade was in the second quarter of the eighteenth century, when tobacco imports increased ninefold, to 45 million lbs per annum.

The Scots were also involved in sugar importation and the slave trade, becoming heavily involved after 1750 in the British Caribbean. The Jamaican historian Edward Long believed that Jamaica was 'greatly indebted to North Britain, as very nearly one third of the inhabitants are either natives of that country or descendants from those who were'. Long overestimated in his 1774 History of Jamaica how many Scots there were in Jamaica. In the early nineteenth century, Scots made between 30 and 40 per cent of white inhabitants in Jamaica and the new sugar frontier of British Guiana. They were often among the wealthiest people in these colonies. Sir John Gladstone, the father of the British statesman William Gladstone, was a prime example of Scottish merchant success as a planter. He used profits from Baltic trading to invest heavily in sugar plantations in Demerara, where he owned well over 1,000 slaves and made a large fortune which after the emancipation of slaves in the British Empire in 1834 he used to continue his plantation profits by sponsoring indentured labour to come to British Guiana from India. T.M. Device argues that 'the Caribbean connection, therefore, can be regarded as a factor in Scotland's "great leap forward" of the eighteenth century. The islands provided markets for the country's booming textile manufacture, and the sojourners who returned home with their profits put much of their capital into Scottish industry and landownership'.[15]

Scots were traders, doctors and, in the height of the Scottish Enlightenment, the principal intellectuals of the Atlantic World. Among the luminaries were David Hume, William Robertson and Adam Smith. They were also soldiers. In one of the numerous ironies that punctuate the history of the Atlantic World, the Highlanders who were the firm opponents of Britain in 1745 became principal supporters of the British army soon after that conflict had ended. They were recruited in very large numbers to serve as soldiers in British North America in the Seven Years' War, the American Revolution and the French Revolutionary and Napoleonic Wars. The death of clanship made the Highlands more militarized in the second half of the eighteenth century than before 1745. In the 1790s, between 37,000 and 48,000 Highlanders from a population of between 250,000 and 300,000 people were in military uniform. Scottish soldiers were mostly ordinary recruits but among their ranks were some high-ranking officers. An extreme example was John Campbell, Earl of Loudoun, who, despite few obvious signs of military genius, rose to become Commander-in-chief of the British forces in North America during the Seven Years' War, until relieved from command when his mediocrity became painfully clear.

The raising of these Highland regiments marked a period of profound change in Highland history which shows how involvement in the Atlantic World could, on occasion, be of great benefit to certain regions and European peoples. Involvement in the Atlantic compensated ordinary Highlanders for adverse social changes which were making life increasingly hard for them in Scotland. Traditional clan society was swept away after 1745 and was replaced by landlordism, increased rents, indebtedness and clearance, all justified by that catch-all eighteenth-century term, 'improvement'. As Matthew Dziennik states, 'a long history of government centralization, integration, state-backed patronage, and social change in the Highlands, dating back at least as far as the reign of James VI and I, was significantly strengthened by the moment of imperial commitment after 1756'.[16]

Highlanders had their own reasons for wanting to be soldiers in North America. They were promised free land once their term of service was complete. And many Highlanders got such free land, taken off the Native Americans they had fought against in colonial wars. Soldiers were happy with the deal. They were so enthusiastic about colonial opportunities given to them in places like New York they inspired over 10,000 of their country people to leave for North America in the late 1760s and early 1770s. Dziennik argues that Scottish Gaels after 1745 came to have a genuine belief in the moral and political necessity of imperialism. They also identified with its exploitative aspects, not seeing any commonality between themselves and Native Americans, no matter what previous generations of intellectuals had thought. Geoffrey Plank notes that 'Highlanders wold assert themselves and alter their reputation ... after large numbers of Gaelic speakers began moving into distant, contested zones in North America during the Seven Years' War'.[17]

The state's need for soldiers defined the place of the Highlands within late eighteenth-century Britain. It offered rural Highlanders money they had never had before. Indeed, Highland recruitment of soldiers served as 'the primary vehicle of regional responses to the emergence of the British state as the dominant authority in the Gaelic world'.[18] Once again, as is a theme in this book, the state was a big winner in the reshaping of the Highland world modified by Atlantic influences after 1745.

NOTES

1   Filippo de Vivo, 'Crossroads Region: The Mediterranean,' in Jerry H. Bentley et al., eds., *The Cambridge World History* vol. 6, part 1, *The Construction of a Global World, 1400–1800 CE* (Cambridge: Cambridge University Press, 2015), 431.

2   J.H. Elliott, *Spain, Europe and the Wider World, 1500–1800* (New Haven: Yale University Press, 2009), ch. 6. This section is very indebted to Elliott's interpretation of European empire in the New World.

3   Ibid., 112.

4   Benjamin Schmidt, 'The Dutch Atlantic: From Provincialism to Globalism,' in Jack P. Greene and Philip D. Morgan, eds., *Atlantic History: A Critical Appraisal* (New York: Oxford University Press, 2009), 180; Pieter Emmer and Wim Klooster, 'The Dutch Atlantic, 1600–1800: Expansion without Empire,' *Itinerario* 23 (1999), 48–69. Klooster has stepped back from the most strident expression of this argument. See Klooster, *The Dutch Moment: War, Trade, and Settlement in the Seventeenth-Century Atlantic World* (Ithaca: Cornell University Press, 2016).

5   John Gallagher and Ronald Robinson, 'The Imperialism of Free Trade,' *Economic History Review* 6 (1953), 1–15.

6   Elliott, *Spain, Europe and the Wider World*, 130.

7   Jack A. Goldstone, 'The Problem of the "Early Modern" World,' *Journal of the Economic and Social History of the Orient* 41 (1998), 249–84.

8   Eric Hobsbawm, 'The General Crisis of the European Economy in the Seventeenth Century,' *Past & Present* 5 (1954), 33–53; 6 (1954), 44–65; Hugh Trevor-Roper, 'The General Crisis of the Seventeenth-Century,' *Past & Present* 16 (1959), 31–64.

9   Geoffrey Parker, 'Crisis and Catastrophe: The Global Crisis of the Seventeenth Century Reconsidered,' *American Historical Review* 113 (2008), 1077.

10 Daron Acemoglu, Simon Johnson and James Robinson, 'The Rise of Europe: Atlantic Trade, Institutional Change, and Economic Growth,' *American Economic Review* 95 (2005), 546–79.

11 Jan De Vries, 'The Economic Crisis of the Seventeenth Century after Fifty Years,' *Journal of Interdisciplinary History* 40 (2009), 181.

12 Jan De Vries and Ad van der Woude, *The First Modern Economy: Success, Failure and Perseverance in the Dutch Economy, 1500–1815* (New York: Cambridge University Press, 1997).

13 Douglas Watt, *The Price of Scotland: Darien, Union and the Wealth of Nations* (Edinburgh: Luath Press, 2007).
14 Andrew Thompson, 'Empire and the British State,' in Sarah Stockwell, ed., *The British Empire: Themes and Perspectives* (Oxford: Oxford University Press, 2008), ch.4.
15 T.M. Devine and Philipp R. Rossner, 'Scots in the Atlantic Economy, 1600–1800,' in John M. Mackenzie and T.M. Devine, eds., *Scotland and the British Empire* (Oxford: Oxford University Press, 2016), 52–53.
16 Matthew P. Dziennik, *The Fatal Land: War, Empire, and the Highland Soldier in British America* (New Haven: Yale University Press, 2015), 5.
17 Ibid., 17–18; Geoffrey Plank, *Rebellion and Savagery: The Jacobite Rising of 1745 and the British Empire* (Philadelphia: University of Pennsylvania Press, 2006), 146.
18 Dziennik, *Fatal Land*, 223.

BIBLIOGRAPHY

Oxford Online Bibliographies – Atlantic Trade and the European Economy; Early Modern Portugal; Early Modern Spain; France and Empire; Hanoverian Britain; London; Northern Europe and the Atlantic World; Scotland and the Atlantic World; The Atlantic and the Mediterranean; Western Europe and the Atlantic World.

David Abulafia, *The Great Sea: A Human History of the Mediterranean* (London: Penguin, 2011).

Pierre Boule, *Race et esclavage dans la France de l'ancien Régime* (Paris: Perrin, 2002).

J.H. Elliott, *Spain, Europe and the Wider World, 1500–1800* (New Haven: Yale University Press, 2009).

Jack A. Goldstone, 'Efflorescences and Economic Growth in World History: Rethinking the "Rise of the West" and the British Industrial Revolution,' *Journal of World History* 13 (2002), 323–89.

Serge Gruzinski, *Les quatre parties du monde: histoire d'une mondialisation* (Paris: Martiniére, 2004).

Wim Klooster, *The Dutch Moment: War, Trade, and Settlement in the Seventeenth-Century Atlantic World* (Ithaca: Cornell University Press, 2016).

Karen Ordahl Kupperman, ed. *America in European Consciousness* (Chapel Hill: University of North Carolina Press, 1995).

John M. Mackenzie and T.M. Devine, eds., *Scotland and the British Empire* (Oxford: Oxford University Press, 2016).

Geoffrey Parker, *Global Crisis: War, Climate Change, and Catastrophe in the Seventeenth Century* (New Haven: Yale University Press, 2013).

Kenneth Pomeranz, *The Great Divergence: China, Europe, and the Making of the Modern World Economy* (Princeton: Princeton University Press, 2005).

Nuala Zahedieh, *The Capital and the Colonies: London and the Atlantic Economy 1660–1700* (Cambridge: Cambridge University Press, 2010).

10

SOUTH AMERICA AND THE CARIBBEAN

ENVIRONMENT

The Caribbean was the first contact zone in Atlantic America. Central America and South America were respectively the second and third, with significant contacts between Africans, Native Americans and Europeans happening well before similar contacts in North America. How do we make sense of this vast area over a long period of time? One entrée is through exploring non-human actors, notably insects – which had a surprisingly important role in shaping human interactions in this space. Insects were most important in shaping historical patterns in the large area that historians have termed 'neo-Africa'. This region covered the large space between Bahia and the Chesapeake and was not especially hospitable to human habitation – population decline, rather than population growth, marked the experience of the region. It was a tropical and semi-tropical region in which slavery was established early and became essential to the political and economic functioning of societies that developed. The slave ships that supplied the labour necessary to maintain this slave system also carried Aedes Aegypti mosquitoes, the primary vector of the yellow fever virus and a carrier of falciparum malaria. The mosquito, as John McNeill has shown, profoundly influenced settlement patterns in 'neo-Africa', as what the mosquito brought to the Americas were very lethal to people, especially Europeans who were not used to these diseases.[1]

Yellow fever and malaria had long been hyperendemic in West Africa, so that all those who survived childhood there were fully immune to yellow fever and maximally resistant to malaria. Neither Native Americans nor Europeans had such immunity and died in droves when yellow fever epidemics occurred, as in the Caribbean from the 1690s. An example of how devastating yellow fever could be and how mortality shaped settlement patterns was at Kourou in French Guiana in 1763–1764. As Emma Rothschild has detailed, an ambitious French plan to create in northern South America a colony full of Europeans growing provisions for the booming colony of Saint-Domingue, just as New England served as a source of supplies for Jamaica, became a 'horrible tragedy', like the Scottish effort to colonize Darien in Panama in 1697–1698, when almost every European migrant succumbed to yellow fever.[2]

Yellow fever made warfare precarious, as conquests had to be made quickly before non-immune soldiers succumbed to the ravages of disease. A quick conquest worked for the British in Havana in 1762 but did not work so well in the British siege of Cartagena in 1741 and operated most disastrously for the French in the Haitian Revolution between 1795 and 1804.[3] This tendency for European soldiers to die from yellow fever kept Spanish America Spanish after 1655, despite several determined attempts to wage war against Spain and its tropical empire. It also helped to keep Jamaica safe from French and Spanish invasion in 1782. A large invading force of 25,000, harboured in Port au Prince in Saint-Domingue, was decimated by disease, so that 7,000 soldiers died in just a few weeks. This level of mortality made this aborted invasion the deadliest conflict of the entire American Revolution.

A more prosaic insect that created havoc in this neo-African world was the humble sugar ant. Ants presented a major threat to sugar cane that was the foundation of the Caribbean and northeastern Brazilian economies. Contemporaries were more aware of ants and other insects than we are. There was an explosion of interest in entomology, or the study of insects, in the eighteenth-century Atlantic. Insects were usually just nuisances. On occasion, they created havoc on a catastrophic scale. Matthew Mulcahy and Stuart Schwartz have described how insects caused devastation in Guadeloupe in 1657 (due to a caterpillar infestation), leading to famine. In the Greater Antilles, what planters called a 'blast', probably caused by insects, ended hopes of building a plantation economy around the cacao tree. It stopped plantation agriculture almost dead in Santo Domingo (present-day Dominican Republic) and encouraged Jamaicans at a crucial time in their transition to a full-fledged plantation economy to concentrate on sugar, rather than cacao.[4]

Ants were particularly troublesome in the developed plantation economy, especially in the 1770s when crops could be destroyed by ants and planters made bankrupt. Many planters from Martinique and Grenada were so affected by sugar ant infestation that they went with their slaves to undeveloped Trinidad, taking advantage of incentives from Spain. New species of cane brought from the Pacific proved very vulnerable to ant invasion, even though they were desirable varieties of cane as they brought increased yields. European nations offered huge prizes for anyone who could solve the problem of ants but the many attempts to find a solution were all mostly unsuccessful. What was most instrumental in reducing the infestation of sugar ants was another environmental threat to plantations. A great hurricane in 1780 in Barbados and Jamaica seemed to have one positive result, the destruction of ant communities.

Entomology was a subject that became more popular and more scientific as Europeans tried to work out how to stop insects from threatening the economic prosperity of the Caribbean. Plantations themselves, of course, were essential factors in causing insect infestation. Sugar monoculture reduced plant diversity and led to forest clearances, preventing vegetation regeneration. It created new ecological balances and new landscapes in which insect pests could flourish. The contribution that plantations made to environmental change and to insect infestation was studied most effectively by the British naturalist, Henry Smeathman (1742–1786), whose career in Africa and the West Indies has been excellently explored by Deirdre Coleman. Smeathman made a study of ants and while he had no answers for ant infestation on plantations, he developed an ingenious theory that used the structure, order and industry of a termite mound as a model for a cooperative colonial settlement that would 'improve' the tropics. Smeathman also observed how another 'alien' species – the enslaved African – was a malign consequence of the plantation system and by extrapolating from his study of ants to his experience of slavery in the British Caribbean became an early abolitionist.[5] It was in this 'neo-Africa' of the Caribbean when the first efforts to get rid of the slave trade and then slavery were made, transforming relations in this large area in the Atlantic World.

SPANISH AMERICA

Spanish America settled down after the tumults of the Conquest period and was relatively peaceful in the seventeenth and eighteenth centuries. Spain itself experienced lots of difficulties in this period, as did Portugal, but those difficulties did not translate into Spanish America, where increasing economic diversity occurred within a region that retained its dominant position among European empires in the Americas, without facing significant challenge until the early nineteenth century. By 1750, Spanish possessions in the America were much greater than the possessions of other European empires and included things not seen elsewhere, such as impressive cities, universities and cathedrals.

Population growth was impressive. The Native American population recovered in this period, except in borderland areas such as northern New Spain, which suffered the same bouts of mortality as had occurred elsewhere during the Conquest. Total population surged from 1.5 million in 1650 to 3 million a century later and then boomed again to 6 million by

1810. Thus, population growth in Spanish America kept pace even with the extraordinary increase in population in British North America. Population growth was strongest in the two main viceroyalties of New Spain and Peru, but growth elsewhere led to a new viceroyalty, New Granada, being created for territories north of Peru. First created in 1718–1719, New Granada lasted only four years in its first iteration but was re-established in 1739. It was joined by a viceroyalty for possessions south of Peru, Rio de la Plata, in 1776.

Murdo MacLeod makes the important point that we need to distinguish between 'near' and 'far' Atlantics when thinking about Spanish America in this period.[6] The 'near' Atlantic included the Caribbean and coastal Venezuela, places with good harbours that were close to Europe and thus closely integrated into Atlantic commerce. The 'far' Atlantic included Mexico, Peru and New Granada, with economies based on mineral extraction and where internal economic development was probably more important than connections to the Atlantic. The territories of Central Mexico fell between 'near' and 'far' Atlantic categories. Nevertheless, there was enough diversity within these regions so that we can see that in all areas there were both a need for well-developed regional economies and a necessary involvement in transatlantic trade.

Venezuela, part of the 'near' Atlantic, exemplifies how 'near' and 'far' Atlantics were interrelated. It participated in both intercolonial and transatlantic trade. The colony began with providing wheat and flour to Caribbean islands before specializing at the end of the sixteenth century in tobacco and cacao production. The lure of profits in cacao brought in significant Spanish migration, leading to the development of a major city in Caracas. The economy and society hummed along for most of the early eighteenth century, very dependent on Britain, which was the chief supplier of slaves to the colony and which provided the means whereby Venezuelans got good prices for their cacao in Mexico. The end of the British *asiento* in 1739 brought depression and discontent to Venezuela. Smuggling from the Dutch entrepôts of Curaçao and Bonaire greatly increased, and commerce declined rapidly in Venezuela itself. The result was a revolt in 1749, as described in more detail below. It was quickly put down, but it led to a review of political and commercial arrangements in Venezuela by the Spanish Crown. A royal commercial monopoly and wide-ranging administrative reforms brought the Habsburg-era mode of consensual accommodation of local interests to an end and led to Venezuela entering a period of Bourbon reform in which control from the imperial state was stronger from 1750 than before. These changes were Spanish responses to developments already occurring in the colony, such as the establishment in the early eighteenth century of a successful cacao trade with Mexico, which justified the Spanish Crown chartering a commercial company to regulate this trade. This reform programme showed, as detailed below, that Spain was more connected with ideas of the Enlightenment – in this case in respect to trade liberalization – than previously thought, through the agency of important Spanish officials such as José de Gálvez. His aim was to increase revenues available to the Crown through opening more trade in Spanish America whereby Spanish Americans could trade with merchants from other European empires. The Crown needed this increased revenue as Spanish American population and territorial growth were expanding rapidly and creating, just as it had done for Britain in North America after 1763, new and expensive defence needs.

SMUGGLING

Trade sometimes created conflict. Problems were especially apparent when the state attempted to crack down upon contraband commerce, which states occasionally thought violated imperial practice, but which colonists tended to think both unproblematic and a mechanism by which neglected regions, such as eighteenth-century Venezuela on the margins of the Spanish Empire, could sustain themselves. As legal Spanish transatlantic shipping continually bypassed their shores for more profitable regions to the west, Venezuelans looked to Dutch, British and French Caribbean islands as desirable markets. As Jesse Cromwell notes, 'coastal Venezuelan subjects and their non-Spanish partners developed a sense of statelessness from the commercial interactions [with other colonial empires] and the relative weakness of the Spanish imperial presence in their lives'.[7]

When the Spanish state unwisely decided to enforce legal commerce and punish smuggling in early 1749, a force of around 500 men gathered in central Caracas under the leadership of Juan Francisco de León, a cacao planter and minor official. Their protest was welcomed with enthusiasm by ordinary Caraqueños but not by royal Spanish officials. But by August, León had a force of between 4,000 and 7,000 men in what became Spanish Americans' most important Creole revolt before the wars of independence in the 1820s. It was a complex event in its causes, events and consequences but it showed three major features of the mid-eighteenth-century Spanish Empire. First, it demonstrated that Spanish American communities, especially in the peripheries, did not think smuggling to be illegal but as part of their rights – they had, in short, a moral economy about what commercial actions were fair and which were unfair, and smuggling was thought to be fair. Second, and following on from this first point, subjects and officials agreed upon acceptable levels of criminality and corruption, which in the absence of formal governmental regulation of illicit transactions functioned as an alternative conceptualization of commercial law. Indeed, making money illegally, if it did not harm others, as what Katherine Browne for the twentieth-century French Caribbean calls 'débrouillardism', which was a socially acceptable lifestyle of making money through avoiding taxes and working off the books, pushed the limits of law while not violating the culturally prescribed limits of the morally defensible.[8] Finally, conflict over illicit trade in the Spanish Atlantic did not harm but benefited empire building. Commerce was an interactive process – the Spanish imperil government needed to accommodate a certain amount of smuggling, as León's forces insisted, while locals had to accept some limits on their economic autonomy. These limitations were tested as early Bourbon reforms in Venezuela to increased government surveillance. The Spanish government tried to picture the León rebellion as a sudden and illegal outbreak of violence, which they admitted might have arisen from utter desolation by participants deprived by government fiat of making a living.

But the government's view was incorrect. The participants in the León rebellion had shared political beliefs in which new laws on how cacao was to be sent to market and shunted into legal commerce seemed to condemn cacao planters to poverty and showed the bias and corruptions of officials with links to the Basque merchants who controlled the legal trade in cacao. The protest by León and his followers was as much about the evils of monopoly and corruption as an attempt to continue the participants' involvement in contraband commerce. León intensified the dispute by forcing the governor of Caracas to flee the town, which left the town vulnerable to slave revolts, it was claimed. The imperial government put down the revolt, with some difficulty, putting León and his sons in chains and transported them to Spain, where León soon died. His sons served lengthy prison sentences, as did twenty-eight other men.

Resentment against this heavy-handed action lasted for decades, with Venezuelans regarding the government monopoly that was the Caracas Company as an intruder into local affairs, which prosecuted unfairly poor inhabitants and their foreign trading partners for smuggling while not allowing these people the entry into the cacao trade that would have made smuggling less attractive. Eventually, Spanish trade liberalization in the form of commerce libre decrees (free commerce), began in 1765 and expanded in 1778, broke the company and it ceased operations. The León Rebellion showed smuggling's importance in the gradual evolution of a local creole identity. Venezuelan protests against the Caracas Company forced rebels to define who they were and how their identity was tied up in their beliefs in commercial autonomy.

It is going too far to see the León Rebellion as a failed independence movement or a precursor to Latin American revolt, but the episode does show how smuggling informed Creole constructions of moral economy, autonomous commercial trade and the identity of Creoles in a changing environment of increased state intervention into and control of well-established patterns of doing business in marginal Atlantic places. Smuggling, Cromwell argues, 'acted as a safety valve to relieve the pressures of imperial relationships. Those who tampered with contraband trade risked the explosion or subversion of these compacts.'[9]

SPANIARDS AND NATIVE AMERICANS

Among the factors that helped provide stability in this expanding Spanish America was a stabilization in the Native American population and a modus vivendi between the Spanish and Native American communities about how the relationship between both groups should work. It was an uneasy alliance, however, of interests that remained fundamentally opposed to each other. The historical information about Native Americans in the post-conquest era has greatly increased in recent decades. There has been a renaissance in recent historiography about Native Americans in the post-conquest era. Most accounts of Native Americans in the early modern period in Spanish America concentrate on the densely settled areas of central Mexico. One of the most significant historiographical advances in Atlantic history in the last generation has been the rediscovery of abundant Nahua texts in the Nahuatl language. Scholars working on these texts have shown that older notions that Native Americans in Central America had largely disappeared or had been rendered mute by a European imperial expansion that destroyed American indigenous cultures are wildly off the mark. A civilizational apocalypse did occur for Native Americans in the Caribbean, but not in the major centres of Native American settlement in central Mexico and the Andes.

James Lockhart pioneered the translation of hundreds of Nahuatl language sources and showed that while Native American communities were burdened by colonialism, they remained vital and resilient well into the eighteenth century and with continuing cultural self-assertions to keep the Nahual people and their language flourishing. Camilla Townsend has recently written an absorbing account of Nahual texts that extends Lockhart's researches to show the extent to which Nahuas were able to keep their culture and language alive in the post-conquest period. The focus of these texts was very much on the local community – Nahuals defined themselves by local attachment and were hostile to getting involved in more national and global trends. Most texts were written by small-town intellectuals and men of local standing, eager to boost their local communities. They wrote, Townsend declares, 'to protect their communities and its ways against all comers, to bend with changing times but never break'.[10] Their stories show the conflicted ways in which Native Americans had to react to Spaniards, sometimes as enemies, sometimes as allies. One vivid example of a friendship that developed in Tecamachallo, now a suburb of Mexico City, between the Nahua nobleman and adept in the genre of xiuhpoualli in which the best Nahuatl-language texts are written, was don Mateo Sánchez and the Franciscan monk, Francisco de Toral. Their correspondence reveals a complicated and intense relationship quite typical of men of their class that is subtler than collusion between a colonizer and a member of a co-opted conquered elite. It shows that the relationship was a friendship between two men of similar mien who found connections in their shared commitment to advancing the interests of their community and in their desire to protect that community against outside threats, whether those threats came from Nahua or from Spaniards.

This new work using Native American languages has been concerned with settled and urban Mexicans rather than wandering and rural peoples. Some interesting research, however, is being done on Native Americans in the arid lands of the borderlands' region of northern New Spain – present day north Mexico, California and Arizona. Borderlands are places of considerable historical interest as they encompass contested spaces where different cultural traditions and peoples meet and clash. They did so in this region because Spain came to see this area both as an opportunity to get fresh mineral wealth and as inherently problematic. It was a place with hostile Native Americans whom they depended upon but whom they found hard to control or bend to their will. Geography shaped human interactions in this borderland space, with tribal lands following the trajectories of river valleys. And this borderland was not really a 'frontier' as we customarily think of the frontier when considering the nineteenth-century American west. Colonial borderlands in northern New Spain were made from scattered settlements in a huge territory mainly controlled by unassimilated Native Americans. Spaniards needed Native Americans more than the other way around. They needed Native American labour for mining and Native American foods for sustenance in landscapes where agriculture was challenging.

Despite that dependence on Native Americans, however, Spaniards treated Native Americans with contempt. They used the threat and reality of violence to take advantage of rapidly declining populations – Sinaloa, Ostimini and Sonara in northern New Spain saw population drop from 408,000 in 1530 to 44,300 in 1790. They used violence especially often during periods of drought and epidemic. As Native Americans became weaker, Spaniards became stronger. The process is best described as a rhythm of advance and retreat, marking a pattern of relationships and reciprocal actions in which each side tested each other repeatedly in small conflicts. The process generally went forward in three stages. First, Native Americans from different river valleys joined together to observe mission towns and Spanish soldiers and reported back to home villages the strengths and weaknesses of these new strangers who had invaded their lands. To an extent, this stage saw Native Americans merging together as a single unit and putting aside their local differences to concentrate on a common enemy. Second, Spaniards tried to deal with Native Americans through their *caciques*, or chiefs. They actively sought indigenous allies to attract new converts to Christianity in Jesuit missions, to recover fugitives from mining camps and agricultural estates, and to put down rebellions. They tried to divide *caciques* from each other, rewarding allies with gifts of clothing, tools and especially horses. Third, during subsistence crises occasioned by drought or flooding, Spaniards took advantage of Native American disarray to force *caciques* to give them land and labour in return for Spanish American assistance. Through this multi-stage process, which lasted in northern New Spain for more than two centuries and which was marked throughout by episodes of terrifying violence, the Spaniards and Native Americans created together borderlands as places where there were webs of interdependency and contestation within fluctuating and hybrid spaces.

Spanish colonial rule was always tenuous. Spain could not coerce Native Americans to do what they wanted, except in rare times of emergency, but always had to negotiate, often from a position of weakness before the eighteenth century. By the late eighteenth century, the balance of power had shifted much more in their favour than before and allowed Spanish authorities to impose their will on Native Americans increasingly often. These negotiations were only made possible through the transitory alliance of Native American leaders, military officers and church officials, colonial settlers, and a mixed population of free and coerced labourers. Spain succeeded in establishing sovereignty over these areas by the early eighteenth century, its main ally being the disease which afflicted Native Americans, but it was also helped by Jesuit missionaries who helped assimilate Native Americans to Spanish customs and assisted the owners of mines and farms in getting Native American labourers. Nevertheless, Native American *rancherios*, or communities, maintained territorial and ethnic integrity, even as the arrival of mines, missions, labour migrations and Native American enslavement meant that Spanish and Native American societies overlapped, to Native American disadvantage. One reason for this uneasy collaboration where Native Americans stayed rather than were dispersed, as in westward expansion in Canada and the United States, is that Spanish colonists were more interested in Native American labour than in their land. The aridity of the landscape in this area thus meant that Native American communities continued to exist, albeit in diminished form, even after Spain had taken control of power in the region.[11]

PORTUGUESE AMERICA

The period between 1650 and 1750 also saw stability in Portugal's Atlantic empire in Brazil. By 1660 Brazil had become firmly Portuguese after the expulsion from 1654 of the Dutch from settlements in northeast Brazil and from their control of Angola in Africa and São Tome in the Atlantic islands off Africa. Henceforth, Portugal became entrenched in the Atlantic in ways that never occurred in its more diverse and inchoate Asian possessions. We can see Portugal's Atlantic commitment in this period in its upsurge in shipbuilding for Atlantic trade from the late seventeenth century onwards, both in Portugal and in Brazil, the latter overtaking Portugal in importance by the end of the eighteenth century. Key to the peculiar nature of the Portuguese Atlantic Empire – it was the only Atlantic Empire in which monarchy was reinforced rather than weakened during the Age of Revolutions, for example, with the locus of power moving from 1808 to Brazil from Portugal – is that the colonies were never as subordinate to the metropolis in this empire as in all the others. By the middle of the eighteenth century, Brazil was clearly more economically and perhaps more politically powerful than Portugal. Portugal's long commitment to Atlantic involvement ironically did not lead to metropolitan wealth and geopolitical influence. Its position in Europe was much weaker in 1755, the year of a devastating earthquake in Lisbon from which Portugal found it hard to recover, than it had been in 1450. It could not defend its interests in Brazil with any conviction – mercantilism and protectionism were conceits rather than realities with smuggling and open violation of Portuguese trade regulations were endemic, even during the reign of Dom João V (r. 1706–1750), the most impressive and dynamic of Portuguese kings during the seventeenth and eighteenth centuries.

The wealth of Brazil, not just in sugar but in mining from the early eighteenth century with the discovery of gold in Minas Gerais, encouraged reasonably substantial migration from Portugal, mostly of single men, and massive importation of Africans. Only Britain sent more migrants to the Americas between 1700 and 1820 than did Portugal: 105,000 from Portugal and 1,535,000 from Africa. The ratio of Europeans to Africans going to Brazil was greater than in any other European Empire save the French and the Dutch empires and in those empires were only so high because virtually no French or Dutch people crossed the Atlantic in the eighteenth century. To accommodate such migration and a growing plantation and mining sector, the Portuguese ruthlessly acquired Native American land, ignoring Native American claims to sovereignty. The population of Brazil resembled that of the British North America, with majority black populations but substantial white minorities, with the significant exception that mixed-race people were a much larger constituency than elsewhere. The ethnic mix in Brazil was distinctive, insofar as independent communities of Maroons in seventeenth-century northeast Brazil, Native Americans in the largely undeveloped interior and Muslim enclaves of enslaved and freed people in Salvador lived in uneasy relationship within an 'official' Portuguese framework. The Portuguese languages, Portuguese modes of behaviour and Catholicism were the accepted standards. Portuguese culture was largely ignored or adapted outside the main centres of Portuguese control such as Salvador, Rio de Janeiro and Sao Paulo. These communities epitomized multicultural exchange and interaction within a diverse cultural mix in which aspects of different cultures merged to create a distinctively Brazilian creole culture. The long tradition of carnival before Lent that developed in northeastern Brazil and in Rio de Janeiro is a lasting manifestation of this dynamic creole culture.

The main trend in Brazil during this period was that the country became increasingly integrated rather than being just scattered pockets of settlement whose major orientation was to Europe rather than to other parts of the country. Salvador and Rio de Janeiro remained core areas but developments in Mato Grosso led to the development of new hinterlands for Sao Paulo and growing links between the north and the south of the large colony. The northeast remained a monoculture economy but elsewhere in the eighteenth century economic diversification was considerable as cities grew and the expansion of mining opened new areas of settlement in Minas Gerais, where manumission rates of slaves were greater than anywhere else, making free people of colour a socially and increasingly politically important group. Nevertheless, slavery was essential to Brazil and became more essential as the eighteenth century progressed: slavery and the Catholic Church were the only institutions that continued from first European settlement until the end of slavery in 1888. Brazilian wealth became increasingly significant for Portugal: Brazilian gold saving it from economic disaster in the 1690s and 1740 and Brazilian diamonds performing the same role in the 1720s. Portugal, however, had poor infrastructure and no manufacturing, meaning it had to rely increasingly on Britain for basics like grain, foodstuffs and manufactures. It led to a significant balance of payments problem which was partly alleviated by allowing Britain more access to Brazilian markets. By 1800, Brazil was almost as much a dependency of Britain as of Portugal.

One sign of this shift from Portugal to Britain was the move of the Brazilian capital in 1763 from Salvador to Rio de Janeiro. Rio was the centre of transatlantic trade, the home of the biggest Atlantic merchants and the centre of the slave trade. The accession of Dom José I in 1750 to the Portuguese throne saw, as with the Bourbon reforms in Spanish America, a reinvigorated mercantilist policy designed to increase state revenues and channel Brazilian trade to the home country. The major force behind this move was the marquis of Pombal (1699–1782), a devotee of the Enlightenment who advanced policies of secularization in Portugal, the replacement of hereditary nobles in Portuguese government by commercially oriented merchants, and a raft of legislation designed to integrate northern Brazil more fully into the main currents of Atlantic commerce. Pombal was exactly the sort of statesman needed to drag Portugal out of its long torpor, but he was no more successful than the equally dynamic Dom João V in trying to enforce state monopolies and mercantilism. Indeed, by advancing merchants to positions of authority he undermined his own intentions, as these merchants tended to be motivated by their own goals for profit rather than the national goals Pombal promoted. The result was less mercantilism and more autonomy, especially in Brazil where colonists became increasingly nimble in evading their traditional commercial obligations to the crown. Slave traders, especially, had enough money to act independently of state control and metropolitan financing. Commerce became thus central to an endemic culture of evasion of the state that was a special characteristic of Brazil in the late eighteenth century.

THE CARIBBEAN

Barry Higman starts a chapter on plantation people in the seventeenth-century Caribbean with the arresting statement that 'by the beginning of the seventeenth century, European colonization had reduced the Caribbean islands to a blank canvas. In truth it was not so much a blank canvas as one that had been thickly painted by a series of hands, scoured and scraped, then smeared with a rough bloody cloth, and cleaned again of yet another attempted landscape. The people and the civilizations that had flourished in the Greater Antilles before Columbus had been virtually obliterated. They had not been replaced by any new substantial population or any new form of civilization'.[12] Alan Karras, by contrast, argues that the post-Columbian Caribbean was a crucible of modern world history, a 'harbinger of world historical developments that would take place centuries later' such as 'implantation and colonization, global migration, enslavement, extraction, economic transformation and integration, as well as "very briefly" revolution and state building'.[13] He argues for the importance of Caribbean slavery in fuelling European economic development by allowing Europeans to use money that might have paid for wage labour to produce sugar for other economic purposes.

Both Higman and Karras can be reconciled. The aftermath of the Columbian apocalypse in the Greater Antilles allowed for a new form of economic regime emerging in the Caribbean base on sugar and slavery and resulting in the plantation complex. This lethal combination is described at length elsewhere in this volume. It mostly took place in French and British colonies before 1790. The Spanish did not concentrate their attentions on the Caribbean until the fall of Saint-Domingue, when Cuba became for the first time a major sugar producer. Before then, Spain merely holding onto its Caribbean holdings was an achievement.

What also marked the Caribbean was colonialism, which began earlier and ended later there than everywhere else in the Atlantic World. The Age of Revolutions did not result in liberation or independence with the important exception of Haiti. Government remained located in Europe and what limited political autonomy there was in the region was held tightly in the grip of wealthy white male slave holders. The sole exception were Maroon communities in Jamaica and Surinam where black people controlled aspects of their lives. Surprisingly, given the extent of war in the region which was almost constant in the eighteenth century, colonies changed hands between empires very seldom. No large island, for example, was transferred between European empires after the conquest of Jamaica in 1655. Planters and merchants were happy with their colonial dependency until the 1790s when the twin forces of revolution and abolitionism made the white elite realize that a world without slavery and without planter rule was entirely possible. By this time, however, it was too late as whites were thoroughly embedded in a whole structure of European security which made it impossible for them to break free from imperial control. Jamaica's wealthiest planter, Simon Taylor, for example, might fulminate in the late 1790s that 'there can never be either peace to, or security in, any of the islands while Pitt and Wilberforce were agitating to an end of the slave trade' and thus 'constantly sounding the trumpet of rebellion among the negroes' but he was powerless to do anything than rage against the injustices he believed planters were facing. His fortunes and the fortunes of his island were so tied up with Britain's colonial authority that no action was possible except private complaint.[14]

The quintessential Caribbean slave societies in the eighteenth century were the Greater Antilles colonies of Jamaica and Saint-Domingue. Both colonies were extremely profitable but socially monstrous slave societies that had perfected a form of economic organization – the plantation machine, employing a mechanistic metaphor favoured in Enlightenment thought – that operated on a global scale. This machine was a proto-industrial wealth-making regime, which produced a distinctive social structure, both in the countryside where there were 'factories in the field' and in vibrant towns such as Cap Français and Kingston, with the slave trade pouring in money and people so that merchants became rich and powerful. These colonies were modern societies with an overwhelming commitment by their white residents on capitalist accumulation. They were also extraordinarily brutal places. The ethos of both places was a peculiar combination of libertinism and authoritarianism, in which the authority of masters over slaves was frequently greater than the authority of the imperial state and its legal institutions. Both masters and slaves lived in uneasy tension which occasionally exploded into open and violent resistance, as in Tacky's Revolt in 1760 in Jamaica and in the Haitian Revolution of 1791.

These were very difficult societies for contemporaries to understand. Vincent Brown argues that death defined the cultural ambience of such colonies better than anything else. Everyone seemed to be dying – whites from disease, blacks from overwork.[15] They were also extraordinarily unequal places, where the enslaved suffered a standard of living that placed them at the bottom of human experience in the 1770s. Arriving in Saint-Domingue inspired both desire and disgust in Alexandre-Stanislas de Wimpffen in the late 1780s. He was entranced by the beauty of the landscape and beautiful 'mulatresses' who 'combine the explosiveness of saltpeter with an exuberance of desire, that, scorning all, drives them to pursue, acquire and nourish pleasure'. What he mostly saw, however, was a world turned upside-down, where morality was absent, and which was based on the pursuit of profit, not religious virtue, social cohesion or imperial loyalty: 'It seems in Saint-Domingue violent agitations of the heart take the place of principles; except for illusions of love, dreams of pleasure, extravagances of luxury and greed, the heart knows no other adorations.'[16]

Not everyone in these colonies were free whites or enslaved blacks. During the second half of the eighteenth century, a substantial body of free people of colour emerged, more often female than male and concentrated in towns rather than the countryside. It was not as substantial a population as in Brazil, but it was an increasing factor in colonial politics in Saint-Domingue, where, unlike Jamaica, free people of colour often amassed considerable wealth. The quadroon Vincent Ogé, a leader of the early stages of the Haitian Revolution who was executed in February 1791 by being broken upon the wheel, may have been worth 350,000 livres or £15,000 in the early 1780s, an amount of wealth equivalent to that of a Parisian merchant.

By the second half of the eighteenth century, these colonies entered the period of their greatest prosperity. They had established culturally vibrant, dynamic and economically valuable imperial possessions. The enslaved people in these colonies had developed their own cultures which were created in opposition to the cultures that Europeans had and which they were able to develop mostly unimpeded by slave holder concerns about how enslaved people kept intact many of the African customs, notably in religious practice and family relationships. Planters were overwhelmingly concerned with making money and had a limited commitment to the societies they lived in – they were 'passengers only', with little desires to make a permanent home in the Caribbean but wanting most of all to return in some style to their metropolitan homelands. Consequently, they cared little about enslaved peoples' interior lives but viewed them only as units of labour that produced wealth for them. Ironically, planters' lack of concern for enslaved people gave some space whereby enslaved people could create their own cultural patterns free from white intrusion.

Sidney Mintz has argued that the process of enslavement and displacement of Africans from Africa to the Caribbean produced fundamental changes in their outlook and personality that he describes by the shorthand term 'creolization'. Creolization, he argues 'was a reaction of people to the terrible constraints of enslavement and the resulting ethnic disorganization'. It was an attempt by the victims to respond creatively to their condition. In addition, it seems that in this creative culture building slaves had to build collective social institutions within slavery. As he notes, 'memories had to be aggregated collectively to build shared social practices. Such processes of rebuilding, of informing daily lives with new meanings, were modernizing experiences'. Finally, the cultural displacement arising from movement from Africa was so great 'that the creolization process that followed became a rich but unrecognized source understanding for any theory of human culture'.[17]

As Mintz reminds us, the slave culture that emerged out of creolization arose from necessity. Slaves were viciously mistreated, yet they had problems that they had to solve straight away to endow their daily lives with meaning. The enslaved had lost touch with their ancestral cultures through displacement and trauma. The losses came first. Then came a rebuilding of institutions to replace, incompletely, what had been lost. What was not lost was memory, including language, motor habits and culturally inscribed material like religious belief or music or dance. Mintz notes that 'memory, creativity and collective effort made possible the re-institutionalization of African-American lifeways'. They could not reconstitute what they had left behind but through creolization devised new cultural practices which, Mintz argues, formed a process of modernization. He concludes that 'Caribbean people were modernized by enslavement, by forced transportation in large, ethnically mixed groups, by massing in time-conscious enterprises, by the reshuffling of gender roles, by constant oppression, and by the need to reconstitute their cultural forms anew, and under pressure. This was happening to people from societies of a different sort from the ones into which they were brought; they were thrust into what were remarkably industrial settings for their times, with their smokestacks, mills and raging fires. Finally, they were controlled primarily by physical violence. They learned how to live under constant repression'.[18]

ABOLITION OF SLAVERY

Jamaican and Saint-Domingue slaveholders were supremely confident that the plantation societies they had created not only were economically beneficial to their metropolitan overlords but also would continue to be supported by European empires into the indeterminate future. In the 1790s, as Saint-Domingue imploded into slave rebellion, investors poured into Jamaica to buy land and plantations at inflated prices. Even more often, people headed to colonies acquired by the British from the French, Spanish and Dutch such as Trinidad, Berbice and Demerara. They were not fools to do so. Established opinion believed that there was a great future in slavery. That was a common belief right until slavery ended. Adam Smith cautioned his students in the 1770s that slavery would last for centuries, even though he disapproved of it on economic let alone moral grounds. Sir John Gladstone, investing heavily in Demerara from 1812, continued to invest in plantation economies as abolition occurred and during emancipation made concrete his belief in the survival of a profitable plantation system by organizing for Asian indentured labour to be shipped to his estates. Abraham Lincoln, the author of the Emancipation Proclamation in the United States in 1863, argued in 1858 that slavery was likely to only end in 1958.

How slavery went from being thought of as essential to Atlantic prosperity with virtually no-one contemplating its end any time soon to being demolished in Britain in less than a generation of protest and in France and the Netherlands within two or three generations is a contentious topic, which can only be touched on briefly in this book. The historical explanations for its demise are of three kinds, all advanced in debates over

British abolition, an event which has occasioned the most impassioned and impressive arguments around this historiographical controversy. The date when abolitionism emerged as a movement is clear. It happened during the Seven Years' War, with Quakers the most prominent advocates of abolition in its earliest stages. They did so ostensibly for religious reasons, at first connected with their longstanding adherence to pacifism but soon intertwined with philosophical debates over the morality of holding slaves against their will and political debates about reducing the power of slaveholders within British politics. Before the mid-eighteenth century, concerns about slavery and even more so efforts to end it were limited. Bartolomé Las Casas in the sixteenth century objected to the brutality of Native American enslavement (although his interest was in the immorality of violence, he was less concerned about whether slavery was legitimate or not). A few seventeenth-century radical religious reformers noted that slavery was immoral, with these thinkers most prominent in the English Civil War when people determined to fight for liberty became anxious and confused about whether supporting liberty meant attacking slavery, though their arguments were placed in odd places and were so highly hypothetical in tone that it suggested that the argument was entirely intellectual without having any practical implications.[19]

Nineteenth-century and early twentieth-century British historians tended to accept the views of abolitionists themselves about the causes and consequences of abolition movements as being spontaneous outbreaks of moral indignation against an activity identified as sinful and wicked. The ultimate cause of abolitionism was revulsion against slave traders, against slavery and against slave holders and how they violated God's will to treat others as they would like to be treated themselves. British Christians adopted the 'golden rule' of doing unto others what you want to be done to yourself. Their successful opposition to first the slave trade and then slavery was a rare instance of the workings of divine providence, so it was argued a century ago, and served as a moral justification for British moral meddling in the world during the heyday of nineteenth-century imperialism.

In 1944, Eric Williams, later prime minister of Trinidad and Tobago, changed the terms of debate by arguing that the reason for the abolition of the slave trade and then slavery lay in economics. The slave trade and the institution of slavery were ended, he contended, when the success of the Industrial Revolution, which Williams thought was largely funded through profits invested into industry by Lancashire slave traders, made investing in slavery less urgent and showed that the costs of protecting the West Indies and giving them commercial advantages in selling their rum and sugar to Britain were too great to sustain. Thus, Britain abolished the slave trade and slavery for self-interested economic interests and got out of Caribbean slavery just as the plantation complex was losing steam. Roger Anstey responded in the 1970s with a reassertion of the religious dimension in abolitionism, arguing that abolition emerged out of changes in evangelical Protestant religion which insisted on Christians being active in the world and demonstrating their Christian beliefs by attacking sinful practices. Moreover, these evangelical conservatives proved very adept, as John Oldfield has shown, in mobilizing popular opinion against slavery, using tools of popular protest that have subsequently been applied to most European and American social protests, especially petitioning parliament and strategic boycotts for moral reasons. David Brion Davis has combined both religious and economic imperative in arguing that British abolition was an ideological crusade among a new group of middling Britons with connections to the new attitudes engendered by increasing industrialization. This group believed in free market principles and in the market discipline that industrial activity instilled in workers, owners and consumers. They were quite comfortable in accepting poor conditions for the English working class in infernal cotton mills while insisting that slavery was wrong because it deprived enslaved people of autonomy over how they chose to work and live.[20]

What is remarkable about the abolition of the slave trade in Britain is the speed by which it became a popular movement and the success of the methods that abolitionists used to attack the institution. It was a movement that before the 1780s attracted only a few religious zealots and some free black people, like the writer and Methodist, Olaudah Equiano. A spate of influential antislavery polemics by James Ramsay and Thomas Clarkson in the mid-1780s; a fuss over the cause célèbre of the *Zong* case of 1783, in which slave holders claimed for insurance for captives who had been deliberately murdered for that purpose; and the formation of an anti-slavery organization in 1787 that decided to adopt a durable patter of protest that led to mass popular mobilization made a marginal issue very mainstream. It took only two years (1787–1788) for the idea that the slave trade should be abolished to become massively popular in England. Abolitionists were very nearly successful in persuading parliament to end the slave trade in 1791, but fears held by conservatives of the danger of allowing any reform in the treacherous years of the French Revolution meant that abolitionists had to wait until 1806 when the geopolitics of allowing abolition had shifted dramatically in favour of antislavery activists following France's loss of Saint-Domingue (1804) and its loss of naval mastery in the Battle of Trafalgar (1805). One significant feature of the abolitionist movement was that it provided a space for women – increasingly considered the repositories of virtue and thus ideally suited to play a role in moral campaigning – to enter politics. Women were especially important in a pioneering consumer movement to boycott sugar.

Abolition faced fierce opposition from slave holders, and the British state continued to acquire fresh territory ideal for slavery in the Caribbean in the 1800s and 1810s. Abolition also suffered a setback when Napoleon reinstated slavery after it had been abolished in 1794 during the radical phase of the French Revolution. But during the first three decades of the nineteenth century slavery became less popular within parts of the Atlantic (while expanding greatly in the United States, Brazil and Cuba in what is called 'second slavery'). By 1825, most mainland Spanish American states had abolished their slave trades, had liberated enslaved elderly people and enacted gradual emancipation laws that freed children of slaves from birth. Encouraged by these events, abolitionists first in Britain and then in France reinvigorated their opposition to slavery, moving away from ideas of amelioration (the idea that slavery could continue but had to be made more humane) to ideas of immediate abolition.

In the British Empire, such ideas of immediate abolition were made more powerful by the actions of enslaved people themselves, as in Demerara in 1823 and in Jamaica in 1831–1832 where religiously motivated slaves led large slave revolts that were so brutally put down by slave owners and the colonial state that it alienated the few supporters slave holders had left in Britain. A final massive petition campaign in 1833 led to the abolition of slavery, although its radical implications were weakened by the implementation of an apprenticeship system whereby ex-slaves would not become fully free until 1838 and by a compensation scheme whereby £20 million was given to slave owners for the 'loss' of their property while none was given to slaves.

French abolitionists saw what Britain had done and formed the French Society for the Abolition of Slavery in 1834. It was a conservative society, determined to distance itself from the revolutionary slave revolt in Haiti and was unwilling to engage in popular mobilization campaigns which had been so successful in Britain. The second French slave emancipation in 1848 came, like the first in 1794, either from above rather because of popular pressure or from the actions of enslaved people. Neither Spain nor Portugal followed suit and neither had antislavery movements of any consequence. What was most important in hindering the slave trade in both empires was the power of the British navy, which in the first half of the nineteenth century was used as a force to stop foreign slave ships from taking captives to Americas. The liberated slaves were returned to Africa, often to Liberia, where there were colonies of freed slaves from America and the West Indies.

EMANCIPATION

Slavery took, however, a long time to die. It took an extremely bloody Civil War between 1861 and 1865 for slavery in the United States to end. Slavery ended even later in Iberian America. Indeed, events elsewhere made slavery stronger in nineteenth-century Brazil and Cuba than it had been before. As Ada Ferrer explains, 'at a basic level, liberation in Saint-Domingue helped entrench its denial in Cuba. As slavery and colonialism collapsed in the French colony, the Spanish island underwent transformations that were almost the mirror image of Haiti's. The sugar no longer produced in

Saint-Domingue was now produced in Cuba ... Two decades after Haitian independence, Cuba had emerged as the world's largest producer of sugar and one of the great consumers of enslaved Africans in the nineteenth-century world.'[21] By 1841, the number of slaves in Cuba peaked at 436,000, which was 43.3 per cent of the population, the largest enslaved population ever in the Caribbean, although well behind contemporary enslaved population figures in the United States.

It was only in the mid-nineteenth century the plantation societies of Brazil and Cuba faced abolitionist challenges. We have dealt with Cuban antislavery and independence in Chapter 7. In Brazil, abolition came even later, on 13 May 1888, which is one date we might take as the end of a certain kind of Atlantic history. It resulted, as in Cuba, from a long-term legislative process, though in Brazil without an accompanying war. It also came more from the people than in Cuba, with slaves and ex-slaves prominent in their own self-liberation. What is noticeable about abolitionism in Brazil is that it emerged and was most important in areas where slave holders were most powerful. No such push for abolition ever came from the slave societies of the British Caribbean or the American South. Slave owners in Brazil responded vigorously against abolition but faced a losing battle from the 1870s, when slavery was ending largely by itself, as manumission rates soared. Where planters were successful is what concerned them most, stopping black political participation – they were so successful in doing this that Brazil has yet to have a black president despite having the largest population by far of people of African heritage in the Western Hemisphere.

What were the effects of emancipation? The results were decidedly mixed. The Haitian Revolution liberated one-third of the Caribbean slave population in 1804 but not many ex-slaves prospered afterwards. For slave holders elsewhere, moreover, Haiti became a by word for anarchy. Both Simon Bolivar and Thomas Jefferson were whites whose view of Haiti was one characterized by fear and horror. The example of Haiti, however, inspired slaves in other place to think of revolt. The most remarkable such case was the conspiracy in Havana in 1812 of the free black wood worker, José Antonia Aponte (c. 1760–1812). Aponte drew pictures celebrating the black heroes of Haiti and promised his supporters that Henri Christophe, the emperor of Haiti, would give him help – an illusory promise, as it turned out.[22]

In other parts of the Caribbean, ex-slaves gained some benefits from emancipation even while the plantation economies they were part of suffered general decline or collapsed. Workers refused to work as they had done under slavery, and planters had to make concessions over wages, provision grounds and the ownership of houses. Perhaps the area where ex-slaves had most success was in family relations. Men and women insisted that the gender roles under slavery, where women worked in the fields without much help given when pregnant, would have to change, with women insisting that they needed time off work to raise and look after families.

Sidney Mintz has been an especially influential scholar in analysing the transformations that resulted from emancipation. He argues that in Jamaica, Haiti and Puerto Rico ex-slaves wanted above all land and autonomy from white pressure. Land was an important way of ensuring that autonomy. They were prepared to work within the plantation economy, but on their own terms and for specific reasons, such as getting a surplus on top of the subsistence they got from peasant production. In short, they moved, as Mintz states, from being a proletariat to becoming a peasantry.[23] Their attempts to become a peasantry, however, were only partially successful. The results of emancipation were not just disappointing to planters, whose racist views about the mental and moral capacity of Afro-Caribbean ex-slaves meant that they willed them to the self-defeating assumption that ex-slaves would never work unless forced to do so.

That scepticism spread to people in France and Britain. In Britain, the generation that led the nation to the abolition of slavery got old and died. Their place was taken by men and women less sympathetic to black desires for freedom. They were influenced by what they saw as failures in emancipation, which they attributed not to problems in state management of emancipation (the true answer) but to deficiencies in the black character. Blacks were increasingly described as work-shy, sexually obsessed, mentally incapable and uncivilizable. This new generation of scientific racists, headed by men such as Thomas Carlyle and including the novelist Anthony Trollope and the historian James Froude, pointed to how sugar production had fallen dramatically in Haiti, Louisiana, northeast Brazil and Surinam within five years of emancipation (though they seldom mentioned Cuba, where production of sugar increased by 25 per cent in the first five years after emancipation).[24] Unlike the United States, post-emancipation disillusionment by rulers did not lead to formal segregation of the ruled, but informal segregation and discrimination proved insidious legacies of the centuries-long history of slavery.

NOTES

1 John R. McNeill, *Mosquito Empires: Ecology and War in the Greater Caribbean, 1620–1914* (New York: Cambridge University Press, 2010).
2 Emma Rothschild, 'A Horrible Tragedy in the French Atlantic,' *Past & Present* 192 (2006), 67–108.
3 Elena Schneider, *The Occupation of Havana: War, Trade, and Slavery in the Atlantic World* (Chapel Hill: University of North Carolina Press, 2018).
4 Matthew Mulcahy and Stuart Schwartz, 'Nature's Battalions: Insects as Agricultural Pests in the Early Modern Caribbean,' *William and Mary Quarterly* 75 (2018), 433–64.
5 Deirdre Coleman, *Henry Smeathman, Flycatcher: Natural History, Slavery, and Empire in the Late Eighteenth Century* (Liverpool: Liverpool University Press, 2018).

6   Murdo MacLeod, *Spanish Central America: A Socioeconomic History, 1520–1720* (Austin: University of Texas Press, 2008), 199.
7   Jesse Cromwell, *The Smugglers' World: Illicit Trade and Atlantic Communities in Eighteenth-Century Venezuela* (Chapel Hill: University of North Carolina Press, 2018), 12.
8   Katherine Browne, *Creole Economies: Caribbean Cunning under the French Flag* (Austin: University of Texas Press, 2004), 11.
9   Cromwell, *Smugglers' World*, 307.
10 James Lockhart, *The Nahuas after the Conquest* (Stanford: Stanford University Press, 1992); Camilla Townsend, *Annals of Native America: How the Nations of Colonial Mexico Kept Their History Alive* (New York: Oxford University Press, 2016), 1.
11 Cynthia Radding, *Wandering Peoples: Colonialism, Ethnic Spaces and Ecological Frontiers in North-Western Mexico, 1700–1850* (Durham: Duke University Press, 1997).
12 B.W. Higman, *A Concise History of the Caribbean* (New York: Cambridge University Press, 2011), 97.
13 Alan Karras, 'The Caribbean Region: Crucible for Modern World History,' in Jerry H. Bentley et al., eds., *The Cambridge World History* vol. VI, part 1 (Cambridge: Cambridge University Press, 2015), 393.
14 Christer Petley, *White Fury: A Jamaican Slaveholder and the Age of Revolution* (Oxford: Oxford University Press, 2018), 177.
15 Vincent Brown, *The Reaper's Garden: Death and Power in the World of Atlantic Slavery* (Cambridge, MA: Harvard University Press, 2008).
16 Trevor Burnard and John Garrigus, *The Plantation Machine; British Jamaica and French Saint-Domingue and Atlantic Capitalism* (Philadelphia: University of Pennsylvania Press, 2016), 26.
17 Sidney W. Mintz, *Three Ancient Colonies: Caribbean Themes and Variations* (Cambridge, MA: Harvard University Press, 2010), 197–98.
18 Ibid., 204–05.
19 John Donoghue, '"Out of the Land of Bondage": The English Revolution and the Atlantic Origins of Abolition,' *American Historical Review* 115 (2010), 943–74.
20 Robert Forbes, '"Truth Systematised": The Changed Debate over Slavery and Abolition, 1761–1916,' in Timothy Patrick McCarthy and John Stauffer, eds., *Prophets of Protest: Reconsidering the History of American Abolitionism* (New York: New Press, 2006), 3–22. Christer Petley, *White Fury: A Jamaican Slaveholder and the Age of Revolution* (Oxford: Oxford University Press, 2018); Christopher Leslie Brown, 'Abolition of the Atlantic Slave Trade,' in Gad Heuman and Trevor Burnard, eds., *The Routledge History of Slavery* (London: Routledge, 2011), 281–97.
21 Ada Ferrer, *Freedom's Mirror: Cuba and Haiti in the Age of Revolution* (New York: Cambridge University Press, 2014), 10.
22 Matt D. Childs, *The 1812 Aponte Rebellion in Cuba* (Chapel Hill: University of North Carolina Press).
23 Sidney Mintz, 'Slavery and the Rise of Peasantry,' *Historical Reflections* 6 (1979), 215–42.
24 The decline in sugar production was respectively 98.3, 75.2, 32.8 and 38.2 per cent. Christopher Schmidt-Nowara, 'The Transition from Slavery to Freedom

in the Americas after 1804,' in David Eltis et al., eds., *The Cambridge World History of Slavery* vol. 4 (Cambridge: Cambridge University Press, 2017), 481.

BIBLIOGRAPHY

Oxford Online Bibliographies – Abolition of Slavery; Abolitionism and Africa; Brazil; Colonial Governance in Spanish America; Creolization; Cuba; Iberian Port Cities; Mexico; Spanish Frontiers; The Caribbean.

Christopher Leslie Brown, *Moral Capital: Foundations of British Abolitionism* (Chapel Hill: University of North Carolina Press, 2006).

Trevor Burnard and John Garrigus, *The Plantation Machine; British Jamaica and French Saint-Domingue and Atlantic Capitalism* (Philadelphia: University of Pennsylvania Press, 2016).

Celso Thomas Castilho, *Slave Emancipation and Transformation in Brazilian Political Citizenship* (Pittsburgh: University of Pittsburgh Press, 2016).

Camillia Cowling, *Conceiving Freedom: Women of Color, Gender, and the Abolition of Slavery in Havana and Rio de Janeiro* (Chapel Hill: University of North Carolina Press, 2013).

Seymour Drescher, *Capitalism and Slavery: British Mobilization in Comparative Perspective* (New York: Oxford University Press, 1986).

Ada Ferrer, *Freedom's Mirror: Cuba and Haiti in the Age of Revolution* (New York: Cambridge University Press, 2014).

Adrian Masters, '"A Thousand Invisible Architects": Vassals, the Petition and Response System and the Creation of Spanish Caste Legislation,' *Hispanic American Historical Review* 98 (2018), 377–406.

Enrique López Mesa, *Tabaco, mito, y esclaves: Apuntes Cubanos de historia agriaria* (Havana: Ciencia Sociales, 2015).

Joseph C. Miller, *Way of Death: Merchant Capitalism and the Angolan Slave Trade, 1730–1830* (Madison, WI: University of Wisconsin, 1988).

Matthew Mulcahy, *Hubs of Empire: The Southeastern Lowcountry and British Caribbean* (Baltimore: Johns Hopkins University Press, 2014).

Gabriel Paquette, *Imperial Portugal in the Age of Atlantic Revolutions: The Luso-Brazilian World, c.1770–1850* (New York: Cambridge University Press, 2014).

Jeremy Popkin, *'You Are All Free': The Haitian Revolution and the Abolition of Slavery* (New York: Cambridge University Press, 2010).

Christopher Schmidt-Nowara, *Empire and Antislavery: Spain, Cuba and Puerto Rico* (Pittsburgh: University of Pittsburgh Press, 1999).

Bartolomé Yun-, as noteCasalilla, *Iberian World Empires and the Globalization of the World, 1415–1668* (Basingstoke: Palgrave Macmillan, 2018).

11

NORTH AMERICA

EARLY SETTLEMENT

The English and Welsh (from 1707, after the union with Scotland, the British) were latecomers to colonization in the Americas. Henry VII was keen on exploration in the Western Ocean and gave Christopher Columbus some attention in the 1480s, but he could not persuade English merchants to replicate the exploratory voyages made by Bristol merchants to the North Atlantic in 1480–1481. The disastrous reign of his son, Henry VIII, saw the English turn away from the Atlantic World. It was only in the second half of the sixteenth century that the English showed some interest in the Atlantic. The Scottish were firmly oriented towards Europe and made no concerted involvement in the Atlantic World at a governmental level until a group of Scottish merchants and speculators, led by William Paterson, founder of the Bank of England, sought to develop a colony – Darien – in the Isthmus of Panama in the late 1690s, to disastrous effect, virtually bankrupting the kingdom and paving for way for union with England and Wales. It was, however, under the Scottish king James VI, who became James I of England and Wales on the death of Henry's daughter Elizabeth I, that the first permanent settlement of English colonists in the America occurred. English colonization began with the unpropitious establishment of a colony on the edges of the Chesapeake Bay in 1607. This colony, called Jamestown after the English and Scottish monarch, in the colony of Virginia, named after Elizabeth, was almost a catastrophic failure, nearly destroyed by Native Americans, falling quickly into disorder and anarchy, followed by military tyrant. But it survived, mainly due to the successful planting of the highly desired crop of tobacco, resulting in a half century of further colonization by private interests and, by 1655 with

Oliver Cromwell's Western Design to capture Spanish possessions in the West Indies, into the first English Empire in the Americas.[1]

Before 1607, however, English involvement in the Atlantic World was slight. The only significant focus of attention was on seeking an illusory northwest passage in northern Canada and the Arctic to Asia, thus ideally shortening greatly sea and land routes from the British Isles to the source of spices and textiles. Otherwise, the English left the Atlantic Ocean to Iberians. Despite the urgings of propagandists such as Richard Hakluyt, who advocated for English settlement and imperial advancement in the Atlantic to counter Spanish European dominance, the English were reluctant under Elizabeth I to engage in colonization in North America or the West Indies. Their activities in this region were confined to privateering expeditions led by famous 'sea-dogs' from southwest England, such as Francis Drake, John Hawkins and especially Walter Raleigh. These activities were often useful in stealing from the Spanish and as such were semi-countenanced by the English state. Elizabeth I was reluctant, however, to spend money on expensive Atlantic voyaging. Her government gave tacit consent to privateering raids but advanced little to no monetary support.[2]

The absence of English state support for colonizing activities until the late seventeenth century meant that seventeenth-century English colonization had a distinct flavour that separated it out from Iberian colonization. The state was relatively little involved in most of the colonizing activities that followed the establishment of a colony by the Virginia Company, a chartered joint-stock company in which London investors shared the risk of colonization in return for supposedly high returns (investors were sadly disappointed in their desire for fortunes from most American schemes of colonization by private individuals in the seventeenth century). In the sixteenth century, state support for colonization was entirely absent. The result was that by 1600 English colonization had resulted in just an active and profitable seasonal pursuit of cod in the North Atlantic which led to temporary settlement by the English in Newfoundland and a failed attempt at colonization in Roanoke in North Carolina in 1587. This latter attempt at colonization was probably doomed through Native Americans attacking English colonists, forcing them to either flee, be assimilated into Native American households or, for the most part, be killed.

NATIVE AMERICANS AND EUROPEAN CONTACT

The fate of the colonists at Roanoke draws attention that the English did not arrive in an empty land. In what is now the United States, there were probably 5–8 million Native Americans at the time of the Columbian conquest; if we add in Native Americans in what is now Canada, the numbers go to over 10 million. That population was very diverse. Excluding Athapaskan and Aleut-Induit language groups, which were individually specific and largely separate from other language formations, there were ten distinct language family groups leading to hundreds of different Indian languages in North America. Unlike South America, the diversity in languages was not matched by a similar diversity in socio-economic organization. Most North American Indians lived in small communal bands and survived (and indeed prospered) through hunting and gathering, in which gender roles were firmly differentiated and which were closely connected to a dense world of sacred iconography and ritual.

These rituals were the fundamental building blocks of Native American identity and to their sense of belonging to the land. Europeans saw their hunter-gatherer characteristics and mistakenly thought that this showed they had no attachment to land, because American land was not settled and cultivated in ways Europeans though appropriate. Native Americans, however, had close relationships with the spaces they occupied and resisted fiercely, and often successfully, European incursions into their territory. These battles over land, settlement and culture formed the backdrop to European settlement during the period of Atlantic history, especially in the seventeenth century, when British colonization was being established and when Native Americans were the dominant force almost everywhere on the North American continent, save in coastal Virginia and in Atlantic New England.[3]

Antagonism between Native Americans in seventeenth-century Virginia and New England was among the fiercest such antagonisms in Atlantic history, bearing direct comparison with how Native Americans were treated on Hispaniola in the early sixteenth century. Some scholars have termed the relationship between English settlers and Native Americans as genocidal in nature. That is too sweeping a claim because, as Richard White showed in his pioneering work on the Middle Ground – places where Native Americans and Europeans met, as in the early eighteenth-century Great Lakes region of North America, on terms of wary egalitarianism and where agreements had to be negotiated and affirmed through difficult but necessary forms of cultural diplomacy – relations between Native Americans and Europeans encompassed a great deal more than just bouts of extreme violence from each side.[4]

The conventional definition of genocide means that one side must intentionally want to 'destroy' or 'eliminate' a racially or ethnically defined people. Such intention was rare in North America. It probably did exist, however, in early Virginia, between 1622 and 1632, after a rebellion by the Powhatan chief, Opechanough, which had nearly destroyed the infant colony.[5] Official policy was genocidal in intent in these years and relations between Native Americans and Europeans both hostile and brutal. Similar genocidal policies operated in New England, as in the ferocious Pequot War in 1637, where the Pilgrim leader William Bradford gleefully celebrated the death by burning of Native American villages containing men, women and children. They were in place even more so in 1676, in King Philip's War, pitting European colonists against the Wampanoag chief, Metacom, who adopted the English name Philip and who succeeded in uniting several Native American tribes in a desperate and it eventuated fruitless attempt to combat European colonization encroaching upon Native American territory. That war was marked by extreme acts of barbarism, committed by both New England settlers and Native Americans, which made a few Puritan divines question whether indeed the mission of New Englanders in Massachusetts was unfolding according to God's plan.

But we should not believe that Native American history, and violence in North America, started with Englishmen coming to Roanoke, North Carolina. Native American history was not unmoving and static. As in Central and South America, some groups of North American Native Americans had long and complicated histories before the arrival of Columbus. These histories were usually developed not in isolation from other native American groupings but in constant dialogue with other peoples. Neither geographic distance nor linguistic barriers halted the spread of materials, peoples, beliefs and technologies in the centuries before European arrival. On occasion, Native American peoples developed significant civilizations that evolved out of hunter-gathering and which sometimes rose and collapsed before European (first Spanish, then English and French) arrival in the late sixteenth through seventeenth centuries. For example, as hinted at in Chapter 1, the Anasazi tribes created in the Chaco Canyon of modern Colorado a vibrant network of villages that communicated closely with each other and which connected perhaps 15,000 people in dense trade networks. That system arose in the tenth century and lasted for nearly 300 years, before collapsing due to difficulties arising from drought, which undermined elite power over how production was controlled, and how trade was regulated. The smaller pueblos (or villages) that the Spanish encountered in the sixteenth century and which they thought had been the basis of Anasazi social organization for time immemorial were thus of relatively recent origin.

Similarly, in the eastern woodlands of North America, from the Mississippi Valley to the Atlantic coast, where Native American contact with Europeans was first and most profound, diversity of social and economic organization within growing populations who benefited from the prosperity of the region and abundance of easily obtainable food supplies, even before agriculture became the principal mode of food production, was palpable. That diversity changed because of a switch to agriculture. Some eastern societies resembled the Anasazi in becoming highly centralized. As in the Chaco Canyon, these societies flourished for several centuries before becoming too large and hierarchical for many members, leading groups to disperse and rearrange themselves in smaller-scale villages. The impact of disease upon such populations – death from European diseases arrived well before Europeans themselves and thus Europeans arrived into not so much in an empty land but a widowed landscape, where Native American populations were in sometimes rapid population decline – accentuated a move from large-scale to small-scale societies. The result was a bewildering number of different Native American societies, all with clear and different identities but which were highly aware of each other and in constant interchange, notably over trade. Quite often that interchange led to war: Europeans were able to take advantage in North America, as the Spanish had done in Mexico and Peru, of pre-existing tensions within Native American communities and play one Native American group off against another.

Their ultimate success against Native Americans was neither foreordained nor easy to accomplish. The seventeenth century was marked in North America by constant violence and bloodshed. The English shared with the Spanish who were supposedly their enemies a shared Conquistador mentality of glorying in conquest almost for its own sake. We can see this attitude expressed right from the start of settlement. In 1607, for example, William Brewster declared, in language reminiscent of Hernan Cortés, 'Nowe is the kinge[s] majesty offered. The most Statlye, Riche kingdom in the world, nevar possesse by anye Christian prynce, be you one meanes among manye to Further our Secondyinge, to Conquer this land.' With these attitudes, it is not surprising that English settlers responded ferociously when Native Americans dared to intrude upon their colonialist fantasies. The Puritan divine, Cotton Mather, for example, waxed hysterical in how he thought of Native Americans in the aftermath of bloody warfare in New England from 1676 to the 1690s. He fulminated that 'Those *Devils Incarnate* have Tyed their *Captives* unto Trees, and first cutting off their ears, and then have broiled their whole *Bodies*, with slow Fires, dancing the mean while about them, and cutting out dollops of their flesh'.

As Susan Juster observes, the extreme language used by English settlers about the cruelty of Native Americans and their innate savagery was copied from anti-Catholic rhetoric embodied in John Foxe's Protestant recording of Catholic atrocities, *The Book of Martyrs* (1563). As she argues, 'the rage expressed in the desecration of Indian bodies and mission chapels derived in part from a deep well of spiritual anxieties and animosities whose source lay in the bloody European past as in the unsettled American present'.[6] Europeans not only termed Native Americans by the inaccurate title of 'Indians', confusing them with Southeast Asians but understood the iconography of native American religion and resistance within frameworks derived from the tumults of the Reformation. It is harder to understand what Native Americans thought of Europeans, given the one-sided nature of historical evidence, but what we can find suggests that they too thought of their foes within intellectual systems of conflict and cooperation with other Native Americans forged over many years of contact.

The main theme in the settlement and colonization of North America is that eventually Native American land became English, British or French land. That process evolved over at least a century on the tidewater regions of the

Atlantic coast and longer elsewhere. The process by which European settlers took over Native American land was bloody, contested and uneven in how it occurred. By the middle of the eighteenth century, however, the eastern woodlands and Atlantic coast of what became the United States and Canada were firmly under the control of European settlers. The principal reason for European success was demographic – Native American populations kept declining, a process that continued well after colonial British North America had become a postcolonial nation. By 1900, the Native American population of the United States had reduced to 237,000, a 95 per cent drop from pre-Columbian times. That nadir of Native American experience, however, lay in the future. During the seventeenth and eighteenth centuries, some Native American peoples did not just survive but developed their own imperial formations which prevented European intrusion into their territory and which were themselves intrusive onto the lands of less richly endowed Native American populations.

The most noticeable example of a Native American empire arising in conjunction with European empires was the Comanche empire of southwestern Texas and New Mexico, chronicled by Pekka Hämäläinen. The Comanches were a powerful assortment of Native American peoples who lived on the southern plains and who were determined to use importations from Europe – guns and horses, in particular – to wage war against opponents, known to outsiders as Apaches. By 1800, when their power began to decline, Comanches numbered about 20,000, which was twice the number of other Native Americans in the region and more than the Spanish residents in what was ostensibly part of the Spanish Empire and then the United States, but which was, in fact, an aggressively expanding Native American realm deserving of the name 'empire'. Their rise is explicable through the Comanches' successful management of their ecological environment, including animals native to the Americas, like bison, and animals from the outside, like horses, to wage war to acquire horses, women, children and excellent hunting territory and ever more firearms. Their empire eventually crumbled, mainly due to the prime weapon Europeans had against Native Americans – disease – but for the hundred or so years that the Comanche empire prevailed their success showed how it was possible for Native Americans to devise creative responses to the dangers and the opportunities unleashed by European contact.[7]

ENDURING NATIVE AMERICAN POWER

We often think of European colonization of the Americas as a one-way process. This equation of European power with European conquest comes in part from the nature of the sources we use – the great majority created by Europeans, not by Native Americans, as noted previously. It also comes in part from how we have traditionally neglected Native American forms of power and especially indigenous forms of territoriality. Native Americans did not view land claims and sovereignty as did Europeans, but they knew precisely where their domains began and where others ended. If their definitions were governed by behaviours and traditions rather than contracts or nationality that did not make these definitions any less real. As Pekka Hämäläinen notes, 'from one bridgehead to another and across the [North American] continent's edge, European pretensions to empire crashed against indigenous territoriality'.[8] Thus, in New Mexico and Texas, Spanish colonists altered their intentions to deal with the reality of Indian power. When the French looked at maps of seventeenth- and eighteenth-century Louisiana, it seemed limitless, but the reality was that the French were confined to small spaces by powerful indigenous confederations – France operated in the Americas under significant constraints from the reality that in the Pays d'en Haut region west of Montreal and extending to the Great Lakes.

Native American peoples maintained their territorial power well into the period of European colonization throughout the Americas. It meant that European settler societies were limited to small pockets of settlement, primarily on the Atlantic coast. These pockets of colonial power exerted an influence deep into the continent – we should not make the mistake when acknowledging Native American power in the colonial period of underestimating how severe a challenge growing European power was to traditional power relations even in the North American interior where Europeans were not present. But the majority of the great interior remained largely closed to European settlement until after the American Revolution. English settlers remained huddled on the Atlantic coast well into the eighteenth century; advances west were incremental well into the eighteenth century; and the so-called 'backcountry' settlements around the Appalachian Mountains from Pennsylvania to Georgia formed a distinct region separated from societies on the coast by culture as much as by space, where relations with native Americans were especially intense. Spanish colonialism in North America expanded in the eighteenth century from Florida, Texas and New Mexico into the lower Mississippi Valley and into California but, just as with French settlement, which did not move from the St. Lawrence and Mississippi Valleys, Native Americans kept both sets of colonials physically constrained. As Pekka Hämäläinen concludes, 'spearheads of colonial expansion morphed into defensive ethnic enclaves, and imperial frontiers softened into borderlands where indigenous forms of social control not only prevailed but often dominated'.[9]

One reason why European settlers found it hard to breach Native American–controlled areas was that Native Americans, just like Europeans, were formidable warriors with societies oriented around warfare. Europeans tended to interpret this martial quality in deeply negative fashion, alleging that Native Americans were naturally cruel due to their irreligion and lack of civilization. But Europeans admitted that martial skills were highly valued among Native Americans and that young men believed that exploits on the warpath were important determinants of national prestige. The New York politician Cadwallader Colden stated, 'It is not for the Sake of Tribute that they make War but from the Notions of Glory, which they have ever most strongly imprinted in their Minds.' In short, if you wanted to make it in Native American societies, then you needed to be a successful warrior.

War served other functions in Native American culture more than prestige. It was a way of acquiring captives to maintain or to increase population. But Native Americans approached war differently from Europeans. They valued victory but did not think death in battle glorious. Benjamin West's depiction of a respectful Iroquois chieftain mourning the death of General Wolfe in 1759 as a heroic act is a fanciful invention. Europeans marvelled at how Iroquois would retreat from engagements on the brink of success if they suffered a few deaths. For the Iroquois, as Daniel Richter observes, 'such a campaign was no victory; casualties would subvert the purpose of warfare as a means of restocking the population'.[10] The differing attitudes to death in battle between Native Americans and Europeans encouraged the latter to consider the former cowardly – a great mistake on their part, as they usually found when they encountered battle-hardened and aggressively expansionist Native American confederations like the Iroquois and the Cherokee, where European violence was met and matched by violence from their adversaries. The Iroquois, for example, were formidable warriors, skilled in firearms and tenacious in defending their land and their people from attack.

Europeans also failed to realize that they were often not the major object of attention within Native American geopolitics. Previous historical processes did not just stop when European colonization started. Of course, European disease, firearms and animals like horses intensified Native American conflicts as disputes over trade, especially the 'beaver wars' of the late seventeenth and early eighteenth centuries in the Pays d'en haut, made economic motives central to Native American conflicts for the first time. But many Native American wars were conducted between different Native American nations. In the seventeenth century, for example, Mohawks, Senecas, Onondagas and Huron in British New York and French Canada fought constantly, with economic factors being added to, rather than replacing, older cultural motives for confrontation. One of those older motives was the desire to get captives for mourning (the torture and execution of captives to assuage mourners' grief) and for population replacement. The latter imperative became more urgent as disease affected Native American populations ever more deeply as colonization proceeded. Until the mid-1670s in this region, war continued to perform useful functions for the Iroquois. It was only after this period when the focus of warfare decisively turned away from inter-Native American conflict to antagonism and conflict with Europeans.

The reason for this change was a change in power relations on much of the North American continent. Settler power increased in the early eighteenth century as population levels dramatically increased through natural reproduction in the region north of Maryland and to an extent in the American South. The fur trade became a greater part of the settler economy and European pressure on Native American economic alliances increased, making alliances made between the two groups ever more problematic and more often breached, usually by Europeans. The turning point for the Iroquois came around 1700, when Anglo-French control for the interior of North America cut off the fur trade, causing great harm to local Native American economies, while European raiding parties destroyed vital crops and villages. But, as Richter notes, Native Americans were not helpless in the face of unprecedented onslaughts from Europeans. They adjusted their patterns of warfare, reduced domestic factionalism and swapped diplomacy for war (leading to a 'grand settlement' of 1701 between Iroquois and the French in 1701 that kept a truce between the two parties). Richter notes that 'through most of the first half of the eighteenth century, [Iroquois leaders] pursued a policy of neutrality between the empires with a dexterity that the English never, and the French only seldom, comprehended'.[11]

What happened in the American Northeast was a local variation on an Atlantic pattern. James Merrell has shown how the Catawbas, a relatively small confederacy in the North Carolina piedmont were able to maintain their territorial boundaries against Europeans – whom they called 'nothings' – until the end of the American Revolution and perhaps the early nineteenth century, thus demarcating limits for English colonialism in a vital area of expansion into the interior. The Catawba were less concerned about European incursions into their lands but threats from the Iroquois hundreds of miles north. The Iroquois in the early eighteenth century had become an aggressive imperialist power, whose actions against fellow Native Americans were more disturbing to these tribes than were the less worrying and occasional attacks they faced from Europeans. The Catawba found it relatively easy to repel Europeans until late in the eighteenth century.[12] The even larger southern confederations of the Cherokee, Creeks, Choctaws and Chickasaws felt even less constrained in their geopolitical ambitions by threats from Europeans than the smaller Catawba Native group. They lived in areas well distant from American expansion until the development of the cotton frontier in the early nineteenth century and their focus was on stopping each other from dominating the southeast region of North America. For most of the seventeenth and early eighteenth centuries, the ambitions for dominance of each group were kept in check by the power of the other groups in the South. The result was continued but significant low-level violence as each southern confederation of Native Americans fought with each other to achieve unrealized hegemonic aims. By the middle of the eighteenth century, however, the Creeks became more dominant than the other groups, which meant that they attracted other smaller Native American groups like the Seminole and Alabama to attach themselves to the Creeks for protection. The other major group in the region, the Cherokee, reacted by signing peace treaties with the Creek in the 1740s and 1750s, giving the region a degree of peace until the American Revolution that had not been present before. These formidable nations, however, attracted attention from the Iroquois who, as well as threatening Native American groups in the Great Lakes region, shifted their raiding for slaves into the southeast. As Pekka Hämäläinen argues, in the first half of the eighteenth century 'the Native Southeast was a "tribal zone," a militarized landscape where lethal microbes, new technologies of killing, and colliding colonial interests fueled wars that were only seemingly local. But Southeastern Indians kept fighting and killing one another not only because they were so vulnerable to external forces, but also because they remained so powerful.'[13]

ENVIRONMENTAL CONDITIONS

The European settlement of North America was conditioned by the ecology of the continent and itself shaped significant ecological change over time. Much of North America, excluding the far north Arctic and deserts in the southwest, was eminently suitable for cultivation. If we just confine ourselves to settlement done during the Atlantic period of colonization in the seventeenth and eighteenth centuries, we can divide North America into three large zones. The first – smallest and least important but vital in the sixteenth century as a kickstart to colonization – was in the far north, between Greenland and the Great Banks of Newfoundland, where fish were abundant and were fished so intensively that by the nineteenth century cod stocks had greatly diminished. The second, larger and more obviously suitable land for cultivation, were temperate lands ranging from Quebec to Baltimore. In this region, European colonists developed modest economies based on shipping and semi-subsistence agriculture that sustained rapidly growing families. The economies of the region were largely self-sufficient insofar as they provided food for themselves but little for export. It was a region heavily involved, however, in the Atlantic World, with its residents prospering from every aspect of Atlantic commerce, from slavery to whaling. These activities were focused on thriving Atlantic ports such as Boston, New York and Philadelphia, where transatlantic merchants traded extensively with the West Indies and secondarily with Britain. These ports were also central to a major development in North American history, which was the advent of industrialization after 1800, a process which made the northeast of North America the wealthiest region of the world by the mid-nineteenth-century, when our story ends.

It was also a region of the world that was especially demographically propitious for white settlement. Despite attracting very few immigrants relative to other parts of British America, the population of New England and the Middle Colonies (from New York to Delaware) boomed in the eighteenth century, so that by the time of the American Revolution there were 1.1 million white residents and a relatively small number of Africans (predominantly enslaved but some freed) in the region. The demographic success of the region was celebrated by Benjamin Franklin, a scientist among his many accomplishments, who was undoubtedly the single most famous colonial American before George Washington. Writing in 1760, during the Seven Years' War, his *Observations Concerning the Increase of Mankind* was an encomium to the imperial benefits of a fast advancing European population. He crowed that rapid population increase meant that in North America there 'will in another Century be more than the People of England, the greatest Number of *Englishmen* will be on this Side of the Water. What an Accession of Power to the *British* Empire by Sea as well as by Land! What Increase of Trade and Navigation! What Numbers of Ships and Seamen!'

The final region was the biggest and most prosperous. Extending from Maryland through to northeastern South America, it was a region devoted to plantation agriculture based upon slave production. It is so important a region of the Atlantic World, given its reliance on slavery and on its economic value to European empire that it is treated in a separate chapter in this book. It first became important in British North America during the colonization of Virginia when in the 1610s colonists realized that the land was suitable for producing tobacco, a crop with a high demand in Europe. In 1619, Virginia received what was probably the first shipment of African captives and by the 1650s had joined the small but historically significant island of Barbados in transforming itself from a society largely full of white planters and English and Irish indentured servants into a racially divided society where whites reaped the advantages to be gained from plantation agriculture (tobacco in the Chesapeake; rice and indigo in the Carolinas; sugar and rum predominantly, but also cacao, cotton and ginger, in the West Indies) while imported Africans consigned to lifetime and hereditary enslavement did the bulk of the work. By 1770, the population of the Chesapeake and Lower South was 1 million, of whom just over 400,000 were black while there were just 10,000 people in Louisiana in 1763, of whom 6,000 were black.

The settlement of these regions by the British and French took place during a period of significant ecological global crisis, the period of the 'Little Ice Age', where the world, including North America, experienced some of the coldest weather, notably in the decades between 1590 and 1610 and again in the 1640s and 1690s. Not coincidentally these were periods of considerable political antagonism throughout the Atlantic World, leading respectively to the beginnings of settlement in North America, to a political implosion whereby a Britain preoccupied with civil unrest left English colonies in the Americas to develop outside effective metropolitan oversight, and a reassertion of imperial power following the Glorious Revolution in England, Scotland and Ireland in 1688. Overall, however, the acquisition by England of colonies in the seventeenth century had the environmental effect of avoiding Malthusian crisis in the British Isles (Thomas Malthus in 1798 predicted that rising European populations would face famine as population increased exponentially while resources increased only arithmetically). What North America and the Caribbean provided the metropolis with was 'ghost acres' whereby fewer acres than should have been the case had to be devoted to European agricultural production. Fish, grain and timber from America and, to a lesser extent, the calories that were contained in plantation crops like sugar and rice permitted an escape for Europeans from growth constraints that were not available anywhere else on the planet.

As John McNeill insists, colonization in North America meant that 'Atlantic Europe sidestepped the constraints of the pre-industrial organic energy regime' by using an 'energy subsidy' from the Americas that kept Malthusian scenarios of famine and dearth away. He concludes that 'Atlantic American ecosystems subsidised the overstrained ones of Atlantic Europe after 1600, allowing escape from stagnation and eventually allowing a sustained economic growth that made the tiny societies of northwestern Europe the most dynamic and soon the most powerful in the world'.[14] Nowhere was that ecological benefit more pronounced than in Britain, which received profits and products from slave-powered plantation economies as well as having in its northern regions a growing and affluent market of consumers eager to buy British manufactured eighteenth century. The price of European happiness was largely paid by Native Americans, whose land allowed for expansion of agriculture and increases in population in North America, and by Africans, whose labour in the American South and West Indies allowed the ecological revolutions that so benefitted Europe to take place in American plantation zones.

THE CHARACTER OF EARLY ENGLISH AND FRENCH COLONIZATION

The English colonists who moved to North America in the first half of the seventeenth century were not from a cross-section of English society. For a start, very few of them were women: the ratio of male migrants to female migrants in the places of largest emigration, such as Virginia and Barbados, was perhaps 9 to 1. It was only in the peculiar circumstances of the 'Great Migration' of English Puritans to Massachusetts in the late 1620s and early 1630s that women came in comparatively large numbers. Women went to Massachusetts out of religious conviction and to support husbands and children seeking to build a new Zion in the relatively inhospitable environs of New England. Their presence and the healthy disease environment of

New England meant that low levels of migration to this region still resulted in substantial population gain. Elsewhere, women were low in numbers. Little work has been done on why women found moving to English America unappealing but it is probably due to a mixture of push factors (better opportunities in domestic service in England than in Virginia) and pull factors (the business of colonization was unappealing when what women would be expected to do – field work as well as running a household with few resources and the strong possibility of sexual exploitation in societies with a superfluity of men and few legal protections for poor women – was unpleasant). Dire demographic conditions among white colonists in the seventeenth-century Chesapeake and Caribbean did allow some women the chance to 'marry, bury, marry again and grow rich', as some observers callously commented and which Daniel Defoe made central to his story of Moll Flanders, a fallen woman made good in Virginia. But the realities of raising families without a male protector in environments where children frequently died made coming to America uninviting for most women, especially as gender norms made it harder than for men for women to make their fortune and potentially return home.[15]

The small number of European female migrants, especially those who came to North America free and uncoerced, meant that even more than for men most women arriving in North America from other parts of the Atlantic World were coerced – either indentured servants or, more often, enslaved women. Indeed, the modal female arriving in North America was a young Biafran sent as a slave to the Lower South. The disparity between women and men in the Atlantic slave trade was much less than among European migrants, with perhaps 29 per cent of enslaved people arriving in the Chesapeake and Carolinas in the eighteenth-century being women and about 36 per cent being female (including girls). The African population was always a more gender-balanced stream of migration than the European stream, meaning that increased importation of slaves went along with a demographic transition to a native-born white population around 1700 to make the most male-dominated region in seventeenth-century North America – the Chesapeake – as gender balanced by 1720 as were the northern colonies of British and French North America.

The first European settlers in seventeenth-century North America were not just male. They were remarkably cosmopolitan adventurers who brought with them ideas about colonization drawn from experiences in other places of English colonization, notably Ireland (where 200,000 English and Scots migrated in the seventeenth century). Others had been involved with English trade in the Mediterranean and occasionally with commercial ventures in the Indian Ocean World. These colonial globetrotters, as Alison Games describes them, played an outside role, as the initial residents of English settlements in North America, in shaping religion, trade, labour and culture. The most famous example of such a globetrotter was John Smith – a man with a very common name but an extraordinarily unusual life. Before becoming one of the initial settlers in Jamestown from 1607 and a visitor to New England in the 1620s, Smith had been a soldier of fortune in Europe, becoming enslaved in the Ottoman Empire. His experiences in Europe and in Ireland allowed him great scope to shape the development of early Virginia. So too, Thomas Dale, the tyrannical first governor of Virginia, had been a soldier for hire in Europe who spent several years being a mercenary for the Dutch. After Virginia, he joined the East India Company, dying in its service in India. Ostensibly, he had turned his attention from tackling Iberian hegemony through establishing an English colony in the Chesapeake to thwarting the trading enterprises of other European empires besides the English in the Indian Ocean. It is difficult to see, however, that changes in circumstances altered his overall inclinations – which were not so much as to establish colonies in the New World as to benefit from Atlantic trading opportunities.

It took many years and many changes of policy for English settlements in North America to become colonies giving something valuable to the Crown, such as revenue from desirable exports. In the early years English colonization was largely private in nature with relatively minimal state involvement. The aim of early English settlers in Virginia in 1607 was that they would establish towns on the Spanish model in the Caribbean from which settlers would exploit relations with Native Americans and would find silver to trade with Europe. Virginia was never meant to be a place of permanent English settlement. In its first few years, the ill-equipped Englishmen who went there expected their residence to become a trading factory, as was being established (with more success) by Europeans in early seventeenth-century Indonesia, Japan and India. It also resembled what the English were doing in West Africa. That Virginia was meant to be a trading factory rather than a colony helps explain the nature of early cultural contacts with Native Americans. As in Africa, English colonists tried to learn languages and cultural practices to make trade easier. They also sought sexual contacts with native Americans, as was common for European merchants and slave traders in West Africa, partly for exploitation of local networks and probably also for companionship in lands with fewer white women and with lax sexual mores. The famous marriage between John Rolfe and the Native American 'princess', Pocahontas, was one such example of cultural exchange achieved through a sexual relationship. Rolfe certainly thought that his marriage to a well-connected Native American girl would aid him in developing commercial relations with Native Americans in Virginia.[16]

One result of this kind of colonization – done by globetrotters, working for private companies, rather than for the Crown – was that English colonization, especially outside New England, where the settlement had a more obviously religious rationale than in the Chesapeake, was different to how colonization had developed in Iberian America. The institutions of Spain and Portugal, from municipal councils to legal systems, came with the first settlers and were soon implemented as fundamental features structuring Iberian colonial life. In English America, by contrast, the Crown pursued imperialism indirectly, through joint-stock companies where investors, usually from London, took all the risk and claimed all the profits of settlement. Apart from essential royal monopolies, English commercial companies had enormous latitude to create their own worlds overseas. The result was an astonishing range of colonial and commercial experiments in North America, a range that never entirely disappeared, despite the strident efforts of government officials from the time of the Restoration of the English and Scottish monarchy in 1660 to impose order upon an unruly colonial atmosphere. In contrast to Spanish America, English colonies exhibited a wide range of behaviours and characteristics which defeated imperial attempts to make colonial administration uniform.

The Iberian Atlantic World found English and French colonization very challenging to its sense of itself. English colonization was not just different to that of Iberian America but was a dangerous intrusion into a world Spain and Portugal claimed for itself. Spain chose to react rather than passively sit aside. For example, in 1565 there was a brutal extinction of a French colony in Florida by Pedro Menéndez de Avilés. This massacre, widely reported as an outrage in Protestant Europe, convinced Protestant colonists, like the English, that the Spanish monarch Philip II was the devil himself and that they needed to settle in northern regions, away from Spanish settlement.

English colonizers embarked upon a remarkable propaganda exercise in favour of the virtues of colonization which celebrated the religious and patriotic character of private commercial activities, casting what people were doing for profit into an anti-Spanish national enterprise that would not just make participants money but spread the Protestant Gospel, enhance English wealth and power, and improve the waste spaces of Atlantic America through raising lucrative and desired crops like tobacco. By 1624, just before a major push for settlement by the English into New England and the Caribbean, English, and to a lesser extent, French, colonization had broken the Iberian monopoly over a New World, creating a vast new supernatural space which brought the four continents of the Atlantic World together. In this space, the English had not just developed economic infrastructures and rudimentary societies but had implanted something very dear to English hearts – a system of government with a representative assembly that was set within an expanding English world of political liberties. Most of the people in seventeenth-century English colonies, white and black, were not free but the colonies they established were fiercely devoted to the preservation of English liberties and English concepts of freedom.

The first Africans to arrive in North America were also cosmopolitans and different in kind and influence than most Africans who arrived in the continent once the plantation system was established fully in the last quarter of the seventeenth century. The initial shipment of Africans coming to Virginia probably arrived in 1619 with only a few more coming into the

Chesapeake before the 1660s. Most of the first arrivals were transported into the region by the Dutch, dribbling into Chesapeake rivers in small lots that were seldom greater in number than twenty Africans. These Africans were a diverse lot. Only a small proportion came directly from Africa. The majority had already spent time in the New World, usually in Spanish America, were familiar with Christianity (and sometimes were Christian themselves, which was problematic for English colonists wanting to justify the enslavement of Africans on religious rather than racial grounds) and other European cultural norms and were generally highly skilled linguists. For the first fifty years of settlement, these cosmopolitan men worked side by side with white labourers as tobacco workers and had a variety of statuses besides being slaves in societies in which slave status was not codified until the 1660s. Small in number, these enslaved people were large in influence. The multiplicity of their origins and the diversity of their experiences ensured that the earliest racial interactions between whites and blacks were part of a general process of creolization, where African inheritances of a manifold kind intersected with New World experience to quickly create a distinctive, and truly American, enslaved culture.

The story of Anthony Johnson, sold to the English at Jamestown in 1721, is that of an Atlantic creole. He started as a labourer alongside white indentured servants on a tobacco plantation, surviving in his first year the 1622 Native American raid that nearly destroyed the colony. He was a highly regarded servant who was allowed by his master to farm independently while a slave, to marry and have his children become baptized and to eventually gain his and his children's freedom. One sign of his incorporation into a fledgling Chesapeake society was the Anglicization of his name, from Antonio to Anthony. By 1651, he had earned a 250-acre head-right grant for sponsoring the entry of servants into the eastern shore of Maryland. When in 1653 his plantation burned to the ground, he asked and received a substantial tax abatement. He died in 1670, with grandchildren and a strong sense of his independence and self-worth. When challenged by a local elite planter to deny he was slothful, Johnson declared, 'I know myne owne ground and I will worke when I please and play when I please.'

Such assertions of authority soon ended, however. By the late seventeenth century, the period of Atlantic creoles had ended and almost all people of African descent had been deprived of their freedom and made into, at best, second-class subjects, without any rights that white people had to consider. The diversity of the early years in African experience in North America had collapsed and black experience had narrowed and become more like the experiences of enslaved people in the Caribbean and South America. Africans arriving into the Carolinas, for example, after 1680 found themselves arriving into societies very similar to those found in Barbados and Jamaica. As Ira Berlin puts it, 'the demand for slaves was greater, the importation of slaves more massive, and degradation of black life swifter and deeper'. They lived lives of greater desperation in both Carolina and the

Chesapeake after 1700 than before and faced the constant threat of violence more than Anthony Johnson had done. As Berlin continues, 'Chesapeake slaves faced the pillory, whipping post, and gallows far more frequently and in far larger numbers than before.' Those punishments were both cruel, ingenious and humiliating as when the Virginian great planter William Byrd forced a bedwetting slave to drink a 'pint of piss'.[17]

Nevertheless, the experiences of enslaved Africans in North America were distinctive in one important respect from their compatriots elsewhere in the Atlantic World. Alone of the major slave holding regions of the Atlantic, North American slaves experienced demographic success. By the American Revolution not only were most enslaved people in North America born in America rather than Africa but planters in the Chesapeake and the Carolinas could contemplate ending the Atlantic slave trade and relying instead on natural increase of slaves and an increasingly flourishing domestic slave trade to maintain enslaved populations. One major result of this unusual demographic regime was a greater amount of creolization, or adaptation to the dominant Euro-African culture. How much enslaved people conformed to European ways and adapted that culture in syncretic ways to develop distinctive African-American cultures differed according to region. In the Northern colonies, blacks were a distinct minority, widely dispersed and in constant interaction with whites. They adapted themselves to European cultural norms more than was the case in the Lowcountry tidewater, where Africans or African-Americans were in the majority. Interactions with native-born slaves rather than with whites were the primary means whereby Africans were acculturated around 1700 in the Chesapeake, likely increasing the speed by which a creole culture developed in that region. By contrast, increased importation of Africans into the Carolinas between 1750 and 1776 and an influx of Africans into the American North, an influx which seems to have led to Northern blacks becoming aware of their African origins, probably meant that African-American cultures in these areas became more obviously African just before the American Revolution. Creolization, it seems clear, proceeded at different paces and in different rhythms in different places. Everywhere, however, Africans and their descendants were forced to reshape African ideas and practices in the light of the necessities of local North American life. As Berlin notes, 'for most Africans, as for their white counterparts, identity was a garment which might be worn or discarded. Choice as well as imposition or birthright, determined who the new arrivals might be. In short, identity formation for African slaves was neither automatic nor unreflective, neither uniform nor unilinear.'[18]

COLONIAL CONSOLIDATION

The diversity of early settlement patterns in British North America was never eradicated and they never lost the extensive political autonomy they acquired in the 1640s when the English Civil War caused an implosion at the imperial centre that left colonies to fend for themselves. After 1660, Charles II tried to impose more uniformity on the colonies but his efforts and even more so the efforts of his ineffectual and authoritarian brother, James II, failed. As Stephen Saunders Webb notes, the lessons of the English Glorious Revolution of 1688 suggested the uselessness and danger of administrative centralization. The remarkable dynamism of North American colonies in the early eighteenth century as economies based on slave labour started to become highly profitable and which allowed for an integration of the Atlantic economy around slavery and slave-produced crops validated for powerful native-born American elites the wisdom of a set of arrangements with the Crown which made them virtually semi-autonomous entities.[19] By the 1760s, many of the Americans declaring for Revolution were therefore committed to a concept of negative liberty which meant 'freedom from a number of political and social evils, including arbitrary government power' with a tendency to see 'government as malevolent'.

Before the 1760s, therefore, the imperial touch in North America was light. Britain largely left the colonies alone, abandoning in practice but not in theory late Stuart attempts to bring the colonies under firm centralized control. The result was strong and continued economic growth and remarkable political stability. That stability was remarkable given that the wealth of North America and the diverse origins of European settlement patterns meant that many colonies, notably in the Middle Colonies of New York, New Jersey and Pennsylvania, exhibited sizeable religious and ethnic diversity as thousands of emigrants from continental Europe transformed the population of the regions. Everywhere throughout British North America in the eighteenth century, powerful local creole elites established and dominated strong representative institutions founded as replicas of British models, especially the Houses of Parliament, in which they proclaimed their adherence to liberties they believed their British inheritance. Those liberties, it was argued, had been confirmed in Britain by the constitutional settlement of the Glorious Revolution.

Simultaneously and fervently, they also expressed their allegiance to the Hanoverian monarchy, which was a political manifestation of Protestant supremacy and which represented a major form of resistance to the supposed malign influence of Catholic despotism as personified in the rule of Louis XIV and his successors as French monarchs. American colonists eagerly supported Britain in their many wars against France from the 1690s, culminating in the Seven Years' War, fought largely in North America between 1756 and 1763 and which resulted in the establishment of British dominance in the continent. Even before then, however, American colonists participated in Britain's colonial wars against Spain and France, as in the attack on Cartegena in 1741 and in the siege of Havana in 1762 where thousands of soldiers from New England sacrificed their lives to disease in the British imperial cause.

Divisions in the eighteenth century between colonists were evident in differences between a growing wealthy elite and increasing numbers of poor people and especially between a largely prosperous white population which by the eve of the American Revolution had the highest living standards of any population on earth and an impoverished and unhealthy black population where living standards were very poor. Religion also proved divisive as much as it also provided colonials with sources of meaning and perhaps a sense of themselves as an American people who were different from European forebears. A burst of evangelical revivalism (the Great Awakening) within Protestant denominations led by celebrity preachers from England like George Whitefield who attracted enormous audiences throughout North America in the 1720s and 1730s not just transformed the nature of American religion, making it more obviously emotional and individual and possibly foreshadowing an attachment to egalitarian democratic politics but caused a breach between evangelicals and more conventional Anglicans, notably in the American South. These Anglicans found such emotional religiosity disturbing and against a social order based around politeness, emotional restraint, deference to established authority in the church as well as in politics, and adherence to hierarchical inherited social order.

But what impresses most about this period of remarkable and sustained growth in all areas in the first half of the eighteenth-century is the degree to which these diverse North American British societies developed along similar lines and converged culturally around a shared attachment to English social and political values. One means by which this convergence was achieved was through the expansion of the world of goods and the development of a commercial culture based upon the extensive importation of consumer goods from Britain that gave a stylistic uniformity to British American culture. Just as important was the rise to authority in every colony of creole elites who by mid-century not only dominated politics but were also the arbiters of social style. That style was that of English gentlemen. Anxious above all to be genteel and English, colonial elites had a shared devotion to gentility, improvement and Anglicization that linked them to elites in Britain and which also made each colony increasingly like each other. Ironically, it was this convergence around adherence to English norms of behaviour which helped diverse colonies converge together sufficiently to have a shared outraged response to changes in imperial actions in the 1760s that served as an important precondition for revolution in 1776.

The dark undercurrent to this story of colonial success was slavery and the suppression of Native Americans. White Americans' attitudes to Native Americans were almost uniformly hostile by the middle of the eighteenth century, with colonists in frontier regions openly declaring that Native Americans were barbaric savages and advocating policies of genocide to remove Native Americans from land they coveted. The Seven Years' War exacerbated such tendencies, leading to outbreaks of severe frontier violence such as Pontiac's War in the Ohio Valley in 1763. Native Americans were inspired in their opposition to colonists' encroachment on their land and advocacy of genocidal policies by religious prophets who since the 1740s had been preaching rejection of the European Atlantic World. Millenarian fervour led to shocking violence. In Pontiac's War in 1763, for example, Native Americans destroyed most British military posts west of the Appalachians, killing, capturing or evicting colonists they believed were squatting on their land. Colonists in the American interior swore revenge. They felt betrayed by the British Proclamation of 1763, which attempted to ban westward settlement in the west and which they believed validated the savagery of Pontiac and allies by refusing to punish Native Americans for the violence they had inflicted on colonists. The Quebec Act of 1774, which was not only thought outrageous for its encouragement of Catholic settlers in New France but which, by expanding the boundaries of that province southwards to the Ohio River, denied access to speculators in Indian land – the most notable being the Virginian, George Washington – was lambasted for depriving settlers of property they thought was rightfully theirs due to the military success of the Seven Years' War. The Quebec Act became a major grievance leading to the American Revolution.

Slavery underscored British North American prosperity. The gentility of colonial elites derived directly in the South and indirectly in the North from the increasingly efficient and brutal exploitation of enslaved labour. Whites and blacks may have been intimately connected in relationships that were both close and negotiated, but these negotiations were unbalanced, allowing a savage master to exploit and traumatize vulnerable, isolated and malnourished Africans. American slavery was better than slavery in the Caribbean, mainly because fewer enslaved people worked in sugar and mostly because native-born enslaved communities could forge cultural ties that left them less dependent than slaves in the West Indies on the whims of masters. But that is saying very little. American slaves lived miserable lives, as whites well knew.

Planters achieved great success in their creation of a vicious plantation system. Their monopolization of the weapons of coercion meant that slave resistance was mostly futile, meaning that slave rebellions were few and easily suppressed. But the threat of enslaved violence was constant. The climate of fear that governed relations between masters and enslaved persons permeated all social interactions, even those not involving blacks and whites but whites or blacks alone. White reliance on slavery rendered colonial claims of improvement and gentility extremely problematic. We need to remember that Thomas Jefferson, the author of the primary document of the founding of the United States, the Declaration of Independence in 1776, may have proclaimed Americans as entitled to pursue happiness and as so entitled able to seek their claims to be accepted by European nations but his life depended from its start in 1743 to its end in 1826 on the labour of the slaves he owned and who looked after him as a child and built the coffin he was buried in.

FRENCH COLONIZATION

Of course, Anglicization could never be complete in North America because until well into the nineteenth century, the region was a place of competing European empires, alongside a continuing Native American presence. The most important European empire besides the British in North America was the French. The French were also latecomers to settlement in the Americas and were much less involved in colonization than the English. Their major settlements in North America were in Quebec and Louisiana with considerable involvement in the fur trade in the interior of North America. One significant difference between French and British colonization is that relatively fewer French people were willing to come to the Americas. France was the largest nation in Western Europe throughout the period of Atlantic history yet the proportion of its residents who were willing to brave an Atlantic crossing was small. Only 45,000 French people moved to Americas in the seventeenth century compared to nearly 400,000 Britons. This small level of migration meant that French America did not form the kind of settler colonies that marked British colonization, although population increase in Quebec was almost as remarkable as in New England, leading to a population of mostly white French-speaking people of 70,000 at the end of the French regime in 1759–1760.

French America was less integrated than British America, mainly due to geography. In North America, there was a predominantly rural society consisting of free Europeans interacting with Native Americans, chronically short of money and settlers and not very valuable to the metropolis. Canada gave no significant agricultural surplus to France and did not provide all that much to the main place of French colonization, which was a vibrant plantation economy based on slave labour in the Greater Antilles in the Caribbean. Louisiana might have been geographically part of North America, but it was culturally and economically an extension of this Caribbean system. Canada, by contrast, was largely self-sufficient and thus unimportant in most aspects of French geopolitics. Once Canada was lost in 1763, France considered it useless to keep Louisiana and ceded it to Spain. The future for the continent was clear: it was to be English-speaking and English-oriented, developing eventually into the independent nation of the United States and the British colony of Canada.

NOTES

1   Carla Pestana, *The English Conquest of Jamaica: Oliver Cromwell's Bid for Empire* (Cambridge, MA: Harvard University Press, 2017).
2   Peter C. Mancall, *Hakluyt's Promise: An Elizabethan's Obsession with America* (New Haven: Yale University Press, 2007).

3   James H. Merrell, *The Indians' New World: Catawba and Their Neighbors from European Contact through the Era of Removal* (Chapel Hill: University of North Carolina Press, 1989).
4   Susan Sleeper-Smith, ed. 'Forum: The Middle Ground Revisited,' *William and Mary Quarterly* 63 (2006), 3–96.
5   Bernard Sheehan, *Savages and Civility: Indians and Englishmen in Colonial Virginia* (Cambridge: Cambridge University Press, 1980).
6   Susan Juster, *Sacred Violence in Early America* (Philadelphia: University of Pennsylvania Press, 2016).
7   Pekka Hämäläinen, *The Comanche Empire* (New Haven: Yale University Press, 2009).
8   Pekka Hämäläinen, 'The Shapes of Power: Indians, Europeans, and North American Worlds from the Seventeenth to the Nineteenth Century,' in Juliana Barr and Edward Countryman, eds., *Contested Spaces of Early America* (Philadelphia: University of Pennsylvania Press, 2014), 31–68.
9   Ibid., 37.
10 Daniel K. Richter, *Trade, Land, Power: The Struggle for Eastern North America* (Philadelphia: University of Pennsylvania, 2013), 75.
11 Ibid., 90.
12 James H. Merrell, 'Indians' New World: The Catawba Experience,' *William and Mary Quarterly* 3d ser. 41 (1984), 539–49.
13 Hämäläinen, 'Shapes of Power,' 65.
14 J.R. McNeill, 'The Ecological Atlantic,' in Nicholas Canny and Philip Morgan, eds., *The Oxford Handbook of Atlantic History* (Oxford: Oxford University Press, 2013), 302–03.
15 Trevor Burnard and Ann Little, 'Where the Boy's Aren't: Women as Reluctant Migrants but Rational Actors in Early America,' in Jay Kleinberg, ed., *Revisioning Women's History* (New Brunswick, New Jersey: Rutgers University Press, 2007), 12–29.
16 Alison Games, 'Beyond the Atlantic: English Globetrotters and Transoceanic Connections,' *William and Mary Quarterly* 63 (2006), 675–92.
17 Ira Berlin, *Many Thousands Gone: The First Two Centuries of Slavery in North America* (Cambridge. MA: Harvard University Press, 1998).
18 Ibid., 103–05.
19 Stephen Saunders Webb, 'William Blathwayt, Imperial Fixer,' *William and Mary Quarterly* 3d ser. 25 (1968), 3–21.

BIBLIOGRAPHY

Oxford Online Bibliographies entries – British Atlantic World; Colonization of English America; Settlement and Region in British America, 1607–1763; Britain and Empire, 1685–1730; The Economy of British America; French Atlantic; New France and Louisiana; The Acadian Diaspora.
David Armitage and Michael Braddick, eds., *The British Atlantic World, 1500–1800* (New York: Palgrave Macmillan, 2002).
Joyce E. Chaplin, 'Expansion and Exceptionalism in Early American History,' *Journal of American History* 89 (2003), 1431–55.

Edward Countryman, 'Indians, the Colonial Order, and the Social Significance of the American Revolution,' *William and Mary Quarterly* 3d ser. 53 (1996), 342–62.

David Eltis, *The Rise of Atlantic Slavery in the Americas* (New York: Cambridge University Press, 2000).

Alison F. Games, *The Web of Empire: English Cosmopolitans in an Age of Expansion, 1560–1660* (New York: Oxford University Press, 2008).

Gilles Havard, *Empire et métissages. Indiens at Français dans le Pays d'en Haut, 1660–1715* (Sillery, Quebec: Septentrion, 2003).

Eric Hinderaker and Rebecca Horn, 'Territorial Crossings: Histories and Historiographies of the Early Americas,' *William and Mar Quarterly* 3d ser. 67 (2010), 395–432.

Paul W. Mapp, *The Elusive West and the Contest for Empire, 1713–1763* (Chapel Hill: University of North Carolina Press, 2011).

Daniel Richter, *Facing East from Indian Country: A Native History* (Cambridge: Cambridge University Press, 2001).

Lorena S. Walsh, 'Slavery in the North American Mainland Colonies,' in David Eltis and Stanley L. Engerman, eds., *The Cambridge World History of Slavery* vol. 3 *AD 1420–AD 1804* (Cambridge: Cambridge University Press, 2011), 407–30.

Michael Witgen, *An Infinity of Nations: How the Native New World Shaped Early America* (Philadelphia: University of Pennsylvania Press, 2012).

12

PLANTATIONS

A GLOBAL INSTITUTION

The plantation complex was a global institution. It was initiated in Europe; was realized in the tropical and semi-tropical regions of the Americas; involved Asia both as a source of capital and as a source of labour; and was focused strongly on Africa, from where most plantation labourers came. It extended eventually in the nineteenth century into the Pacific and Australia. Plantations were depicted by Karl Marx as inherently backward and a way station on the march from feudalism to capitalism. They were thought of by romantic defenders of the system, exemplified in the 1930s film *Gone with the Wind* as like feudal estates with picturesque slave quarters and the mills being centres of energetic cooperation overseen by stern (but benign) masters. This view of plantations was a misconception. These were modern institutions in which the violence that marked every feature of the institution was not atavistic but instrumental – designed to aid complex and sophisticated chains of production.

It was the imperative force behind the Atlantic slave trade, bringing 12.5 million captives from Africa, of whom 10.5 million arrived in the Americas. They laboured in a large geographic region that stretched from the Rio Grande do Sol in southern Brazil to the Mason-Dixon line in southern Pennsylvania in the United States. Did it add anything much to human experience? David Eltis claims no, rather derisively claiming that the whole history of the plantation can be attributed to Europe's sweet tooth with the plantation adding relatively little to European and North American economic well-being.[1] Historians of Africa, as discussed in Chapter 8, tend to think that the plantation system not only added nothing to African well-being but actively corrupted African politics and harmed economic development. But such views underestimate the influence of the plantation on the development of capitalist institutions in Europe; on changing consumption patterns that added to the industrious revolution that Jan de Vries has described as a precursor to the Industrial Revolution; and on making the Americas profitable and workable. As Barbara Solow argues, 'it was slavery that made the empty lands of the Western Hemisphere valuable producers of commodities and valuable markets for Europe and North America'.[2] David Eltis, Frank L. Lewis and David Richardson contend that the plantation sector was the most dynamic part of the New World economy before 1800, with rates of economic growth that corresponded well to rates of economic growth in industrializing Britain and the United States and with strong productivity gains, especially in the second half of the eighteenth century.[3]

The rise of the plantation system played an important role in the establishment of chattel slavery in the Americas as a way of replacing using indentured labour from Europe to grow tropical produce. Racial prejudice made planters reluctant at first to buy African slaves. But plantation agriculture required workers and increasingly white labour was unavailable, as potential migrants learned how bad conditions were on plantations for workers and as better alternatives for work became available in Europe. In Virginia, the result of decreasing supplies of indentured workers from the 1650s along with the establishment of the Royal African Company in the 1660s, which reduced the price of Africans in the slave trade and increased the supply of such slaves, encouraged them to move wholeheartedly and quickly into purchasing Africans and making them slaves. Africans offered the prospect of a perpetual agricultural workforce in ways that European indentured servants did not. And throughout the Atlantic World, planters learned from other plantation systems how to make slavery an essential feature of new and more brutal work regimes. Gender was crucial in this process. In Europe, women were generally not assigned to agricultural work. That was not true for women in Africa and even less so in the Americas. Europeans expressed increasingly derogatory views about the bodies of African women to justify African enslavement. They argued that an African woman's work was interrupted by neither childbirth nor hard labour. They could even work while nursing children due to how their breasts hung down in ways that facilitated easy suckling of infants. The ultimate claim behind these images of women giving birth without pain and needing little time to recover from childbirth showed that they were ideal workers and that, though human, their humanity was strange and deformed. It helped, also, that early legislation in the mid-seventeenth century in Barbados, Virginia and Martinique confirmed that all children born of black women were automatically slaves themselves, even if the fathers of these children were free and white. Economic utility trumped paternal rights.

DISTINCTIVE FEATURES

Philip Curtin outlines six features that define the mature plantation complex. The most important feature was the labour force, which was normally an enslaved population of people of African descent. That population was generally not self-sustaining (except in the United States from the mid-eighteenth century) and thus relied on the slave trade to replenish populations. Plantations were capitalist enterprises, even if they retained some aspect of feudalism, especially in Brazil where plantations were oriented around *engenhos*, or sugar mills, where *lavradores de canha*, small farmers who grew cane, took their canes to mills where it was milled by *senhores de engenhos*. These capitalist enterprises produced for distant markets in Europe and were this dependent on the vagaries of long-distance trade. Finally, plantation societies were colonial societies, with political control lying in Europe. Plantation societies thus were linked to a European empire and through that country to the European state system.

There were two models of plantations, both in major sugar producing regions (although plantation agriculture was not confined to sugar as planters produced such crops as tobacco, rice, coffee and cotton). It was an institution which evolved over time, from its Atlantic beginnings in the Canary Islands, to Brazil, to Barbados and then throughout the Greater Caribbean and North America. Brazilians were the first people in the Americas to develop a plantation system, but they were handicapped by their lack of access to capital and by devising a plantation system that did not benefit much from economies of scale and which was complicated by having to move sugar from planter-owned fields to independently owned mills. As prices for sugar slumped in the 1620s, and as slave resistance became more prevalent in a period when the Dutch were assailing Portuguese power, the Brazilian sugar industry declined into a century and a half period of stability and low profits. Their place as plantation leaders was usurped by the French and British who were better integrated than the Portuguese into North Atlantic commercial networks.

The small island of Barbados played a vital role in mid-seventeenth transformations of the plantation system. Sugar had already become a desired item of consumption in England by the early seventeenth century, moving from a luxury item to an ordinary product that everyone could buy and consume. Barbados proved to be the crucible in which the mature plantation system was incubated. Barbadian planters' crucial innovation was to move away from the dispersed system common in Brazil to a system in which they integrated the growing and processing of sugar cane. Their system was a large integrated plantation staffed by Europeans willing to inflict harsh discipline on enslaved people and containing at least a hundred and often more enslaved Africans. Economies of scale quickly ensued. The key innovation was not slavery but the adoption of a form of labour organization – ganged labour where slaves worked in lockstep discipline under the liberal use of the whip – that could produce enough sugar to bring wealth substantial enough for substantial reinvestment. This system was so successful that it quickly spread throughout English/British and French America. It was successful because enslaved people were worked very intensively, labouring for 3,288 hours per year in late eighteenth-century Jamaica, which was well above average hours worked by agricultural labourers in Europe.

The switch to the integrated plantation and to gang labour was contested by Africans. Slaves hated working in gangs and detested the regimentation that gang labour forced upon them. A slave rebel in Barbados declared as he was being executed that 'the Devel was in the English-man, that he makes everything work, he makes the Negro work, the Horse work, the wood work, the Water work and the winde work'. Masters achieved their aims through relentless brutality. Such repression generally worked. Slave resistance on plantations was usually low level and seldom erupted into violence. When it did, as in a big slave revolt in Jamaica in 1760, rebels were treated with a calculated brutality that made European observers flinch and wonder whether planters deserved the appellation of being thought properly British, French or Dutch.

'A KILLING MACHINE'

Where plantations were most effective and efficient and where the power of masters over the slaves that comprised the labour that made plantations work was not constrained by either morality or outside pressure, such as in the eighteenth-century Greater Antilles, they were killing fields. The numbers condemn the complex. Marcus Rediker describes how death stalked the Atlantic slave trade, the mechanism by which labour was provided to fuel plantations' insatiable desire for labour. Plantations ate up unfortunate individuals enmeshed in the system through hard work and poor material conditions. He concludes, chillingly: 'Another way to look at the loss of life would be to say that an estimated 14 million people were enslaved to produce a "yield" of nine million longer-surviving Atlantic workers.'[4]

The sugar plantation – the culmination in most ways of the plantation complex – was a 'killing machine' with the benefits of sugar as a crucial factor in modern economic growth being balanced by the many-sided relationship between the plantations and death. The violence and destruction of the plantation complex were not reminiscent of backward economic systems. There was almost no resemblance in plantation systems to feudalism or to Greek or Roman slavery, despite planters' penchant to give their enslaved workers heroic Greek names, thus adding a touch of condescending mockery to enslaved people's daily torments. The plantation, in fact, anticipated by centuries the quite different oppression that marked labour in the Industrial

Revolution. It was, in fact, a very modern system. Sidney Mintz sees the plantations as a symbol of 'precocious modernity'. He argues that by forcibly drawing together people from many cultures and by forcing them to work relentlessly on the plantations where workers created new cultural forms under terrible conditions, the planter class transformed slaves into new and essentially modern people. The work regimen, Mintz notes, made the slaves into 'anonymous units of labour – alienated, expendable, and interchangeable – as if they lacked individuality or any personal past'. They were, culturally, people without history: 'their reborn and distinctive individuality arose partly in reaction to the nearly total loss of historical continuity'.[5]

What was true regarding culture was also true with respect to the economy. Paul Cheney's exploration of the plantation economy of Saint-Domingue in the booming years in the 1780s before the Haitian Revolution of 1791–1804 – probably the purest manifestation of the plantation system in world history – explains that the plantation complex was a peculiar manifestation of early modern capitalist accumulation. He argues that the Antillean plantation system 'was a central component of the commercial revolution experienced in northern European countries over the long eighteenth century'. He employs mechanistic metaphors, as was common for Enlightenment thinkers, to describe the plantation system, seeing the Saint Domingue plantation complex as a great and complex machine operating on dangerously narrow tolerances. Samuel Martin, a mid-eighteenth-century planter from Antigua, argued in similar terms, noting that 'a plantation ought to be considered as a well-constructed machine, compounded of various wheels, turning different ways, and yet all contributing to the great end proposed; but if any one part runs too fast or too slow in proportion to the rest, the main purpose is defeated'.[6]

Why were sugar plantations such dreadful places to work and thrive? Barry Higman explains it as being due to how planters worked out ways to work slaves to their limits. The work of cultivation and harvest went on together, the factory or mill operating continuously for much of the year. The tasks sugar workers were asked to do were arduous and dangerous and were performed in the fields by gangs who were whipped by drivers to keep up work rates. The nature of gangs was also distinctive insofar as they were dominated by females. Most women on plantations worked as field labourers with only a few women become 'privileged' slaves, such as domestics (thought that job often meant accepting sexual exploitation as a byproduct of the job). Men were more likely than women to become 'privileged' slaves with some respite from monotonous field labour. The demands of working in sugar for women in child-bearing years were so great as to seriously harm prospects of getting pregnant and of bearing a child past infancy. Moreover, at least in the Greater Antilles, planters expected slaves to grow their own food in the limited time that had away from plantation labour. The result was severe nutritional pressure that was aggravated by periodic environmental disasters, such as hurricanes and even more by man-made events, such as war. Plantations relied so heavily on imports of food from elsewhere to supplement meagre attempts at self-sufficiency that they operated even in good times at the very edge of sustainability.[7]

When things went wrong with this system, as in the British West Indies during the American Revolution and in the French Caribbean during the Seven Years' War, famine, starvation and excess enslaved deaths were the result. Under pressure from abolitionists in Europe, sugar planters in the early nineteenth century were encouraged to adopt measures of amelioration, making plantation life easier and improving fertility rates through some recognition of pregnancy. But such solicitation of slaves' welfare came late in the plantation period. While the Atlantic slave trade flourished, planters preferred to work slaves as hard as they could and make up demographic losses through buying fresh inputs of labour from Africa. That led to rising slave prices – which most planters did not mind as it made their enslaved property increasingly more valuable.

THE CULTURE OF THE PLANTATION

Plantations tended to grow first near the coasts of islands. Jamaica and Saint-Domingue were classic examples of this kind of development, with settlement not going into the mountainous interiors until fifty to eighty years after initial European settlement by the British and French. Slavery was not always the first kind of economic organization developed, with plantations in Barbados, for example, beginning when the dominant element in the labour force was indentured servants. But slavery soon began to dominate. It was sustained by pervasive violence, something crucial to the plantation system. Plantation societies were divided socially and economically in ways that made them qualitatively different to European, African or Asian societies. They tended also to be intellectual backwaters, deficient in every respect except for the wealth they produced, wealth which tended to increase as you moved south from the northern limits in the northern Chesapeake, became concentrated in the Caribbean, and only slowly declined as the plantation system moved to central and southern Brazil.

The plantation complex created two enduring social types: the planter and the slave. Neither social type, of course, was synonymous with the plantation. Slaves had existed from time immemorial and in most societies and had seldom worked in plantation societies before the mid-seventeenth century. And slaves were just as likely to be white as they were black – the derivation in English for 'slave', of course is 'slav', implying slaves were identified in Western society as being Russian more than being African. In the early modern period, increasingly it was Africans who were slaves and they, of course, were overwhelmingly black. 'Race' was a complicating factor in social structure. The arrival in the Americas of numerous Africans meant that differences in appearance would become connected with who one was and how much wealth or power a person had or did not. Such differences militated against a sense of common identity. Indeed, communities of whites and of blacks were made much more separate and at the same time internally more coherent by the ways in which race was perceived. The racial division between the owners of plantations and the workers on those plantations perpetuated and enhanced pernicious forms of racism that made whiteness a socially desirable characteristic and blackness a socially derided category accompanied by multiple legally enforceable forms of racial discrimination that persisted well after slavery ended and many people of African-American descent had ceased to be plantation workers.

Money was almost as significant in shaping master–slave relations. Planters were rich, or at least much richer than slaves who were overwhelmingly poor – in the Americas from the seventeenth to late nineteenth centuries being perhaps the largest group of very poor people in the region. Planters relied on their slaves for their wealth and were thus concerned mostly to make sure that slaves worked hard for them. They expected slaves to be obedient and devised a variety of means alongside state-sponsored violence that at bottom upheld their authority to impress upon slaves that they were helpless, worthless and dependent upon the planter's goodwill. That goodwill was often in short supply as planters lashed out at slaves and sexually exploited them even while they relied on them as workers.

Everywhere slaves were psychologically damaged. Occasionally they rebelled but that act entailed great risks. Except in Haiti, where rebellion eventually succeeded in overthrowing white rule but at the cost of perhaps a hundred thousand enslaved lives, rebellions always failed. The planter response to slaves who dared challenge their authority was savage and uncompromising. The aftermath, for example, of the Demerara slave rebellion of 1823 saw many slaves executed and their head left on gibbets to remind slaves returned to plantations of the awesomeness of planter powers. These displays of what Vincent Brown calls 'spectacular terror' regularly punctuated plantation life.[8]

The plantation system was a complex social order where violence was ever-present but in which personal interactions were very important in shaping power relations. Plantation slavery was a negotiated relationship between one group, slave owners (often planters) who had most of the power but could not always get their own way, and another group, slaves, who were severely handicapped in trying to establish lives for themselves independent of the master's control. Slaves, however, always had a few weapons they could deploy– weapons of the weak, uniting slaves with other subaltern groups in history, such as peasants and bandits, in respect to how people without power had means of working within a system to try and gain small advantages for themselves. Slaves took advantage especially of the temporalities involved in working practices, especially on sugar estates, that meant that speed was often of the essence, notably in harvest time. But they found establishing ways in which slave management practices could be side-stepped to be difficult so long as planters controlled the political process. One reason why slavery endured so long in the American South and in Brazil is that planters were largely left alone to dispense plantation justice to enslaved people and were not countermanded when they used excessive violence to compel enslaved people to do their will. Planters exercised considerable political power, power they used to protect the plantation system and their own position in society. Most of the presidents of the United States before the Civil War, for example, were planters with a commitment to maintaining and sometimes expanding the system of slavery that underpinned their wealth and status.

It was in the working out of this negotiated relationship that the theory of the plantation – that masters ordered, and slaves obeyed – was contradicted in practice. Masters were meant to be in control but in fact they depended so much upon slaves for their material comforts that this opened a space for slaves to try and change the conditions of their enslavement. In this respect, slaves employed strategies of opposition, tactics designed not so much as to overthrow their enslavement but to make the conditions of their lives a little more bearable. Slaves also attempted to create lives for themselves outside of the plantation system, recreating in the Americas social, political and religious lives that they had left behind in their African homelands. They succeeded in making such alternative lives remarkably frequently, with religious practices such as vodou in Saint-Domingue, obeah in Jamaica and syncretic African-Catholic mixes in Brazil taking strong root in slave communities despite official discouragement. Everywhere, however, slaves struggled just to survive. They were undernourished, deprived of sleep, were often beaten and learned to survive under these conditions. Everywhere, slaves struggled against alienation, uncertainty and flux in living and working arrangements. They found it harder than any other group of plantation workers to maintain their traditions in religious, family and cultural lives. But these traditions did survive, encouraging the growth of vigorous enslaved Creole communities. One of the major consequences of the plantation system in its mature form in the Americas was to introduce African culture into this part of the world. The cultural forms developed by plantation slaves have shaped societies in the Americas in dramatic and long-lasting ways – religious practice and musical expression, for example, cannot be disentangled from their roots among enslaved people in plantation settings.

ECONOMIC PERFORMANCE

In the 1770s, the plantation complex was at its pre-industrial peak. Its economic performance was extraordinary. Plantation produce amounted to around 40 per cent of the trade circulating around the Atlantic. It was slave-produced goods which integrated the Atlantic system, and which made it so dynamic in the eighteenth century. Even those places that had neither slaves nor plantations were involved in providing goods and services that supported plantation economies. The annual value of colonial exports, most of which came from plantations, in 1774 was £5.6 million for British America, £5.2 million for French America and £1.8 million for Brazil.

The wealth from the plantations made some people – almost always white men – very rich. Whites in Jamaica were nearly fifty times as wealthy as the average person in Jamaica and the very wealthiest planters, like Simon Taylor (1740–1813), were among the richest people in the British Empire. Taylor died with a fortune worth over £1 million, including well over 1,000 slaves. The French plantation system was even more profitable than the British system. The French started to outperform the British in the plantation sector by the second half of the eighteenth century. Their success can be attributed to greater state support, better resources and more effective use of infrastructure improvements, especially in irrigation. By the 1780s, Saint Domingue had become the wealthiest place on earth. But that wealth was highly unequally distributed. Planter wealth depended on black immiseration. Slaves in Jamaica when the plantation system was most profitable were barely given enough wages in respect to food (much of which they had to grow themselves), medicine and clothing to keep themselves above subsistence. When provisions from overseas became harder to obtain, as during the American Revolution, that bare subsistence turned into famine and destitution.

In short, planter wealth came out of enslaved people's misery. The systematic exploitation of enslaved labour by imperial states gives an urgency and legitimacy to contemporary requests by Caribbean governments for compensation for slavery. The amounts owed are easy to work out: each Jamaican slave produced about £18 profit per annum for his or her owner but received only £4–5 in goods and services in return. If we assume a fair wage would have been £10, thus still allowing planters good profits and enslaved people a modicum of comfort, then the collective difference between wages received and rightful wages gives some precise monetary figure that could be used to work out reparation costs in the present.

What was the economic performance of plantation economies and in what ways did plantation wealth contribute to the development of capitalism and industrialization? The link between plantation profits derived from slavery and the slave trade was probably limited, as planters tended not to invest their profits in industry but in conspicuous consumption, expensive country houses and some investment in financial institutions. But as detailed in Chapter 7 'ghost acres' in the plantation New World allowed Europeans to devote more attention to manufacturing. The most important contribution of plantations to European wealth creation was probably in the areas of technical innovations in finance and insurance because of the complications arising from long-distance trade.

Another question was whether the plantation system was in decline by the end of the eighteenth century. One view is the plantation system had inherent weaknesses that meant that it had within it the seeds of its own destruction. Few historians now hold to this view, as work on what is called 'second slavery' in nineteenth-century Brazil, the United States and especially Cuba has shown that planters and the plantation economy were remarkably adaptable to new circumstances. The rise of industrial economies in Western Europe and the northern United States and Canada from the late eighteenth century showed that industrialization produced enormous profits and extraordinary economic growth by historical standards. Plantation societies by the nineteenth century were not as comparatively dynamic as they had been in the early eighteenth century but by most standards they were doing very well and becoming ever more important to European economies. In 1800, the contribution to national GDP made by the economic activity of plantation economies, slavery and the slave trade was around 10 per cent in Britain, perhaps double what it had been in the second quarter of the eighteenth century. When Britain abolished the slave trade in 1807, they were not cutting their losses from an economic system in decline and costing them money. They were deciding to abolish a flourishing industry on moral grounds that inflicted serious harm on the British economy and much greater harm on the West Indian economies in which plantation agriculture was dominant. That calculus was true for all European empires that abolished the slave trade and slavery and even more true for the United States when it went to war against a slaveholding secessionist Confederate state in 1861. As in Cuba, where an industrial form of slavery developed in the nineteenth century which was highly profitable and very adaptable, the plantation system in the American South was attacked when it was at one of its peaks of productivity. The vitality of the plantation system in the American South in the 1850s seemed so strong that planters notoriously declared that their importance to the economy of the world's leading power, Britain, was so important that no-one would dare interfere with American planters. Opponents of American planters thought much the same. It took a calamitous Civil War from 1861 to destroy the system at the cost of over 600,000 lives and even then slavery was only ended by a presidential decree that was probably illegitimate under the rules of a pro-slavery Constitution and was only put into place as an extraordinary war measure.

NOTES

1   David Eltis, *The Rise of African Slavery in the Americas* (Cambridge: Cambridge University Press, 2000).
2   Barbara L. Solow, *Slavery and the Rise of the Atlantic System* (Cambridge: Cambridge University Press, 1991), 1.
3   David Eltis, Frank L. Lewis and David Richardson, 'Slave Prices, the African Slave Trade and Productivity in the Caribbean,' *Economic History Review* 58 (2005), 673–74.

4   Marcus Rediker, *The Slave Ship: A Human History* (London: Penguin, 2007), 5.
5   Sidney Mintz, *Three Ancient Cultures: Caribbean Themes and Variations* (Cambridge, MA: Harvard University Press, 2013), 10–11.
6   Paul Cheney, *Cul de Sac: Patrimony, Capitalism and Slavery in French Saint Domingue* (Chicago: University of Chicago Press, 2017).
7   B.W. Higman, 'Demographic Trends', in David Eltis et al., eds., *The Cambridge World History of Slavery* vol. 4, *AD 1804–AD 2016* (Cambridge: Cambridge University Press, 2017), 5.
8   Vincent Brown, *The Reaper's Garden: Death and Power in the World of Atlantic Slavery* (Cambridge, MA: Harvard University Press, 2008).

BIBLIOGRAPHY

Oxford Online Bibliographies – Atlantic Slavery, Church and Slavery, Cotton, Domestic Slave Trades; Law and Slavery; Material Cultures of Slavery; Plantations; Slave Rebellions; Slavery and Gender; Slavery in British America; Slavery in Danish America; Slavery in Dutch America; Slavery in French America; Slavery in Spanish America.

B.J. Barickman, *A Bahian Counterpoint: Sugar, Tobacco, Cassava, and Slavery in the Recôncavo, 1780–1860* (Stanford: Stanford University Press, 1998).

Robin Blackburn, *The American Crucible: Slavery, Emancipation and Human Rights* (London: Verso, 2011).

Trevor Burnard, *Planters, Merchants and Slaves: Plantation Societies in British America, 1750–1820* (Chicago: University of Chicago Press, 2015).

Philip D. Curtin, *The Rise and Fall of the Plantation Complex: Essays in Atlantic History* (New York: Cambridge University Press, 1990).

Gabriel Debien, *Les esclaves aux Antilles françaises XVIIe au XVIIIe siècles* (Basse Terre, France: Sociéte d'histoire de la Guadeloupe, 1974).

Max Edelson, *Plantation Enterprise in Colonial South Carolina* (Cambridge, MA: Harvard University Press, 2006).

David Eltis and Stanley L. Engerman, eds., *The Cambridge World History of Slavery* vol. 3, *AD 1400–AD 1804* (Cambridge: Cambridge University Press, 2011).

David Eltis, Stanley L. Engerman, Seymour Drescher, and David Richardson, eds., *The Cambridge World History of Slavery* vol. 4, *AD 1804–AD 2016* (Cambridge: Cambridge University Press, 2017).

Sandra Graham, *Caetana Says No: Women's Stories from a Brazilian Slave Society* (Cambridge: Cambridge University Press, 2002).

Sidney Mintz, *Sweetness and Power: The Place of Sugar in Modern History* (New York: Vikig, 1985).

Stuart B. Schwartz, *Tropical Babylons: Sugar and the Making of the Atlantic World, 1450–1650* (Chapel Hill: University of North Carolina Press, 2004).

Lorena S. Walsh, *Motives of Honor, Pleasure and Profit: Plantation Management in the Colonial Chesapeake, 1607–1763* (Chapel Hill: University of North Carolina Press, 2010).

PART FOUR

Atlantic Themes

13

WAR AND VIOLENCE

A VIOLENT WORLD

The rise of the Atlantic World was accompanied by an increase in the use and intensity of violence almost everywhere. That increasing violence was only sometimes associated with the Atlantic per se. The wars of religion that swept Europe in the sixteenth and seventeenth centuries, for example, were not very Atlantic in origins, course or consequences. Nevertheless, even when the conflicts were not especially Atlantic, they sometimes were influenced by Atlantic events. For example, after Hernan Cortes destroyed the Aztecs in 1519, he used his experiences in Mexico to devastate Algiers in 1541. It is possible that the threshold for violence was lowered as men with Atlantic experience used their near-genocidal conduct to Native Americans to conduct war that was more brutal than usual in European and African settings. As Jean-Frédéric Schaub notes, 'reports about atrocities and engravings describing tortures were very popular in the first two centuries of print. These textual and graphic materials concerning conquest in America, religious war in Europe, and captivity in Africa and elsewhere created a unified web of representation.'[1]

The rise of Atlantic connections also gave a different meaning to violence, suggesting to contemporaries that violence was instrumental insofar as it helped to knit together places that had been previously separate. One radical novelty for Europeans in this period was a comprehension that the world was in a process of unification, under largely Western European leadership, and that unification involved the universalization of brutality. This realization was an important factor in how Europeans were able to impose their will on Native Americans. It was hard for people in the Americas and Africa to see European violence against them and against each other as anything other than some malign characteristic of horrible people. Their turn to violence to defend themselves was essentially reactive and rooted in local circumstances. Europeans had an advantage, as they were the active actors in violent encounters and could grasp, if dimly, what Native Americans and Africans found difficult to grasp, that European violence had a larger and global imperative as part of ways of connecting the world together.

Violence also moved in Europe and then in the Americas from being either part of ordinary tensions in life or part of circumscribed military action to being more obviously ideological, involving the mass murder of groups of people deemed in some way unfit to occupy space. In short, normal patterns of atrocities and massacres morphed into more deliberate attempts to obliterate human societies from the earth. Both the Spanish and the English adopted policies of mass murder. The expulsion of Muslims from Granada during the *Reconquista* between 1482 and 1492 and the forced conversion of Muslims and Jews by Cardinal Francisco Cisneros (1436–1517) between 1500 and 1506 were the backdrop to continual attempts to persecute those individuals who resisted or who reverted to their ancestral faith. In 1568–1570, civil war erupted in Granada against such practices. The Spanish response was ruthless and merciless: Morisco society was crushed and ethnic cleansing of suspect Christians and non-Christians was rapid and effective. English brutality towards Irish Catholics who rebelled against them in the 1590s and in 1641 was equally brutal and equally based on a policy of extermination rather than just military defeat. These internal episodes of mass murder quickly extended into the Atlantic World, with the Portuguese trying with some success to destroy the native Guanche of the Canary Islands and the remarkably successful effort by the Spanish, greatly aided by disease, to empty Hispaniola of Native Americans entirely.

To an extent, violence in the Atlantic by Europeans was just an extension of ordinary violence in Europe and was of an order that was common in Africa and the Americas. Every society on the Atlantic World was a violent one and some of the most celebrated societies in Africa and the Americas matched European violence quite easily. The Aztec empire, for example, was built on an edifice of human sacrifice which horrified the Spanish when they encountered it. The slave trading kingdom of Dahomey also practised human sacrifice and there are many accounts from horrified European slave traders of witnessing public ceremonies that concluded with mass beheadings, designed to show the king's subjects the awesome power of royal authority. Yet somehow violence in the Atlantic was also new, insofar as depictions of it fed a European population's inexhaustible appetite for tales of brutality and atrocity. The brutality of the Atlantic World was highlighted in books, the most famous being Bartolomé Las Casas's mid-sixteenth-century account of Spanish cruelty and policies of Native American extermination in the Caribbean. It was graphic material, made more graphic when depicted visually in the hugely popular illustrated version with engravings by Theodore de Bry in 1598. This version both supported the developing notion of the Black Legend – the belief that the Spanish were a preternaturally cruel people – and whetted the European imagination in seeing the Atlantic as a place where violence exceeded normal limits. The success of Las Casas in the sixteenth century was emulated by the enormous popularity of Alexander Exquemelin's *The Buccaneers of America* (1678) and *The General History of the Pyrates* (1724), written by Charles Johnson, which was probably a pseudonym for Daniel Defoe. These books gave a receptive reading public grisly tales of pirates behaving badly and were suffused by violence, indicating that life in the Atlantic was life beyond the pale of normal civilized behaviour.

RELIGION AND VIOLENCE

One of the sad facts about Atlantic history is that religion was not always a force for good but was often a progenitor for evil. Christian missionaries, for example, were not just involved in seeking the conversion of non-Christians but were proponents and enactors of religiously inflected violence. The most obvious example of how they used violence as a vehicle for imposing conformity with violence was through the implementation in the Americas of the European institution that enforced religious orthodoxy as the Catholic church interpreted it, the Inquisition. Spanish clergy and especially members of missionary orders like the Franciscans, the Dominicans and the Jesuits espoused in their conversion efforts in the Americas a militant Catholicism where adherence to established tenets was crucial.

Native Americans and poor Spanish colonists could hardly have been expected to understand what was allowed under Catholicism as determined by religious authorities in Rome. The Catholic Church demanded extreme discipline because of the paternalism of the early church in Latin America. Missionaries believed that they were bringing the news of the gospel to child-like Native Americans who, paradoxically, were both full of sin which needed to be eradicated, by force if necessary, and people who in their innocence were the people of earth closest to the state of bliss that was the biblical Garden of Eden. Conversion had a practical application, as well. Protestant evangelists and Catholic missionaries both agreed that one reason why it was necessary to convert Native Americans to Christianity was that Christian Native Americans could be used as allies against non-Christian Native Americans in European wars against American indigenes. That assumption was as often tested as it was fulfilled but the hope of gaining allies was frequently behind missionary efforts. These efforts were complicated as well by the equation of being 'Christian' with being 'civilized'. Becoming Christian usually involved more than just accepting Christian doctrines. It meant adopting European ways of life and European cultural assumptions, including assumptions about marriage and sexuality that Native Americans thought bizarre and unnecessary. Violence often ensued through the Inquisition when Native Americans or African-Americans became Christian but refused to abandon sexual practices that were forbidden in Christian doctrine, such as fornication outside marriage, sodomy and polygynous relationships.

The Wars of Religion in sixteenth-century Europe heightened the possibility of religious violence by encouraging eschatological visions of a world about to end and the imminent arrival of the antichrist as foretold in the Bible. Long identification in religious texts of the lands and peoples of the Americas as being closely associated with the Devil – the idea was not just that the Devil was in the hearts of non-Christians in the Americas but that the Devil had made his earthly dwelling there – encouraged colonists to use violence in their dealings with Native Americans and, to an extent, with African slaves. It was easy to try and enforce religious orthodoxy through violence when you felt the Apocalypse was soon to arrive and thus that what you were involved with in the Americas was the first stage in a 'cosmic war' that involved 'martyrs' in the Christian struggle against demons. Christian doctrine persuaded Europeans that they were fighting the Lord's battles when they confronted Native Americans over land expropriation and led them to see their actions within a powerful and doctrinally attractive religious iconography of sacrifice and martyrdom. As Brian Sandberg explains, 'European colonists' personal religiosity and faith became entangled in an all-encompassing struggle that provided powerful religious justifications for violence, and even holy war, in colonial warfare throughout the early modern world.'[2]

Of course, Native Americans were no less religious than Europeans and just as inclined to place their violent actions within a religious framework. H.E. Martel shows how in the celebrated example of the Tupinamba people of Brazil, widely known in Europe as actively practising cannibals, that the Tupinamba manipulated their fearsome image as a way of manipulating the religious tendencies of Europeans to their own advantage. The German, Hans Staden, was held captive by the Tupinamba for ten months in 1552.[3] His account of his captivity claimed that the Tupinamba were cannibals. Scholars divide as to whether this claim of cannibalism was justified. I think it is. What is clear, however, is that the Tupinamba used the rumours that they were cannibals to feed European obsession with dreaded cannibals that earned them respect within a colonial discourse where cannibalism was especially feared and within a related European discourse over Protestant attacks on the Catholic interpretation of the Christian Eucharist as symbolically cannibalistic. In short, the Tupinamba 'played' cannibal for their own ends, keeping European visitors at a disadvantage through their anxiety about being eaten. As Neil Whitehead explains, 'the cannibal sign was quite overtly manipulated by indigenous populations, in the face of colonial obsessions'.[4] Fear of violence could be as effective as a form of resistance as violence itself.

A feature of Atlantic wars was that there was an absence of restraint as authorized in customary rules of warfare promulgated in Europe and a routine use of excessive violence, usually on both sides. Native Americans customarily resorted to torture, as noted previously in this book, often done within religious ceremonies, when dealing with prisoners. The absence of restraint was also apparent, if less frequent, in European warfare and was inevitably associated with wars of an ideological nature, which in sixteenth- and seventeenth-century Atlantic settings usually involved a religious dimension. The worst examples of atrocities in both Europe and America usually occurred when soldiers were participating in religious warfare as in the Thirty Years' War, 1618–1648, and as they demonstrated their religious zeal against ideological enemies. One reason among many why European violence in Africa did not lead to wars and war crimes was that this religious dimension to conflict was missing in that continent. It was different in the Americas. If you were a Christian awaiting the Apocalypse, waging war against Native Americans signified participation in the struggle against the anti-Christ and meant that no quarter was given or expected. Nicholas Canny comments that in both Ireland and Virginia, the English resorted quickly and successfully to schemes of ethnic cleansing and near-genocidal extermination.

Soldiers from the British Isles who had participated in the atrocities of the Wars of the Three Kingdoms in the 1640s were probably very prepared to practise war in the Americas without restraint, as occurred in King Phillip's War in New England in 1675 when the country was laid waste, no mercy was shown on either side and normal rules of military engagement were abandoned, to the shock of Puritan divines who felt the bloodshed invalidated New England claims to be a godly place with a special mission to establish a society based on biblical values in the New World. The soldiers who participated in these mid-century wars in Europe and America had seen how the conventional limits on warfare between Christians had been weakened, leading to bitter religious hatreds and an increase in religious and ethnic violence. Moreover, English colonization coincided with religious strife in the British Isles between Catholic Ireland, Calvinist Scotland and a religiously mixed and divided England. The atrocities soldiers participated in back in Europe were transferred to the New World. Canny notes that English colonists used 'the same pretexts for the extermination of the Indians' as the English had done in the mid-sixteenth century for 'the slaughter of numbers of the Irish'.[5]

MILITARY REVOLUTION

How wars were fought in Europe and the Atlantic World was influenced by what historians call the Military Revolution. The term, first posited by Michael Roberts in 1955, has been elaborated upon by Clifford Rogers and

Geoffrey Parker as a way of describing rapid bursts of military innovation followed by long periods of incremental change. Rogers describes the process as being a 'punctuated equilibrium evolution', in which first infantry developed means of overcoming cavalry; then moved to armies using gunpowder weapons effectively; and then proceeded to the creation in the late seventeenth centuries of permanent standing armies in major European states like Britain and France, with armies and navies becoming the nerve centres of bureaucratized states and expansive empires.[6] The Military Revolution was very much an European invention and one that made it better able to expand its power against non-western tribes, nations and empires. War became deadlier, more expensive, and more exportable outside Europe. War also became more destructive of life and property as armies became larger, navies more powerful, and with guns that made ships lethal to enemies.

Thus, warfare in Europe became qualitatively different to war conducted in other parts of the Atlantic World by the late seventeenth century. In West Africa, for example, African war technology did not advance along the same ways as in Europe. Africans relied on hand-powered weapons, such as swords and bows and arrows, and on fortifications for defence. In many ways, they did not need to adapt their methods of warfare, as Europe did not challenge African rule except sporadically before the mid-nineteenth century. War in Africa was frequent, but the effects of war were similar as in medieval Europe – people tended to try and limit the effects of war and treated war with fear and respect, shaping war aims to benefit themselves and mostly capturing rather than killing enemies. Battles were infrequent and most conflict was done in skirmishes, raids and ambushes, some of which increasingly occurred as part of plans to increase the supply of captives available for the Atlantic slave trade. The Military Revolution made a large difference to the European ability to impose their will on others. The increasing lethality of war in sixteenth- and seventeenth-century Europe encouraged states to invest heavily in armed forces and orient growing state bureaucracy around the needs of warfare – what historians have called the invention of 'fiscal-military' states. Africans and Native Americans quickly learned to use European weapons and, as noted elsewhere in this chapter, remained formidable opponents of European aggression. But, as Ira Gruber argues, 'nearly all lacked that combination of economic, political, and cultural resources that allowed Europeans to go beyond a tactical application of new weapons to enhance the power and security of their states and establish global empires'.[7]

There were technological changes which accompanied the military revolution, a revolution characterized by larger armies, more military expenditure and new military tactics. One major change was a move during Britain's wars with France and Spain in the 1690s and 1700s away from the musket-pike combination, in which soldiers with muskets were accompanied by soldiers carrying pikes, to the fusion presented by firearms-mounting bayonets, in which each soldier had the same weapon, and marched in strict formation. A shift at the same time from matchlock to flintlock muskets made muskets more reliable and enlarged the range of the ordinary soldier. Infantry became the most important part of European armies, with soldiers increasingly able to withstand cavalry attacks. Drilled incessantly and governed by extremely fierce discipline, which exceeded in ferocity even what slaves had to endure on plantations and where obedience to officers was strictly and brutally enforced, rank and file soldiers were not just well-armed but were able to keep to their posts much more readily in the past, thus increasing their effectiveness against other types of warfare. The eighteenth-century British or French army was a formidable adversary and was seldom beaten in battle situations by less conventional forces. The strength of the British and French armies underlay their remarkable imperial success in the eighteenth century. That the British army eventually was more formidable than even the French army under Napoleon is the main reason, even more than its burgeoning industrial wealth, why it became from 1815 the strongest state in the world and the most powerful empire.

The Military Revolution is usually thought of as a phenomenon that flourished between 1560 and 1660 but the eighteenth century was also important in initiating changes in military organization and effectiveness. Naval changes dominate the story in this century, with the British navy learning how to project power at a distance, thus allowing conflict to move towards a global dimension. Britain's mastery of the sea in the eighteenth century became clear as early as the War of Spanish Succession (1702–1713) and was continually enhanced during the almost continuous wars that Britain engaged in with France between 1689 and 1815. A key date was 1747 when British victory in two naval battles off Cape Finisterre off the west coast of Galicia in Spain showed that Britain was not just the most superior naval power in Europe but had advantages in technology and administration that no other naval power, even the French (who invested heavily in their navies from the mid-eighteenth century) could match.

Why was British naval power so lastingly strong? Their advantages lay in their having more ships than the French and in their ability to build and equip those ships quickly and effectively, having an extensive and effective administrative system, having strong public finances and having generally good naval leadership. The British navy was relatively meritocratic (more than the British army and much more so than the French navy), with some possibility of men from ordinary backgrounds getting good commands, although high command still tended to be confined to men from aristocratic backgrounds. The two great British naval heroes – George, Lord Rodney (1718–1792) and Horatio, Lord Nelson (1758–1805) of the American Revolution and the Napoleonic Wars – both came from middling backgrounds rather than from the upper reaches of society. Britain also committed more money to fighting war on sea than did France, which was more inclined to favour war on land. That preference for war at sea probably reflected Britain's position as an island empire and reflected the importance of Atlantic commerce in its eighteenth-century national economy. Britain used its navy to wreck colonial commerce, as it did very effectively when blockading Saint-Domingue in the late 1750s and capturing the seemingly impregnable redoubt of Havana in 1762 near the end of the Seven Years' War.

PIRACY

Parallel to warfare becoming more organized and more explicitly part of state formation, one major area of conflict in the Atlantic World was a place of anarchy, with opportunities open to individuals only loosely attached to European state. The Atlantic Ocean was a place where piracy was abundant. Pirates were very important in the creation of the Atlantic World and were indirectly tied to expansionist state building which helped integrate that world in the early eighteenth century. Ironically, pirates were a group that were quickly dispensed with once their purpose was served. The Golden Age of piracy, celebrated in Hollywood and popular culture, dating from 1713 to around 1730, was the period when European states all agreed to make piracy a capital crime rather than a means of enhancing state power, as had been the case for the previous two centuries.

Pirates from different European states attacked those from another in the early Atlantic World, becoming central to patterns of warfare at sea. Sometimes they combined to attack the richest state, usually Spain. On occasion, as with the Elizabethan 'sea-dogs' like Sir Francis Drake, John Hawkins and Sir Walter Raleigh, they even had tacit permission from their own government to be pirates. In these cases, they were given 'letters of marque and reprisal' to attack foreign enemy shipping. If they had such a license, they were termed a privateer, and could be lauded as heroes by their country; if they had no such license, they were deemed pirates, and thus were liable to arrest and grisly execution.

Piracy can be defined as robbery on the high-seas. It involved at least the threat of violence, if not actual violence, and was especially common in the Caribbean in the sixteenth and seventeenth centuries. The emergence of piracy was a major nuisance for Spain, above all. But, as Alan Karras notes, 'the non-Spanish pirates nevertheless served a tremendously important purpose in the settlement of the Western Hemisphere. Not only did the pirates' base for raiding and plunder eventually lead to permanent settlements that would later become non-Spanish colonies in places like Florida and Carolina, but the pirates' actions also led to a partial redistribution of the New World's wealth from Spain to more worthy European states who competed with it, in the mercantile system.'[8]

The legal status of piracy was ambivalent. In the seventeenth century, the word 'piracy' was applied to many things, including mutiny, shipboard crimes and raiding without government permission. Sometimes piracy was legal; sometimes not. Mariners became skilled at walking the unclear lines that existed between legitimacy and illegitimacy, also being aware that being on the wrong side of the line could end up with them in court. As Lauren Benton notes, mariners who worried about being classified as being pirates 'engaged in frequent legal posturing ... [and had] some shared knowledge of defence arguments that might be effective, and even when far from home gave considerable thought to strategies for preserving the pretence of legality'.[9]

One common argument they made was that they had been forced into piracy against their will, either through deception or through coercion. Indeed, pleas of coercion became literary devices in the increasingly popular literature celebrating pirates' deeds and misdeeds: good men went to sea and fell into bad company. It was an essentially conservative response, however, to claims against piracy, indicating support for the authority of ship captains and the legitimacy of ship discipline. People accused of piracy generally accepted the prevailing assumptions that piracy (as opposed to privateering) was indeed high crime – few pirates defended themselves claiming piracy was a worthwhile and defensible manner of life. Mariners and pirates knew they sailed in the Atlantic Ocean where their ties to nationality were both vital and a matter of interpretation. Shaping that interpretation could literally be a matter of life and death for men and the occasional woman accused of piracy on the high-seas. But the testimony of people accused of pirates did have important legal consequences, transforming European law about the status of the 'high-seas' and forming an important link in the development of international law. The founding jurist of international law, Hugo Grotius (1583–1645), for example, made several significant interventions about how piracy was to be defined and how law at sea might be reconciled with law on land. The result was that the 'high-seas' and the Atlantic and Indian oceans came to be regarded as a region of law outside the normal boundaries of national sovereignty and thus the first truly international places, where the laws of several jurisdictions might apply.

The nomenclature of the terms associated with piracy is revealing about the indeterminate status of pirates within European law. The term 'pirate' was an epithet, designed to condemn high-seas robbers. The more common and respectable terms were 'corsairs', 'privateers' and 'buccaneers', who were to be considered as working within the law, rather than outside it. Various nations excelled at high-seas piracy. The French were the main scourge of the Spanish up to 1560 and were then largely replaced by the English until the death of their erstwhile Protector, Elizabeth I, in 1603. The English in turn were replaced by the Dutch until around 1640.

The most important period of piracy in the Atlantic, and the period of piracy which has shaped the imagination of the world about what pirates were like, was in the second half of the seventeenth century, when freelance 'villains of all nations' became buccaneers and ran amok in the Caribbean, seriously disrupting Spanish trade and threatening Spanish power in the region. Buccaneers were often crucial, as in the pirate haven on Jamaica with its pirate capital of Port Royal, where Henry Morgan was based, in providing what might be considered 'start-up capital' from plunder that was employed in building up plantations and buying slaves. Their pirating raids became more daring in the 1660s, culminating in Morgan's sack in 1671 of Panama City, from which enormous quantities of bullion were transferred from the Spanish Caribbean to fledging colonies of the English.

Eventually, European nations grew tired of the disorder that inevitably accompanies buccaneering and grew readier to listen to Spanish complaints about the practice, especially as the Spanish themselves moved away from diplomatic protest and turned towards reprisal raiding in the 1690s. The end of the War for Spanish Succession in 1713 left the Atlantic with no European nation wanting to continue piracy, as the custom had become seen to be too destructive of international amity to continue and as, just as importantly, the need for 'start-up' capital from plunder had faded in importance. The end of the war, however, left on the Atlantic Ocean many naval veterans who had maritime skills but limited opportunities for employment. Some turned to work on the plantations; others became pirates. The most famous British pirates – Edward 'Blackbeard' Teach, Charles Rackham, William Kidd and the female pirates, Anne Bonny and Mary Read – were prominent in this period. Britain, however, was determined to root out piracy through its ever more powerful Royal Navy and made the capture and execution of pirates a primary objective in asserting their control over the high-seas. Most famous pirates had the proverbial merry and short life, either being killed or hanged (often in chains, so that their bodies could be left on display as grisly examples of what was done to pirates when caught), as the Royal Navy tightened its grip upon the seas.

What type of person became a pirate? People at the time attempted to say they were people apart, *hostis humani generis*, or 'Enemies not of one Nation or of one Sort of people only, but of all Mankind'. They were thus categorized as traitors, meaning, as Judge Sir Leoline Jenkins, the author of the above statement, declared in 1668, that 'Everybody is commissioned and is to be armed against them, as against Rebels and Traytors, to subdue and root them out'. Recent analyses, however, suggest that pirates were not so much hardened criminal predators, though some certainly were, without supporters on land and thus alone and isolated at sea, but were connected to communities on land who gave them support, even if that support was selective, sometimes arbitrary and could be withdrawn when circumstances changed. William Kidd (1645–1701), a local hero in New York, and a successful pirate or buccaneer in both the Indian and Atlantic Oceans, found out how fickle support on land could be, when he went from being lauded as a hero to being tried and executed as his support on land evaporated while he was at sea and oblivious to changing political circumstances.

We can see how useful pirates might be to communities on land (before they outlived their usefulness) in assessing their place in the seventeenth-century English empire. In the first half of the seventeenth century, profits from maritime plunder were crucial in kick-starting colonization in Ireland and the Americas, with windfall profits helping cover the price of settlement. One of the most prominent such privateers was Sir William Phips (1651–1695), whose rapid rise from obscurity to prominence showed how pirates were some of the rare people who could transcend usual social hierarchies – they were, like Henry Morgan, the celebrities of their day, with wealth and fame that set them apart from others. Phips was born poor in northern New England (now Maine), and rather miraculously discovered a Spanish treasure wreck which made him very rich and New England prosperous. He became a local hero and a royal governor who launched a not especially successful assault on New France in the 1690s.

Jamaica was where pirates gathered in this period, being as much a pirate as a planting society in the 1660s and 1670s. By the 1680s, however, the pirates' nest of Port Royal had become hostile to pirates and English plunderers sailed north to places in English North America such as Newport and Charleston. These communities not only harboured pirates; after 1688 they financed pirate ventures, ostensibly as part of strategies in England and Britain's war with France. But after 1696, pressure from the English state made these communities become less welcome to pirates. They did so because legitimate and remunerative activities at sea became more common and violence at sea came to be problematic while the anarchic planter did not fit community visions of the future development of settler societies as respectable places. In addition, free trade in slaves after the demise of the Royal African Company from 1708 made pirates at first superfluous and then a social problem. The 1690s were crucial in establishing England as a coherent and integrated maritime empire where pirates were no longer necessary. Once pirates had no connection to communities on land, they found it hard to get supplies and impossible to access social and sexual pleasures. Not surprisingly, they were soon able to sustain themselves and took to preying on the communities that had previously supported them. Once pirates became a special sociological type – men who spoke their own language, had distinctive clothing and an unusual culture – their fate as marginal and disposable outsiders was soon sealed.

BRITAIN VS. FRANCE AND THE SEVEN YEARS' WAR

In the eighteenth century, the most important consequence of the militarization of European societies was the Second Hundred Years' War between France and Britain. Both nations engaged in a virtual arms race in this period. Britain concentrated on strengthening its navy so that by the 1750s it had a fleet of over 300 warships and strong naval bases in British America. The French and Spanish governments responded vigorously to what they saw as British threats to their European position and expanded their navies. By 1760, these three European empires had two-thirds of the world's fighting fleet. France concentrated on securing its position in Europe by building a massive army. Louis XIV (1638–1715) financed an army of 340,000 by the 1690s. As with sea-power, other nations responded so that by around 1710 there were 1 million men in arms in Western Europe. In this period, Atlantic wars were most fought in Europe but during the eighteenth century wars were increasingly fought in the Americas, often with colonists doing most of the fighting. It was only in the Seven Years' War that Europe sent large armed forces to the Americas. After a long peace between 1713 and 1739, Britain, France and Spain engaged in a series of wars between 1739 and 1748. These wars were not unimportant – they were far more than skirmishes – but the aims of protagonists were generally limited. Neither France nor Britain tried to capture the territories of the other and mostly tried to destroy plantations, disrupt trade and try and make their position within the circuits of Atlantic commerce stronger. These wars were in effect largely military means of fighting for greater commercial dominance in an Atlantic World when such commerce was becoming ever more vital.

The war that started in the Ohio Valley in 1754, one in which a youthful British Military officer called George Washington (1732–1799) played an important role in provoking the start of conflict, was different. When war began in earnest in 1756, it became the first global war (although to say such a thing betrays a certain Atlantic-centricism, as significant parts of the world such as East Africa, China and the Ottoman empire were not affected very much by this conflict between European empires in the Americas, Europe, West Africa and South Asia). Because the result of this war led directly to the American Revolution, later generations tended to think of it as a largely imperial conflict. That is a mistake. As Daniel Baugh comments, 'the ultimate object of statesmen in London ... was to maintain and increase security, power and influence in Europe'.[10] Statesmen in Paris felt the same way. Britain was a European power and its first concern in diplomacy and warfare was always about how its actions would affect its position in Europe.

Even William Pitt (1708–1778), the prime minister largely responsible for British victory and sometimes thought of as Britain's first great imperial statesman, was obsessed with how to improve Britain's position in Europe. For Pitt and his French counterpart, Ètienne-François de Choiseul, Duc de Choiseul (1719–1785), colonies were the means of securing security and influence in Europe. Britain was determined that France would not dominate Europe and established its political system of absolute monarchy so that European liberties, in the British views, would be destroyed. France, on its part, feared that British global expansion and the remarkable growth of its colonies, which stimulated British manufacturing and filled British state coffers, enabling it to fight expensive wars, would enable Britain to usurp France's position in Europe. Both nations connected their concerns over their rival gaining European hegemony to the increasing importance of American colonies in developing European trade networks. Thus, it was very likely in the 1750s that any war between France and Britain would start outside Europe – that it emerged from a local conflict in the backwoods of the Ohio Valley is not as surprising as it initially seems, if we look at the war in the ways that American historians have often looked at it, as being an entirely American War (the French and Indian War) rather than a war with significant European consequences. That the Seven Years' War originated in the borderlands of America shows the extent to which the Atlantic World had become an integrated unit by the mid-eighteenth century.

The Seven Years' War was a massive triumph for Britain but a triumph with significant pyrrhic aspects. Britain succeeded beyond its wildest expectations between 1756 and 1763 either due to the wise policies of Pitt or because piecemeal responses to unfolding situations turned out surprisingly well. The war proceeded in two phases. From 1756 to 1758, Britain did poorly. From the 'annus mirabilis' of 1759, when Britain won battle after battle and made conquests worldwide under Pitt's inspired leadership, the tide turned decisively to Britain's advantage. The three most important victories were those by General James Wolfe (1727–1759) on the Battle of the Plains of Abraham below Quebec City, which ended most of French colonization in the northern part of North America; that of Robert Clive (1725–1774) at the Battle of Plassey in India, initiating control of large parts of India under the East India Company; and the 1762 conquest of Havana in Cuba, a huge shock to the confidence of Spain in the security of its American possessions.

The problem with all three of these victories is that it induced a hubris among British statesmen, who started to believe, against Pitt's advice, that they were invincible and that European allies were largely unnecessary. The result was that in the 1760s and 1770s Britain had no serious ally in Europe. France and Spain were determined to gain revenge against Britain for the humiliations they had suffered from 1759 to 1762. They got their chance in the American Revolution. In retrospect, the outcome of the Seven Years' War was a clear demonstration that British global supremacy rested on Britain having European allies. But Europeans now saw Britain and its growing global hegemony after 1763 as a mortal threat to their own position. And the war was so enormously expensive that even Britain, the Atlantic power with the best resources to fight war without bankrupting itself, was sorely stretched, meaning that it embarked on plans to make colonists in British America sustain more of the expenses of defending imperial possessions, leading from 1765 to colonial revolt. In addition, the result of the war was to alienate Britain from its Native American allies who felt betrayed by the Peace of Paris in 1763.

NATIVE AMERICAN RESISTANCE

An important feature of the wars between Britain and France in the eighteenth century was that they involved Native Americans on both sides. Ironically, the value of Native American military assistance escalated as French-British imperial competition from 1689 to 1763, a period coinciding with seeing Native Americans as uncivilizable. The defeat of the French in 1763 made it easier for the British to diminish the importance of their Native American allies, even as settlers increased their violent assaults on Native American land. But Native Americans were in fact indispensable to both sides during eighteenth-century imperial wars. They provided intelligence reports, for example, so that Europeans could learn of enemy movements. Initially, the British had fewer Native American allies, leading to punishing raids on British settlement in the interior regions of Pennsylvania and Virginia. Their successful naval blockade from 1759, however, changed the direction of Native American allegiance. The French could not provide trade to Native Americans due to the blockade. The result was a movement over to the British, with the most important moves being by the Mohawk and Cherokees.

Native Americans were to be seriously disappointed by the British once war had ended. Britain's failure after 1760 to maintain diplomatic relationships and to restrain settler violence led to what is called Pontiac's War of 1763 but which was a multi-tribal uprising of Native Americans against the British. Similar uprisings also developed between 1759 and 1761 in South Carolina. Settlement of the disputes was only solved, partially, by the Royal Proclamation of 1763, which set aside the trans-Appalachian West as Native American land. This Proclamation solved one problem but created another. It thwarted the ambitions of white settlers to acquire western lands and put them at odds with an integrated, centrally controlled sphere of imperial authority, thus becoming a cause of the American Revolution.

A recent efflorescence in understanding Native American warfare in North America reminds us that we cannot see warfare in the eighteenth-century Atlantic World through the eyes of Europeans only. Eventually, the Native Americans in the Great Lakes and the Ohio Valley who had participated in Pontiac's War and other conflicts after the end of the Seven Years' War lost their lands to the United States. That loss of land happened when these Native Americans were abandoned by their British allies in the Peace of Paris of 1783, following the American Revolution. Britain transferred the Ohio country to the United States without reference to the Native American people who lived there. But in the mid-eighteenth century, Native Americans still retained much power in the region. In 1763, the British had taken possession of French territory from the St. Lawrence to the Mississippi rivers. But Native Americans in this region made it clear to the British that 'although you have conquered the French you have not conquered us'.

Native Americans were powerful forces shaping imperial outcomes well into the eighteenth century. As Colin Calloway notes, 'in 1755, Indians in the Ohio country destroyed the biggest army Britain had dispatched to North America; in 1791 they destroyed the only army the United States possessed'.[11] General Edward Bradddock was defeated at the Battle of the Monongahela in 1755 mainly by Native Americans. Inadequately trained British troops met Native American soldiers with French Canadian officers who were experienced in fighting and in leading Native Americans. General John Forbes succeeded where Braddock had failed by negotiating peace with Native Americans in the region rather than engaging them in war. The French hub of Fort Duquesne quickly collapsed.

This collapse did not mean that the Ohio nations had ceded their country to anyone. When General Jeffrey Amherst ignored the advice of the dying General Forbes to listen to Native Americans and refused to engage in gift-giving, the Native Americans of Ohio nearly obliterated the British Empire west of the Appalachians. And, as Calloway argues, 'they made sure the British understood the causes of the conflict'. Before warriors of the Seneca nation killed a British commander, 'they made him write down their list of grievances: lack of trade, high prices, and British expansionism'.[12] This land was Indian country, whatever the Peace of Paris said. The power of Native Americans in the Ohio Valley was not easily swept aside.

Even after they had been betrayed by the British in the Peace of Paris, Native Americans in the Ohio Valley fought against American westward movement, defeating General Arthur St. Clair in 1791, killing 630 American soldiers with a multinational army executing a carefully coordinated battle plan. For a while, St. Clair's defeat seemed to threaten the very survival of the new United States, occurring when separatist movements in the West were proceeding toward alliance with Spain and as the British in Canada watched to see if they could move back into northwestern Ohio. Native Americans crowed that they held Americans 'in the most Supreme Degree of Contempt'. It was vainglorious boasting. General Anthony Wayne defeated a weakened confederacy at the Battle of Fallen Timbers in 1794 and the British failed to support Native Americans as they had promised to do. In 1795, Native Americans ceded most of Ohio to the United States. Their defeat at Fallen Timbers, however, should not blind us to the fact that Native Americans were often successful in their struggles to keep their land for longer than is customarily thought.

Indeed, some Native American empires used violence and warfare to dominate their own region and to resist colonial domination for centuries. That was what was the case for the Iroquois in the northeast, the Lakotas on the Dakotas and the Comanche in southwest North America. As Pekka Hämäläinen has shown, the Comanches forged an empire in the late eighteenth century and early nineteenth century with three components that allied warfare to economic activity – a trading network, a shifting raiding hinterland that increased the number of horses Comanche had and which were vital to Comanche military power, and a flexible frontier policy that incorporated neighbouring groups into their empires. Spanish colonists could not withstand the pull of the Comanches' political economy and their military might. European settlement in the area the Comanche controlled was stopped for many years. Indeed, the Comanche remained powerful in the American southwest until the 1860s, when population loss and adverse environmental issues reduced their powers.[13] The lesson to learn here is that Europeans did not have it all their own way when trying to subdue Native American opposition and warfare was a principal means whereby Native Americans preserved their sovereignty against a growing economic power.

NOTES

1   Jean-Frédéric Schaub, 'Violence in the Atlantic: Sixteenth and Seventeenth Centuries,' in Nicholas Canny and Philip D. Morgan, eds., *The Oxford Handbook of the Atlantic World 1450–1850* (Oxford: Oxford University Press, 2011), 114.
2   Bryan Sandberg, 'Beyond Encounters; Religion, Ethnicity, and Violence in the Early Modern World, 1492–1700,' *Journal of World History* 17 (2006), 15.
3   H.E. Martel, 'Hans Staden's Captive Soul: Identity, Imperialism and Rumors of Cannibalism in Sixteenth-Century Brazil,' *Journal of World History* 17 (2006), 51–69.
4   Neil Whitehead, 'Hans Staden and the Cultural Politics of Cannibalism,' *Hispanic American Historical Review* 80 (2000), 750.
5   Nicholas P. Canny, 'The Ideology of English Colonization: From Ireland to America,' *William and Mary Quarterly* 3d ser. 30 (1973), 596–97.
6   Clifford Rogers, ed. *The Military Revolution Debate: Readings in the Military Transformation of Early Modern Europe* (Boulder: University of Colorado Press, 1995).
7   Ira Gruber, 'Atlantic Warfare,' in Nicholas Canny and Philip D. Morgan, eds., *The Oxford Handbook of the Atlantic World 1450–1850* (Oxford: Oxford University Press, 2011), 427.
8   Alan L. Karras, *Smuggling: Contraband and Corruption in World History* (Lanham, MD: Rowman and Littlefield, 2010), 23.
9   Lauren Benton, 'Legal Spaces of Empire: Piracy and the Origins of Ocean Regionalism,' *Comparative Studies in Society and History* 47 (2005), 707.
10   Daniel Baugh, *The Global Seven Years' War, 1754 to 1763* (London: Longman, 2011), 1.
11   Colin Calloway, 'Red Power and Homeland Security: Native Nations and the Limits of Empire in the Ohio Country,' in Michael A. McDonald and Kate Fullager, eds., *Facing Empire: Indigenous Experiences in a Revolutionary Age* (Baltimore: Johns Hopkins University Press, 2018), 145.
12   Ibid., 151–2.
13   Pekka Hämäläinen, 'The Politics of Grass: European Expansion, Ecological Change, and Indigenous Power in the Southwest Borderlands,' *William and Mary Quarterly* 3d ser. 67 (2010), 173–208.

BIBLIOGRAPHY

Oxford Online Bibliography – Arsenals; Fiscal-Military State; Medicine and Warfare; Piracy; Sailors; Soldiers; Violence; War and Trade; Warfare; Warfare in 17th-century North America.

Fred Anderson, *The Crucible of War: The Seven Years' War and the Fate of Empire in British North America, 1754–1764* (New York: Alfred A. Knopf, 2000).

Jeremy Black, *Beyond the Military Revolution: War in the Seventeenth-Century World* (Basingstoke: Macmillan, 2011).

Colin Calloway, *The Victory with No Name: The Native American Defeat of the First American Army* (New York: Oxford University Press, 2015).

Guy Chet, *The Ocean Is a Wilderness: Atlantic Piracy and the Limits of State Authority, 1688–1756* (Amherst: University of Massachusetts Press, 2014).

Barbara Donegan, 'Atrocity, War Crime, and Treason in the English Civil War,' *American Historical Review* 99 (1994), 1137–64.

Gregory Dowd, *War under Heaven: Pontiac, the Indian Nations and the British Empire* (Baltimore: Johns Hopkins University Press, 2002).

Jan Glete, *War and the State in Early Modern Europe* (London: Routledge, 2001).

Mark Hanna, *Pirate Nests and the Rise of the British Empire, 1570–1640* (Chapel Hill: University of North Carolina Press, 2015).

Michael A. McDonnell, *Masters of Empire: Great Lake Indians and the Making of America* (New York: Hill and Wang, 2015).

Geoffrey Parker, *The Military Revolution: Military Innovation and the Rise of the West, 1500–1800* (Cambridge: Cambridge University Press, 1988).

James Sharpe, *A Fiery and Furious People: A History of Violence in England* (London: Penguin, 2016).

John Thornton, *Warfare in Atlantic Africa, 1500–1800* (London: Routledge, 1999).

14

THE MOVEMENT OF THINGS

MERCHANTS

Among the special Atlantic 'types' – sailors, slaves, pirates – the 'merchant' holds a special place. The Atlantic presented great opportunities to investors in Europe and a windfall to a few fortunate people in Africa who engaged in trade with Europeans. In general, it was merchants who took advantage of these opportunities. Moreover, the merchants who profited most from Atlantic trade were those on the margin, as established merchants in Europe and Africa tended in the fifteenth century to be linked into more established trading relationships with people in the Mediterranean or in the Ottoman Empire and in the Levant. The Atlantic World is a classic example of Joseph Schumpeter's observation that innovation seldom comes from older industries but comes out of new initiatives, grows up alongside existing commerce and then displaces established interests. Merchants investing in the New World, whether they came from sixteenth-century Genoa, seventeenth-century Amsterdam, or eighteenth-century Nantes or Bordeaux, tended to be from marginal positions in society and were willing to take greater risks than people from more comfortable backgrounds. It is a noticeable feature of Atlantic commerce that old landed and aristocratic elites were seldom involved in the Atlantic World. Very few of the leading aristocrats in England, including the Cavendishes, the Russells and the Stanleys, invested in the Atlantic. English and British royal involvement, save for James II's personal involvement in the government of the New York province named after him and the Royal African Company in which he was very interested, in the Atlantic World was sporadic and without much personal interaction.

There were good reasons not to be involved in Atlantic commerce: it was very risky to send ships across the Atlantic Ocean and the possibility of high profits went alongside the likelihood of financial ruin. Ships sank, people overseas cheated others with impunity, legal systems of recovery were inadequate, and banks and insurers could charge extortionate rates when Atlantic commerce became dangerous, as during wartime. Theodore Rabb, in a famous article from 1974, argued that 'the proclivity for taking large risks, against heavy odds, was a fundamental characteristic of the early-modern merchant. It was entirely in keeping with his outlook, that he should have approached overseas enterprise in an almost reckless frame of mind'.[1]

Merchants in the Netherlands tended to continue in their existing European trade relationships with merchants in the Baltic or Scandinavia. A few men from established merchant families were willing to risk being involved in Atlantic trade, joining forces in chartered companies. They were joined by merchants from the southern Netherland and Sephardic Jews, both of which groups were new entrepreneurs, keen to innovate, and willing to entertain high levels of risk. Jews were closely connected to Portuguese merchants and used those contacts to establish information networks of considerable sophistication. Most of these men had relatively little capital or access to credit, a problem for a capital-intensive business. They got around this in the seventeenth century through joining together in joint-stock companies, thus spreading the risk and getting enough capital for heavy start-up costs. These companies faded by the end of the seventeenth century, usually because they could not get debtors to pay quickly enough, meaning that capital was tied up unproductively. The solution to the problem of credit was a new financial instrument, the bill of exchange, in which an American commodity produced by an indebted planter was consigned to a European merchant with the bill of exchange being used by the merchant to pay for goods to be sent on credit from Europe to the planter. This transfer of the financing of Atlantic trade from European merchants to American planters allowed for the great expansion of private commerce in the Atlantic in the eighteenth century through leveraging significant new assets. The broad trend was for European capital to move into American production.

ATLANTIC TRADE OVER TIME

There were three models of trade in the Atlantic World: Spanish, Dutch and the English/French model. Spain adopted from the start an imperial model where from 1503, under rules called La Casa Contratación, Atlantic commerce was subject to monopolistic rules. These monopolies were hard to control but the intention of Spain and to an extent Portugal was clear. As David Hancock comments, 'The Spanish monarchy monopolised commerce, created an organisation to manage it, established a fleet system to protect it, and gave Seville merchant guilds the charge of – and profit from – exploiting trade.'² The general idea was the notion of 'mercantilism' where overseas trade was organized by the state in a highly protectionist way intended to advance national self-sufficiency. Spain found it hard to enforce such strict state control, however, and rules were flouted with increasing impunity, with smuggling rife throughout the Spanish American empire, and increasing over time. The Spanish also were unable to develop their own slave trade and subcontracted this trade to various European nations in the *asiento* system.

The Dutch model started off as an imperial one, like the Spanish and Portuguese models, but quickly was transformed into one where the Dutch acted as intermediaries to other states, supplying, for example, slaves and provisions to Portuguese plantations in Brazil and Surinam by the 1630s. The French and English operated a different model still. They organized their trade in the seventeenth century as monopolies within a mercantilist framework that allowed for a measure of private trading, under a regulatory framework – codified in l'exclusif in France and in the 1651 Navigation Acts in England. These frameworks worked well for both countries in the second half of the seventeenth century but came under increasing strain from the 1690s as the Atlantic became the pivot of empire for the English and as France developed cod fisheries in the Bay of Biscay and Brittany and a profitable triangular trade in fish between France, Newfoundland and Iberia. The chartered companies proved largely unable to satisfy increased demand and private trading in both countries took over from state-sponsored commerce by the early eighteenth century.

During the first three quarters of the eighteenth century, Atlantic commerce increased considerably in both France and Britain. In Britain, Atlantic imports grew sixfold and exports by 6 and 10 per cent respectively between 1700 and 1775. More and more of British overseas trade went to the Americas in this period, amounting to one-third of all overseas trade by 1775. France's Atlantic trade simultaneously increased exponentially in this period but unlike Britain whose increase came to a sudden halt in the 1790s, when the Haitian Revolution destroyed commerce from its most productive colony, Saint-Domingue. In addition, it lost Martinique and Guadeloupe in the Caribbean before regaining them in reduced state after 1814. The Netherlands prospered as well during the eighteenth century from Atlantic trade under its intermediation model. The value of its Atlantic commerce was twice in 1750 what it had been in 1636.

Iberian trade in the Atlantic was erratic. Spain's government was ineffective in the early eighteenth century and it was only after its defeat in the Seven Years' War in 1763 that its government made concerted reforms to the organization of its empire and especially to its by now antiquated system of Atlantic commerce. What Spain wanted to do was reconstitute its empire so that private profits increased, and state revenues were great enough to allow Spain to emulate the fiscal policy of Britain. What was needed was an 'active' model of empire to replace a 'passive' one, a system of commercial colonization to supplant the spoils of conquest. What emerged was a more decentred commercial empire where imperial regulation was less intrusive than previously. Centralization of government decreased; trade within Spanish America increased. One important consequence was a dramatic increase in the slave trade to Spanish America and Brazil. The Haitian Revolution and the abolition of slavery in the British Empire in 1807 did not, however, see the Atlantic slave trade decline but rather saw captive Africans moved from one part of the Atlantic to another.

The problem that Spain had was that there was an imbalance between what Spain could provide America and what America could provide Spain. Between 1778 and 1796 exports from Spain to America rose about four times but imports from America to Spain increased tenfold. Only Spain's continuing capacity to import precious metals allowed it to pay for manufactured goods from Britain and France. The disaster for Spain and Portugal of Napoleonic invasion after 1807 severely curtailed trade from Spain to America. It was only trade with the United States and the settlement of British merchants in strategic Latin American cities that stopped economic disaster for the new Latin American republics. Nevertheless, economic woes in the early nineteenth century meant that relative income per capita in Latin America fell considerably relative to that in the United States between 1800 and 1830. That gap in wealth has not yet disappeared.

The big winner in Atlantic trade by the first half of the nineteenth century was Britain. Its burgeoning Industrial Revolution allowed it to send manufacturing goods to its colonies and to Ireland and then to the United States after 1790. The United States and the republics of Latin America became informal colonies of Britain, costing little in imperial upkeep but buying large amounts of British goods. By the turn of the eighteenth century, British imports from Asia were about the same as those from the Atlantic. But exports to Asia were tiny compared to what was sent to the Americas. Imports from the Americas could be paid for by manufactured goods, for which Americans in both North and South America had an insatiable demand. Britain outpaced the Dutch who in the mid-seventeenth century had exported more manufactured goods within Europe than England. But by the eighteenth century the Dutch could not penetrate Iberian markets as could the British and were excluded from British America. The British made lots of money from overseas trade but profits from slave-generated Atlantic trade probably did relatively little to cause the Industrial Revolution – the causes were mostly connected to British internal economic development. Nevertheless, the growth of population in the Americas, their increasing wealth and their eagerness to copy European consumption fashions were a massive stimulus to industrial output. Thus, much of the expansion of European industrial production was stimulated by demand throughout the late eighteenth- and early nineteenth-century Atlantic World.

RUM

We can see how trade works at both the macro and the micro level in the Atlantic World through a case study of rum production and consumption. Estimating the increase of Atlantic trade by volume tells us a great deal but to understand how trade goods from the Atlantic changed the patterns of everyday life we need to assess the impact of individual commodities and how people experienced those commodities when they purchased them. Let's examine the meanings behind that quintessential Atlantic drink, rum punch. Rum was a by-product of sugar and making it was a skilled process, involving blending and distilling coarse molasses. The making of it required 'much labour', as Richard Ligon commented in mid-seventeenth-century Barbados, but also a close connection with the environment.

If we are to understand the relationship between the production of commodities and their consumption we first need to decentralize humans from the process and think about the total ecosystem through which 'work' was done. The rum produced on Caribbean sugar plantations can be defined as much by abstracted energy transfers as by human slavery. The energy transfers required to produce rum were biological in three ways: agri-ecological work for sugar cane to grow; human labour to tend, harvest and process sugar; and then microbial work for the yeast to take sugar and ferment it into alcohol. Enslaved people not only did work as conventionally thought of. They were embedded into multiple natural systems which itself did work, such as providing sunlight as energy so that sugar cane could grow. The environment was the slave's companion and his or her enemy, acting against them regarding heat and disease. Slaves toiled under a hot sun, fighting back thick verdant growth, engaged in arduous digging or 'holing' of Caribbean soil, and planted and harvested cane. It was a miserable business. The ex-slave Ashton Warner declared that working as a sugar worker was 'the worst of all punishments – the lowest step of disgrace … It is a dreadful state of slavery … I declare before Almighty God that I wold rather die than submit to it'. When Europeans and settlers drank rum punch, they were indirectly involving themselves with processes and environments and peoples from the far distant Caribbean.[3]

The anthropologist Sidney Mintz sums up the complicated relationship between humans and the environment in producing rum, showing that there was a disconnect between those making the ingredients for rum punch and those consuming the drink. He wrote:

> The chemical and mechanical transformations by which substances are bent to human use and unrecognizable to those that know them in nature have marked our relationship for nature almost as long as we have been human … But the division of labour by which such transformations are realised can impart additional mystery to the technical processes. When

the locus of manufacture and that of use are as little known to each other as the process of manufacture and use themselves, the mystery will deepen.[4]

As with today, when we seldom think about how our clothes might be produced under sweatshop conditions, the disassociation between drinking rum punch and realizing that the rum was produced through brutal treatment of enslaved people was very strong. Only a few ethically minded people refused to eat sugar or drink rum as a protest against slavery.

Eighteenth-century rum drinkers were probably more aware of the imperial and commercial implications of rum consumption than they were aware of it being produced by slaves. Rum was a popular drink in the British Empire with a third of rum exports from Barbados going to Britain in 1748 and over half going to British North America, and the rest mostly consumed by whites and blacks alike in the Caribbean. Barbados alone produced 1.5 million gallons of rum in 1768. In North America, it is estimated, perhaps over ambitiously, that the average white man drank 21 gallons of rum a year around the time of the American Revolution. Rum was very much the chief drink in British American taverns. It was usually drunk mixed with water, lemons and lots of sugar, with its principal ingredients, all direct products of transatlantic trade.

Drinking rum gave out strong social messages, given that a bowl of rum punch was designed to be shared with others and tended to be drunk in convivial fashion in taverns and in face-to-face occasions of male sociability. If women in the eighteenth century favoured drinking tea, men preferred drinking rum. Rum drinkers seldom made the link between what they were drinking and the people who produced rum. Philip Waldeck, for example, was a German visitor to Jamaica in late 1778. On arrival, he told of how 'two boat-loads of black girls came on the ship with all sorts of things to sell'. He bought citrus fruit from them and proceeded to mix a bowl of rum punch 'which here in its native land can be thoroughly enjoyed'. He was a happy man: 'we took old Jamaica rum, said to be the best in the world, lemons which grow fresh here ... and sugar grown here ... drinking this punch ... we again forgot all unpleasantness, all dangers, all that we had been through at sea'. Even though Waldeck lamented the 'miserable existence' of sugar cane workers in later writings, arguing that 'we have no advantage over them except we are white and they are black', he did not make the link between his enjoyment of rum punch and the horrors of Jamaican slavery.

There were, however, a few Europeans who linked slave-produced alcohol to the iniquities of enslavement. The New England clergyman, Cotton Mather, argued in a 1708 sermon that drinking too much rum was like enslavement. A man who drank too much was like a slave who needed to 'shake off these Chains; they are the Chains of Darkness'. The abolitionist Anthony Benezet made a more direct link to African chattel slavery in

1774 when he argued that sending alcohol to Africa made Africans so desirous of buying rum that they resorted to the slave trade. It was as 'if the poor negroes have been … bewitched and prevailed upon to captivate their unhappy country people, in order to bring them to European market'. Drink, as Benezet recognized, and as Peter Mancall has described for Native Americans, could be highly destructive of social and economic relationships for people previously unused to it.[5]

THE MEANING OF FOOD

The Columbian exchange brought new foods into the Atlantic which people had not eaten before. In general, people find eating new foods challenging rather than exciting. That was certainly true in the early period of Atlantic history. New foods could prove unsettling as it was commonly assumed in Europe, where humoral understandings of medicine (that the body had four 'humours' and that the purpose of medicine was to keep these humours in balance) underpinned ideas about bodily functions, that if one ate unfamiliar foods this would affect a person's health. It also might mean that a person would become transformed into the sort of person who usually ate such foods. In short, if you ate like a Native American, you became a Native American. Food was central to early modern thought about bodily difference – you were what you ate. Early modern Spaniards believed that eating non-European food might alter the European body. Eating the correct food was thus essential to maintain European identity because both diets and bodies were fluid rather than fixed and liable to change once the balance of humours in the body were altered, either by moving into unfamiliar climates (such as going from a temperate to a tropical climate) or by diet.

When Spaniards thought about Native American bodies, they were unimpressed, thinking them inferior in composition to more virile Spanish bodies. According to humoral theory, Native Americans were phlegmatic and inclined to melancholy, unlike the choleric Spaniards. Some of this difference was due, it was believed, to climate and New World 'airs'. But even more of this bodily deficiency was due to the bad foods that Native Americans consumed. Food was considered to play an important role in correcting humoral imbalance. If you were melancholic and thus 'dry and cold', then you should eat hot, moist foods, like sugar. Spaniards who thought about such things warned that if the Spanish in the New World experimented with Native American foods they would become unhealthy. Increasing mortality among Spanish settlers only confirmed such theories. Foods such as maize, they believed, were inherently unhealthy, a belief they kept to even after maize came to be the chief part of the diet of settlers and became a crop that proved a hugely successful implant into Mediterranean diet regimes. It was a matter of faith that eating Native American foods made you sick. A dieting manual from 1586 claimed that 'the root called cassava, from which the Indians make bread, is mortal poison to those from these parts who navigate over here'.

For this reason, Spaniards were willing to pay large sums to bring from Spain traditional food, such as the Iberian trio of bread, wine and olive oil. The first two foods were crucial not just within diets but in religious ceremonies, being part of the Eucharist in which the body of Jesus Christ was turned into nourishment for Christian believers. These foodstuffs were not just good for you but symbolized in real form Catholic civilization and as such were as necessary in the New World as in the Old World. In addition, growing European crops in the Americas showed that if such crops could flourish, so too could Europeans – plants were a test of how well the Spanish would do in the Americas. One issue, however, in abjuring Native American food was that many New World crops were delectable. Everyone loved eating pineapples while tomatoes and chillies were widely praised. And, of course, maize was successfully sent, along with potatoes, to Europe, transforming European diets and preventing famine. Spaniards admitted that these foods were good to eat but insisted that they should be eaten only in limited quantities. Maize, for example, did not produce 'proper' bread, after all, which was only possible using wheat.

Given that Spaniards believed that diet shaped the human body so that a Spaniard might turn into a Native American if she adopted a diet of Native American foods, their understanding of the human body was that it was mutable and porous and that Atlantic peoples could become interchangeable if care was not taken to insulate oneself from being contaminated by the cultures that one encountered on Atlantic peregrinations. As Rebecca Earle notes, 'It is for this reason that chroniclers and officials devoted so much attention to documenting the cultivation of Old World crops in the Americas, and the sons of conquistadors proudly recited the names of the European plants that their fathers had introduced, for these foods were the bulwark that separated the colonisers from the colonised.'[6] Transforming the Americas so that as much as possible they resembled the landscape and the cultures that had been left behind was therefore not just a way in which European settlers in the Americas marked their occupation of the land and made themselves comfortable with trappings of what they considered to be civilization. It was also a means whereby Europeans could foil the degenerative tendencies of the New World, tendencies which prevailed as orthodox thinking in Europe and the Americas until the late eighteenth century. Things changed when discoveries in natural science, such as the recognition that the largest trees in the world were in western North America (redwoods) and that the largest animals (dinosaurs) to have ever walked the earth live in North America, showed that it was not true that everything declined in a New World setting, including the human body. Writers like Thomas Jefferson seized upon these natural facts to argue that the New World was designed to eventually supplant the tired civilization of the Old, now that European settler populations were established in America and were flourishing.

Many of the most important Atlantic exchanges in Europe as well in the Americas revolved around the new foods introduced as part of the Columbian exchange. The important role of the food trade in Atlantic commerce is self-evident. Edibles constituted most of the value of overseas trade in countries like eighteenth-century Britain. The taxes on these commodities helped sustain the fiscal-military state that allowed Britain to expand its global empire without bankrupting itself. Custom duties on sugar in the 1760s, for example, were enough to fund the pride of the British state, the British navy with its worldwide presence and ability to project power over France and Spain. Nevertheless, food had other meanings that were more symbolic than economic or geopolitical. It helped Britons in the eighteenth century make strong identification with their empire, in part because food coming from other parts of the Atlantic World was more ubiquitous in people's lives than reading about empire. People read books occasionally; they consumed sugar, smoked tobacco and drank coffee every day.

The market for Atlantic foods was large and growing ever more important during the eighteenth century. Annual consumption of sugar in Britain increased 25-fold between 1650 and 1800. Increasingly, everyone had access to tropical goods through effective and extensive domestic trading networks. By 1750, grocers' shops abounded in Britain, even in small villages distant from Atlantic ports, selling sugar, coffee, tobacco (and tea from India and China) to an ever-larger clientele. People were willing to work harder in what historians call the 'industrious revolution', in which desires for items of consumption spurred increase in production, so that they could afford to buy edibles such as sugar that might satisfy their sweet tooth and be used in ceremonies that added meaning to life. What is a birthday, for example, without a cake, and what is a cake without sugar?

Understanding what consumers thought they were doing when they were consuming Atlantic goods and appreciating the extent to which consumers connected such products to the places where they were grown and to the people who produced them are difficult to assess, though we know that advertisers played on British associations of certain New World products with their places of origin to sell goods more effectively. Advertising itself shaped how these foods came to have symbolic meanings that increased an awareness of the Atlantic World. First, tropical food lacked a deep-rooted history in Britain, allowing advertisers to invest from scratch Atlantic associations to certain Atlantic products. Advertisements for tobacco, for example, usually made the point that the tobacco was grown in Virginia and used imagery of Native Americans (though seldom the enslaved African Americans who grew the tobacco consumers were smoking) to demonstrate the excellence of the product they were hawking. Second, Britons relied upon national marketing campaigns to encourage them to buy such goods. Advertisements for tobacco, for example, were the same for consumers in Cumbria as in London, suggesting a national shared

pastime rather than something that had any local associations. Third, the
economic machinery getting such things as Jamaican sugar to a farmer's
wife in Cheshire was remarkably efficient, leading to the lowering of costs
and reducing the chance of Atlantic foods becoming associated with British
regional cultures. Atlantic food was a significant means of creating an
image of 'Britishness'. What, for example, could be more British than a cup
of tea sweetened with sugar, even though neither ingredient was ever grown
in the British Isles itself?

Sugar was a bit different, both because the connotations with slavery
were so obvious as to be disturbing and because it had become by the
eighteenth century such an everyday item of consumption. It was difficult to
make grand claims about the specialness of sugar made in the Atlantic when
sugar had been available, albeit in limited quantities, in Britain for centuries
before the Atlantic World had been initiated. In addition, unlike tobacco
or even coffee, sugar was so commonplace that it was hard to differentiate
between different kinds of sugar to encourage consumers to choose one
brand over another, although by the nineteenth century producers of brown
sugar from Demerara were successful in attaching the name of the colony to
that kind of sugar import. In general, however, no sugar could be thought of
being of better quality than other sugars.

Britons incorporated these commodities into their existing culture
rather than having them be somehow separate to ordinary life. They did
this exceedingly well – the British pudding became almost completely
disassociated from the places and people who produced the sugar that was
essential to it tasting nice. In a change from the sixteenth century, and
because of the decline of humoral theory as the basis for medicine, the
idea that eating foreign food turned one into a foreigner had faded. British
people came to appreciate food from the Atlantic which was different from
British food. Recipe books abounded with recipes that showed cooks how
to make dishes that approximated how such dishes were made overseas,
such as 'turtle dressed the West Indian way' or 'Carolina rice puddings'.
But it was only after the American Revolution that such direct linkages
with the British Empire in the Atlantic and increasingly in India (curry
became a quintessential British dish, for example, even if how it was made
would have been unfamiliar to South Asians) were customarily made. Their
appearance then suggests the importance of the earlier Seven Years' War
as a watershed for popular notions of empire. As Troy Bickham notes,
'The proliferation of empire-related recipes, which consistently emphasised
authenticity, suggests a genuine widespread interest in engaging in sensory
investigations of overseas cultures.'[7] This investigations were conducted
either in new public museums, such as the newly founded British Library,
established by Hans Sloane, using profits derived from the profits of
Jamaican sugar plantations, or at dinner tables, where Atlantic products
were prominent.

COTTON

The two most important commodities shipped from the Americas were cotton and sugar. What is interesting about cotton is that it was very far from being an exclusively, or even mainly, Atlantic commodity. It had been part of the world economy since *c.* 1000, although it became important only after 1300, when weavers in India developed a sophisticated series of regional industries that spread into China, southeast Asia, east Africa and by the early modern period into Europe. Before cotton began to be produced in the Americas, Indian cotton became globalized through the efforts of European traders sending textiles to Africa and the Americas. Eventually, however, Europeans, first in Britain, in the late eighteenth century and as part of the Industrial Revolution, moved from trading cotton to manufacturing it, replacing Indian cottons with products of its own making.

We need to look at cotton in the Atlantic World in two ways, as part of trade and as part of manufacturing. Cotton was central to the Atlantic slave trade and to European trading relationships with West Africa. The Portuguese started selling Indian cottons in North Africa and the Levant in the 1580s and in the early sixteenth century started selling low-quality Indian textiles in West Africa that were exchanged mostly for slaves at high rates of profit. Indian cloth sold to buy a slave in Angola cost 20 cruzados, but the slave could be sold for 100 cruzados in Brazil and for 160 cruzados in Mexico or Cuba. West Africans had sophisticated tastes and Europeans quickly learned what they liked – brightly coloured cloth with shapes and checks – and what they did not like – painted calicoes. Merchants needed to be very attuned to the changing fashions of the marketplace in Africa, as in Europe and in the Americas.

The trade became very important. It was first organized through state-sponsored companies, like the Dutch West India Company. After 1800, most trade was conducted with private merchants and was considerable. Between 1699 and 1800, cloth accounted for 68 per cent of all commodities exported from Britain to Africa and perhaps an even-larger percentage of Dutch trade with India. In the 1740s, when Indian cloth was most popular in West Africa, it accounted up to 60 per cent of all cottons exported to Africa from Britain while Asian textiles sent by France to West Africa was worth 1.4 million livres (£60,000) per annum. Imported textiles were probably a luxury product. David Eltis estimated that only a small proportion of West Africans wore imported cloth in the 1780s, with the amount of cloth imported in that decade amounting to just 0.4 yards per person.[8] But the people who wore such cloth were rich people and the Africans most connected to Atlantic commerce, suggesting that the cultural importance of wearing imported cloth from Asia was outsized.

Cloth was also sent in large quantities to the Americas, with Indian and Chinese clothing coming direct from the Pacific Manila-Acapulco route being very fashionable among poorer whites in eighteenth-century Spanish America. Enslaved people also liked to wear Asian textiles and adapted them to their own use, often in ways that alarmed colonial authorities who thought that enslaved people should not show in their dress any sartorial flair. We can see the frequent use of cotton clothing in the popular casta paintings, which showed in brilliant style the mixed ethnic background of the Latin American population. In addition, North Americans emulated Latin Americans as consumers of cotton, with textiles forming an important part in what T.H. Breen has called the 'empire of goods' which marked British American life immediately before the American Revolution. As well as cloth, British Americans were avid consumers of such things as earthenware, silks, pewter and guns, manufactured in Britain and exported in exchange for agricultural products, and, where available, Spanish and Portuguese silver and good.[9] In both places, this consumption connected consumers more closely than almost anything else to fashion in their ancestral or imagined homelands.

A major shift occurred in the middle of the eighteenth century when British manufacturers, notably in Manchester, a town which exploded in population after about 1750, began to produce their own cloth in the new cotton mills that were so central to the Industrial Revolution centred in that town and region. It is important to note that the growth of cotton production in Britain was not just a change in production. It was related closely to changes in consumption patterns. One reason why the British started to produce their own clothing was that Indian producers were slow to adapt to changing Atlantic fashions. Women consumers in Britain and in the Atlantic World initially found Indian cottons very attractive but over time became less enamoured of what India was providing them. European copies of Indian patterns which suited European women's tastes, and which accorded with standards of European dress and decoration, became increasingly popular to the extent that manufacturers came to realize that they could cut out India entirely and sell garments made in Europe that had been 'Europeanised'. As with today, most wearers of clothes cared little about where clothes came from and were much more interested in whether the clothes they bought accorded with fashion. Colourful printed cottons, first coming from India and then from Manchester, spread throughout the population in ways that silks, which were expensive and thus luxury items, could not. These cottons mimicked the design and visual effect of silks at a reasonable price.

In addition, Europeans had an interest in finding new and abundant supplies of raw cotton, so they were not so dependent on Asian trading networks that they felt engaged in price gouging. For most of the early modern period, Europe suffered from endemic supply problems with respect to gaining raw cotton. The Mediterranean could not produce enough cotton in the fourteenth century and neither could the small Atlantic islands of Cabo Verde, Sao Taigo and Fogo in the fifteenth century. Cotton started to get produced in the Americas in the sixteenth century. It was a slow process getting planters in the Americas to produce cotton, probably because compared to sugar and tobacco, which were immediate hits with consumers in Europe, cotton was not in high demand in Europe until the eighteenth century, when men and especially women started to find cotton clothing desirable.

The development of plantation slavery was highly beneficial for cotton production, as it provided the necessary cheap labour that made the growing of cotton profitable. The West Indies was the first major area where cotton was produced in sufficiently large quantities to allow for a step change in cotton manufacturing in Britain. Some small islands, such as Carriacou in the Grenadines in the southern Caribbean, turned themselves almost entirely to cotton in the 1780s. Cotton was a good crop for smaller planters to grow as it did not require the capital necessary to start a sugar plantation. Between 1783 and 1797, for example, the Spanish in Trinidad brought in hundreds of French settlers who developed 500 new plantations, most of which were cultivated in cotton.

The West Indies provided British industrialists with reasonable quantities of cotton, but the production of raw cotton was still limited by the laborious means by which it was picked. Technology made a major difference. In 1794, Eli Whitney in the United States invented a cotton ginning machine, which enabled cotton to be processed in markedly greater amounts than previously. His invention allowed the United States, which was previously marginal to cotton production, to become the greatest cotton producer in the world by the 1810s. The United States had abundant land in the Deep South of the new country which proved perfect for cotton cultivation, given both rapid westward expansion into fertile land previously occupied by Native Americans and given that the American South had a labour system based on black chattel slavery.

What was exceptional about nineteenth-century American cotton production was, first, its remarkable expansion from virtually nothing to world dominance. Production jumped from 334,000 bales in 1820 to 1.35 million bales in 1840 and to 2.4 million bales in 1850, with over half of this crop being produced in the newly settled states of Alabama, Mississippi and Louisiana. Cotton production led to a new and very intensive slave trade internal to the United States, with perhaps 850,000 enslaved people sold to planters in Lower State from their birthplaces in states in the Upper South where there was a demographic surplus in the slave population. These imported slaves departed from a slave system that was relatively benign by Atlantic standards (though no slave system anywhere was all that pleasant) to much harsher conditions in southern cotton fields where aggressively entrepreneurial planters worked slaves hard to make great profits. Their work was made harder by having to often carve out fresh plantation land from primeval forests.

Eventually, the United States began its own cotton industry in New England in the second quarter of the nineteenth century. But for most of the first half of the nineteenth century, most American cotton went to Lancashire, England. The cotton industry was incredibly geographically concentrated. In 1841, 70 per cent of 1,105 cotton mills in Britain were in Lancashire, employing 40,000 workers. One-third of the Lancashire working population worked in the cotton industry between 1800 and 1840. Raw cotton in this period stayed cheap (and got cheaper over time) while American planters continued to make lots of money. How was this possible? The conundrum is explained by efficiencies developing in the cotton industry in Britain and increased productivity in slave picked cotton in the United States. Productivity gains were mostly due to the adoption of new varieties of cotton in the 1820s and early 1830s, which both allowed higher yields and which were easier to pick and process. Declining costs of transport were also significant as sailing ships gave way to steamships, keeping the price of raw cotton low as larger amounts could be shipped more quickly to Britain and raising productivity rates.

Cotton was crucial for the prosperity of the infant United States – half of American exports in 1850 were of cotton. But where cotton was most important in transforming society and economy was in Britain, a place where cotton was impossible to grow. Largely through cotton (and coal), the economy of a small island became several times larger than the needs of its own people. As Douglas Farnie observes, 'The external functions fulfilled by the [cotton] industry became more significant than its domestic functions.'[10] Cotton enabled Britain to open a large gap between it and France, who failed to develop strong commercial ties with the United States, despite its alliance with America in its War for Independence. By 1816, the export of British cotton textiles was three times that of French exports. Britain sent lots of textiles to Europe, Latin America (an especially strong market), Africa and, ironically, Asia, from where cottons had previously come before British imperial policies worked to deindustrialize India.

Giorgio Riello explains that in the nineteenth century – 'truly a century of cloth' – the impact of textiles on Britain's push to global dominance was multifaceted. As he argues,

> The advantages provided by technological innovation, industrialisation, and increasing productivity were translated in commercial terms into the shaping of a system of exchange heavily reliant on European products, capital and entrepreneurship. The importance of trade was not limited to high returns or investment or on the expansion of national industrial structures: it also stimulated backward linkages to other parts of the country's manufacturing economy, in particular iron, coal, and the mechanical industry; it facilitated the building of internal infrastructures in shipping and engineering, and enabled the development of insurance and financial intermediaries.[11]

In short, Britain's rise to global dominance and the source of how it led Europe in the 'Great Divergence' in overtaking China economically has a great deal to do with cotton and its place in a growing Atlantic economy.

MATERIAL CULTURE

How was cloth used and what did the wearing of cotton fabrics mean for people? Clothing is more than just something that is part of local, national and international economies. It is also more than just a cover for nakedness (and being naked is itself a form of dress, as Spanish conquistadores made clear when they justified the expropriation of Native American land and labour because Native Americans went about without clothing, thus showing themselves to be barbarians). It conveys meanings about personal style, aspirations for cultural expression, and information able to be absorbed easily and visually by others about wealth and status. A consequence of the opening of the Atlantic was that merchants could bring fabrics and garments to a wide number of locations. The Atlantic had a bewildering variety of dress materials in its various locations. These dress regimes ranged from woven-fabric textiles (wool, linen, silk, cotton), to furs and animal skins, and even to clothes fashioned out of bark of trees. It is noticeable that when travellers tried to describe the places where they had been and the people they had encountered, they very often focused on what men and women wore or did not wear. European commentators did more than describe dress; they assigned value and meaning to it, based on European prejudices about what clothing should be like. They did so because how people dressed was taken to be an obvious sign of whether they were civilized.

In Western Europe, people wore woven-fabric cloth, usually wool and linen before the eighteenth century, then cotton. They tended to cover the whole body with clothing, including their heads, with only faces and hands exposed to sight. Dress was very gendered, sometimes extremely obviously, as with the fashion among elites in the sixteenth century for men to wear codpieces. Dress was colourful, with red and blue colours favoured, and was the more colourful the wealthier the person was. In some circumstances, however, as among Puritans in the seventeenth-century British Isles or among pious sixteenth-century Spaniards, dress could be deliberately sombre and dominated by black hues.

Women dressed in long skirts with a short jacket with sleeves or a bodice on top. They also wore stockings and footwear plus a cap or hat and often an apron and cloak to wear outside in colder climates. Male clothing was more varied, with doublets, breeches, hose or stockings, and a cloak. In some time periods, like the late seventeenth century, men wore elaborate wigs and clothes that were beautiful but highly impractical. Wearing clothes in which doing work was difficult or impossible was a means of expressing gentility – the gap between the polite and the plebeian was governed in European and settler societies by dress codes, with the genteel favouring fashion over utility.

Africans also wore textile-based apparel, at least if they were well-off. Otherwise, they adopted dress regimes that Europeans thought strange and denoting savagery. They were much less inclined than Europeans to cover the whole body with clothing, which is not surprising given the hot climates most lived in. The lack of bodily coverage was sometimes accompanied by bodily decoration, such as elaborate multicoloured body painting. As in Europe, many West African societies had sumptuary laws, whereby dress was regulated so that people were fined if they were wearing clothes which were too grand for their status. Clothing was also a way whereby Europeans and Africans could interact – there was some, though limited, adoption of European dress by wealthier Africans, especially in places like the Kongo, where Catholicism was strong.

Native Americans were different again. They tended not to wear woven fabrics but dressed in animal skins, furs and bark of trees. They customarily did not cover much of their bodies with clothing and in some areas, as among the Tupinamba in Brazil, were generally unclothed, without even covering male genitals. Bodily adornment, including extensive tattooing, as well as body painting and the use of decorative accessories, was common. Native Americans differentiated themselves on grounds of status through clothing less than what was usual in Europe, although chieftains and shamans generally had some markings that made them stand out within their societies. Dress tended to be most important for ritual occasions. The Tupinamba, for example, put on clothing, such as fancy robes, for festive occasions, notably for ceremonies where they allegedly (or probably, as it is more likely than not that they were indeed cannibals in certain ritualistic situations) ate war prisoners who had been ceremoniously killed. Of course, Native Americans also dressed according to the weather. In the Arctic, for example, furs were used to keep the body warm.

The impact of Atlantic interactions on dress regimes was considerable and dress changed over time as people learned about ways of dressing from other people. In general, Europeans were less willing than Africans or Native Americans to modify their dress to fit new environments. Europeans thought that adapting other people's dress regimes might make people think them to be savages. Adopting European dress, on the other hand, symbolized for Native Americans less that they shared European ideas about modesty and civility within dress regimes than showed an acceptance of European and settler ascendancy over them. Whenever Europeans seemed to be 'winning', then Native Americans adopted clothing that was European in design, function and meaning. By the middle of the eighteenth century, Native Americans living within or alongside European communities in North America had largely laid aside their own clothing except for ritual occasions and had taken to wearing clothes of European derivation. Slaves, too, tended to dress in versions of European dress as they became more and more creolized to life in enslavement.

That does not mean, however, that enslaved people and Native Americans were just passive receivers of dress rules handed down to them by Europeans who had political and economic power over them. They proved ingenious in shaping European dress in ways that reflected their own cultural preferences. Handkerchiefs became headwraps, for example, and shirts were worn as jackets. Aspects of Native American or African culture remained within adopted dress regimes in practices anthropologists characterize as syncretism – the selective adaptation of one cultural form by retentions of other cultural forms. In general, dress regimes went from Europe to the rest of the Atlantic rather than the other way around. Europeans resisted adopting clothing from America or Africa, although in the seventeenth century there was a craze for beaver hats, which helped stimulate the fur industry in Canada and the interior borderlands of northern British America. But items from the Atlantic like moccasins or clothes made from animal skin or bark never became popular. Perhaps the main influence of the Atlantic on European and settler populations' dress regimes is that clothing became lighter, smoother, more multihued and with more varied patterns. It certainly became more colourful. As Robert Du Plessis concludes, while diversity in dress regimes in the Atlantic World led some European manufacturers to embrace change, 'in the aggregate, Atlantic demand served to sustain well-established industries and practices as much as – even more than – to promote new and technologically innovative processes and products'.[12]

It was only in the nineteenth century that Western dress came to become the standard form of dress throughout the Atlantic World. In 1780, the leading men in the world were dressed in a variety of garments; by the late nineteenth century a growing number of powerful men wore Western dress in public and varieties of Western dress were seen adorning almost everyone in the Atlantic World. The trend was less obvious among working class, peasants and subaltern men and even less obvious among women, where varieties of dress regimes persisted over time. The trend, however, was towards uniformity and towards European standards of decorum. Enslaved women who commonly went about open-breasted in the eighteenth century wore demure, if often very poor-quality clothes, when picking cotton in the antebellum American South. Uniformity in dress regimes was aided by fashion and advertising but reflected above all the visual representation of the economic and geopolitical dominance of Europe and the northern United States in the nineteenth-century world. Nevertheless, the process was not just a one-way adoption of European bodily practices or European food. Multilateral links between different world societies meant that, for example, Asian commerce and the American slave plantation were connected: eighteenth-century Caribbean slaves were fed on Asian white rice and clothed in Indian cotton. Globalization accompanied the rise of Western Europe to global dominance.

NOTES

1 Theodore K. Rabb, 'The Expansion of Europe and the Spirit of Capitalism,' *Historical Journal* 17 (1974), 679.
2 David Hancock, 'Atlantic Trade and Commodities, 1402–1815,' in Nicholas Canny and Philip D. Morgan, ed., *The Oxford Handbook of the Atlantic World 1450–1850* (Oxford: Oxford University Press, 2013).
3 Neil Oatsvall and Vaughn Scribner, '"The Devil Was in the Englishman That He Makes Everything Work": Implementing the Concept of "Work" to Reevaluate Sugar Production and Consumption in the Early Modern British Atlantic World,' *Agricultural History* 92 (2018), 461–90.
4 Sidney Mintz, *Sweetness and Power: The Place of Sugar in Modern History* (New York: Penguin, 1985), xxiii.
5 Peter Mancall, *Deadly Medicine: Indians and Alcohol in Early America* (Ithaca: Cornell University Press, 1995).
6 Rebecca Earle, '"If You Eat Their Food …:" Diets and Bodies in Early Colonial Spanish America,' *American Historical Review* 115 (2010), 713.
7 Troy Bickham, 'Eating the Empire: Intersections of Food, Cookery and Imperialism in Eighteenth-Century Britain,' *Past & Present* 198 (2008), 108–09.
8 David Eltis, 'Precolonial Western Africa and the Atlantic Economy,' in Barbara L. Solow, ed., *Slavery and the Rise of the Atlantic System* (Cambridge: Cambridge University Press, 1991), 107.
9 T.H. Breen, 'An Empire of Goods: Their Anglicisation of Colonial America, 1690–1776,' *Journal of British Studies* 25 (1986), 485–90.
10 Douglas Farnie, 'Cotton Industry,' in Joel Mokyr, ed., *Oxford Encyclopedia of Economic History* II (Oxford: Oxford University Press, 2003), 21.
11 Giorgio Riello, *Cotton: The Fabric That Made the Modern World* (Cambridge: Cambridge University Press, 2013), 267, 271–72.
12 Robert S. Du Plessis, *The Material Atlantic: Clothing, Commerce, and Colonization in the Atlantic World, 1650–1800* (Cambridge: Cambridge University Press, 2016), 242–43.

BIBLIOGRAPHY

Oxford Online Bibliographies – Atlantic Trade and the European Economy; Clothing; Cotton; Domestic Production and Consumption; Economy and Consumption; Food; Insurance; Material Culture; Merchants; Merchants' Networks; Rum; Sugar, Tobacco; Wine.
Maxine Berg, 'In Pursuit of Luxury: Global History and British Consumer Goods in the Eighteenth Century,' *Past and Present* 132 (2004), 85–142.
Steeve O. Buckridge, *Language of Dress: Resistance and Accommodation in Jamaica, 1760–1890* (Kingston: University of West Indies Press, 2004).
Mariana Candido, *An African Slaving Port and the Atlantic World: Benguela and Its Hinterland* (Cambridge: Cambridge University Press, 2013).

Robert S. Du Plessis, *The Material Atlantic: Clothing, Commerce, and Colonization in the Atlantic World, 1650–1800* (Cambridge: Cambridge University Press, 2016).

Benoit Garnot, *La culture matérielle en France aux XVIe, XVIIe et XVIII siècles* (Paris: Ophrys, 1995).

David Hancock, *Oceans of Wine: Madeira and the Organisation of the Atlantic Market, 1640–1815* (New Haven: Yale University Press, 2009).

B.W. Higman, *Jamaican Food: History, Biology, Culture* (Kingston: University of Qwest Indies Press, 2012).

Sidney Mintz, *Sweetness and Power: The Place of Sugar in Modern History* (New York: Penguin, 1985).

Marcy Norton, *Sacred Gifts, Profane Pleasures: A History of Tobacco and Chocolate in the Atlantic World* (Ithaca: Cornell University Press, 2010).

Giorgio Riello, *Cotton: The Fabric That Made the Modern World* (Cambridge: Cambridge University Press, 2013).

15

THE ATLANTIC IN GLOBAL CONSCIOUSNESS

COLLECTING

European travellers to the New World understood that people back home were curious about the worlds they had not seen but had only had described to them. In 1520, Hernán Cortés sent back to Spain objects from the New World as presents to the Habsburg monarch, Charles V, including gold and silver (much of which was later melted down to pay for wars), gems and elaborate works made up of feathers. It was these objects that formed a famous Spanish *wunderkammen*, or cabinet of curiosities, starting a kind of institution that by the nineteenth century had developed into the modern museum. The rise of collecting between the sixteenth and eighteenth centuries reflected more than just the 'discovery' of the Americas. It also was stimulated by the rediscovery of classical antiquity in the Renaissance. But New World discoveries were crucial to the collecting impulse. That was true in Europe but also had some adherents among Native Americans while African merchants and princes were keen on collecting Indian cloth and Chinese porcelain.

Collecting went side by side with the expansion of print, allowing collectors to disseminate images of their possessions to a wide audience. Collecting took place in multiple forms, across many media and at various economic levels. Indeed, collecting exotic materials had a transmedia quality as images crossed from medium to medium, from travel books to atlases, to decorative arts and to museums. Collecting took place from the start of Atlantic encounters but exploded in the late seventeenth century when the output of exotic materials greatly intensified, especially in descriptive materials. Benjamin Schmidt explores this intensification in looking at how the humble parasol, once associated with the East but by the late seventeenth century becoming a symbol of the New World, became omnipresent in prints, collections and literature. He argues that the origin of the parasol as being Atlantic comes from its placement in a map, Nicolaes Visscher's *Totius Americae* (1650), where a parasol was placed in a cartouche that was meant to show America providing its riches to the rest of the world. The parasol, he suggests, was thus transformed from a symbol of Oriental power into a marker of American identity.[1]

Once established as a symbol of America, the parasol was launched on what art historian calls an 'iconic circuit', a circuit that was 'an economy of representations in which images of a certain kind circulated between different media in which pictures were involved'.[2] We see the parasol everywhere after 1650 as a way of symbolizing the exotic non-European world. One example is a clock decorated with tropical scenes from Daniel Defoe's famous novel, *Robinson Crusoe*. Crusoe holds a parasol over his servant Man Friday (rather incongruously given the status implications involved), with his servant significantly Africanized in features. The exotic if very everyday item of the parasol was in this case as in the novel a signifier of the Atlantic World while set in no man's land, an unknown island in the Caribbean.

Objects needed to be interpreted when they entered collections. What did Europeans think of Cortés's treasures? Of course, Cortés did not just send back gifts to Spain without an ulterior motive. He wanted to get Charles V's approval for his unauthorized conquest of Mexico and pardon for his murder of a fellow monarch while disarming criticism at court that he knew was already there about the cruelty and barbarism of how he had behaved towards Montezuma. Initially, he presented precious objects as gifts from a newly encountered, potential client kingdom and as a way of making Charles V a greater monarch than any other European, African or American prince. Charles showed his appreciation by regifting some of the Mexican treasures to his brother Ferdinand, a ruler he put in place to command his possessions in central Europe. The gifts that were sent to him in 1524 symbolized imperial authority, including eleven pieces of Aztec treasure.

It was not just treasure that was collected. Europeans were fascinated by American bodies, as we have already seen. People living in Europe were anxious to see Native Americans in person. They did so almost immediately and the Native Americans they gazed upon as objects in themselves were sensations in European courts. Columbus took Native Americans as slaves back to Spain after his first voyage while Sebastian Cabot in 1502 brought Native Americans to England for the first time. Richard Hakluyt the younger in 1589 cited a first-hand account that claimed that when these Native Americans arrived they were 'clothed in beasts Skins, and did eater awe flesh, and spake such speech, that no man could understand them, and in their demeanour like to brute beasts'. But after two years in the royal court, the same observer declared that 'I could not discerne [them] from Englishmen, till I was learned what they were'. The lesson was that the bodies of Native Americans, exposed to English air and food, could become transformed into the bodies that were English.

By the seventeenth century, perhaps 1,600 Native Americans, hailing from Brazil to the Arctic, had travelled to Europe. Artists went to work to provide visual descriptions of many of them. In short, the collecting of Native Americans moved from collecting actual bodies to collecting them visually. The most famous set of images in England made of Native Americans were watercolours done by John White, later turned into engravings by Theodore de Bry, painted in Roanoke in North Carolina in 1587, showing Carolina Algonquians in domestic settings. They were portrayed in heroic and sympathetic form, confirming that before the start of permanent settlement by the English in Virginia in 1607 the English had largely positive views of Native Americans. They saw them as part of a general human race, civilizable and improvable. White did not depict his subjects as racialized 'others' nor did he see them as monsters who lived beyond human experience. At the very start of colonization, the English fascination with Native American bodies and how images of them were collected gave out hope that the English encounters with them during colonization might be based on a degree of mutual respect.

That representation changed in the seventeenth century, a century where interest in collecting material to do with Native Americans dramatically declined. It was only in the late eighteenth century that the collecting and classifying impulse returned. The new interest arose because Native Americans were beginning to be viewed by European and American thinkers as a 'vanishing race', who needed to be studied before they disappeared from the earth. The most remarkable study done at this time of Native Americans that attempted to understand their origins so as to contribute to intellectual discussions over how to classify them within new classifications of humans derived from the taxonomies devised by the Swedish botanist Carl Linnaeus (1707–1778) was made by Thomas Jefferson in *Notes on the State of Virginia* (1787), written while he was the American representative in Paris.

His account of Native Americans, unlike his treatment of African Americans, was generally favourable, if paternalistic, as he gave the first archaeological treatment of Native American remains from a study he conducted on Indian bones buried near his Virginia estate. His main aim was to establish that the origins of Native Americans were that they were people who had come to America from Siberia crossing the Bering Strait. He used Indian bones to make this and other findings. There is no sign, sadly, that he preserved the remains he had disturbed – respect for the Native American body did not extend as far as respecting their feelings about the sanctity of their ancestors. His actions were like those that were increasingly taken by museums in the nineteenth century.

The final great age of collecting came in the early nineteenth century when the disciplines of anthropology and archaeology were developed so that the whole world could be studied and classified. Europeans turned to making trips to Latin America to use archaeological findings to make a systematic inventory of the natural world so that a global classification system, including different human races, could be made, in the fashion of Linnaeus. Scientific institutions were keen to send explorers and naturalists out to get specimens for them to display. For example, naturalist, Alcide d'Orbigny, was sent by a French museum to South America in 1826 to search for ceramics, many of which he transported back to France to form the basis of a great collection, that might cast light on pre-Columbian history. D'Orbigny used the information he had gleaned from his excavations and ceramic acquisitions to rethink the idea of separate pre-Columbian races.

RELIGION

Knowledge of the Atlantic World came about in part by objects but also in part by ideas. No ideas were more important than religious concepts as religious belief structured the contours of everyday life in ways that make the early modern period fundamentally different from life in developed countries in the twenty-first century. One difficulty that arises in assessing the Atlantic implications of religious change in this period is that internal changes within parts of the Atlantic World were so great as to make transnational changes seem not that important. In Europe, the Reformation transformed religious attitudes. In the Americas, demographic disaster caused a massive crisis of faith for bewildered Native Americans and which greatly facilitated European efforts to convert Native Americans to Christianity. Religious change was also profound in West Africa, with Islamic revolutions in the eighteenth century appearing all over north-west Africa, in which jihads took place and Muslim clerics displaced existing elites as rulers, culminating in the creation of the Sokoto caliphate in 1804. All these developments deserve extensive treatment but for the sake of space, and because European changes in religious belief had larger global effects, we'll concentrate on Europe in assessing the effect of the creation of an Atlantic World on religious belief.

These internal changes were all influenced by the dramatic changes of scale in the contacts between cultures and civilizations that followed Columbus's voyages to the Caribbean. Christian Europe had to rethink its ideas about what was the best way to honour God, and indeed to rethink what the nature of God and His plan for the world might be. European ideas about religion had some diversity about them before the Reformation but were all derived from a common root, the Judaic civilization of the Near

East that had led to the three great religions of Europe and the Near East – Judaism, Christianity and Islam. What Columbus found in the Americas had more than geographical implications; it made Europeans think hard about religious beliefs that had hardened into unquestioned doctrine. It was very difficult to fit a whole new spectrum of previously unknown religious attitudes into traditional Christian religious practices. Suddenly, religions were viewed in an objective rather than a subjective way. It was more difficult after 1500 for Europeans to view Christendom as a universal faith and easier to view religious belief in relativist terms, as being the expression of the values of specific societies rather than God's direction to people imbued with Christian values. This relativist notion of religion caused an intellectual crisis for European thinkers which became especially apparent in the religious thought in the early Enlightenment.

The new approach to comparative religion in early modern and Enlightenment Europe suggested that all religions reflected an essential unity in humankind. Thinkers wrestled with what that meant and how that could be reconciled with schema that listed peoples of the world with respect to how civilized they were for the rest of the Atlantic period (and to a degree until today). What, for example, did idolatry mean if Bartolomé Las Casas was right in the mid-sixteenth century when he stated that 'idol worship was human' and thus not against one of the Ten Commandments? As Guy Stroumsa explains,

> In earlier times, religion had always remained a binary concept, centered upon the Augustinian opposition between *vera* and *falsa religio*. Together with the devaluation of Christianity, both implicit and explicit, the discovery of so many and so different forms of religion permitted, paradoxically, the development of a single concept of religion. From then on, religion would be perceived, primarily, as a central aspect of any society, endowed with a different function in each one of them. Religion had become part of collective identity, and the study of religion would see, gradually, intellectual curiosity take over polemical animus.[3]

This crisis of faith, however, came after a major expansion of Christianity in the Atlantic World. It occurred to a limited extent in Africa, where the Kingdom of Kongo was Catholic from late medieval times and to a much greater extent in the Americas. In the Americas there were two models of Christian expansion: conquest by the Spanish in Spanish America and colonial settlement, as done by the British and French in North America. In Spanish America and in Portuguese Brazil, Catholicism was largely imposed on Native Americans from above, as part of the price paid for conquest to a dispossessed people whose indigenous forms of religious expression and religious institutions had been suppressed, with that suppression reinforced by persecution by the Inquisition. Spanish strategies of forced conversion were largely successful, at least insofar as

Native Americans had become at least nominally Catholic as early as the beginning of the seventeenth century.

The Spanish invested more resources in evangelization than Protestant European empires, with the French occupying a midway position between both poles of missionary activity. Protestant missions were less well endowed than their Catholic counterparts, giving Catholics large advantage over Protestants in converting Native Americans. It was only in 1640, for example, that the first Protestant catechism in a Native American language was written, composed by a Swedish Lutheran minister in New Sweden in modern Delaware. Catholic writers in Latin America had been writing Native American language catechisms from the mid-sixteenth century. Moreover, Catholic priests were also less concerned than Protestant ministers in ensuring that their converts knew and adhered to Christian doctrine, accepting conversion even when they doubted that there had been any acceptance in the heart of Christian belief.

Protestants were especially reluctant to convert their enslaved populations. Slaveholders thought that the legitimacy of slavery would be threatened if Africans adopted Christianity. Before the early eighteenth century, the English tended to share Islamic beliefs that one could not enslave co-religionists. That changed as slavery became more established and race, rather than religion, became the principal justification for why people might be enslaved. The evangelization of the enslaved was a slow process in the English-speaking Protestant world. It was only from the late eighteenth century that the enslaved population in the British West Indies and the United States started to be converted to Protestantism. Conversion was strongly associated with notions of civilization, meaning that it was no coincidence that Christian conversion accompanied shifts in the demographic composition of enslaved populations towards most slaves being Creoles rather than Africans.[4] In the nineteenth century, however, American slaveholders came to think that encouraging Christianity among slaves would foster a sense of obedience that would assist them in their increasingly paternalistic vision of slavery – the idea being that as one needed Christians to be obedient to God, so too enslaved people owed duty and thanks to masters who acted as supposedly benevolent fathers to slaves envisioned as being akin to children. That belief in Christian slaves coming to accept enslavement in this world in the hope of salvation in the next proved misplaced. By the early nineteenth century, enslaved people in the British Caribbean and the American South took their own reading of the Bible in radical directions, seeing in the Christian message in the Gospels a message contrary to that fed to them by their masters, that God saw every Christian as a human with expectations of freedom on earth as much as in heaven. Slave rebellions in the nineteenth-century Protestant world, as in Demerara in 1823, in Jamaica in 1831–1832 and in Virginia in 1832, all had an important religious dimension and were led by men like Jack Gladstone, Samuel Sharp and Nat Turner who were fervent Christians who believed the message of the Bible-justified slave revolt.

A distinctive feature of religion in the Atlantic was that it was a syncretic process of cultural adaptation in which religious beliefs from one religious system were fused with beliefs from another religious system to create a new, fused religious culture. We can see this syncretic religious impulse in examining the transformations of African-American religion by the enslaved in the Americas. Whatever their religion adopted in the Americas, Africans and their descendants retained aspects of inherited African religion in their religious practice. Divination was one such practice brought over from Africa to the Americas. James Sweet has shown how divination was combined with Catholicism in a penetrating study of Domingo Álvares, an enslaved African-turned freedman, who was born in Benin around 1710, became a religious adept in Africa, and after becoming enslaved and sent to north-east Brazil in 1830, finally became a healer with a large following of mostly Africans in Rio de Janeiro. He ran foul of local authorities and was taken to Portugal under the Inquisition under charges of witchcraft.

Evidence gained from him under torture provide a first-hand insight into how an African took his beliefs in such things as divination from Africa, adapted those beliefs to fit in with evolving Catholic thought as interpreted by the enslaved, and developed a composite African and European religion that satisfied the needs of his compatriots (and which also provided Domingo with a tidy income). The Inquisition records show he had a strong connection to Brazilian Vodun (like vodou in Haiti and obeah in the British Caribbean), the religion of most people in his native Benin. He cured people using herbs and roots but also organized Vodun rituals (it was these rituals that got him into trouble, as authorities thought he was using witchcraft to stir up enslaved resistance to white authority). What is interesting about Álvares, as well as him being one of the rare slaves in the eighteenth century whom we know much about, is how easily he created and then moved between separate African identities – Nago, Cobu, Mina and Angolan – using religious practices as a form of survival and cultural identification. His skilful shape-shifting moves between different religious customs confirmed his status within enslaved and free black communities as a powerful religious figure able to bring spiritual relief to slaves and alleviate their sufferings under enslavement. Sweet concludes that 'the cultural flexibility that was a necessary response to the conditions of enslavement in Africa simply continued in the diaspora, as categories of identification expanded to meet new social realities'.[5]

An even more telling example of an African adopting a syncretic view of religion was, in the case of Makandal, a slave rebel in Saint-Domingue who was burned to death in 1757 but who inspired slaveholders and generations of Haitian slaves to see him as a fearsome poisoner, creating havoc among whites in northern sugar-planting regions. The stories about him poisoning many whites in revenge are far-fetched. Recent research sees him less as a rebel than as a shaman. Like Domingo Álvares, he was a religious adept, gaining a reputation among fellow slaves as a healer who was willing to use his religious powers to assist slaves in various kinds of problems that afflicted them. What distinguished him from other healers was that he exposed slaves to a different kind of African religion, one that used items that masters as well as enslaved people thought had religious value. He carried with him small bags containing charms, powders and potions. These bags often included a small lead crucifix, soaked it was said in holy water. Makandal was a charismatic leader in a Congo-influenced tradition, in which African and European religious symbols were combined. He aroused fear in his white captors because his spiritually charged bundles contained 'their' symbols, incorporating Christian iconography with African meanings. He was probably more a religious mendicant than a rebellious poisoner – but he was more dangerous given this circumstance. His execution for witchcraft showed that Europeans thought that African religion had spiritual and political power and that sorcerers were effective conduits for potentially larger rebellions. Settlers were as prone to having their religious beliefs influenced by African ideas as Africans were as likely to adopt Christian ideas and practices.

Makandal was seen by settlers as a malicious poisoner who used religion to foment sedition. Concerns about poisoning by malcontents were also prevalent in early modern Europe and led to considerable anxiety that witchcraft was widespread. Most Europeans believed that witches existed and were working their black magic until the early Enlightenment when accusations of witchcraft began to be denounced as contrary to philosophies based upon reason. The popular European view of the 'witch' included the idea that she regularly used poison. The peak of the European witch craze was in the late sixteenth through mid-seventeenth centuries within Protestant countries. By the time that the plantation system boomed in the late seventeenth century and early eighteenth century, witchcraft was beginning to become decriminalized and laws were being passed in Europe stopping prosecutions for witchcraft.

The same process whereby witchcraft was rendered no longer part of civilized society did not occur in plantation America. Indeed, witchcraft became racialized as something that Africans did which Europeans did not do. The irony was that in Africa itself witchcraft was not a terribly prominent part of early modern African thinking – belief in witchcraft became more prevalent from the start of colonization in the mid-nineteenth century. Africans were more inclined to believe that individuals could manipulate spiritual power for a range of ethically problematic purposes. Africans who were brought to the Americas, however, shared with Europeans a sense that harm could be done to people through occult means, sometimes through the invocation of poison (although most accusations of poisoning were like accusations of witchcraft in early modern Europe – highly unlikely to be true given how difficult it was to effectively use poison as a weapon). In the Caribbean, planters warned that slaves would use spiritual weapons against them. Vincent Brown explains that in mid-eighteenth century

Jamaica settlers migrating from a continent that had stopped believing in witches came to adopt the beliefs of the enslaved people they oppressed that Africans engaged in sorcery. He states that masters and slaves 'each appropriated from the other symbolic practices that carried social and spiritual power; the use of powerful cultural categories and symbols did not necessarily correspond to their distinct and originary uses in Africa or Europe, even when they were put to distinct and irreconcilable purposes by blacks and whites'.[6]

What convinced Jamaican planters that witchcraft was real while a myth in Europe was how they had experienced African religious men – people who practised obeah – in slave rebellion. In 1760, slaves in several parts of Jamaica revolted against white authority. They nearly succeeded in upturning white authority. They were aided in their rebellion by what Edward Long called 'a famous obeah man or priest', who Long thought was 'the chief instigator and oracle of the insurgents'. Like Makandal, obeah men drew on African ritual and religious knowledge, while incorporating Christian iconography, to encourage, planters thought, slaves to rebel. The Jamaican response was swift: a law against obeah was passed, punishing with death people known to practise it. The law drew on the concept of witchcraft in British law to suppress obeah as dangerous, individualizing a collective practice by making obeah a criminal activity. Obeah was not finally decriminalized until well into the twenty-first century. Practising obeah or any suspicion of poisoning was used by colonial authorities as an excuse to interfere in the religious lives of the enslaved. Usually, planters turned a blind eye to its practice in everyday life. But its establishment as a crime shows how religion and social control were connected in white Jamaican minds. As Diana Paton comments, 'the establishment of obeah as a crime ... left the legacy of a legal construct that, after slavery ended, would be mobilised in an effort to cultural and culturally transform the population'.[7]

FROM ATLANTIC TO WORLD HISTORY: ECONOMICS

In 2020, the two-decade obsession with globalization that followed the fall of the Berlin Wall and the collapse of communism between 1989 and 1991 seems to be ending, with populist agitation about the inequalities that globalization engenders and concerns about immigration rendering national identity problematic showing that there can be a significant backlash to the phenomenon. The current climate should make those of us who study Atlantic history take pause, as one of the characteristics of Atlantic history is that it takes historical progress towards globalization as a given and sometimes, its critics say, is too quick to celebrate that march towards world uniformity without recognizing what is lost as the world becomes increasingly the same wherever one goes. Changes in how we view the contemporary effects of globalization make us question whether globalization is both inevitable and historically longstanding. This questioning does not mean, however, that historians see modern globalization as unprecedented – we are aware that there was world history in the early modern period just as much as in the early twenty-first century.

Where historians have divided opinions is over whether the Atlantic World and its related cousin, the Indian Ocean World, had combined sufficiently during the period in which we customarily date Atlantic history, from the mid-fifteenth to the mid-nineteenth century to form an integrated world economy (though not a world culture – that has not, thankfully, yet occurred, allowing for diversity in cultural forms to still flourish). Historians disagree especially about when and if such a global convergence did happen. Adam Smith in *The Wealth of Nations* (1776) considered that the two most important events in recorded history since the death of Jesus Christ were the 'discovery' of the Americas by Christopher Columbus in 1492 and the establishment of a viable route to the Indies by Vasco da Gama in 1498. The doyen of world history, William H. McNeill, concurred, stating that 'the year 1500 marks an important turning point in world history ... the European discoveries made the oceans of the earth into highways for their commerce'.[8]

World historians tend to follow Smith and McNeill in seeing world history emerging out of the Atlantic World in the early modern period. Jerry Bentley, for example, suggests that 1500 inaugurated 'a genuinely global epoch of world history'.[9] Indeed, Dennis Flynn and Arturo Giráldez even pinpoint the birth of globalization to a specific year – 1571 – and place – Manila. They argue that world history started 'in 1571 with the establishment of direct and permanent linkages between the Americas and East Asia with the development of the Manila-Acapulco trade'.[10]

Economic historians are not convinced that world history started so early, and in my opinion, they have the better of the argument. They admit that the Atlantic World makes sense as a cultural if not an economic unit from around 1700 but they do not want to make the leap from accepting the reality of an Atlantic World to seeing the world integrated in the early modern period. Most Atlantic historians date the integration of an Atlantic World so that it became a definable entity from around 1700. Nicholas Canny and Philip Morgan argue that it was in the eighteenth century when the Atlantic World became integrated, as seen in the creation of a common seaborne culture with a dramatic increase in shipping volumes, more reliable and predictable shipping, with massive improvements in communication. They argue that 'the density of economic exchanges deepened and thickened to the point where each "national development" contributed to the enrichment of all'. Geography-facilitated integration, they posit, as did imperialism, the increasing sophistication of native-born American populations, and the integrating experience of war as methods of warfare merged. The most important forms of integration, however, were economic. Canny and Morgan suggest that the three revolutions described for this period – the sugar revolution, the consumer revolution and the information revolution (to which might be added a financial revolution) – show that the period around 1700 saw as much change, though around the integration rather than the dissolution of an Atlantic World, as did the more heralded changes in the later age of political revolutions.[11]

Economic historians tend to view world history as emerging out of the technical innovations of the Industrial Revolution. Their argument is rather abstract, and mathematical, being based around economic theories of international price convergence. Kevin O'Rourke and Jeffrey Williamson claim that a world economy came about only from the 1820s as it was only through the technological changes of the early nineteenth century which made 'possible the movement of bulk commodities between continents so much more cheaply that domestic prices, and domestic resource allocation, were significantly affected by international trade'. They argue that it was the nineteenth-century transport revolution that precipitated the 'decline in the international dispersion of commodity prices' which they argue is 'the only irrefutable evidence that globalisation is taking place'. O'Rourke and Williamson accept that the voyages of Columbus and Da Gama were important, generating the Columbian exchange. But they deny that these voyages led to globalization. As they argue, 'for the economic implications of the Voyages of Discovery to be fully realised required the peopling of frontiers and the application of European capital to those frontiers. But, more importantly, it also required the breakdown of monopolies controlling long distance trade, and a technological revolution.'[12]

If there was no global economy before 1820, was there an Atlantic system that was itself integrated before 1800? Canny and Morgan cautiously suggest some degree of Atlantic integration after 1700. Pieter Emmer disagrees. He accepts that the Atlantic World had some cultural unity between 1500 and 1800 but insists that economic integration was limited. The economies of Europe, Africa and the New World were largely independent from each other with no more than 2 per cent of their gross national product being generated by intergenerational trade. He concludes:

Only the European trading forts along the coast of West Africa, the plantations in the New World and certain Atlantic port cities in Western Europe were so interconnected that we can speak of a slave trade cum plantation section in which one section could not survive without the other. The economic impact of this system was too small to affect the economies of the three Atlantic continents at large with the possible exception of Great Britain during the second half of the eighteenth century.[13]

Indeed, it is probable that the Atlantic economic system declined over time. Most countries always mainly engage in trade with their nearest neighbours, rather than with transatlantic partners. David Eltis argues:

> After a massive switch to transatlantic trade in the century or so after transatlantic contact was first established, the normal trend thereafter for most societies was a long secular shift back towards intra-Africa or intra-American trade, and perhaps above all, a return to a focus on domestic sources of demand for goods and supplies of factors of production. In the sense that most economies around the Atlantic have become more developed over time and the more developed the economy, the more important are its domestic relative to external markets, globalisation and Atlantic history are myths.[14]

An important implication of this argument, that the peripheries of overseas investment and trade are peripheral to overall wealth and economic growth, is that the most important period of Atlantic history is the earliest period, where one continent – Europe – made windfall gains through acquiring both large quantities of American silver which it used to force itself into trade with China which had previously been closed to it and even more from the acquisition of 'ghost acres' in the Americas stolen from a Native American population in rapid decline. Once equilibrium had been restored in the Americas, economic integration slowed, with only the slave trade connecting the Atlantic World together and then in limited fashion. By 1700, the percentage of gross national product taken up by slavery, the slave trade and American plantations (other trade was negligible till around 1800) in Britain, the only country where an Atlantic economy could be said to exist, was around 6 per cent. This was important but not vital to the British economy. Research has not revealed a European percentage in Atlantic trade, but it was undoubtedly less, perhaps 2 per cent as Emmer suggests, with the percentage probably even less in Africa. The value of European imports into West Africa could not have been more than 5 per cent of the value of Africa's internal production, and this percentage both assumes that Africa produced no more than subsistence, which is unlikely, and that the western coastal regions of this continent were a disproportionately great part of the African economy, which is also unlikely.[15]

The Atlantic World did, however, have a constellation of values and initiatives that eventually led to the making of the modern world. It involved a predominance of coerced labour before free labour became important in the mid-nineteenth century. It was also a place where there was intense debate about who was an 'insider' and thus entitled to the privileges of belonging to a place, nation or empire, and who was an 'outsider', and thus someone whose rights did not need to be considered. But some areas of life, notably in gender relations and in ideas about family structures, were brought within a similar Atlantic rubric. That rubric had a peculiar aspect to it: as societies increasingly came into greater contact with each other, they became internally more complex and more stratified but converged together in ways that meant the nineteenth century was more uniform, especially with respect to what C.A. Bayley calls 'bodily practice'.[16]

We have seen how that uniformity was expressed by the end of the Atlantic period in dress. It was also apparent in the realm of language. The most important area where we see Atlantic convergence is in the realm of communications and ideology. The nineteenth century was the age of the newspaper and the telegraph, sending not just information but ideas around the world in ways that were incredibly more rapid than in the past. People in the nineteenth century may not have been able to travel as quickly as we do across the world but intellectually they were already on the way to becoming global citizens. Of course, that was true for the rich, rather than for the poor, and more likely for Europeans and for men than for non-Westerners and for women. As noted in Chapter 1, modern nationalism coming out of the French Revolution became global after 1850, with advocates of the rights of people to have national self-determination spreading throughout the Atlantic World, first in the United States, then in the non-Caribbean Spanish America, and by the end of our period in Brazil and the Caribbean. Nationalism took longer to take hold in Africa, where the nineteenth century saw the start of colonization and arbitrary divisions of diverse regions of tribes and nations to suit the fancies of European empires. In short, we should not see the Atlantic World as the beginnings of a global economy, but rather a cultural manifestation in which values from one part of the Atlantic World moved to another.

FROM ATLANTIC TO WORLD HISTORY: CULTURAL INTEGRATION

Let's take two examples of how the making of an Atlantic World saw the transfer of values and culture from one place to another: food and music. Food, as we have seen, was central to Atlantic integration as so many of the products that Europeans wanted from the Americas were foodstuffs and most African slaves were employed in the agricultural production of tropical luxury foodstuffs. The consumption of goods from both Asia and the Atlantic – tea, coffee, sugar, tobacco, porcelain and cotton textiles – increased dramatically in Western Europe from the late seventeenth century through the French Revolution. In the eighteenth century, we see a remarkable revolution of people's tastes and purchases away from products of local agriculture and industry towards products imported from abroad. By the mid-eighteenth century, many Europeans had become Atlantic citizens regarding what they consumed. As Anne McCant notes for mid-eighteenth-century Britain and the Netherlands, 'demand for colonial commodities was strong enough to support commodity sale prices at a level that continued to cover the high cost of transhipment', thus counteracting O'Rourke and Williamson's contention that demand was confined only to the rich and thus not very important. She suggests that changing living standards of workers, where they consumed ever-larger quantities of Atlantic foodstuffs, had a large, not 'trivial', impact on European import demand. She concludes that 'although a paucity of source materials will continue to make it difficult for historians to quantify with precision the size and scope of the early modern demand for colonial groceries and Asian manufactures, we risk misunderstanding a critical moment in the globalising process if we fail to recognise the power of that demand to radically transform European patterns of consumption as well as its processes of production'.[17]

We can see cultural integration in the Atlantic World in other ways as well, such as in convergence of cultural idioms in musical expression. Laurent Dubois has used the African instrument that became in America the banjo to outline how trans-culture works in practice. He sees the banjo as a symbol of exchange and encounter and a 'central corner and condenser of images of the plantation, of slavery, and of degradation'.[18] The banjo was a form of lute, at least that is how European travellers described it, commonly used in Africa, often to communicate with the spirits of ancestors. It came quickly to the Americas, arriving with the first slave ships. Jean-Baptiste Labat, a French monk, described how the banjo was used on Martinique and Guadeloupe in the mid-1690s to help Africans perform a dance called a *calenda*, which Labat found disturbingly erotic. As part of the dance, men and women thrust their thighs and stomachs together in what Labat thought was a provocative manner.

Hans Sloane saw similar dances in Jamaica in the late seventeenth century. Sloane was the rare European in the tropics who was interested in understanding and documenting the cultural and spiritual lives of enslaved Africans. He was at the hub of a new habit of collecting that eventually led in his case to the founding of the British Museum. Among the treasures he gave that museum were 300 bound volumes of dried plant specimens, as well as items devoted to plantation slavery – a bullet belonging to a free black Jamaican maroon; whips, clothing and weapons; and a gift sent 'as a token of friendship and esteem' by a Virginia planter which was 'some tissue he had removed from the vagina of a slave girl'.

He also was one of the earliest chroniclers of African music, publishing a musical notation for three Afro-American songs. The Africans who sang these songs came from many regions in Africa and thus had to adopt their inherited musical memories to those of others. Richard Rath describes this process as one of creolization where an intensive process of negotiation between different sound ways had to take place in a situation conditioned by exile, intrusive oversight and the confrontation with an extremely oppressive slave system. Rath shows that what Sloane recorded was a very specific moment in which 'Koromanti, Papas and Angolans' were 'using instrument sounds and their voices to forge identities as Africans'.[19] Through this process new and explicitly Caribbean music was created in which a modified African instrument, the banjo, was used to create different musical styles that were African in origin and Caribbean in expression.

In North America, the banjo was commonly used in the Pinkster celebrations in New York City in the 1790s and 1800s. The Pinkster was a festival of Dutch origin which had been taken over and adapted by African Americans. They created dances and music that was overseen by an African-born slave called King Charles 'whose authority is absolute, and whose will is law'. Charles was dressed like an outlandish British general. Thousands of New York City African Americans, both free and enslaved – observers thought that nine in ten blacks participated – sang African songs, beat banjos and had a great time. Whites watched blacks perform, with amusement, excitement and sometimes with shock, as African Americans inverted customary racial order in a carnival reminiscent of a European charivari.

In Dutch Surinam in 1774, the English observer John Stedman watched as a group of recent Africans from Angola danced to banjo music. He was scandalized by the dance which he wrote 'consists from first to last in such a Scene of Wanton, and Lascivious gestures, as nothing but a heated imagination and Constant Practice could enable them to perform'. Slaves 'become more and more Active and Animated, til [sic] they are bathed in lather like Post Horses, and their Passions are wound up to such a degree … that Nature being overcome they are ready to drop into Convulsions'. He was especially disturbed that whites watched these 'indelicate' performances 'without the least reserve'. Stedman, of course, was unlikely to know what subversive measures slaves were sending out during these musical performances. The music and dance surely worked on several different levels, depending on whether one was black or white. In the crucibles of creolizing culture, music was a means of creating connection and solidarity between Africans and, if briefly, between whites and blacks. They were performed during a long-term process of accommodation, assimilation and resistance by Africans to European cultural forms that signify the middle to late eighteenth century as being a time of tremendous cultural diversity. The banjo might be thought of as being both an old and a new instrument, one that preserved cultural traditions, and which created new forms of cultural expression that were creole in form. It was African but also American, and it took listeners back and then moved them forward. It connected many African musical traditions within a Caribbean and then an American context.

Dancing became an issue of debate between defenders and attackers of slavery in the late eighteenth century. Proslavery writers claimed that enslaved people sang and danced because they live happily in 'a scene of festivity and mirth', pleased that they had left behind them the barbarities of Africa. Thomas Clarkson, the ardent abolitionist, disagreed. Slaves' dancing were not, he argued, the sign of 'any uncommon degree of happiness' but showed 'an uncommon depression of the spirits' which drove the enslaved to 'even sacrifice their rest, for the sake of experiencing for a moment a more joyful oblivion of their cares'.

Other writers were less concerned about whether slaves danced because they were happy than about whether their music was worthy of the name. The West Indian planter historian Bryan Edwards declared in 1793 that the music of the enslaved was merely imitative. 'An opinion prevails in Europe', he wrote, 'that they possess organs peculiarly adopted to the science of musick, but this I believe is an ill-founded idea'. Enslaved Africans were poor singers, in his opinion, and while reasonably proficient musicians on ordinary instruments, he had never 'seen or heard of a Negro who could truly be called a fine performer on any capital instrument ... In general they prefer a loud and continual noise to the finest harmony, and frequently consume the whole night in beating on a board with a stick', this being 'one of their chief musical instruments'.

But Edwards was unable to persuade white listeners that black music was terrible and that they should not listen to it. The banjo became central to all kinds of music in the Americas, both white and black created. It is central to the music of Haiti, in Twoubado, or Troubadour, music popular in rural areas and performed during Vodou ritual ceremonies. It was central in the nineteenth-century tradition of minstrelsy, a very popular music hall form of entertainment where Europeans mimicked African-American performance tradition. In contemporary America, it is central within folk music, bluegrass music and much country music coming out of Nashville. The greatest recent banjo player was Peter Seeger (1919–2014), born into relative privilege and Harvard-educated who used the banjo to join with Woody Guthrie in classic protest songs that have defined American popular music in the last half century. The banjo is currently enjoying a revival with musicians like Rhiannon Giddens of the Carolina Chocolate Drops carrying on the long tradition of banjo playing and connecting it to African-American music from slavery days.

But let's end this book with a reference to what I believe is the quintessential American song and one that would be at the top of any album of Atlantic-inflected songs. This song is 'Oh! Susanna', written by the American popular songwriter Stephen Foster in 1847. It has a famous chorus: 'Oh! Susanna, do not cry for me; I come from Alabama wid a banjo on my knee.' The chorus links together in one phrase Africa and America. Foster loved African-American music or what he called 'negro melody'. He possibly was inspired to write the song after hearing a slave ballad that was a comic lament about being caught up in the nineteenth-century American domestic slave trade, about a slave not leaving from, but coming to, Alabama. 'Oh! Susanna' became a staple of minstrel shows in America, Europe and Australia. It was a song that was a form of mimicry, but we can view it as a symbol of how deep Atlantic roots had struck by the middle of the nineteenth century. It is a song written by a person of European heritage using the voice of a descendant of Africans wanting to leave a place with a Native American name and which had once been Native American land. The song remains popular throughout the Atlantic World, being probably the only song from before 1900 that is regularly sung and to which people know the words. The connections made by the movement of things, ideas and most of all people throughout an Atlantic World initiated in the mid-fifteenth century and which have some contemporary and modern echoes make this a topic and an historical subfield worth studying.

NOTES

1   Benjamin Schmidt, 'Collecting Global Icons: The Case of the Exotic Parasol,' in Daniela Bleichmar and Peter C. Mancall, eds., *Collecting across Cultures: Material Exchanges in the Early Modern Atlantic World* (Philadelphia: University of Pennsylvania Press, 2011), 31–57.

2   Craig Clunas, *Pictures and Visuality in Early Modern China* (London: Reaktion, 1997), 46.

3   Guy Stoumsa, 'The Scholarly Discovery of Religion in Early Modern Times,' in Jerry H. Bentley et al., eds., *The Cambridge World History* vol. VI, part 2, *The Construction of a Global World, 1400–1800 CE* (Cambridge: Cambridge University Press, 2015), 319.

4   Sylvia R. Frey and Betty Wood, *Come Shouting to Zion: African American Protestantism in the American South and the British Caribbean to 1830* (Chapel Hill: University of North Carolina Press, 1993).

5   James H. Sweet, 'Mistaken Identities? Olaudah Equiano, Domingos Álvares, and the Methodological Challenges of Studying the African Diaspora,' *American Historical Review* 114 (2009), 279–306.

6   Vincent Brown, 'Spiritual Terror and Sacred Authority in Jamaican Slave Society,' *Slavery & Abolition* 24 (2003), 50.

7   Diana Paton, 'Witchcraft, Poison, Law and Atlantic Slavery,' *William and Mary Quarterly* 69 (2012), 235–64.

8   William H. McNeill, *A World History* 4th ed. (Oxford: Oxford University Press, 1999), 295.

9   Jerry Bentley, 'AHR Forum – Cross-Cultural Interaction and Periodization in World History,' *American Historical Review*, 101 (1996), 768–69.

10 Dennis O. Flynn and Arturo Giraldez, 'Path Dependence: Time Lags and the Birth of Globalisation: A Critique of O'Rourke and Williamson,' *European Review of Economic History* 8 (2004), 99.

11 Nicholas Canny and Philip Morgan, *The Oxford Handbook of the Atlantic World 1450–1850* (Oxford: Oxford University Press, 2013), 11–13.

12 Kevin O'Rourke and Jeffrey Williamson, 'When Did Globalisation Begin?,' *European Review of Economic History* 6 (2002), 45.

13 Pieter Emmer, 'The Myth of Early Globalisation: The Atlantic Economy, 1500–1800,' *European Review* 11 (2003), 38.

14 David Eltis, 'Atlantic History in Global Perspective,' *Itinerario* 23 (1999), 143.

15 Eltis and Lawrence C. Jennings, 'Trade between Western Africa and the Atlantic World in the Pre-Colonial Era,' *American Historical Review* 93 (1988), 953–59.

16 C.A. Bayly, *The Birth of the Modern World 1780–1914* (Oxford: Blackwell, 2004), 12–22.
17 Anne E.C. McCants, 'Exotic Goods, Popular Consumption, and the Standard of Living: Thinking about Globalization in the Early Modern World,' *Journal of World History* 18 (2007), 462.
18 Laurent Dubois, *The Banjo: America's African Instrument* (Cambridge: Harvard University Press, 2016), 5.
19 Richard Cullen Rath, *How Early America Sounded* (Ithaca: Cornell University Press, 2003).

BIBLIOGRAPHY

Oxford Online Bibliographies – African Religion and Culture; Catholicism; Evangelicalism and Conversion; Global History; History of Science; Jewish Diaspora; Missionaries; Music and Music Making; Native Americans in Europe; Religion; Religious Networks; Witchcraft.

C.A. Bayly, *The Birth of the Modern World 1780–1914* (Oxford: Blackwell, 2004).

Daniela Bleichmar and Peter C. Mancall, eds., *Collecting across Cultures: Material Exchanges in the Early Modern Atlantic World* (Philadelphia: University of Pennsylvania Press, 2011).

James Delbourgo, *Collecting the World: Hans Sloane and the Origins of the British Museum* (Cambridge, MA: Harvard University Press, 2017).

Laurent Dubois, *The Banjo: America's African Instrument* (Cambridge: Harvard University Press, 2016).

Susanne Lachenicht, *Hugenotten in Europa und Nordamerika: Migration und Integration in der Frühen Neuzelt* (Frankfurt and New York: Campus Verlag, 2010).

Anne E.C. McCants, 'Exotic Goods, Popular Consumption, and the Standard of Living: Thinking about Globalization in the Early Modern World,' *Journal of World History* 18 (2007), 433–62.

Sidney Mintz, *Three Ancient Colonies; Caribbean Themes and Variations* (Cambridge, MA: Harvard University Press, 2010).

J.R. Oldfield, *Transatlantic Abolitionism in the Age of Revolution: An International History of Antislavery, c. 1787–1820* (Cambridge: Cambridge University Press, 2013).

Anthony Pagden, *Natural Man: The American Indian and the Origins of Comparative Ethnology* (Cambridge: Cambridge University Press, 1981).

Diana Paton, *The Cultural Politics of Obeah: Religion, Colonialism and Modernity in the Caribbean World* (Cambridge: Cambridge University Press, 2015).

Carole Shammas, *The Pre-Industrial Consumer in England and America* (Oxford: Oxford University Press, 1990).

Guy G. Stroumsa, *A New Science: The Discovery of Religion in the Age of Reason* (Cambridge, MA: Cambridge University Press, 2010).

James H. Sweet, *Recreating African Culture, Kinship, and Religion in the African-Portuguese World, 1441–1770* (Chapel Hill: University of North Carolina Press, 2003).

INDEX